INTO ACTION
1960–2014
IRISH PEACEKEEPERS UNDER FIRE

Lieutenant Colonel Dan Harvey has served on operations at home and abroad for over thirty-five years to date. He is the author of *Soldiers of the Short Grass: A History of the Curragh Camp* (Merrion Press, 2016) and has previously written about major incidents involving Irish Defence Forces members on active overseas peacekeeping services, including *Peace Enforcers: The EU Intervention in Chad* (2011) and *Peacekeepers: Irish Soldiers in the Lebanon* (2001).

From Cork to the Congo,
from Galway to the Gaza Strip,
from this legislative assembly to the United Nations,
Ireland is sending its most talented men,
to do the world's most important work,
the work of peace.

President John F. Kennedy's address to Dáil Éireann and Seanad Éireann, 28 June 1963

This book is dedicated to those 'most talented men' and women, our Irish Peacekeepers, and especially their families, who for over sixty years and ongoing are 'doing the world's most important work, the work of peace'.

INTO ACTION 1960–2014
ACTION
IRISH PEACEKEEPERS UNDER FIRE

DAN HARVEY

FOREWORD BY KEVIN MYERS

MERRION PRESS

First published in 2017 by
Merrion Press
10 George's Street
Newbridge
Co. Kildare
Ireland
www.merrionpress.ie

© 2017, Dan Harvey

978-1-78537-111-0 (Paper)
978-1-78537-112-7 (Cloth)
978-1-78537-113-4 (Kindle)
978-1-78537-114-1 (Epub)
978-1-78537-122-6 (PDF)

British Library Cataloguing in Publication Data
An entry can be found on request

Library of Congress Cataloging in Publication Data
An entry can be found on request

All rights reserved. Without limiting the rights under copyright reserved alone, no part of this publication may be reproduced, stored in or introduced into a retrieval system, or transmitted, in any form or by any means (electronic, mechanical, photocopying, recording or otherwise) without the prior written permission of both the copyright owner and the above publisher of this book.

Interior design by www.jminfotechindia.com

Typeset in Minion Pro 11.5/14 pt
Cover design by www.phoenix-graphicdesign.com

Cover/jacket front: A lull in hostilities. Despite the severe pressure, morale in C Company remained high. Courtesy of Comdt Ned Kelly (retd) Destroyed Christian militia half-track at entrance to UN Post 6-15 Platoon HQ at At-Tiri, Lebanon, April 1980. Courtesy of Comdt Ned Kelly (retd).

Cover/jacket back: Members of 33rd Irish Battalion boarding a US Air Force C-124 Globemaster transport plane at Baldonnel Aerodrome, 18 August 1960. Courtesy of the Military Archives, Dublin.

Printed in Ireland by SPRINT-print Ltd

Contents

Maps		vi
Abbreviations		x
Foreword by Kevin Myers		xiii
Introduction: A New Departure		xv
Part I	**Congo (1960–4)**	
Chapter 1	Chaos in the Congo (Niemba)	3
Chapter 2	Company in Defence (Jadotville)	25
Chapter 3	The Battle for the Tunnel (Élisabethville)	49
Part II	**Lebanon (1980)**	
Chapter 4	Attack on At-Tiri	111
Part III	**Kosovo (2004)**	
Chapter 5	Blocking Position	207
Part IV	**Chad (2008)**	
Chapter 6	The Dead Heart of Africa	235
Part V	**Syria (2013–14)**	
Chapter 7	Hull Down	291
Epilogue		297
Roll of Honour		298
Author's Note		302
Acknowledgements		306
Index		308

Maps

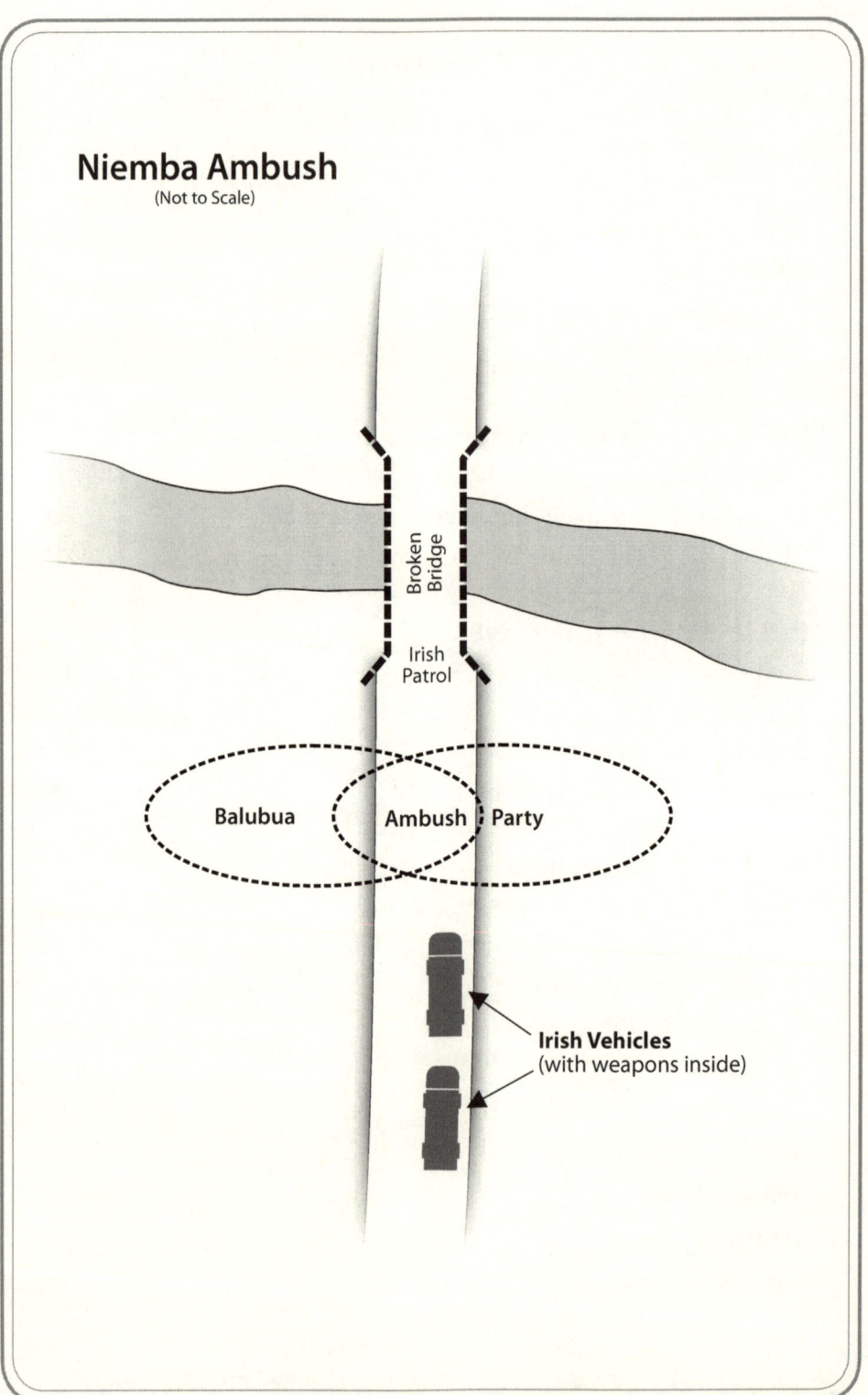

Maps | vii

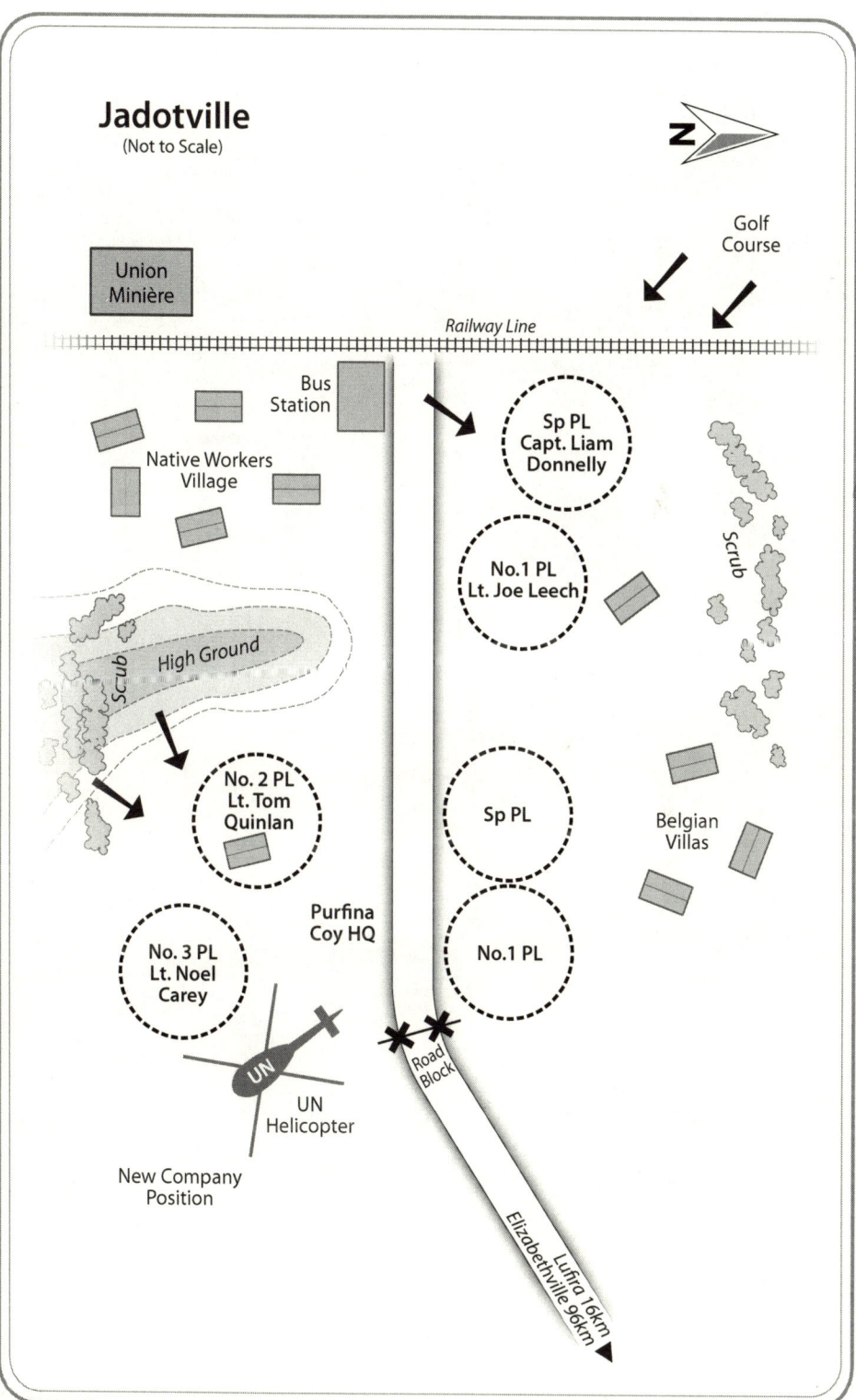

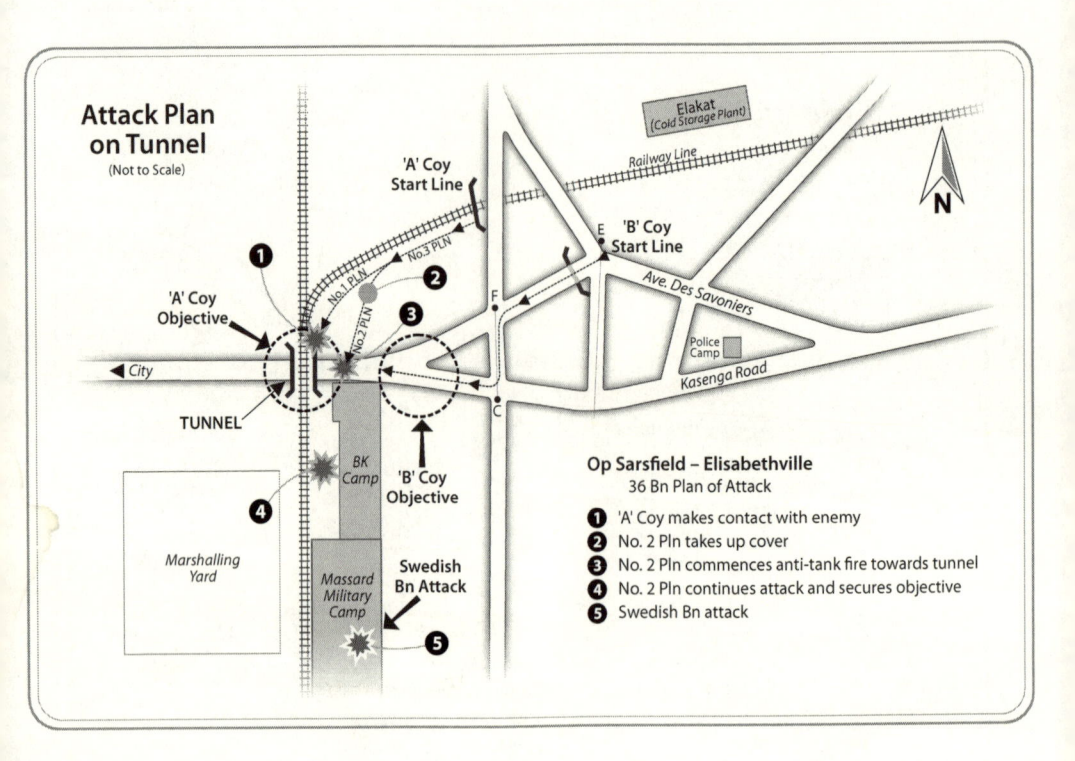

viii | *Maps*

Attack Plan on Tunnel
(Not to Scale)

- 'A' Coy Start Line
- 'B' Coy Start Line
- No.1 PLN
- No.3 PLN
- No.2 PLN
- 'A' Coy Objective
- City
- TUNNEL
- BK Camp
- 'B' Coy Objective
- Marshalling Yard
- Massard Military Camp
- Swedish Bn Attack
- Elakat (Cold Storage Plant)
- Railway Line
- Ave. Des Savoniers
- Police Camp
- Kasenga Road

Op Sarsfield – Elisabethville
36 Bn Plan of Attack

1. 'A' Coy makes contact with enemy
2. No. 2 Pln takes up cover
3. No. 2 Pln commences anti-tank fire towards tunnel
4. No. 2 Pln continues attack and secures objective
5. Swedish Bn attack

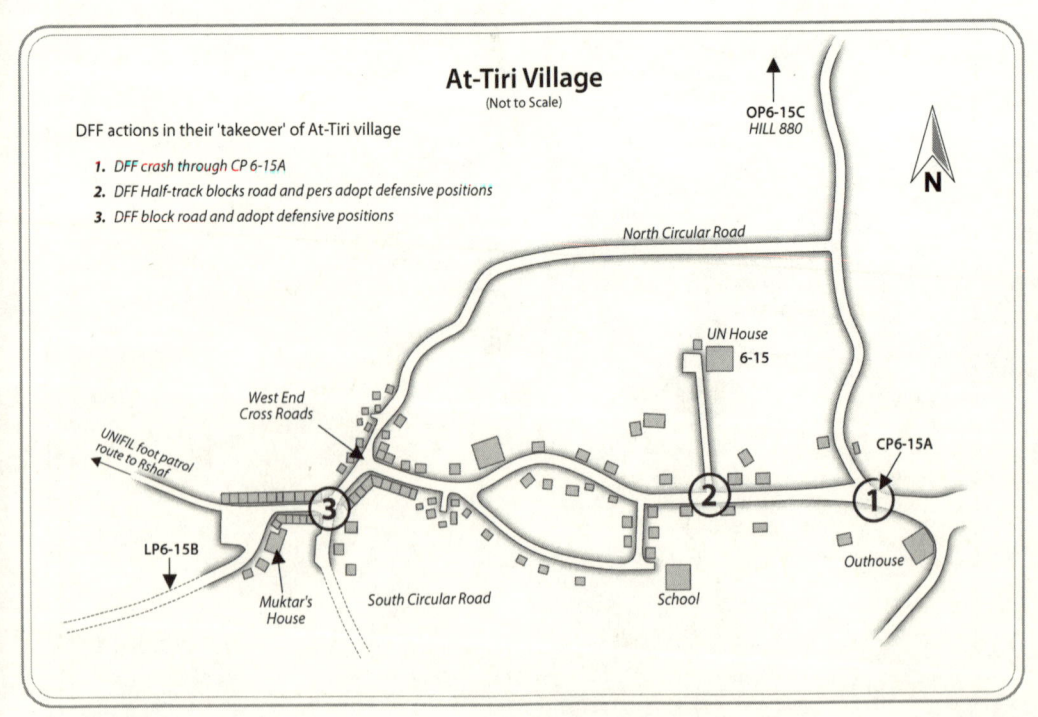

At-Tiri Village
(Not to Scale)

DFF actions in their 'takeover' of At-Tiri village

1. *DFF crash through CP 6-15A*
2. *DFF Half-track blocks road and pers adopt defensive positions*
3. *DFF block road and adopt defensive positions*

- OP6-15C HILL 880
- North Circular Road
- UN House 6-15
- West End Cross Roads
- UNIFIL foot patrol route to Rshaf
- LP6-15B
- Muktar's House
- South Circular Road
- School
- CP6-15A
- Outhouse

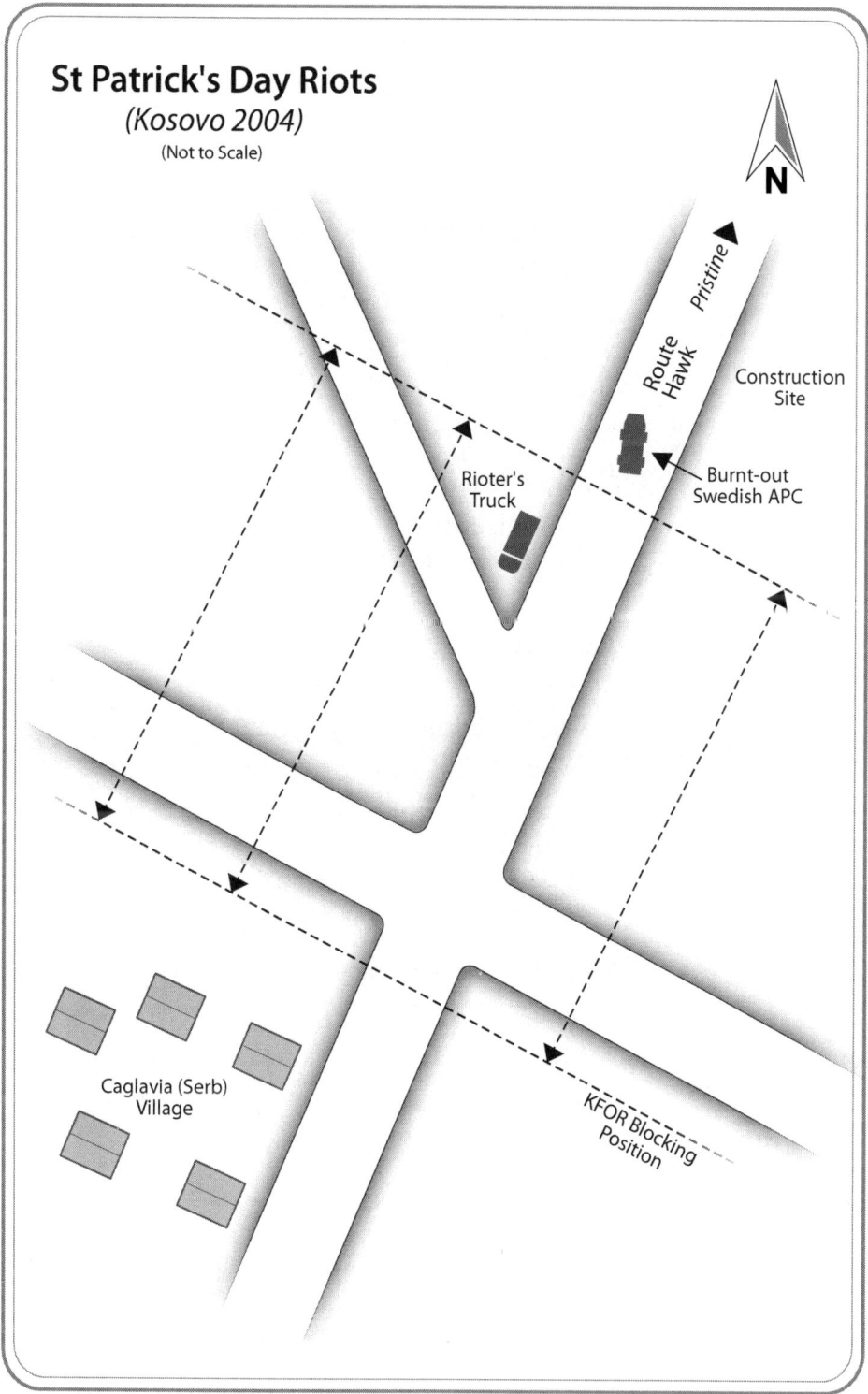

Maps | ix

Abbreviations

ANC	Armée Nationale Congolaise (the army of the newly independent Democratic Republic of Congo)
AO	Area of Operations
AOR	Area of Responsibility
APC	Armoured Personnel Carrier
APOD	Airport of Disembarkation
CASEVAC	Casualty Evacuation
CB	Counter Battery (mortar fire)
DFF	De Facto Forces, or the South Lebanese Army (an Israeli-backed Christian militia)
DFS	Department of Field Support
DPKO	Department of Peacekeeping Operations
DROPS	Demountable rack offload and pickup systems
EEC	European Economic Community
ESDP	European Security and Defence Policy
EUFOR	European Union Force in Chad and Central African Republic
EULEX	European Rule of Law Mission (Kosovo)
FHQ	Force Headquarters
FLN	Front de Libération Nationale
FMR	Force Mobile Reserve
FN	Fabrique Nationale (Belgian Arms Manufacturer)
FOO	Forward Observation Officer
GPMG	General purpose machine gun
HMG	Heavy machine gun
HQ	Headquarters
IDF	Israeli Defence Force

Irish Batt	Irish Battalion
IDP	Internally Displaced Person (a displaced person who moves but does not cross a border)
IUNVA	Irish United Nations Veterans Association
JAMBO	Katangese Gendarmerie
JEM	Justice and Equality Movement
JOC	Joint Operations Centre
KFOR	Kosovo Force
LAUIS	Locals armed and uniformed by the Israelis (a pro-Israeli militia)
LP	Listening Post
MEDEVAC	Medical Evacuation
MIA	Missing in Action
MINURCAT	United Nations Mission in Central African Republic and Chad
MFC	Mobile Fire Controller
MRE	Mission readiness exercise
MOU	Memorandum of Understanding
NATO	North Atlantic Treaty Organisation
NCO	Non-commissioned Officer (Corporals and Sergeants mostly)
NGO	Non-governmental organisation
OC	Officer Commanding
OHQ	Operational Headquarters (link between Military Strategic and Force Headquarters)
ONUC	Operations des Nations Unies au Congo (United Nations Operation in Congo)
OP	Observation Post
OP CMDR	Operational Commander
PfP	Partnership for Peace (an arrangement whereby non-NATO members may participate with NATO members on certain peacekeeping missions)

PLO	Palestinian Liberation Organisation
RCO	Raising and Concentration Order
Recce	Reconnaissance
RE-ORG	Reorganisation location for attackers having secured an objective
SASE	Safe and Secure Environment
SLA	South Lebanese Army (a pro-Israeli militia)
SLA/M	Sudan Liberation Army/Movement
SOFA	Status of Forces Agreement
SPOD	Sea Port of Disembarkation
SRV	Special Reconnaissance Vehicle
SRAAW	Short Range Anti-Armour Weapon
TA	Technical Agreement
UNAMID	United Nations African Mission in Darfur
UNDOF	United Nations Disengagement Observation Force
UNHCR	United Nations High Commission for Refugees
UNIFIL	United Nations Interim Force in Lebanon
UNIFYCYP	United Nations Peacekeeping Force in Cyprus
UNMIK	United Nations Mission in Kosovo
UNTSI	United Nations Training School Ireland (Military College, Curragh Camp, Co. Kildare, Ireland)
UNTSO OGL	United Nations Truce Supervision Organisation, Observer Group Lebanon

Foreword

No one ever became a soldier in order to be a full-time peacekeeper. A soldier is a warrior, whose primary skill is in the taking of life. To do that efficiently he must obey orders and accept the hierarchy that administers them. These ingredients – the ability to deliver lethal force and a culture of command and submission – enable armies to have other functions that are beyond the scope of most civilian organisations. One of these is peacekeeping, but this is a secondary role and it is one of the misfortunes of the Army of the Republic that this secondary duty is now widely perceived as its primary function.

It most emphatically is not. Those who wear the uniform of the Republic are its true embodiment. They are its soldiers, who accept the lawful commands of the state in its protection and in its service. Whereas An Garda Siochána serves the citizens and enforces the law, the Army defends the Republic – in both the military sense and in the civic sphere – especially in times of emergency. But what underwrites and enables these duties is the ability and willingness of the soldiers of the Republic to take life in its service, and to place their own in harm's way.

Many men and women like danger. The truth is that large numbers of Irishmen, in the service of many states, have always courted death. This is one reason why Irishmen make great soldiers. But it is the willingness to obey and to use disciplined violence that transforms what might otherwise be a thrill-seeking rabble into an army. And an army is only an army when its members enter a contract that is predicated on killing, and its associated skills.

The many peacekeeping missions that our Army has undertaken for nigh-on sixty years have usually been free of the situations that invoke the killing contract. But that is in large part because armed locals who might otherwise be tempted to use force are usually in no doubt about the consequences if they do. In the absence of violence, a good army will display its martial skills in surrogate but very visible ways: vigilance, discipline, obedience and an easy confidence in the bearing of firearms. These are the vital signals that prevent an armed but passive witness from becoming an active player.

When these messages fail to communicate their underlying purpose, or are ignored, the peacekeeper must revert to his primary duty, the one he or she, by nature, likes best; that of being a soldier whose safety catch is off, looking for a target. When this happens, the enemy will see a quite different soldier from the affable, smiling person who was so obliging at roadblocks and who helped administer the TB jab. This character will, if need be, kill you.

Peacekeepers are not social workers with guns, through whom the local militia would drive with scorn. They can only keep the peace because they can also end it. Dan Harvey has written this fascinating description of when Irish peacekeeping efforts – for whatever reason – no longer kept the peace, and so it was time for fighting. No one joins the Defence Forces without hoping for something like this. Why? Because, at bottom, it's something that Irish soldiers are good at. Excellent at minding the peace, and just as good at concluding the ambitions and even the heartbeat of those who want to end it.

Kevin Myers, January 2017

INTRODUCTION

A New Departure

The Irish Defence Forces' involvement in overseas peacekeeping service was to prove the single biggest development in their history. It was also to involve its members in a number of significant critical moments, when Irish soldiers as peacekeepers, inserted into volatile and violent, often difficult, dangerous and deteriorating situations, walked the very fine line between peacekeeping and war-fighting, the need to return fire and otherwise using measured force as a last resort in self-defence.

Peacekeepers are often asked to do what politics and diplomacy have not done. Partisan, belligerent protagonists have often been part of the reality faced by Irish peacekeepers in an array of highly varied and intricate mission areas. Irish Peacekeepers, using patience, persistence, impartiality and professionalism have addressed the effects of complicity, complexity, crisis and conflict. Despite some setbacks, problems and difficulties, peacekeeping works and the Irish are good at it. On occasion, the Irish Defence Forces, with nearly 60 years participation as peacekeepers, 85,000 individual tours of duty in over 70 United Nations (UN) or UN-approved missions, and 86 Defence Force members paying the ultimate price, have experienced circumstances when a demonstration of resolve became necessary. Ireland is one of the most consistent European contributors to the UN and is one of the most successful contributors to UN-mandated Peace Support Operations. They are well regarded by those with whom they operate and the various peoples of the mission areas in which they have found themselves. Today it is taken for granted that Irish soldiers should serve alongside those of other nations in UN peacekeeping missions worldwide, yet when first requested to do so it was an entirely 'New Departure' and Ireland moved into the mainstream of then current world events.

What is hardest won is most savoured, and often in the histories of different nations that is peace. That is why, when frequently coming from conflict, it is crucial that once gained peace is maintained. Peace facilitates stability, bringing normality into peoples' everyday lives and generating good governance and economic development. Lose peace and hope and a peoples' future will become severely jeopardised. That is why, coming from fragile political–military circumstances, a fledgling peace sometimes needs the presence of a peacekeeping force to maintain and nurture it. There are, however, certain critical variables that affect the always uncertain feasibility of a peacekeeping force achieving a successful outcome. Among the issues influencing the situation are, and remain to be, a clear and workable mandate; the nature of the conflict; consent of the parties involved; the physical environment; the extent of international support; and both the appropriate configuration and means available to the peacekeeping force.

The degree to which all or most of these determinants were present and played out had a significant bearing on what the peacekeeping force was able to achieve. The absence of any one, or more of these factors, adversely affected the context in which the peacekeeping force was able to perform. This had often and all too frequently been the case, resulting in the peacekeeping force of which the Irish were members being tasked to keep a peace where there was, in fact, no peace to be kept. Throughout the Irish Defence Forces' rich experience of peacekeeping in many mission areas throughout the world, confrontation was sometimes part of this 'strange soldiering' involvement. Irish peacekeepers have been severely challenged, tested, and become embroiled in some noteworthy actions. Irish peacekeepers have seen action in the Congo (Niemba, Jadotville and 'The Tunnel' at Élisabethville); in Lebanon (At-Tiri); in Kosovo (the St Patrick's Day Riots of 2004); in Chad; and more recently in Syria.

Interestingly, an analysis of these engagements illustrates the presence of some distinguishing commonalities, such as unexpected 'mission command'; sub-unit involvement; leadership; the value of training; strategic implications of a tactical incident; and not to overstate it, bravery. These incidents were all the more remarkable because the Irish, adhering to peacekeepers' strict rules of engagement, had to act against protagonists engaging without such rules.

'Peacekeeping' is not mentioned in the UN Charter, it evolved out of necessity. So what was a 'New Departure' for the United Nations also became one for the Irish, and for six decades this Irish participation has greatly contributed to peace throughout the world.

Departure for the Congo. Members of 33rd Irish Battalion boarding a United States Air Force C-124 Globemaster transport plane at Baldonnel Aerodrome, 18 August 1960. Courtesy of the Military Archives, Dublin

PART I
CONGO (1960–4)

CHAPTER 1

Chaos in the Congo (Niemba)

Congo's vast natural resources of mineral wealth were in stark contrast to its people's poverty. An enormous country, Congo's former colonial history had been brutal, yet its independence in 1960 swiftly brought it towards, then beyond, the brink of bloodshed. A huge humanitarian tragedy was in the offing and the country itself faced fragmentation. Now Katanga, its primary province, was perched perilously on the precipice of pandemonium.

Soldiers from seventeen countries, including Ireland – all member states of the United Nations – had contributed to a peacekeeping force attempting to stabilise the situation before it imploded. That such an undertaking had come to pass owed its origins to when the European powers – Germany, Britain, France, Belgium and Italy some seventy-six years previously at the Berlin Conference hosted by Otto Von Bismarck in November 1884, entrusted the Congo not to Belgium per se, but rather uniquely to the personal control of King Leopold II of Belgium. Unwilling to risk hostilities over the, as yet, unclaimed regions of Africa, the European colonists were happy to amicably divide up what was left.

Initially a loss maker, Congo's bountiful wild rubber was soon exploited, resulting in huge personal financial gains for Leopold II by satisfying the demand for tyres for the newly emergent and thriving car industry. In their quest for ever-increasing quotas of rubber produce, zealous overseers inflicted appalling abuses and atrocities on the native Congolese when failing to meet these laid-down quotas.

Congo's abundance of raw materials – timber, ivory, rubber and vast quantities of minerals – were quickly monopolised by Belgian firms paying high dividends to Leopold for the privilege. Inevitably, envious competing interest from others, including British businesses unable to gain a highly lucrative market share, exploited the concerns of outspoken missionaries over the shockingly inhumane treatment of the Congolese and raised such concerns in the British Parliament. As a result, in mid-1903 Roger Casement, at the British Consul in the Congo, was directed to conduct an investigation. By the year's end, after a thorough, systematic and highly conscientious undertaking, his report laid bare in graphic detail the maltreatment being meted out to the Congolese, including the severing of hands which were then preserved by a smoking process – proof of money not wasted on bullets. Casement's report earned him a knighthood and caused widespread condemnation and criticism of Leopold II. The resultant international hue and cry led to Belgium itself being given control of Leopold II's personal African fiefdom. However, the horrors did not fade overnight.

Diamonds, uranium and other minerals from Congo's seemingly inexhaustible supply of valuable natural resources soon replaced timber, ivory and wild rubber as income-earning exports for the Belgians. It was shortly after the First World War that the province of Katanga, where vast resources of copper had been discovered in 1913, attracted

An Irish search party arrives at the broken bridge ambush site over the River Luweyeye at Niemba.   Courtesy of the Military Archives, Dublin

fortune-seeking European and American mining and mineral firms led by Union Minière, a large Anglo-Belgian concern. It became one of the most highly lucrative mining centres in the world, accounting for 50 per cent of Congo's wealth.

The preservation of potential ongoing returns focussed the attention of these corporations as the region prepared to enter the countdown to its post-colonial era. However, while other colonial countries had prepared their respective indigenous populations to ease the transition towards independence, Belgium undertook no such preparations for the Congo. Theirs was the presumption of continuance through utter necessity. Disastrously, they believed that the existing white administrative level would continue to administer. There were few Africans in positions of responsibility in the Congo and its 25,000-strong army was commanded by in excess of 1,000 Belgian officers. On being granted independence, this army became the Armée Nationale Congolaise (ANC). Its layer of white command was removed and with it, it has to be said, control. In addition, some 200 Congolese tribes were just released from Belgian control.

Granted sudden independence, the Congo – with huge mineral wealth but no public administration layer – was unable to impose control on its so-called army to ensure stability and security – its new government's first duty – and the result was chaos. This disintegration arose directly from two speeches, the first by King Baudouin of Belgium, the second by Patrice Lumumba, the new prime minister of the Congo. In his address to the Congolese, Baudouin encouraged them to be deserving of the advantages granted by his grandfather, Leopold II, a personage hugely disliked throughout Congo. Insulted, Patrice Lumumba set aside his prepared conciliatory speech, instead delivering an impassioned denunciation of the Belgians, which had immediate repercussions. Political opportunists seized the momentum, the army mutinied and many tribesmen sought reprisals for generations of white supremacy.

There were some 10,000 Belgians living in Congo and many white families, previously associated with mining and plantations, became targets for robbery, rape and murder. Lumumba, not anxious to seek the assistance of Belgium, hinted he might contact China for support. He did in fact communicate with the Russians but then, advised by

Congo's US Ambassador, turned instead to the UN. The old colonial power, Belgium, now had a pretext for intervention – the protection of its citizens – and sent in paratroopers who took possession of Élisabethville, the epicentre of the mineral-rich province of Katanga and one with much international interest. The following day, 9 July 1960, Moise Tshombe declared Katanga's independence. Alarmed by possible Russian involvement at the height of the Cold War, the US exerted pressure on the UN leadership and Security Council Resolution S/4387 was adopted on 14 July 1960. Within a fortnight the Irish were on their way, marching into the madness of tribal strife, anarchy and a web of economically motivated vested self-interests – and even an undertow of Cold War machinations.

Precious metals were at the heart of the madness, some of which were used in the manufacture of jet engines and radar apparatus. Moreover, Katanga supplied a tenth of the world's copper and over half of the world's cobalt. There was also uranium and many minerals, including large quantities of diamonds. Thus 10 per cent of Congo's population generated 50 per cent of the nation's income and the Katangese wanted to protect their interests, as did those European entities that had much to lose and more to gain. Enter the boots of the *Casques bleus* – the Blue Helmets of the UN – onto Central African soil and headlong into the Congolese maelstrom. The UN was in at the deep end from the beginning and the pace of events was moving rapidly.

Reality Check

In the thick bush and tall grass either side of the Manono road, on both sides of the damaged 20-foot bridge over the River Luweyeye thirteen miles from Niemba, a large Baluba war party, baptised with 'magic water' and hyped up by ritual words, lay in wait for an eleven-man patrol from the 33rd Irish Battalion, sent to the Congo as part of a UN peacekeeping mission and under the command of Lieutenant Kevin Gleeson. The Baluba tribesmen were determined that the Irish would not go beyond the broken bridge and had received explicit instructions from Grand Chief Kasanga-Niemba to that effect. The Baluba war party, led by ex-Congolese Premier Sergeant Lualaba, had ripped most of the large wooden decking planks off the bridge, throwing them into the river below. Now, with a patient determination to kill, they silently waited for the arrival of the Irish peacekeepers.

When the eleven-man Irish patrol arrived at the bridge they left their vehicles to inspect the broken structure and were taken completely by surprise when the group of Baluba tribesmen appeared suddenly out of the dense head-high elephant grass. Carrying bows, with arrows whose tips, it was largely believed, had been dipped in the fatal venom of the black mamba snake, as well as spears, hatchets, knives and clubs, the tribesmen quickly formed into a war party. Six abreast the Balubas strode forward, perhaps forty in all with as many more hidden in the thick undergrowth. Without warning they started screaming and shouting and flung themselves wildly at the hapless Irish patrol. Firing a hail of arrows, they set upon the Irish, yelling raucously and roaring. The overwhelming number and sheer aggression of their opponents shocked the unsuspecting Irishmen who, having gone forward from their vehicles to inspect the bridge had left most of their weapons behind. The rapidly advancing Balubas moved between the Irish and their two vehicles and cut off recourse to their only means of survival – their weapons – which were agonisingly close yet still out of reach. With the few weapons they had the Irish patrol fought for their lives, a desperate defence against being bludgeoned and hacked to death.

Neither Lieutenant Kevin Gleeson nor Sergeant Hugh Gaynor, in Niemba since early October and familiar with Baluba activity, suspected the broken bridge to be a Baluba ambush position. The majority of the other nine on the patrol, newly arrived in Niemba from Kamina the previous day and unfamiliar with the area, did not know what to expect.

The Balubas, a newly established group of highly assertive warriors, was attempting to consolidate its position in the area and had erected numerous roadblocks in an attempt to impede the presence of the Katangan Gendarmerie. They had previously come under attack from pro-Katangan and allied forces and the roadblocks were an attempt to keep their attackers at bay. They therefore resented the UN's removal of their only defence.

The previous day, a combined contingent of Irish troops under Commandant PD Hogan joined with Lieutenant Gleeson and some of his platoon, a combined strength of forty from all ranks, and travelled north-south to join a concurrently moving south-north patrol under

Lieutenant Kevin Gleeson's Platoon prior to departure to Congo, July 1960. Kevin Gleeson is in the front row, sixth from left. Courtesy of the Military Archives, Dublin

Commandant Barry. Their task was to simultaneously clear all obstacles encountered en route and to rendezvous at noon at Senge Tshimbo. They made a contingency that both patrols, whether or not they successfully linked up, were to begin their respective return journeys at 1300 hours. In the event they did not meet. Commandant Hogan's and Lieutenant Gleeson's patrol made slower progress than Commandant Barry's, encountering and clearing no fewer than eight felled trees and having to bridge or fill in five trenches cut across the route, resulting in them covering only thirteen miles in just under seven hours. This brought them to the bridge over the River Luweyeye, where unknown to them they were not alone. Only a few metres away, hidden amongst the scrub, bush and high grasses, was the expectant Baluba war party.

Sergeant Lualaba was also taken by surprise. He was looking at a bigger than expected Irish convoy, eight vehicles instead of the normal one or two, and a large a group of Irish peacekeepers. He was put further off-balance when some of his Baluba lookouts were spotted by some of the Irish troops. For their part the Irish were more concerned with estimating how long it would take to repair the damage to the bridge, which they considered to be several hours work, than worried by the presence of a few natives. Nonetheless, the Balubas were questioned and when they claimed to be pygmies out hunting were given the benefit of the doubt. Too late in the day to begin repairs, the patrol returned to Niemba village.

With Commandant Hogan later departing for Albertville, Lieutenant Gleeson was given orders to continue to patrol the Manono road and see if he could take the patrol as far as Kinsukulu. The following morning, 8 November 1960, Lieutenant Gleeson and ten others were to patrol to the Luweyeye and be confronted with far more than a damaged bridge. Arriving at the bridge mid-afternoon the following day (1500 hours), the eleven-man Irish patrol, a familiarisation exercise for the seven newly-arrived troopers, got out of their vehicles to further investigate the damage to the bridge. Lieutenant Gleeson, Sergeant Gaynor and two others ventured onto the roadway on the far side of the bridge, looking for a possible fording place across the Luweyeye for their vehicles as they went. Suddenly aware of a Baluba presence on that side of the bridge, they sensed something menacing in the tribesmen's demeanour.

Lieutenant Gleeson immediately ordered Sergeant Gaynor back across the river to turn the lead vehicle, a pick-up, back towards Niemba village in the direction they had come. While Sergeant Gaynor was doing this he became aware of a tree being felled across the road behind him, blocking off their retreat. While Sergeant Gaynor was attempting to turn the pick-up, Lieutenant Gleeson and those with him turned back across the river and the Irish formed a single line facing the direction from which they had arrived at the bridge. Coming into full view now was a Baluba war party emerging from the bush onto the roadway, assembling into a formation, six abreast. Facing them, and aware of others behind them, there came the sinking realisation among the Irish and a horrible awareness that a trap had been sprung; it was an ambush, and the Irish patrol was where the Baluba attackers wanted them to be, in the killing area.

Little more than 100 metres, barely the length of a football field, separated the two sides. (See map on p. vi.) The time taken to cover the distance between them would be no more than fifteen or so seconds and it had become all too obvious that the Irish patrol was hopelessly outnumbered. Neither were all the Irish armed, worse, the Bren guns were in the rear of the Land Rover, the second of the two vehicles. The Balubas had achieved complete surprise and too late had the Irish realised the danger. The tense stand-off lasted only for a few seconds. Their hostility palpable, the Baluba warriors hurled themselves at the hapless patrol.

It had all happened in quick succession – from arrival to alert, from alert to ambush, from ambush to attack. As the Balubas advanced they broke into frenzied charge and closed fast on the Irish patrol. Lieutenant Gleeson shouted: 'Hold your fire, we have to wait until they fire first.' Hardly had he spoken when the Balubas, barely twenty metres away, unleashed a hail of arrows. The order to fire was given and those with weapons returned fire immediately. Fifteen Balubas fell dead, nearly as many were wounded, and as many again kept advancing. Suddenly more tribesmen were moving in from the bush, from in front and behind. The Irish troops were in a hopeless situation. 'High ground' was the immediate thought in the Irish minds and Lieutenant Gleeson led his patrol in an attempt to make for a rise, retreating across the river, with the Balubas in pursuit, continuing firing arrows all the time. On reaching the rise, the Irish turned and faced their attackers; here they would make a stand.

With minds racing, hearts pounding, gasping for breath and fearful, the Irish were wounded and in a state of shock. What had been the routine repair of a broken bridge had been used as 'bait' by the Balubas, and it had worked. Such a possibility could not have registered on the patrol's index of suspicion, but the reality they faced, to their horror, was a Baluba war party preparing to move in for the kill. The typical reaction is one of fight or flight and the Irish tried both. Too few in number to begin with, only some had weapons to hand and their ammunition was running out, they tried putting 'stand-off' distance between them and their attackers. The Balubas lined the bank of the river, some ten or fifteen metres away, shouting and continuing to fire. The Irish regrouped on the rise, and Lieutenant Gleeson attempted to speak with the war party, but he received only arrows in return, many of which found their mark. There was realisation among some of the

Commanding Officer's driver examines wreaths at Albertville airport, 18 November 1960.   Courtesy of the Military Archives, Dublin

Irish that they were going to die, especially if they stayed where they were. In any event the Balubas rushed forward and fierce hand-to-hand fighting erupted. The Irish were desperate to survive the onslaught and Dougan, Gaynor, Gleeson, Kelly and McGuinn were killed.

Amazingly, six of the Irish troops managed to fight through the encircling Balubas and a desperate pursuit began as the running battle continued into the bush. The frenzied Balubas wanted to continue killing, while the Irish desperately wanted to evade certain death. Firing as they ran, the surviving Irish peacekeepers clung to the slender hope that if they could outrun their hunters they might yet escape. The skirmish continued in this vein for a short while but the dense bush and the close-packed vegetation was too thick for the Irish troops to navigate quickly. They became dispersed and the pursuit broke down into individual evasive efforts to stay alive. Killeen, Fennell and Farrell were killed while Kenny, through exhaustion, and Fitzpatrick and Browne, through having no other option, found that although the dense growth hindered motion it also provided cover.

In different places and independent of each other, Kenny and Fitzpatrick crawled into the undergrowth, lay still, and hid. They could hear the Balubas looking for them and the noise made by the individual encounters between the Irish and tribesmen around them. The closely-packed vegetation proved a successful sanctuary for Fitzpatrick, while Kenny, although discovered, feigned death. Despite being badly beaten he did not betray his pretence and survived the ordeal. Browne too escaped the chase. He fought himself clear but was not to cheat death. In the immediate aftermath of the ambush, patrols dispatched to the bridge on the non-return of Lieutenant Gleeson and his party discovered Fitzpatrick first, and later, Kenny.

Trooper Browne's fate and body were only discovered two years later. He had succeeded in putting two miles distance between him, the war

Fr Crean HCF saying mass for the Irish deceased of the Niemba ambush at Albertville airport, on their journey homeward to Ireland, November 1960.
Courtesy of the Military Archives, Dublin

party and the ambush site. Heading north, it is believed he sought help from two native women near the village of Tundulu and giving them money asked for food and directions; however, they alerted young warriors who killed him.

The Niemba Ambush was a seminal moment for Ireland and the Defence Forces. It occurred only three months after the first Irish contingent of two battalions (32nd and 33rd) were deployed amid a mood of national exhilaration. The Irish Defence Forces' involvement in UN services overseas was a national tonic as it heralded the dawn of a new outward-looking, more modern Ireland. The sudden deaths of nine of its soldiers, the Defence Force's biggest single loss of life in one tragic overseas incident, then or since, was a stark reality check and a loss of innocence for Ireland. The dead Irish peacekeepers were given a State funeral and over a quarter of a million people turned out in Dublin to witness the funeral cortège as it made its way through the capital to Glasnevin Cemetery.

The Balubas did not know the Irish would not be belligerent, the Irish did not know the Balubas would be, and so there was chaos in the Congo. The Balubas mistakenly considered that because the Irish troops were white they presented the same threat posed to them by the white mercenaries in the pay of Moise Tshombe, a tribal rival. They were soon to learn of the impartiality of the Irish, whose own painful history rendered them free of any colonial baggage and in due course provided much needed protection for the Balubas and other tribes in refugee camps. The naivety of an Irish nation was ended and lessons were learned by the Defence Forces, but the drama and the death in the Congo was set to continue.

Les Affreux – The 'Frightful Ones'

In Africa, the real danger came from the vast inaccessible terrain, the extreme climate and rampant disease. In overcoming these enemies, the opposing soldiers and peacekeepers first had to fight to stay alive before they could engage any human opponent. For UN peacekeepers belligerence was the enemy, its human form ominously manifest in the many mercenaries in the pay of Tshombe. In south west Congo at the close of 1960, Katanga was at war internally with the Balubas and externally with the ANC (Armée Nationale Congolaise), the army of the newly independent Democratic Republic of the Congo, from which Katanga had been trying to break away. Katanga's president, Moise Tshombe, had significantly strengthened the spine of his force with the addition of hundreds of well-armed, highly trained and combat-experienced mercenaries. Their presence provided Tshombe with an assertiveness and a disinclination towards a negotiated détente with the UN; instead their existence inevitably catapulted the Katangese towards conflict with the UN forces.

White mercenaries (Belgian, French, British, Rhodesian, South African, some Germans, almost unavoidably one or two Irish), all soldiers of fortune and ex-military adventure-seeking veterans mostly motivated, if not pure and simply, by money, were recruited across Europe and elsewhere as 'advisors', 'technicians' and 'police officers' for the Katangan Gendarmerie. Their paid participation granted the secessionists an on-the-ground tactical and an overall strategic capability, a potency thrusting the Katangese headlong into combat with the United Nations Operation in the Congo (ONUC).

The mention of mercenaries immediately evokes an almost romantic mystique, but a mercenary is simply an ex-soldier who sells his military skills for money. A soldier is a member of an army and is trained to fight and kill. Tshombe recruited hundreds of these 'dogs of war' to bark for him and deliver a decidedly offensive edge to his forces, thereby strengthening the overall resolve of his Katangan Gendarmerie.

An *Evening Herald* article of the time tells its own tale:

> An ex-French Army Officer was being held today on a charge of trying to recruit 'technicians' to work in the troubled Congo province of Katanga. He was held under a law that prohibits recruiting foreign armies on French soil. Police said he had interviewed several men in his hotel room after running this advertisement in local papers:
>
> CENTRAL AFRICA: *Good pay, former soldiers and young men recently discharged. Those having experience in central Africa preferred. With or without speciality, drivers, radiomen, mechanics. Passport necessary, URGENT.*

Authorities alleged he paid recruits 1,000 francs (£70) as a bonus to sign. Bachelors were paid 1,970 francs a month and married men 2,190 francs.

An Irish mercenary, recruited by interview in a London hotel after answering an advertisement for 'Safari guides', enlisted for $800 a month, over six times what he could otherwise earn elsewhere. During the early stages the inducement was less, at $300 dollars a month, but still an attractive enticement and sufficient to draw the interest of many ex-military men. There were no American mercenaries among them as it was generally believed, incorrectly in fact, that those who enlisted for military service under a foreign flag were in contravention of US law and could have their passports confiscated.

The mercenaries naturally fell into three distinct groups: Belgian, French and the English-speakers – the Compagnie Internationale – mostly from the UK, South Africa and Rhodesia. When off-duty the former two, in particular some of the French, were given to unsoldierly behaviour that gave rise to an unnecessary notoriety. When in the public eye some sought attention by courting a macho-type image: unshaven, long-haired, needlessly in possession of many weapons and wearing well-worn combat fatigues, swaggering from bar to bar in a swashbuckling derring-do fashion. All this gave rise to an exaggerated impression that they were a collection of ill-disciplined, gung-ho hellraisers, a representation not lost on the media, and the phrase 'Les Affreux' – the Frightful Ones – became synonymous with the appearance of some of Katanga's French mercenaries.

In overall command of the mercenaries was a Belgian, Colonel Crevecoeur, and his second in command was Major Matisse. The French group was under Colonel Faulques, formerly a major in the Foreign Legion, a veteran of Dien Bien Phu and fresh from many encounters in Algeria with the Front de Libération Nationale (FLN). Bob Denard (a.k.a. Gilbert Bourgeaud), whose story was widely credited for the feature film *The Wild Geese* (Andrew V McLaglen, 1978) and the novel *Dogs of War* by Frederick Forsyth, was also involved. The Compagnie Internationale was initially commanded by Dick Browne, whose brother was Conservative MP Percy Browne, and included Colonel 'Mad' Mike Hoare and Alistair Wicks among its members. Sometimes confused early on with a unit called the White Legion, this much smaller mercenary outfit were, however, destined to be taken prisoner by UN Ethiopian troops at Kabala in northern Katanga.

The mercenaries were very well equipped, and their armament included brand new weaponry from Belgian manufacturers such as the 7.62mm FN rifle (the British equivalent was the L1A1 Self-Loading Rifle (SLR), or the American M16), the belt-fed 7.62mm General Purpose Machine Gun (GPMG), the FN Browning 9mm High Power Pistol, the 9mm Vigneron M2 and the FN 9mm UZI sub-machine gun.

Speed, noise and immense firepower were the tactics employed by the mercenaries to counter the Baluba. Noise was associated with great power and conveniently was a by-product of the firepower which was used to maximum effect to saturate any Baluba target areas, whether real, possible or even simply suspected. The speed was achieved by being organised into several units known as 'Groupes Mobiles'. At the forefront of each were up to six heavily armed 'Willys Jeeps' with a mounted GPMG or a .3 or .5 Browning Heavy Machine Gun (HMG). With its heavy barrel, the .5 was an updated model of the 1930s design. Two million were initially manufactured and it remains one of the most powerful machine guns in existence. Irish troops were to encounter it, or more precisely, were subjected to its highly disruptive effect, and initially had little equivalent viable response. These highly mobile columns were sometimes spearheaded by light armoured vehicles. Whether jeeps or armoured, or a mix, they were supported by truck-borne Katangese Gendarmerie. The required speed, firepower (noise) and accuracy were delivered to good effect in many whirlwind attacks.

Communications were provided by the PRC-9 short-range backpack radio sets used by the US Army. Powerful radio transmitters were used as rear-links to communicate with the *état-major* (Gendarmerie/mercenary headquarters in Élisabethville) when the various Groupes Mobiles were operating in the Bushveld (a dense bush-filled region in southern Africa) or hemmed in along routes by impenetrable jungle forests, at ranges of up to several hundred kilometres.

The mercenaries were employed to 'pacify' the Balubas and take on the central government's ANC. In the first instance, fighting unsophisticated Balubas demanded an unorthodox approach because of the cultural nature of their comprehension. Uncomplicated, badly organised and poorly armed, they could nevertheless be fanatically brave. Frequently fortified by marijuana and heavily influenced by tribal witch doctors, their preferred tactic was ambush or frontal assault in overwhelming numbers. The prospect of falling prisoner to the Baluba was inconceivable, as they were known to practise grotesque ritual torture, causing the victim excruciating pain and suffering before death. Nor were the Irish immune from the Baluba, their eleven-man patrol having been attacked and nine butchered at or near Niemba. Yet within a matter of some eighteen months it was Irish and Swedish UN troops that were to defend Baluba refugee camps in Élisabethville during the fighting of 1961 and 1962, and at one point some 40,000 Baluba and other tribal refugees were under their protection.

The Baluba had once formed a mighty empire larger than Belgium and Holland combined, which had since waned and by the 1960s they were living as a minority tribe in northern Katanga with a rival, now more powerful tribe, the Lunda. The Bayeke, fierce and warlike, were a third and strong tribe to contend with and ancient tribal rivalries continued to exist. Tshombe was a member of the Lunda royal house and so a natural rival of the Baluba. Since gaining independence, and unrestricted by colonial subjection or obedience to tribal permissions, young adult Balubas had rampaged across northern Katanga, armed with rudimentary weapons and attacking white Belgian settlers and black tribal rivals. These included poisoned arrows and spears, clubs studded with six-inch nails, and sharpened bicycle chains which could shred human flesh to the bone.

Getting to grips internally with the Baluba was one thing – and ongoing – but the time would surely come for military assertiveness in support of the secession. Set against the backdrop of the powerful and competing influences already tearing the Congo apart, three critical circumstances – the death of Congolese Prime Minister Patrice Lumumba, a second UN Security Council Resolution, and the increased activity of the ANC – resulted in events unfolding quickly.

In December 1960, through deception and double-dealing, Patrice Lumumba, along with two others (Maurice Mpola and Joseph Okito), were arrested by Colonel Joseph Mobutu and President Kasavubu of the Leopoldville government and delivered into the hands of his tribal and political opponents, resulting in the announcement of their deaths on 13 February by the Katangese minister of the interior, Godefroid Munongo. Seven days later, on 21 February 1961, the UN Security Council adopted a new resolution allowing the ONUC to use force to restore order and take whatever steps necessary to prevent civil war erupting in the Congo. The UN resolution also demanded the immediate evacuation of all mercenaries and other foreign military and political advisors. The authority for 'the use of force, if necessary, as a last resort' was a mandate to act, changing the nature of the UN forces' rules of engagement from passive peacekeepers (opening fire as a last resort and only if fired upon) to active peace enforcers, allowing a more robust, vigorous, proactive posture. Finally, under Mobutu, the ANC increased their activities, particularly along the internal provincial borders of Kasai and Katanga.

Into this turmoil, Irish Lieutenant General Sean McKeown was appointed Force Commander of ONUC in January 1961. From early to mid-1961, the period following Lumumba's death, order continued to further deteriorate throughout the Congo. Late in August, Lumumba's replacement, Cyrille Adoula, was elected as the new prime minister of the Congo. He immediately announced his intention to end the Katangan secession effort and special legislation was enacted to allow the government to expel foreign officers and mercenaries. To achieve this, Adoula requested the assistance of the UN force sent in to keep the peace and maintain order. In effect he was requesting a more partisan participation than the UN force and its contributing members had anticipated. He wished them to become more measurably immersed in the internal fighting than they had intended and take on a deeper dimension in the developing drama. Had the innocent UN been manipulated unwittingly towards mission creep, allowing an escalation of its role, or was it simply that this was what maintaining order required? For sure, order within Congo could not be restored until the Katangan secession threat was addressed, and order within Katanga could not be resolved until the menace of the mercenary threat was addressed.

The First Battle of Katanga – September 1961

In the likely event of coming into harm's way, the first action required is to remove the source of danger. Before daybreak on 28 August 1961, the UN's Irish, Swedish and Indian battalions were out in force and active in Élisabethville, their objective to pre-emptively oust the foreign military and white mercenaries from the Katangese Gendarmerie's order of battle. The logic of the surprise UN offensive was to outwit them now rather than having to overpower them later. Operation Rampunch, which became known as 'Operation Rum Punch' by the English-speaking peacekeeping forces, was the UN's first direct response to the ever increasing belligerent behaviour of the Katangese. The UN was taking the mercenary fuel from the Katangan fire to contain the Congolese flames.

All mercenary, foreign military and paramilitary forces were targeted for arrest. It was an attempt to reduce the kinetic-effect potential of Tshombe, his Katangan regime and his mercenary-led military force. By defusing his military power and prowess it was intended to cause him to seek a negotiated settlement more earnestly. For the previous six months (January to July 1961) peace talks had – frustratingly – not yielded the desired results and Irishman Dr Conor Cruise O'Brien, appointed as UN Special Representative in Katanga by UN Secretary General Dag Hammarskjöld, was charged to deliver a solution to the reintegration of Katanga back into the Congo. Thwarted by Tshombe's evident determination to keep Katanga independent, Cruise O'Brien was equally – and as stubbornly – determined to bring the secession to an end. Tshombe and his overseas advisors were hoping to outlast the UN initiative, knowing the UN for its part was in the early days of pioneering its peacekeeping policies, making them match their on-the-ground coordination of military, political and diplomatic strategies. The Katangan secession was backed by European commercial patronage, whose own interests lay in ensuring that Katanga's wealth did not fall into the hands of Congolese nationalists. A more forceful posture was required to demonstrate that the UN was serious about ending Katanga's succession and Operation Rampunch was launched.

Well organised and effective, the UN caught many of Élisabethville's mercenaries off-guard with no casualties suffered or inflicted and very few shots fired. The pattern was the same throughout Katanga and initially it was a resounding success; all of the operation's military objectives were achieved, the majority of the mercenaries were captured, Godefroid Munongo, the interior minister, was placed under house arrest, and control of a number of installations was wrestled from Gendarmerie hands. In staging a show of strength, the UN had demonstrated their willingness to forcibly implement the resolution of 21 February and – temporarily at least – seized the initiative from Tshombe.

Meanwhile, on 4 August in north Katanga, another Irish unit, the 1st Infantry Group, took over command of Kamina Base. Their tasks were airfield defence, defending the base and its approaches, general administration of the base and protection of the Kilubi Dam and its hydroelectric station, located some sixty miles north east. In pursuance of that task, B Company, 1st Infantry Group, had taken over Kilubi on 16 August. Lieutenant Michael Minehane (later Major General and Force Commander, United Nations Peacekeeping Force in Cyprus (UNIFYCYP) 1992–94) remembers:

> Things took a serious turn from the 19 August onwards when headquarters in Leopoldville organised what was known as Operation Rampunch. This was [the] UN's plan to haul in all the white mercenaries in Katanga, detain them and repatriate them. For us, that required the immediate setting up of a Detention Centre in Kamina and it also meant that we must be prepared for the hostility which it would give rise to in the Kamina area. The Detention Centre was prepared and our defences were upgraded in anticipation of the inevitable reaction that it would provoke. Detention started in all of Katanga on 28 August and within days we were hosting 150 men [as prisoners]. Tension mounted in Kamina and in the rest of Katanga. Detaining that many rogues created problems for us and we were happy to see a couple of Sabena 707s airlift them out of Kamina between the 9 and 14 September. By 14 [September] we had serious concerns about the intentions of the gendarmerie battalion in Kaminaville.
>
> Our unit had its first experience of action within days. Nobody in their wildest imaginings could have forecast that an attack would come from the air, but it did! A [Katangese Air Force (FAK)] Fouga jet appeared over the base and indicated to our observation tower that he intended to attack us. The pilot discussed likely targets and his general intentions with the staff of the tower. We had to consider some form of defence against this unexpected

threat. The best we could come up with was our Vickers MMGs, which were mounted by our two artillery officers in an anti-aircraft mode for which they were never intended and ill suited. Nonetheless, fire was directed at the Fouga on its next visit. In all, the Fouga paid us about six visits during which he strafed airport buildings and defensive positions. On his second visit to us the pilot indicated that he intended to do damage, that the joking was over. Sure enough he selected a DC-3 on the runway and offloaded his hardware on it. He scored a bull's-eye and the plane went up in flames. This was pretty serious and we were left to ponder the future without defence against a developing and serious threat. He represented our very first taste of warfare, our first shots fired in anger. It was truly a benign introduction to fighting but for any soldier it was a singular experience.

Sporadic fighting had broken out in Élisabethville [and during] the following days there [were] heavy exchanges of fire in the

Katanga Gendarmerie on mobile patrol. Courtesy of the Military Archives, Dublin

city. At Kamina [Base] we were aware of rumblings to the south in Kaminaville. Troops were assembling and their area of interest could only be the strategically important airbase at Kamina. They were eventful days and for me they were about to become even more eventful. My area of responsibility within the company was the support weapons, i.e. MMGs and our tiny 60mm mortars. The company was commanded by Commandant Kevin MacMahon and my platoon was commanded by Captain Thomas Hartigan.

On the late evening of 14 September 1961 I was called to Kevin's office where I received a brief, to the effect that the Swedes at Kaminagate [sic] were under attack by the Gendarmerie, and were in dire need of support. Since mortars were my business, Kevin instructed me to get on up there and give them a hand. Mortars come in a variety of sizes. At 60mm, my three mortars were the smallest made and not likely to impress the Swedes as serious support. We had to help them and soon I was on my way with a crew of Sergeant McCabe, Private Jack McGrath and others.

We rendezvoused with a guide at about ten in the evening and some three miles south of the base. I remember it as a beautiful moonlit night and I vividly recall all the sounds of an African evening, especially the crickets. I remember too, as we moved towards the Swedish position, the voice of a Swedish radio operator in our vehicle, calling to his base: 'Alpha Rudolf, Alpha Rudolf, kum, kum.' Movement forward to the Swedish position was eerie and worrying, since we were in totally strange territory. However, we were led in safety by our Swedish guide. We were extremely happy to find prepared mortar trenches located in a very suitable place just to the rear of the Swedish forward trenches.

Early in the day a company-sized detachment of Gendarmes had tried to penetrate the base along the road. The Swedes fought well and held off the attack. The Gendarmerie took casualties and backed away, leaving behind a large truck laden with ordnance. As dawn broke I was able to observe the truck some 300m from our positions. Its driver was dead in the cab and on top of the cab was another dead soldier who had been manning a machine-gun mounted atop the cab. As the light improved it was possible to see that the Gendarmerie were making serious efforts to recover their truck and its ordnance. By that time my crew was set up and ready for whatever came our way. The Swedish commander came and talked to me about neutralising the truck with mortar fire. I advised him that while he was asking the impossible, we would give it a go. The mortar is essentially a neutralising weapon. It is not a pin-point target weapon. Even the idea of targeting a truck at the distance seemed fanciful. In true artillery style we bracketed the truck – one round just beyond, then one round short and the next landed smack, bang on the truck. The Swedes were delighted and, needless to say, full of admiration for our skills (good fortune)!

On the first day of Operation Rampunch 73 mercenaries were arrested in the province – 41 by the Irish – and by 8 September, 273 non-Congolese personnel in the Katangan Gendarmerie (mercenaries and Belgian officers) had been repatriated, with some 65 awaiting a similar departure. In all, more than 75 per cent of known mercenaries in Katanga were arrested and flown out by the UN. 'The game was up' was how matters were generally perceived among the mercenaries, although it was estimated 104 had slipped the net. The military momentum gained as a result of Operation Rampunch was, however, neither politically nor diplomatically maintained, and so the advantage was lost. Mistakenly, the UN allowed local and Belgian officials to complete the measures the UN had initiated, but these proved unsuccessful. While the operation did see off a large part of the Belgian officer corps of the Katangan Gendarmerie, with additional UN pressure on Belgium, the deported mercenaries flown out by the UN were directly, although discretely, flown back in by Tshombe, only in additional numbers; the game was very much back on.

A by-product of the operation – of no small future significance – was the seizure of fourteen assorted Katangese aircraft (two Sikorsky helicopters, three Alouette helicopters, three Dakotas, four Doves and two Herons). Virtually the entire Katangese air complement had fallen uncontested into UN hands. However, five aircraft not at Élisabethville (two Fouga Magister Jets, two Doves and a Tri-pacer) escaped impoundment and while seriously diminished the skies were still the preserve of the mercenary pilots and, albeit much reduced, they still enjoyed air superiority; in the land of the blind, the one-eyed man is king.

With no UN fighter aircraft available, the Katangan Fouga Magister was master. This combat jet trainer from Aérospatiale, though somewhat obsolete, remained unrivalled in the Congo skies. Swallow-like in appearance, with a highly distinctive butterfly tail, its cruising speed was 750 kph and it had a range of almost 1,000 km. It could strike any target with its rockets and 7.62mm machine guns or bomb it at will; altogether it was a lethal force multiplier. A lone Fouga was itself a serious single prospect to have to deal with and in the hands of Magain, the stocky Flemish–Belgian mercenary pilot, UN ground forces were particularly vulnerable and susceptible to its armaments.

After Operation Rampunch a vicious campaign of anti-UN propaganda was conducted by the Katangese government and anti-UN demonstrations were orchestrated in the centre of Élisabethville. There was also increased Gendarmerie activity and a noticeable intensification in the presence of mercenaries around the city. On 9 September roadblocks sprang up throughout the capital to impede UN troop movements and the following day in Jadotville (Likasi), a quiet mining town 160 km north of Élisabethville, a mercenary-led Gendarmerie force of over 2,000 troops cut off an isolated company of 157 Irish peacekeepers in what was to become known as the Siege of Jadotville.

CHAPTER 2

Company in Defence (Jadotville)

'Enemy attack has commenced, please send strong reinforcements immediately' was the radio message sent from A Company, 35th Irish Battalion in Jadotville to the battalion headquarters sixty miles away in Élisabethville. Their earlier transmission: 'Alert on here', radioed after an initial probing incident, was responded to with: 'Defend yourself with maximum force.' Now, the main attack had begun in earnest. The prelude to the ground assault was an intense, unexpected bombardment of mixed mortar bombs, 75mm artillery shells and heavy machine-gun fire onto the Irish positions. Then the onslaught proper began when over 500 infantry charged in waves toward A Company. By their sheer numbers and momentum alone they looked set to overrun the Irish defences, yet the peacekeepers defended themselves with every weapon available and with every fibre of will they possessed. This was a hard place to be, but the Irish were up for the fight. It was now the turn of the Katangans and mercenaries to be surprised, so stiff was the Irish resistance that their surge forward faltered, then eased off, and then the action was over – for now. Sporadic firing continued but the Irish had held out. Dusk began to fall and with it, to their delight, the Irish could hear the thump and thud of mortars exploding and the distinctive rattle of heavy machine gun fire ten miles away at Lufira Bridge. They knew then that reinforcements were on their way and when the firing ceased all they had to do was await their arrival. They waited, and waited and waited.

Post Operation 'Rum Punch', and with the successful capture of Gendarmerie HQ in Élisabethville on the Sunday morning of September 1961, Commandant Pat Quinlan returned from a 35th Irish Battalion conference to where his troops, A Company, were under canvas around the perimeter of Élisabethville airport, securing it to ensure the airport remained operational in the event of an attack. He announced to his company officers, Captain Liam Donnelly, Support

Platoon, Lieutenant Joe Leech, No. 1 Platoon, Lieutenant Tom Quinlan (no relation), No. 2 Platoon, Lieutenant Noel Carey, No. 3 Platoon, and Company Sergeant Willie Hegarty, that they were to pack up immediately and be ready to move by 1300 hours to a town called Jadotville, sixty miles away. A Company were to be transported by Swedish trucks, as they had no vehicles of their own, and were to be joined by two armoured cars from the cavalry group under Lieutenant Kevin Knightly. Everything was rushed in order to meet the deadline for the arrival of the Swedish transport and in their haste they were told to leave their 81mm mortars and emergency pack rations. These would be sent on later.

A week prior to their move, a Swedish force under Major Meade consisting of one Swedish APC company and B Company, 35th Irish Battalion, was sent to Jadotville on the same mission. In addition they were to patrol towards Kamina and observe and report to Brigade HQ in Élisabethville any build-up of Katangan troops. On arrival, Major Meade was ordered out of Jadotville by the town's Burgermeister (mayor) and, as he found no trouble or rioting in Jadotville, requested to be withdrawn. As B Company were crossing the Lufira Bridge, ten miles from Jadotville in the direction of Élisabethville, they passed their fellow soldiers from A Company, heading towards Jadotville. Naturally, they questioned in their own minds the decision to send A Company to replace two companies who had just decided to withdraw as they saw no rioting in Jadotville. Why was a company being deployed sixty miles from base without adequate transport, logistics or heavy support weapons? It violated every military principle they knew.

Sent to Jadotville to defend the town and its white European population against possible riotous unrest, the Irish were to be made feel unwelcome from their arrival and ultimately had to defend themselves from those they were sent to protect. Instructed to occupy the area by ONUC headquarters, they had done so to prevent atrocities and a massacre, yet soon it would be A Company themselves who would be beleaguered and under siege. The reasons that caused such a deployment have been much ruminated upon ever since. High-level political manoeuvrings, manipulated by the Belgians as a ruse to entrap UN troops, were considered foremost as a possibility. Simply directed to deploy in Jadotville, A Company had no prerogative where they could select the location of their campsite. They just had to take over an area that had initially sufficed for those before them; chosen for accommodation purposes and convenience for quick access to the town's European quarter rather than with any regard to thoughts of tactical defence.

Located on the town's outskirts, in essence it was billet accommodation pure and simple. Consisting of single-storey villas and outhouses centred around the Purfina service station and garage, Support and No. 1 Platoon faced towards the golf course and No. 2 Platoon occupied villas on the left of the road. Company HQ was to the left of Purfina garage, while No. 3 platoon, on the other side, also occupied villas and tents. The distance between the platoons was about 750 metres, an area containing a number of deserted villas. There was a railway crossing at the entrance to the town and to the left was the huge Union Minière Mining Company and hundreds of tin huts on the hilly ground to A Company's left. Close to the area of their positions, for up to 450 metres, was scrubland with high elephant

Preparing a trench for the defence of Jadotville.   Courtesy of the Military Archives, Dublin

grass. All this was conducive to covered concealment for unobserved encroachment by any attacking force and the site was chosen purely for its suitability to accommodate the soldiers rather than any thought of defence, offering its occupiers neither an all-round field of observation nor 360 degree interlocking arcs of fire. In short it would be difficult to defend, and in a short time, unknown to A Company, they were going to have to defend it. This time it would not be the primitive Baluba tribesmen they would be fighting but a mercenary-led force of Katangese Gendarmerie.

Katanga's attraction was its vast copper, cobalt and uranium mineral wealth, and Jadotville was a thriving copper mining town. Its 10,000 or so white Europeans mainly worked in mining or associated services, while 50,000 Katangans, living in the tin huts, were the mine's native workers. About the size of Newbridge, Jadotville's railway line connected to Northern Rhodesia, today Zambia, as part of the copper belt. Post-independence the white Europeans stayed on, maintaining their links with mining and their equally firm links with Belgium.

Digging In

Red, hard-compacted and copper-saturated, the soil was no more ideal than the site to have to dig into. Yet that was what Commandant Quinlan decided A Company's best form of defence would be, in a situation which offered very few advantages. The tense situation, having begun with intimidation, had now become one of danger. Cut off and surrounded, Commandant Quinlan ordered A Company's four platoons to dig in. It was a basic infantry tactic when tasked to hold ground in a conventional warfare scenario, however no one had expected to be doing so as peacekeepers. But under the circumstances his clear presence of mind had a logic to it. It was becoming increasingly likely that A Company would have to put up a defence and he was giving his men the best chance of doing so to best effect. (See map on p. vii.)

Trenches – holes dug into the ground to get in to, fire from, and be protected by – was what 'digging in' was all about. It could not be done haphazardly and there were guiding principles involved, principles that had to be adapted to the terrain and the circumstances. There were other considerations: time and materials available, both for digging-in with and for actual use in trench construction, were also important factors. It has been said that the most important tool any soldier can have is a spoon, since you can dig with it as well as eat. A Company were not reduced to that though, and despite the searing heat and blinding dust set about their task in earnest. The seriousness of the situation was not lost on them, as they knew from their training that digging-in offered them the best defensive option to defeat an enemy attack, providing cover from view, protection from fire and, if their trench included overhead cover, shelter from airbursts and shrapnel. It was crucial that the correct siting of trenches in relation to the terrain and to each other facilitated the optimum possibilities for interlinking, mutually-supporting arcs of fire. An individual trench was required to have a fire-bay and a shelter-bay, with proper overhead cover, and all to be camouflaged.

A ten-man section dictates a combination of two and three-man trenches, with the sections' fire support light machine gun (Bren gun) requiring careful sighting to derive best effect from it. A platoon would have three such sections, plus two-by-two-man trenches at platoon headquarters – the platoon commander and platoon sergeant being in different trenches. The dimensions of an 'infantry trench' are not exact but are usually armpit deep with elbow rests for occupants in the standing position. The use of depth in defence, or as it is also known, 'defence in depth', is essential to prevent enemy exploitation of a penetration, should they overrun the forward trenches. The depth will absorb the enemy's momentum, the penetration progressively destroyed by the fire from those in trenches sited in depth. Sited 'two forward, one back', be it sections, platoons, companies or even battalions, this was how depth and mutual support was achieved.

This was not, however, the alignment allowed under the circumstance experienced by A Company. They were dispersed more than was recommended, strung out in groups of two, two-platoon positions, with 800 metres in between the two, two-platoon groups. The textbook frontage for a company, two platoons forward, one behind, was anywhere between 600 and 1,500 metres. A Company's area of responsibility was a far too large quarter of a mile by a half a mile. Good communications grants good command, and the reverse is also the case. Inter-platoon communications, however, were not readily facilitated by the old No. 88 radios, which were obsolete and whose batteries were awkward and defective.

An obstacle forward of the front trenches to be covered by fire is also very useful, but A Company had no barbed-wire, mines or trip flares. It was now that the absence of their 81mm mortars was acutely felt. A Company did, however, have six 60mm mortars located with Support Platoon, which had a range of 750 metres; as well as two 84mm recoilless rifles with a range of 550 metres used for anti-tank purposes, and two Second World War vintage belt-fed, water-cooled Vickers machine-guns mounted on tripods with a range of 900 metres. Each man had the newly-purchased FN automatic rifle, while NCOs and officers had the Gustav sub-machine gun, and each ten-man section had a light support weapon, the Bren gun. Also available were the two mounted Vickers machine guns with the Armoured Car Section.

Lieutenant Noel Carey recalls the dig-in as follows: 'That evening [Commandant Quinlan] ordered all platoons to dig in, camouflage trenches and hide spoil [dug-out earth]. We worked desperately in [the] stifling heat and hard ground but that night all were dug in and camouflaged by placing scrub and elephant grass over the trenches and removing spoil. Commandant Quinlan personally checked trench positions, all-round protection and fields of fire.' Commandant Pat Quinlan's decision to have A Company dig in was far-seeing, effective and, crucially, was to save Irish lives.

The Noose Tightens

On the morning of Saturday, 9 September, A Company's ration truck was stopped at the Lufira Bridge on its resupply run to Élisabethville and returned empty. Commandant Quinlan ordered Lieutenant Carey to go into Jadotville and see what was happening. Taking the Land Rover and an escort of three NCOs, they were stopped at the closed railway gates. Going forward on foot, Lieutenant Carey was confronted by a large number of armed Katangan troops and a Belgian mercenary officer who refused him entry to the town. Insisting that the UN enjoyed freedom of movement, Carey nonetheless continued to be denied access and was not allowed through. He returned to Commandant Quinlan to inform him of what had occurred and in turn Quinlan reported the matter to Battalion HQ in Élisabethville. In reply, Commandant Quinlan was assured all was well and to stay in situ – A Company were not to withdraw.

The following day, remaining very concerned overnight about the deterioration in the circumstances at Jadotville, Commandant Quinlan sent Captain Liam Donnelly and Medical Officer Commandant Joe Clune to Battalion HQ in Élisabethville to give a first-hand account of A Company's situation. Although they were stopped at Lufira Bridge, they were eventually allowed through when Captain Donnelly pretended to be sick. In Élisabethville, the Officer Commanding 35th Irish Battalion, Lieutenant Colonel Hugh McNamee, and his staff were hosting a dinner for Conor Cruise O'Brien, UN Special Representative in Katanga. On completion of the dinner, Captain Donnelly reported on the up-to-date scenario playing out in Jadotville and of Commandant Quinlan's concern regarding this new situation; most especially that the stated reason for A Company's deployment there no longer held sway. Instead of the need to protect the white population against any threat, they were now threatening the UN Irish troops. Furthermore, they reported that A Company were surrounded by a large formation of mercenary-led Katangan troops, being added to daily, and that Lufira Bridge was effectively blocked. Commandant Quinlan's recommendation was that A Company be withdrawn or substantially reinforced. He was assured that all would be well, that matters were under control and there was no need to worry. With this assurance, Captain Donnelly and Commandant Clune returned across the Lufira Bridge to Jadotville.

The tension continued to mount in Jadotville and the prevailing atmosphere was becoming more pointed by the day as the stand-off continued. A Company's dug-in platoons were well dispersed, perhaps too spread out, but they had to deny tactical advantage to the Katangans, who were continually attempting to encroach into the Irish-occupied area. Rumours of possible attacks by mobs from the surrounding villages heightened the already fraught nerves of the Irish. Neither withdrawn nor reinforced, an encircled A Company waited anxiously for the next development. It would not be long in coming.

The Battle Begins

At 0700 hours on Wednesday 13 September, Lieutenant Carey received a message from Battalion HQ stating, 'Operation Morthor had taken place in Élisabethville. All installations taken over by UN Forces and all quiet. Inform Commandant Quinlan.' The Operation had been organised to remove, once again, all mercenaries from Katanga. This time, however, the Katangans were well informed of UN intentions and several Indian troops were killed while occupying the post office. Nevertheless they captured their objective, having killed a large number of Katanganese, and gunfire was to be heard all over Élisabethville as the Katangan forces and mercenaries resisted fiercely. The UN took casualties, including two members of the Irish Cavalry Corps who were killed after their armoured car was ambushed in the city.

This was the first A Company had known of Operation Morthor, leaving them completely exposed and very vulnerable. Lieutenant Carey informed Commandant Quinlan, who told him to immediately alert all of the platoons. Given the urgency and the distance, Lieutenant Carey drove the Company ambulance to Support Platoon's location. As he arrived he could see a number of trucks at the bus station near Support Platoon and fully armed Katangan troops dismounting. He alerted Support Platoon and moved swiftly on to the immediately adjacent No. 1 Platoon, whose members were going to daily mass, and shouted at them to get to their trenches. While returning in quick order to Company HQ he heard a burst of gunfire, and with his heart pounding inside his chest his natural instinct made him crouch inside the ambulance, believing he was the target. Commandant Quinlan set up his Orders Group (O Group) on the road and gave orders to his platoon commanders to go forward into their respective platoon positions. No. 3 Platoon, Lieutenant Carey's, was tasked with setting up a roadblock at his location and they placed a Land Rover and some oil barrels across the road, covered by an 84mm anti-tank gun. As he was completing the task he thought he heard the unexpected but unmistakable 'pop' of a mortar bomb leaving a mortar barrel. Suddenly, there was a succession of such 'pops' followed by the 'crump' of the initial mortar bomb impacting, followed by several more explosions, all falling into Support Platoon's area. It was not totally unexpected that something would happen, but what did happen was certainly not anticipated! Small arms fire, perhaps, but not this, not mortars, and not so many of them for so long. Worse was to come, with 75mm artillery shells fired from the golf course followed by heavy machine gun fire. There was an unpredicted suddenness about the situation, events were not meant to unfold like this. Yet this is exactly how matters materialised, and they had only just begun.

Action – Reaction

The pounding continued for over an hour. With no inter-platoon communications, a check three days previously having found all the batteries for the No. 88 radio-sets to be dead, it was difficult to gain information concerning possible casualties, or indeed of the general situation prevailing. As suddenly as the bombardment occurred, it stopped. Suddenly, a shout from the forward trench of Lieutenant Carey's Platoon signalled they were under attack from the front.

Lieutenant Carey described the situation:

> I immediately rushed to the forward trench, jumped in and my Section Corporal there was Corporal Sean Foley, who pointed at a scrub area in front of Lieutenant Tom Quinlan's No. 2 Platoon area. I could make out figures coming through the bush in approximately Company strength. Eventually they approached to within 400 yards of us, coming on to No. 2 Platoon who commenced firing directly at the Katangans and mercenaries. We were firing from an enfilade position [at a sideways angle of approximately forty-five degrees] onto them, due to our platoon's relative position to No. 2 Platoon, and my Bren gunner was engaging the targets, as they were now within range and exposed in the open. I found my Gustav sub-machine gun of little use due to its limited range and took over firing the Bren gun, directed by Corporal Foley. Both Companies fired into them as they advanced. The Katangans still came forward. We continued firing, our sustained unfaltering direct volume of fire having its effect. Their attack stuttered, next stalled a little, then completely stopped and they broke back into the bush retreating towards Jadotville.

We were elated with our success. The adrenalin flowed, the various emotions competing for expression: firstly shock, at being under the bombardment, next fear and uncertainty, at a human level, then scared – as you were – of being aware of the challenge of the responsibility of having to lead, of people looking to you, for your reaction to guide their reaction. Once there was a requirement to act I was focussed, because I was part of a team and wanted to be involved in the action. Once I grabbed the Bren gun those around me engaged. I have since often asked myself; did I kill anyone? I honestly do not know, but I've answered it this way: Would I do it again? Absolutely, automatically, without question. We were under attack [so] we were going to fight back. A determination comes out. They had fired on us, tried to kill us, and we were going to respond. The heat and the dust in the trench was stifling and we needed to consume large quantities of water.

Their first time under fire, they all felt that they had acquitted themselves well. However, the company had suffered its first casualty when Private Bill Reidy, forward in No. 1 Platoon position, was wounded in the stomach, a ricochet via his thigh, but overall he had been fortunate as a second bullet struck his ammunition pouch, glancing off a spare magazine contained inside. The bullet was a tracer round, which ignites in flight guiding its firer to the direction of its target, and when it struck Private Reidy it caused his webbing to catch fire. The flames had to be doused before the medic could attend to the bleeding wound, after which Private Reidy was removed to a makeshift casualty station prepared by Company Quartermaster, Sergeant Pat Neville.

Mortaring and machine gun fire continued into No. 1 and Support Platoon areas and Sergeant Tom Kelly decided it was time to make a reply. Aided by information passed previously by Wexfordman Charles Kearney, Belfastman Terry Barbour and Hamish Mathieson from Scotland, all workers with Union Minière, he sought to put the Katangans and mercenaries on the receiving end of an Irish mortar barrage. With the aid of a map he brought the 60mm mortars into play at the extreme limit of their range and coordinated their fire onto the golf club area. Three rounds later, the opposing Katangan 75mm was blown to smithereens. They struck the ammunition supply stacked behind the mortar and up the whole lot went: gun, ammo, and crew. This breathing space, welcome though it was, did not last long.

The infantry onslaught was ongoing throughout the day, one advance involving more than 500 men, but the Katangans continued to be repulsed by the Irish, who inflicted heavy casualties. Heat, fatigue, dust and thirst came to the fore, but before these could be addressed another difficulty arose that required a response. During one assault some snipers had managed to infiltrate into one of the unoccupied villas in the Support Platoon area of the Irish lines. Their firing was becoming a cause for concern but Sergeant John Monaghan had the solution: he employed an 84mm anti-tank gun to good effect and took out the villa, snipers and all. This seemed to settle matters for the day and the Katangans, using an existing phone line to the Purfina Garage, requested a ceasefire to collect their wounded. Commandant Quinlan agreed to their request.

With the approach of dusk, Company Sergeant Jack Prendergast crawled to the trenches occupied by the platoon commanders, informing them that a relief column from Élisabethville was on its way and would be with them by nightfall. The message spread rapidly around the company positions, greeted with relief by everyone for the great news that it was, and the resultant soar of morale was palpable. Having acquitted themselves well, they were going to be reinforced and rescued. As if to confirm their delight, the audible thumps and thuds of mortar fire and other weapons could be heard from the direction of Lufira Bridge. 'Force Keane', Irish troops with Swedish APC support led by Commandant Johnny Keane, was engaged in an offensive action to break through to the besieged A Company.

With the cessation of noise from the bridge, the members of A Company began to wonder how long it would take their rescuers to arrive in Jadotville. As the time passed when 'Force Keane' ought to have appeared, A Company continued to wait. A runner arrived to summon the platoon commanders to a Commanding Officers (COs) conference, to be held in a villa now used as the Company HQ. It was the first time they had seen each other since the commencement of the day's extraordinary hostilities. Commandant Quinlan congratulated each of them on the actions of their respective platoons, but then came the bombshell: their would-be rescuers had returned to Élisabethville. Encountering heavy fire at Lufira Bridge, 'Force Keane' achieved no success in their attempt to overcome it. Stunned, the platoon commanders could not comprehend why 'Force Keane' had not maintained pressure on the bridge's defenders throughout the night and attacked again at first light. Instead, incomprehensibly to the platoon commanders, 'Force Keane' had decided to return to Élisabethville, leaving them, as they saw it, to the mercy of a rapidly growing Katangan force led by mercenaries. By that time the estimated strength of the force opposing them was in the order of 2,000 troops.

After a day of extremes; shock, elation, self-revelation and now devastation, it was with a dreadful feeling that they returned to their trenches. Commandant Quinlan had asked them not to tell their platoons as it could affect morale. Darkness descended, and with it new problems. With no forward protection, such as barbed wire, trip flares or mines, and with scrub coming close to their positions it was difficult to see an enemy approach. They remained on the alert and rotated within individual trenches so the troops could get some rest, but in the cramped space it was difficult. Flares from Verey guns were fired occasionally to light the battlefield, though this was more for morale than effect, as they proved of limited use against the scrub surrounding the Company. During the night the Company cooks did manage to get what was to become known as 'Jadotville Stew' to the trenches, but water was becoming scarce as they were consuming large quantities. Another problem was to contain the reckless firing, as some of the troops became jittery at the slightest sound. Exhaustion began to set in and sleep was necessary but proved elusive.

At first light on 14 September, all Platoon positions came under sporadic machine gun and mortar fire and the minds of A Company once again began to concentrate sharply and focus their attention on whatever the day ahead would bring. Mortar bombs exploded around them as they hugged the cover of their trenches, thankful not to be caught exposed out in the open. Unfortunately, Sergeant Wally Hegarty, No. 2 Platoon, who was moving towards a villa for water when the barrage commenced, was caught without cover. The first two mortar impacts exploded nearby, blowing the roof off the villa, and the third hit him in the legs and buttocks as he desperately dived for cover. Sergeant

Taking a welcome break and a refreshing drink, while 'digging in' at Jadotville.
Courtesy of the Military Archives, Dublin

Hegarty was taken to the casualty station, where he was attended to, and was back in action with his platoon the next day. Meanwhile the mortar fire intensified and Sergeant Kelly and his 60mm mortar crew were once again called into action. With Corporal Foley giving directions, and fall of shot corrections relayed through Lieutenant Carey, after a few ranging rounds Sergeant Kelly ordered rapid fire. There was a flash, a loud explosion, and a cessation of incoming mortar fire.

Around noon, A Company heard the noise of a jet aircraft coming from the direction of Jadotville and suddenly in the bright sunshine they could see a plane fly along the valley in front of their positions, wheel around, and fly over them again, this time more slowly. Some of the company waved, thinking it was a UN aircraft, but it accelerated and flew back towards Jadotville. An hour and a half later they saw the jet again as it flew along the valley, only this time it climbed into the dazzling sun. There was a shout of 'get down' as the plane suddenly swooped on the Purfina garage and strafed the building, blowing out the windows, and dropped two bombs on the courtyard of the garage causing large craters and loud explosions. The target was the petrol pumps and fuel tanks, which was another shock for the beleaguered Company as the last thing they expected was being bombed and strafed by a jet aircraft.

They felt completely vulnerable in their trenches. Dispersed and without good communications, the individual platoons had no idea if there were casualties or not. Only by shouting from trench to trench, platoon by platoon, did they learn that luckily no one was wounded. Commandant Quinlan, who was everywhere, placed the two armoured cars in such a manner as to criss-cross the fire of their Vickers machine guns, leaving Lieutenant Kevin Knightly in charge of their newly ordained anti-aircraft role. Still recovering from the shock of it all, an hour and a half later the Fouga Magister jet was back from its airbase in Kolwezi to bomb them again. The armoured cars put up a barrage of fire but the jet was gone. This time the bombs fell into the bush beside the road.

Darkness descended and fatigue set in, as did the effects of a second day of heat, dust, sunburn, and the shock of being bombed from the air by an enemy jet fighter. A successful infiltration by a number of Katangans saw them reach the villas between the platoons, whereupon they commenced sniping on the Irish. With Captain Liam Donnelly directing, Company Sergeant Prendergast and Sergeant John Monahan put a swift end to the threat with an 84mm anti-tank gun. During this exchange, however, a member of No. 3 Platoon, Private John Manning, was shot in the shoulder and evacuated to the casualty station, which now had three occupants.

Commandant Quinlan now realised that A Company was physically overextended on the ground and in order to ensure an organised shape was maintained, where command and control could be better exercised, he ordered secondary trenches be dug close to No. 2 Platoon's area, which No. 1 and Weapons Platoons would occupy. Within three hours these trenches were constructed and under cover of darkness stealthily occupied. A Company's frontage was reduced to a more manageable 350 metres, its form more like that of an all-round perimeter defence. Now that hostilities were entered into, they would 'occupy' the ground previously inhabited by their fire. Their original positions had, however, served their purpose, in that they had created distance, an area of stand-off between themselves and the Katangans so that during the sequential waves of attacks during the first day they had avoided being overrun.

At night the cooks managed to get bread, 'dog biscuits' and water to the company, and later Commandant Quinlan called a conference for his company officers. The platoon commanders reported a state of high morale among the troops despite the air attack. Commandant Quinlan said that Battalion HQ urged the Company to continue to hold out. He also reported on a phone conversation with the Burgermeister, using a phone in one of the villas, who had asked for a ceasefire to which he had agreed. But the Burgermeister's request to send an ambulance into the area to retrieve casualties was denied as the Commandant suspected a trap. He reported that the water and power had been cut and stressed the need to conserve stored supplies of water. There was still no news of any relief column. Later that night two mercenaries, under the belief that the Irish had all been captured, inadvertently arrived at the roadblock in No. 3 Platoon's area and were duly taken prisoner. Disarmed yet properly treated, they were locked under guard in a room in a villa. A long tense night began, each man wondering what the following day would bring.

Dawn brought the lights of tracer bullets whizzing over the heads of A Company, fired from buildings on a hilltop position over 450 metres away. A Company could not make an effective reply as with the light weapons they had the buildings were out of range. Suddenly, one of Lieutenant Kevin Knightly's armoured cars swooped into No. 3 Platoon's area and fired over 1,000 rounds towards the hilltop. The noise of the rounds clattering off the buildings was great for their morale, as was the cessation of the incoming tracer fire. It was not long, however, before the Fouga Magister jet came back again, this time flying higher than before, perhaps because of the reception it had received from Lieutenant Kevin Knightly's armoured car Vickers gun the previous day. The Magister dropped two bombs into No. 1 Platoon's area, one bomb landing beside a machine gun position on an ant hill, burying the crew, Privates James Tahany and Edward Gormley, both from Sligo. Sergeant John Monaghan, reacting quickly, dug out and pulled a shocked Private Tahany clear and neither he nor Private Gormley

Checking all-round defence and fields of fire of defensive position at Jadotville.
Courtesy of the Military Archives, Dublin

were seriously injured. A second aerial attack later missed its target and exploded on the side of the road. The continual strafing from the air had, however, damaged all of A Company's scarce means of transport,

A shell crater from the bombardment of Jadotville.   Courtesy of the Military Archives, Dublin

eliminating the possibility of an escape. They would have to continue to fight it out on the ground.

Over the previous two days, the enemy had made up to ten attacks on their positions, but A Company knew they had inflicted heavy casualties on their attackers with relatively few, lightly wounded, casualties of their own. In No. 3 Platoon's location, Lieutenant Noel Carey decided to rotate those in the platoon's front trenches, as they had been under most fire for nearly three days with little rest. Then came more incoming 81mm mortar fire, and it was specifically accurate. The first rounds landed 100 metres in front of No. 3 Platoon's forward trench, followed by another salvo which landed the same distance behind the trench. Lieutenant Carey reckoned that if the crews were bracketing their fire correctly, and it seemed certain they were, the trench he and the others were occupying must surely be hit by the next mortar salvo fired. He ordered everyone out of the trench, staying behind to man the Bren gun and ready to put up a defence if the enemy sent in an assault under the cover of this mortar barrage.

As the others rushed for the safety of the shelter of the rear trenches, Lieutenant Carey contemplated his precarious position and thought of his fiancé and family at home in Ireland. It came as little consolation to realise he had actually volunteered for this. Survival was foremost in his mind and with little time for prayers he nonetheless made a hurried pact with Saint Jude (patron saint of hopeless cases) that should he survive, his first child would be called Jude. This first child is now a serving Lieutenant Colonel with the Irish Defence Forces, Lieutenant Colonel Paul Jude Carey. Nonetheless, it was a dreadful feeling to be so defenceless, waiting in dread for the arrival of the next salvo of mortar bombs. To his surprise the mortar fire moved away to his right and he got back to his Platoon HQ trench safely and set about completing the rotation of his platoon among the trenches. They were determined to hold out, and demonstrated this with ongoing mortar, machine gun and small arms exchanges with the enemy throughout the day.

Late afternoon, as was now customary, there was a CO conference at Company HQ. Complimenting the Platoons on their efforts over the previous three days, Commandant Quinlan announced that a relief attempt was on its way. By dusk 'Force Keane 2' would be at Lufira Bridge and they were expected to break through at first light the next day. The platoon Commanders were delighted but went on to report that scarcity of water remained a problem and they were trying desperately to conserve what they had. Food too had become scarce, though despite all this morale remained high. However, the heat, dust and fatigue was taking its toll. Commandant Quinlan informed them that during his frequent phone exchanges with the Burgermeister the threat of a mob from the town attacking them was made repeatedly.

The platoon commanders returned to their trenches and passed on the good news that a relief column was on its way and they could expect to be relieved. Needing to drink, the troops were using tablets to purify the water in their water bottles from which they conservatively sipped throughout the night. It tasted horrible, yet having defied such huge odds nothing could taint the taste of victory they all felt. They stood at their posts eagerly awaiting the morning.

Next morning, Saturday 16 September, the Irish troops watched through tired eyes as the sun came up. All was quiet, then the distinct crunch of mortar rounds impacting and machine gun fire was heard from the direction of Lufira Bridge. A Company were elated; relief at last. The cacophony of machine guns and mortars was music to their ears, a richly orchestrated composition whose arrangement filled their senses, emotions and heads with the thought of freedom. Play it loud, play it long, play it any way you like, just keep playing, and with the final score's joyful crescendo, let the exhilarating climax lift the soul and lift the siege. Then, just as suddenly, the Fouga jet came along the valley. It ignored A Company in Jadotville and instead headed straight for Lufira Bridge. The relief column, 'Force Keane 2', was just as exposed to aerial attack as was A Company. More so, in fact, for they were in the open and not dug in. But would it matter? Would the bombing be accurate? Could 'Force Keane 2', this time with the advantage of an additional Gurkha unit, achieve a favourable outcome where three days earlier 'Force Keane 1' had not? In the event, the combined effect of the Fouga jet's bombing and a heavily reinforced Katangan and mercenary defence caused fatal casualties and chaos. In time 'Force Keane 2' would return to Élisabethville.

As before there were no communications between the relief column and A Company, so it was a while before A Company realised that they were once again having to stand alone. This time it would be under much harder circumstances. Seriously fatigued, dehydrated and with supplies of ammunition running low but not yet exhausted, food scarce and water all but gone, matters were bleak and the prospect grim. After one last sustained exchange it would be down to hand-to-hand fighting or the prospect of a brave but futile bayonet charge! It was as dramatic as that. The situation was critical and no one was sure they could hold out.

Around noon, still unaware of the final outcome of the fighting at Lufira Bridge, A Company heard the blades of a helicopter coming from Élisabethville. It was a UN helicopter, bravely piloted by Norwegian Lieutenant Bjorn Hovden and co-piloted by Swedish Warrant Officer Eric Thors. They had volunteered, at extreme risk to themselves and with the possibility of being shot out of the sky by the Fouga jet, to fly a supply of water to the besieged Irish company. Despite having developed engine problems en route they persisted, and on arrival needed assistance to find a suitable landing place. Aware of the situation, Company Quartermaster Sergeant Pat Neville and Corporal Bob Allen broke cover and laid down bedsheets as markers on some even ground in No. 3 Platoon's area for them to land safely. As they did so they drew a huge volume of fire from the Katangan and mercenary troops. Doing so, however, revealed the position of the newly placed support weapons and with most of what ammunition they had left, the Irish laid down a hail of accurate fire that lasted nearly two hours. Many of the native Katangans fled into the bush, but in the exchange the helicopter was damaged and rendered unfit to fly.

It was soon discovered, cruelly, that the UN pilots had risked their lives in vain as the much-needed water was useless. It had been poured into petrol jerry-cans which had not been sufficiently washed out and the water was undrinkable. The attack faltered and a lull occurred. At this point, Lieutenant Carey's radio operator, Private Myler, asked: 'Sir, would real war be anything like this?' Carey's mood lightened and it was further lifted when, along with the water supply, some mail was delivered and he was one of the lucky ones. Eagerly opening it he found it was a bill for two pounds from a book club back home!

The Irish decided to hit the Katangans and mercenaries again, this time for a full hour with sustained small arms and support weapon fire, and the resolve of the Katangans was broken. It had become a rout, and in order to dissuade others from taking flight into the scrub the white officers were seen shooting their own men, native Katangans, in an attempt to stem the situation. The Irish had won the fire fight but now what? The Burgermeister, similarly unaware of the outcome yet to be reached at Lufira Bridge, contacted Commandant Quinlan asking for a cease fire. From Quinlan's perspective, at that time, he knew that a UN Relief Column had reached Lufira Bridge; a UN helicopter had successfully landed with supplies; A Company were continuing to hold out; and a breakthrough at the Lufira Bridge was imminent.

In reply, from a position of perceived strength, Commandant Quinlan laid down the following conditions; all firing was to cease; a cordon should be set up and a no man's land area, to be patrolled by Katangan Police and A Company; the Fouga jet should be grounded; all Katangan troops to be returned to barracks; water and power supply restored; and, finally, casualties to be evacuated. All these demands were agreed by the Burgermeister and Battalion HQ notified. All A Company wanted to happen now was to greet the Relief Column on their arrival in Jadotville. For the first time in three days they could safely leave their trenches and greet each other, tell of their experiences and take photographs. Some of No. 3 Platoon actually played football with the Katangan police on the roadway beside the Purfina garage.

Late that night Commandant Quinlan called a hurried conference for all officers and Company Sergeant Prendergast. He congratulated them all on their actions over the past few days then to their shock and disbelief he announced that 'Force Keane 2' had returned to Élisabethville. Battalion HQ had sent a message to hold on since UN jets would arrive in Élisabethville soon (in fact it was to take two months for them to arrive). The platoon commanders were not to give this news to their platoons that night as they were fully sure they had won the battle. The platoon commanders spent a sleepless night because they realised their position was now precarious. The initiative had swung to the Katangans, still with a large force disproportionately outnumbering A Company. Their position was indeed hazardous, to say the least.

The Irish had held their ground, fought the Katangans and the mercenaries to a standstill and acceded to a cease fire, which so far was holding. However, the Irish situation was perilous. They were starved, parched and exhausted, without ammunition or reinforcements, unable to resupply and without air cover. Despite the previously agreed arrangements, the Fouga jet reappeared and flew over the Irish positions but did not attack them.

At around 1400 hours on Sunday 17 September, Commandant Quinlan decided to go into Jadotville, with the Swedish co-pilot, Warrant Officer Eric Thors acting as interpreter, to see if he could get the water supply restored. On entering the town, with two Katangan Police as escort, he went into a local bar that was crowded with mercenaries. When they saw him the shout went up: 'Le Majeur Irlandais', and everyone present stood up and saluted. Some showed him their wounds and asked how many Irish had been killed. They were incredulous when they learned that there were none. He returned shortly with some crates of minerals.

Despite this brief respectful exchange, Commandant Quinlan was becoming increasingly concerned for the safety of A Company, as it was noticeable that Katangan troops were encroaching into no man's land, a third violation of the agreement. His difficulty was that in any further negotiations Commandant Quinlan was all too aware that he would not be doing so from a position of strength. He did not have long to muse over matters because he received a message from the Burgermeister that Godefroid Munongo, Minister for the Interior, wished to meet him urgently. He departed with the Chaplain and the interpreter and all were concerned for his safety.

At what turned out to be an angry meeting, Munongo first said the Irish had fought well but they must cease fighting and leave their positions and heavy weapons. He stressed they were cut off and surrounded by 2,000 Katangan troops. Commandant Quinlan stated that the UN were there to restore peace in the Congo and they were only defending themselves from an unprovoked attack. Munongo insisted they vacate their positions on Monday morning or they would be annihilated. Commandant Quinlan stated that UN aircraft were on the way and would bomb Jadotville if the Irish forces were attacked. Munongo knew that this was a bluff and it would take months for UN aircraft to reach Katanga. He gave a final ultimatum to Commandant Quinlan to lay down their weapons or be wiped out. Commandant Quinlan had to inform Minister Munongo of his decision within two hours.

Commandant Quinlan returned to A Company HQ and immediately called an officers conference. It turned out to be a highly charged meeting. Commandant Quinlan outlined the details of the meeting and the demands of Munongo. He congratulated all officers, NCOs and men on their action, and then laid out A Company's precarious position. The troops were exhausted after nearly a weeks' action, under fire; water had been cut off for days and was almost gone; food was low and they had received no resupply since the previous week. Ammunition was nearly completely expended and the two armoured cars could not use their Vickers machine guns as all the locks were damaged, having fired almost 10,000 rounds. It was essential to have this firepower and to break out they would have to travel ten miles through hostile territory to Lufira Bridge and without support fight their way fifty miles back to Élisabethville. Finally, two abortive efforts had already been made to relieve them and it would take a week or more for another effort. Too late for them to hold out without severe casualties.

All officers were asked to give their opinion. The platoon commanders wanted to fight on, but realised how difficult this was under the circumstances. They also realised there was no hope of an escape and their casualties would only get worse. They went through every possibility but there was no hope of early relief. In the end it was left to Commandant Quinlan to make the critical decision. This was a huge judgement call, one the on-ground commander was best placed to make. He had 'mission command' throughout the previous days' perils and had displayed to one and all, friend and foe, that he was a soldier destined for just such an operation. Now he had to have the strength of mind to make a decisive determination. It was one of the most dreadful decisions for any troop commander to make. He contacted Battalion HQ informing them of their situation, to be told that aircraft were on the way and to hold out for a cease fire that was being organised in Élisabethville. He stated that the situation facing A Company was desperate, they were totally surrounded, cut off, running out of ammunition, water and food and needed to be relieved immediately.

After this communication with Battalion HQ it became apparent to him that he had to agree terms with Munongo, who assured him that A Company would be fully protected from reprisals or attack. Courageous decision made, he ordered the platoon commanders to inform their troops. Lieutenant Carey recalls:

> That night I addressed my Platoon with a very heavy heart and I found they did not fully comprehend the seriousness of the situation and were convinced they had won. I ordered them to pack up their kit to be ready to move on Monday morning and we destroyed as many weapons as we could. As I packed my kit with Lieutenant Tom Quinlan that night we were both shocked, shattered and disappointed that after all our fighting and successes it should come down to this. It is indescribable how dreadful was this feeling of uncertainty as to our fate and frustration that we had failed to hold out. Nonetheless, I was still Platoon Commander No. 3 Platoon with responsibility for my men.

This sense of responsibility was shared by all the officers, NCOs and men of A Company, and it would see them through a five and a half week period of captivity that would ultimately bring them all home safely to Ireland, having displayed much bravery and dedication in the cause of peace in the Congo.

CHAPTER 3

The Battle for the Tunnel (Élisabethville)

Baptism of Fire

8 December 1961

'Crump! Crump! Crump!' … the incoming mortar rounds slammed into the Irish camp. It took twenty-six seconds for their firing, flight and fall before they smashed into the Irish position, impacting heavily. The ground shook with each blast, the shrapnel scattering, the hot molten metal menacingly seeking its prey, indiscriminately spreading in search of victims. Newly arrived in Congo, A Company, 36th Battalion, was caught on the wrong side of a mortar barrage. It was savage, raw and violent; deliberate, dangerous and deadly. Corporal Michael Fallon was arbitrarily killed outright when an unlikely, rare direct hit impacted on the roof of the outhouse building in which he was located and he died almost immediately. The mortar barrage accounted for a further five injuries; Sergeant Paddy Mulcahy, Privates Marsh and Gilrain, Troopers Kelly and McMullan. So serious were Trooper McMullan's injuries that he was medically repatriated home to Ireland because of his wounds. Not yet twenty-four hours in Élisabethville, barely two days in the Congo itself, A Company, 36th Battalion had suffered one fatality and five wounded. Their arrival the previous day, though less lethal, had been only slightly less traumatic.

Not Just War But Suicide

7 December 1961

Sustaining over forty hits, with two outboard fuel tanks punctured and the oil system of the starboard inner Pratt & Whitney engine damaged, the United States Air Force (USAF) Douglas C-124 Globemaster II transport aircraft was one of three which received ground fire on approach to landing at Luena Airport, Élisabethville. This was the beginning of the three-week airlift rotation of the main body of the 36th Irish Infantry Battalion to the Congo to replace the 35th Irish Infantry Battalion – the handover duration being extended due to circumstances arising in the region. The 36th Battalion was the sixth Irish unit to deploy in what had already been a year-and-a-half commitment to what altogether became a four-year involvement, comprising twelve Irish units in all. This rotation was to see the scheduled departure and arrival of some twenty Globemaster aircraft, commencing on the 5 December 1961 and ending on Christmas Eve. Originally destined for Albertville, in the Congo's northeast, the twenty-three hour journey took a route whose flight path went from Dublin, over England, France, Italy, the Mediterranean and a first stop at the US Wheelus Field Airbase in Tripoli, Libya. After refuelling the flight went to RAF-run Kano Airbase in Nigeria before finally arriving at Leopoldville in the Congo. After a day's rest and a further 1,200 miles to the south – Congo is a vast country – they reached their destination.

While preparations were under way for landing near Élisabethville, two UN Indian Canberra jets suddenly screamed by, discharging their cannons to engage the Katangese Gendarmerie ground positions in the area around the airport. The Globemaster pilots had to carry out landing procedures according to international code, this being when the pilot has not received finalised landing instructions from air traffic control in the airport control tower. The planes turned into the final leg of their approach and so also out over the hostile Katangese, who let loose a hail of fire from their ground positions. Not yet on the ground, hostilities had begun and A Company were already in the thick of it.

Landing with a trail of aviation fuel vapour spewing behind it from the ruptured fuel tanks, the stricken aircraft made a remarkable landing. More than spectacular, it was miraculous it had not caught fire whilst airborne, considering the heat of the engines and the flammability of the high octane vapour. There to meet them were those whose own tour of duty had been eventful but was now nearing its end: the men of the 35th Battalion. They were on the apron's tarmac, in the airport's buildings, but mostly in slit-trenches, crawl trenches, weapon pits and command posts, defending its perimeter. The aircraft's American crew, taking in this sight and already shaken by their exposure to incoming fire on final approach, commented on the experience that landing in Élisabethville 'wasn't just war, it was suicide'.

Of immediate concern to the aircraft's loadmaster was the real possibility of the soles of the Irish soldiers' hobnail boots causing sparks to fly on contact with the tarmac as they formed rank from the rear of the plane and igniting the fuel now gushing from the wings and vaporising in the heat. They were extremely fortunate not to have been engulfed in a flying fireball on landing, as the requirement to apply the brakes to slow the aircraft often causes sparks. On this occasion none arose and there were instead no casualties among the aircraft's forty-six Irish occupants. The planes took off again during the day, the first on its surviving three engines. The American crew was disinclined to linger in the Congo. For the 120 or so newly arrived members of the 36th Battalion, their first impression was stark, yet this was only a small taste of things to come.

'Sit Rep' (Situation Report) – Freedom of Movement

'A' Company counted the precise number of bullet holes in the USAF Globemaster's airframe, forty-eight in all. Still disbelieving their eventful arrival and bonded in the moment of a share of their good fortune, they quickly understood the US aircrew's collective desire not to remain on the airport's apron to affect repairs. Leaving Africa if at all possible seemed a far more wise, welcome and attractive avenue to any other alternative suggested. Giving them some boxes of pack rations the Irish bade the air crew good luck and farewell, then steeled themselves for the new reality that faced them. They had hit the ground running and were uncertain where it was leading them. What was certain was the main route out of the airport was considered insecure, as sniping continued around the city. Movement to and from the airport for the UN was through 'Route Charlie' (Avenue de Aracarios), a less dangerous alternative.

First reports of new developments in Congo came on 3 and 4 December 1961, two days before their departure from Ireland, as Katangese Gendarmerie, led by mercenaries, became very active in Élisabethville and on roads leading into the city. As a result, all UN and

Irish troops were confined to their respective camps. At this stage the intention had been for the 36th Battalion to concentrate in Albertville and the Nyunzu and Niemba areas, but due to the deteriorating circumstances it became necessary to consider a change in plans and to have the 36th take over from the 35th in Élisabethville. The following day, the Katangese Gendarmerie placed a roadblock on one of the city's main boulevards, blocking access to the airport.

Hardly a random act its significance was to throw down the gauntlet to the UN, in effect saying if you do not control your freedom of movement we are going to do it for you. After some negotiation the Gendarmerie agreed the roadblock would be removed, but it was not and in addition firing commenced in the city. Irish troops around their camp known as 'Leopold Farm', were forced to withdraw to positions closer to the camp. A firm decision was taken in light of these new and grave circumstances to redirect the 36th Battalion to effect relief in situ in Élisabethville. The Katangese Gendarmerie, together with their white mercenary leaders, were determined to ratchet up the pressure on the UN forces. If A Company, newly arrived from Ireland, were in any doubt about the gravity of the situation they were in after the drama of their arrival, it was to become all too obvious over the coming days.

An Uneasy Peace

The abundance of backbone displayed by the Irish at Jadotville was in stark contrast to the dearth of political wisdom that placed them there. Unease existed that the predicament may have been caused by Belgian manipulations in the UN forum, machinations to adversely affect the ONUC's need to address the security of isolated white settlements in Katanga. The tactical deployment of an organisation's military assets ought to serve its political strategic aims in the first instance, and not be unscrupulously manoeuvred by others to their advantage. Troubling also was the UN forces' inappropriately resourced military capabilities to match the assigned tasks. The mission's overall objectives had often seemed uncertain, confused and ill-defined, while the dithering of the political decision-making adversely impeded the speed of the necessary military planning. Even more unsettling were the unexplained enigmatic circumstances surrounding the mystery of the tragic Dag Hammarskjöld plane crash. On 18 September, Hammarskjöld was en route to negotiate a cease fire when his Douglas DC-6 airliner crashed near Ndola, Northern Rhodesia (now Zambia) with no survivors. Accidental, maybe; suspicious, certainly; speculation, endless.

Of enormous and immediate concern in theatre was that by the beginning of December relations between the UN and Katanga government had greatly deteriorated. Katangan Gendarmerie had established a number of roadblocks in the south of the city of Élisabethville, denying the UN freedom of movement in that direction. Subsequent to a series of unsuccessful negotiations, this stalled imposition of an imposed solution in the guise of operations Rampunch and Morthor, and the death of Dag Hammarskjöld in the plane crash, led Dr Conor Cruise O'Brien to voluntarily release himself from his UN assignment in Katanga and he departed the Congo. On 5 December, with A Company busily boarding the three USAF Globemasters at Dublin Airport to commence the 36th Battalion rotation from Ireland, there were reports in the newspapers of an impromptu press conference held in Cruise O'Brien's New York hotel room the previous evening, where he accused the British of covert support for President Tshombe with the aim of getting his regime recognised.

Meanwhile in Élisabethville, also on 5 December, the issue of the removal of the roadblocks was spontaneously combusting. Three days previously a roadblock was set up by Katangan Gendarmerie in the Tunnel, the railway that was the main link in and out of Élisabethville, and a number of UN personnel were 'arrested'. Two Irish officers were fired upon near the roadblock but escaped uninjured. The following day a Swedish UN car was also fired upon, killing the driver and wounding three others. Twenty-four hours later another roadblock was erected at the roundabout on Avenue Saio-Stanley, a particularly sensitive spot lying on the route from UN headquarters to the airport, and a strong Swedish patrol failed to have this obstacle removed.

An outright attack was launched on the Gendarmerie-held roundabout by a company of Indian Gurkhas and a mixed unit of one Irish platoon under Lieutenant Tom Quinlan, with two Ford armoured cars, two sections of Gurkhas and one Swedish APC, all under the command of an Indian, Captain Salaria. This force was ambushed near the old airstrip while en route, about one mile from the roundabout, but after a skirmish succeeded in joining up with the Indian Gurkha company and together reclaimed and freed the Avenue Saio-Stanley roundabout from Gendarmerie possession. The overall cost of this military exercise was one UN soldier and twenty-eight Gendarmerie killed.

Sniping into the Irish HQ, Leopold Farm, began on the same day (5 December), with sporadic mortar fire in the vicinity. Within twenty-four hours, with A Company, 36th Battalion in the air en route to Congo, the bullets were flying in Élisabethville. UN jet fighters also appeared in the sky for the first time and while they did not fire their presence had a striking effect on the morale of the UN forces, particularly the Irish. Bitter memories of the September fighting during Operation Morthor and the handicaps imposed by a single unopposed Katanga Fouga Magister fighter over Jadotville, Lufira and Élisabethville were now assuaged. Now there was an answer to the Katangan strafing and bombing. As a result the few Katangan planes remaining confined themselves to night flying and their bombing was happily inaccurate.

The Irish strength in Élisabethville was now very low. Most of A Company (seventy-two of all ranks) had been rotated out since 29 November, the 35th Battalion's B Company was in Nyunsu and C Company was in Niemba, northern Katanga province. This left only 'HQ' Company, the armoured car group, and a platoon from A Company, 35th Battalion. While 5 December had originally been the date appointed for the final rotation of the 35th Battalion, and all preliminary packing, documentation and arrangements had been completed, plans had to be altered as a result of the situation erupting around them. In the event, final rotation did not start until 18 December. At 1405 hours the following day, 7 December, the 36th Battalion began to arrive.

Greeted by a hail of incoming fire, nearly knocking their lead aircraft from the skies on final approach to landing at Élisabethville airport, Lieutenant-Colonel Michael Hogan, Officer Commanding 36th Battalion, elements of his battalion staff and two platoons of A Company entered Leopold Farm (the Irish camp) and were greeted with a very noisy fire fight immediately outside the post. Fire had been directed at the Irish camp since early morning, when at 0730 hours five mortar bombs dropped into the camp, and fire continued throughout the morning. An Irish UN patrol, tasked with the objective of locating the source of the firing, was unsuccessful and the Katangese pushed forward and were engaged by camp defence. They were beaten off just as the 36th Battalion arrived in camp. While having a meal in the mess, the roof of Leopold Farmhouse was hit by a 37mm shell and Lieutenant-Colonel Hogan's plate was covered in ceiling plaster and debris. Firing by Katangese snipers, machine guns and mortars continued sporadically throughout the afternoon and also through the night. Indian 4.2 inch mortars, located at the Swedish camp, fired throughout the night; some 300 rounds onto the Tunnel and the Katangese Gendarmerie Camp Massart. The Irish were in the direct line of this fire and sleep was out of the question, especially for the newly arrived, uninitiated members of the 36th Battalion, whose first night in Katanga was spent in rain-filled trenches around the camp's perimeter. The Gendarmerie harassment of the Irish continued the next morning, with sniping, mortar and machine gun fire. A fighting patrol was again dispatched and this time a number of snipers were cleared from nearby villas and a group of Gendarmerie, estimated at company strength, was routed. However, a mortar bomb scored a direct hit on an outhouse building in Leopold Farm killing Corporal Michael Fallon and wounding five other members of the 36th Battalion. An uneasy peace shattered, the second Battle of Katanga had begun and unknown to the men of the newly arrived A Company they were all too soon to take centre stage.

Point 'E' – The Liege Crossroads

Their patient determination to kill paid off and the Katangan Gendarmerie ambush set on Stanley Avenue was sprung to good effect. The impact of the anti-tank rounds' direct hit rocked the Swedish UN armoured personnel carrier (APC) on its chassis, the seriously wounded gunner later dying of his injuries. Having been called to a conference of Unit Commanders and Staff Officers at UN Command HQ, Dogra Castle, the APC was transporting officers commanding the Swedish, Indian and two newly arrived Ethiopian battalions and their respective battalion commanders, both Irish battalion commanders (the handover still in progress), and selected staff officers of the various UN battalions. Its occupants were badly shaken, but as the APC was not disabled it limped on to UN Command HQ, only for them to come under heavy mortar fire mid-afternoon. In all approximately 106 rounds fell on the area, though the conference continued in the cellar. For the return journey, four APCs were provided to avoid this rich target presenting itself again in one vehicle and in the event this convoy was also ambushed by a company of Gendarmerie. This time, however, there were no casualties and the four APCs drove smartly through.

With ongoing sniper and mortar fire into the Irish and Swedish camps, the briefing had laid out that the requirement of the UN forces, but particularly the Irish and Swedish, was to push out and enlarge their respective battalion perimeters and so their camp defences. A combined operation was planned to expand UN control of the Élisabethville area in a direction towards the city centre but short of the Tunnel proper. From intercepts it was learned that a major attack on both the Irish and Swedish camps was imminent, but Swedish and Irish mortars went into action on targets at the Tunnel, as later intercepts revealed that the Gendarmerie were 'weakened and becoming discouraged'. The attack never developed.

The night of 9 December was a nerve-racking nightmare for the Irish as all night long Gendarmerie and mercenary mortars and machine guns kept up a continuous concentration of fire on the Irish camp, including harrowing fire from a Greyhound APC. Most mortar rounds fell short but there were some twenty that didn't. The troops again spent the night in their trenches and at this stage most trenches had anything upwards of a foot of water in them. Contrary to expectations no one was injured, but from further intercepts it was learned that the Gendarmerie were reforming once again for an attack on the Irish camp. Irish mortars went into action, successfully, and again the attack did not happen. There was a serious shortage of mortar and anti-tank weapons by this time, as 36th Battalion supplies had been flown to Albertville, their original destination. Over the coming days these armaments and ammunition began to arrive in Élisabethville, but for now the Irish reply to an attack was by measured means, content in the knowledge that the next day would see a more offensive response.

The planned UN expansion operation towards the Liege crossroads, Point 'E', on which the Unit commanders and their staff had been briefed, went into effect the following morning, 10 December, and was preceded by an air strike on the Gendarmerie base, Camp Massart. Silver Swedish Saab fighter jets, nicknamed 'flying barrels' because of their thick fuselage, screamed overhead, expertly piloted, while Indian Canberra bombers strafed other Katangan strongpoints. The capture intact of fourteen Katangese aircraft during operation Rampunch, the majority of their air assets, and the destruction of almost all the remaining aircraft during a crushing air raid on Kolwezi airstrip on 5 December substantially neutralised the Katangese threat from the air and the UN now pressed its advantage to good effect. As in almost all conflicts it is the ground forces, the 'boots on the ground' that have to actually secure the victory. It is this hard, tough, grinding out of on-the-ground fighting by the infantryman that ultimately secures the objective and the day. It is both deadly and dangerous and the issue at hand in Élisabethville was still far from being decided. Since Operation Morthor's unsuccessful conclusion, the UN had been busy ferrying in materials and munitions, manpower and firepower; the build-up was nearing completion.

It takes a form of fatalism to put yourself in direct line of sight. Nonetheless, encouraged by the air strike someone had to step out and be the first susceptible to a hailstorm of possibly pinpoint accurate fire. Those advancing have the difficulty of doing so while at the same time responding to and/or avoiding defensive fire. The men of A Company were without the advantage of surprise, shielded by darkness, nor screened by smoke. They knew all too well that any prepared defences they encountered must be suppressed before they were riddled by bullets and ripped open from top to bottom by the immediate threat ahead of them; unseen, remaining hidden with no visible sign of presence. There is no mood music or a dramatic musical score – nor an enemy that either convivially pops up or conveniently dies – and there is only a split second between being victor or victim. There is only one thing worse than wondering if someone out there is going to try to kill you, and that is knowing it. You can't avoid being afraid; the survival instinct is too strong.

This extreme exposure to fear makes one very aware of the basic elements of self; the tension between having to be in the situation and not wanting to be; the strain of moving forward towards danger wishing instead to turn back and stay in safety; the struggle for courage, lost and found in one moment. Every man feels it, not many show it, but all share it. But how to deal with it? The drill is of cover and movement and in the event of coming under attack is 'fire and movement'.

An infantry company has three platoons; each in turn comprises three sections. The ten-man section is the basic manoeuvre unit and this can be broken into two, one covering the movement of the other,

'X' marks The Tunnel. An aerial view of Élisabethville and A Company's 36th Irish Battalion's avenue of advance.   Courtesy of the Military Archives, Dublin

The Battle for the Tunnel (Élisabethville) | 59

leapfrogging forward ready to give mutual close-range supporting fire to the other, providing an ordered continuity of interlocking fire and movement. Good in theory, practiced in training, rehearsed in exercises. Add the distinct element of fear to cope with and does it work for real? A Company was about to find out.

Corporal Gerald Francis, the lead section commander of the lead platoon, No. 1 Platoon, recalled this unenvied task as a daunting undertaking:

> I knew this was going to be difficult because the avenue along which we had to advance was an open road and we were highly exposed to being fired on. In the open we were going to be very vulnerable [and] I was highly conscious of the ... probability of being fired on first. Chance and circumstance dictated it was me and I was all too aware of the potential dangers and wondered how best to deal with them. Glancing to my left as we advanced early on I noticed, looking down a connecting side road, the Swedes advancing along on a parallel route with APCs.
>
> As they advanced their APCs were pouring 'anticipatory fire' from their twin box-fed Madsen machine guns into anywhere in advance [where] they felt attackers may be lurking so I raised my Carl Gustav sub-machine gun to my shoulder and did likewise and was quickly joined by the Vickers machine gun fire from the two Ford armoured cars. By means then of this 'active defence', while hugely exposed on the move, was how we proceeded, hoping to seize the initiative from any would-be attackers, nullifying their advantage. That there wasn't anyone there or those that were decided the better of taking us on, the net effect was us reaching Liege crossroads without being fired on. The Swedes on the left route, us on the right route, Point 'E' between us.

The Irish battalion perimeter was now extended along Kasenga and Savonniers as far as Liege. B Company had earlier cleared from the Police Camp to the beginnings of Rue De Kasenga, whereupon the Swedes continued. Lieutenant Kiely had been injured by small arms fire. If the firing along the parallel routes had not provoked a direct response from the Gendarmerie then it was because they were only waiting to do so by indirect mortar fire. The 'danger from the sky' was to rain down for days.

Mortar fire is deadly, its lethality derived not so much from its explosive effect, unless it was an unlikely but possible direct hit, rather from the slivers of fragmenting shrapnel subsequent to the shredding of its outer metallic case on impact; a killing radius of around 25–50 metres. The larger the calibre, the greater the killing zone. Mortar bombs are fired – more correctly launched – indirectly, that is not in a straight direct line of sight from firer to target but instead lobbed from a firing line onto a target area, up and over in an indirect flight path following an arch-like trajectory. Mortars themselves are essentially metal tubes with a fixed firing pin inside at its base, the desired direction and distance governed by the angle of elevation at which it is set thereby controlling the fall of shot. The mortar bomb, or round, is dropped down the tube, its base striking the fixed firing pin and projected skywards, the tailfin keeping its direction in flight steady and true. Individual pin-point precision is not required due to the dispersive nature of its deadly debris. Accuracy, especially over distance, can be hampered by poor use of the weapon, varying wind direction or fluctuating wind strengths, and so can cause mortar bombs to fall short, long or wide. Some fall on or near the target area but do not explode. These 'blinds' need careful consideration because they could yet explode by themselves or if inadvertently disturbed. There is also a potential danger that in a rapid fire situation a mortar bomb is slid down the tube and does not launch. Then the firers, thinking it has exited, drop a subsequent mortar bomb down the tube which explodes on contact with the one already in it; this is known as a 'double-feed'.

An indirect fire support weapon's main use is to suppress enemy movement in defence or attack, to subdue their activities, to keep their advance in check, to lay down defensive fire, or to otherwise 'fix' them in position while one's own troops manoeuvre in the advance. 'Harassing fire' – intermittent indiscriminate firing onto a fixed position – can achieve the hoped-for demoralisation of an enemy. Underpinning all this, their main use is to kill.

Fired singularly or in pairs, more often in groups, the more mortar bombs arriving onto a position, the more ground surface is covered, and so in this sense it is an area weapon. Such a grouping of mortars causes them to be referred to collectively and conventionally as a battery, and their fire as mortar battery fire. Their use is not the sole preserve of any one side or the other, often mortar fire is used to respond to an enemy mortar firing line. Such 'counter battery' (CB) fire is conducted by mortars of equal calibre. These duels, however, frequently escalate in the number of mortars employed and use of higher calibre ones for more impact at longer ranges. Because they are fired indirectly, concealed from the enemy's observation, a Mobile Fire Controller (MFC) or 'spotter' gives directions and adjustments of the fall of shot onto the target. For him to do so he has to have direct line of sight onto the target, to see the rounds' impact, how near, far, or wide, and communicate with the mortar firing line to call in the adjustments. Discovering the enemy spotter's likely position and neutralising him is a way of disrupting the process and this makes his job a hazardous one.

Significantly, the Liege crossroads was now in Irish hands and those Gendarmerie accustomed to occupying certain houses from which they opened fire on the Irish camp got a hot reception when they found the houses occupied by the Irish at last light and fled under a hail of fire. Infuriated by the loss of Liege crossroads, a very severe mortar barrage was placed on the Irish positions during the night. Irish mortars replied and approximately 105 mortar bombs fell throughout the battle area. Trooper Sheridan and Corporal Ferguson received shrapnel wounds and Corporal Gorman received a bullet wound; three more added to A Company's casualty roll.

The following day, 11 December, Point 'E', the Liege crossroads, again came under heavy mortar fire. The determined barrage impacts sent dirt flying in a wealth of noise and smoke that sucked the air out of the atmosphere, the combined effect being highly disorienting causing those on the receiving end to feel highly debilitated. The danger caused a panicked scramble for cover, to get behind something – anything – but to get some object, layer or structure between you and the incoming mortar shells; every second urgent as it might be your last, shelter always seeming too far away. Is your dugout deep enough, its top-cover sufficiently protective? Shouting, curses, heart thumping madly – 'thud, bang' after 'thud, bang' after 'thud, bang'. Then silence. An acute silence, a momentary dizzy yet very deep silence, the only disturbance your own thoughts that surely no one else could have survived that. But is it actually over? You stir tentatively. Is it only a lull, will a misfire explode belatedly? You strain to hear the telltale whistle of further incoming shells. Nothing. You peer around, your weapon close at hand. During the barrage there were six direct hits alone on Point 'E'. Yet amid the menacing mayhem, there were lighter moments as well, as Lieutenant Sean Norton describes:

> We were dug-in, defending a strategic crossroads, with our HQ 200m to the rear. An hour before sunset we were subject to a mortar-bomb attack in the form of a creeping barrage, moving from front to rear. As the bombs came nearer [to] the HQ the personnel there were ordered to their trenches.
>
> The first man to reach the large trench at the end of the garden was the head cook. As he was about to jump in he stopped suddenly at the entrance. This caused the others behind him to form a very agitated queue. By now the bombs were ripping up the adjoining garden fences, showering them with debris. Everybody was shouting: 'Jump in!' to which he replied: 'I can't, there's a fucking frog in it.' Needless to say, he was dumped head first in on top of the hapless frog, with his comrades in on top of him.
>
> The Moral? It is not always the obvious that frightens.

Inevitably, accompanying small arms fire poured in from the area of the Tunnel itself and south of Avenue Kasenga. Captain McIntyre, B Company, received a bullet wound while his platoon were assisting A Company. Irish mortars replied.

By day three at Liege crossroads, 12 December – over forty-eight hours since the bombardment commenced – attrition began to take effect. The constant wearing down of stamina, weakening of nerve, wrecking of resolve; these and more are called into question as weariness seeps into the senses. This is where self-belief, confidence and concentration are required and four times during the night Commandant Fitzpatrick, Company Commander of A Company, called for mortar support fire to break up Gendarmerie concentrations in forward positions. Inevitably, Katangese mortars replied and incredibly, unmercifully, unimaginably, Sergeant Paddy Mulcahy was wounded again for an unlikely second time, twice in five days. Tragically these were injuries he was to die from four days later. Privates Woodcock, Desmond and Confrey also took shrapnel wounds during these mortar barrages. At last light, in order to neutralise the Katangese mortar fire, Irish battalion mortars laid down a heavy barrage on Katangese positions. Notwithstanding, intermittent mortar fire fell on all Irish positions during the night. Subsequently these mortar positions were successfully located and fired on by the Irish.

The confrontations during day three were not confined to mortar duels alone – these ongoing exchanges of indirect mortar battery fire and counter battery fire – but also direct small arms encounters with Katangese troops and vehicles. M8 Greyhound armoured cars and 'Willys' jeeps, with all their combined associated armament – 37mm cannon, .3 and .5 calibre HMGs thrown in for good measure – advanced towards Point 'E' and with grim determination were driven off by accurate fire from A Company positions. Though hard pressed at times, the Irish kept up a sustained fire, sending rounds back in the direction of the attackers, who disengaged.

A Company were now well and truly 'blooded'. Under attack on arrival and under constant fire since, with Corporal Fallon killed and five wounded on day one, the advance and holding of Point 'E' was to see Sergeant Mulcahy die of his wounds and nine other assorted casualties from a mix of mortar and small arms fire. All sustained within one week. A Company had received their baptism of fire, which was to be further forged on the crucible that Point 'E' was turning out to be. They were proving silently heroic and resilient in the face of fierce hostility. There are many types of courage and different degrees of bravery, all in essence derived from the overcoming of fear. You do not have to have a weapon in your hand to display it; your actions are intended to help others, not to gain personal recognition. This was seen in a number of instances where individual selfless acts, ordinary in themselves but extraordinary in the time, place and circumstances performed, inspired or at least encouraged others and in this regard were significant. The injured Private Woodcock, despite his wounds and obviously in pain, vulnerable and uncertain of his prognosis, remained calm and urged that other casualties receive medical attention before him. Private James Fallon – brother of Corporal Michael Fallon – insisted on remaining with the company in theatre despite his brother's death on day one, when it was easily understandable that he could return to Ireland. Sergeant Paddy Mulcahy – injured once – refused to leave his platoon and returned to his duties, only to put himself at risk again looking after his men and unfortunately paid the ultimate price. Private James Murray tirelessly provided food to those in exposed positions, even after having one container blown clean out of his hands by a mortar bomb, and continued to maintain an appreciated supply of cooked meals. Medical orderly Corporal Charlie Connolly – regardless of his safety – continued to attend casualties under heavy mortar and small arms fire, bringing medical aid to the wounded, despite the danger involved.

With the UN force fighting for freedom of movement, the capacity of the Katangese to provoke was not yet exhausted and they set up a further roadblock near the large Socopetrol petrol and oil depot on Avenue Usoke in order to secure fuel supplies for themselves and cut off the Irish and Swedish camps from UN Headquarters. Commandant Pat Quinlan, his namesake Lieutenant Tom Quinlan, and elements of A Company of the Jadotville Siege fame, were once again pressed into action within days of being homeward-bound. Passing through defensive fire, the Irish penetrated close to the depot and set a number of storage tanks ablaze with offensive fire. Not satisfied that all the tanks had been destroyed, Commandant Quinlan again approached the depot, this time commando style. He and his squad infiltrated through a swamp, at times up to their waists and even necks in water, to set the remaining much-needed fuel tanks ablaze. Flames rose to an estimated 100 metres, lighting up the countryside and, because of the nightly bombing raids, causing some concern at the airport, some five miles to the northwest. However, no bombing was attempted that night and the blaze continued for four more days.

While this action hampered Katangese motor movement they still retained a bombing capacity, under the direction of mercenary pilot Jerry Puren. A South African, with Second World War bomber service with the South African Air Force, Puren later flew transport planes with the Royal Air Force and saw service during the Berlin Airlift. Recruited as a mercenary in 1961, for the next seven years he was intensely involved in mercenary operations in the Congo, initially on the ground and then an air commander. Later he was an aide to Tshombe himself.

Initially paid $1,000 a month, Puren became one of the very few mercenaries who fought for the Katanga ideal, not solely for the money. Early involvements saw his planes strike against Baluba concentrations, dispersing the Jeunesse warriors along the northern borders of Katanga around Lake Upemba and Kabala. Later, Puren's flights attacked ANC troops of the Central Congolese government crossing Katanga's border from Leopoldville and Stanleyville. Now, having kept a few planes safe from the UN jet fighter attacks on Kolwezi airstrip by holding them in nearby but much smaller airstrips, he was both conducting and directing night attacks on the UN's Élisabethville airport.

He flew a converted Dove aircraft, used as an eight-seater transport or for light cargo deliveries, and rigged a rack system along the interior fuselage to take 12.5 kg bombs, making a hatch in the floor and mounting a plastic bombsight on the floor. By pulling a lever, bombs were dispatched one at a time through the hatch in the floor. By such means, with two Dornier aircraft and Puren in his Dove, the Katangese responded at night to the daytime raids by the UN jets. Thankfully, for the most part, their aim was largely inaccurate, but those below were not to know that until after the fact.

Over the next two days (13–14 December) heavy mortaring continued on all Irish positions. Some of this counter battery fire was in response to Swedish mortars firing from A Company's locale, and during one bombardment Captain Harry Agnew was injured, losing one and a half fingers to shrapnel slivers. At one stage during these heavy exchanges it was agreed with the American Embassy that mortar fire from Irish lines should stop to allow the evacuation of 500 women and children from the Athene schools.

The identification of Katangese mortar positions was vital in the ebb and flow of the ongoing exchanges, which rapidly developed into duels. After three days and nights of almost continuous exposure to heavy incoming mortar barrages, a very definite direction was given with the aim of determining exactly the location of the enemy mortars. It was imperative they were found and neutralised. This involved the mortar OP (Observation Post with the MFC) going to higher ground, but to do so necessitated crossing a road under constant bombardment and having to move the necessary radio equipment, a heavy and cumbersome C-12 Wireless set with two large 6V encased 'wet' batteries to power it. This required crossing the exposed road on no fewer than four occasions, all the while under fire. The observers, Paddy Guerin and the previously injured Paul Ferguson, now gave a new 'fire mission' order with revised directions. The first fall of shot was declared 'near', the second 'on' – remarkable accuracy from the Irish. Thereafter, the enemy mortar line was taken out by A Company counter battery fire. A great deal of damage was inflicted on the Gendarmerie, neutralising its effect. This took a lot of unwanted 'attention' away from the Irish positions along Liege crossroads, and secured a springboard from which to set up the advance on the Tunnel.

On one subsequent occasion, the sighting of a Gendarmerie Greyhound armoured car in a firing position behind a house in Belair – a residential area for white settlers south of Avenue de Kasenga – led to the further discovery of new mortar positions. Surrounded as they were by city residents, the Irish could not direct fire onto them and the Katangese took full advantage of any opportunity afforded in the circumstances. Any such advantage was very short-lived, however, as these exchanges were about to be rapidly overtaken by events and happenings dictated by the UN Force Commander; Operation Unokat was about to be put into effect.

Seize and Hold

It was barely a week since A Company's arrival into Congo and the build up to Operation Unokat, but in terms of experience it had been an electric escalation. They arrived as tentative peacekeepers, immediately became tough peace-enforcers and would soon be tantamount to 'war fighters'. This tacit transformation from timidity through tenacity to temerity had been torrid and traumatic, the journey taut and tense, brutal and bewildering. Shot at on touchdown, subjected to several attacks since and under constant mortar and sniper fire, the Irish had been heavily pounded for the last four days. Having sustained one fatality and suffered several seriously wounded, they were no longer raw recruits and were far from being 'green'. They had gone through something monumental, a situation that had been intense, fast and fluid. Being 'new to the fight' there was an excitement and drama to it, but this was neither history nor Hollywood, it was all too authentic and pressurised. They were beginning to be ground down by their experiences, their tempo degraded, their energy sapped. They were already tired, but the situation demanded a step up in toughness – they had to go toe-to-toe with an 'enemy'.

The undertaking of a conventional offensive military operation was now the task in hand. Taking on this manoeuvre was accompanied by various tactics and techniques, which they had trained for but was now for real. A deliberate full-blown company attack, they were now part of a battalion action, itself a portion of the plan involving a brigade formation operation. The challenge to be accomplished was to be conducted in darkness and within the urban environment of Élisabethville. Fighting in built-up areas is difficult, lengthy and more costly in terms of ammunition and also, potentially, casualties.

The Tunnel, a vital railway bridge intersection with a dual carriageway underpass, controlled a crucial avenue of access into central Élisabethville and was a key point from which to continue the attack and support future operations. The Gendarmerie, under mercenary supervision, had the time, means and weaponry to prepare and fortify selected key buildings and structures as strongpoints; the Tunnel itself ideal for this purpose. The string of mutually supporting bolstered-up buildings and improved protected positions were certain to offer stiff resistance. Due to its nature, a defence of this type is easier to withstand any assault. An attacker faced with fighting in a built-up area will immediately look first and foremost to bypass; next to neutralise, stand off and fire into; then to destroy by artillery, tank or air bombardment. Only as a last and least favoured option would an attacking force conduct an assault. The Tunnel was the centre of gravity of the Katangese defence of Élisabethville; it was on this that everything depended and A Company had to rupture it. Bypassing or reducing it to rubble were not options, the Tunnel had to be seized and held the hard way. It was boots-on-the-ground, troops-on-the-Tunnel time.

A crucial bottleneck, the Tunnel was the single access point, the vital valve controlling the flow to and from the city centre from the south. For approximately 2 km either side it was completely built-up, a critical choke point of strategic importance. To seize requires advance; advance demands forward movement; movement needs impetus; and maintaining impetus under fire is dependent on momentum. It is difficult to keep the continuous tempo of an attack after you have been fired upon at close range. The inclination is to remain under cover and from there return fire. Junior leaders have to push hard and despite training and instruction the tendency is for men to bunch together, to misuse ground and cover; an instinct that has to be fought against throughout such an action. The success of an attack in particular depends on the initiative, energy and determination of the junior leaders in applying the company commander's plan. Giving effect to this offensive spirit is fundamental to getting and keeping men moving towards seizing the opportunities available and gaining the objective. When soldiers come under fire they want reassurance and direction.

The moral strength of the commanders as much as the physical means available is what really gives effect to planned actions. However, the most important weapon in any war is intelligence, and the UN didn't do intelligence. Yet it was effectively at war. It was evident to the Irish that the task that lay ahead was not going to be easily achieved. There are many things that mitigate against such efficiency, some controllable, others not. Knowing the ground, particularly the terrain whereupon sits and surrounds the objective, is important. A Company were without proper maps providing any indication of the nature of the ground or buildings on the objective. Air photographs were not provided, organic fire support weapons – those within the Company were 60mm mortars and medium machine guns – were in short supply, and radio communications were poor. But every commander at every level knows you cannot possibly hope to possess all the advantages all of the time, the reality of the situation you are faced with is often far from the textbook ideal. Notwithstanding, the requirement remains, the objective has to be taken and the mission achieved.

What was a given was that the Katangese Gendarmerie were now a determined, well-equipped force. They were well led by battle-hardened, experienced, ruthless mercenaries who were a thinking adversary with a well-conceived campaign plan. Before this operation the Gendarmerie had been going from strength to strength and implementing this plan granted them a direction towards success. It began with harassing tactics, with close-in firing on UN camps at the time when the Irish and Swedish battalions were rotating. Their aim was to confine these raw new battalions to their camps. Next, they were determined to isolate the UN troops from their supply line; in this they were almost successful. The Irish, Swedish, Ethiopian and Indian battalions were denied routes Alpha and Bravo through Élisabethville. Finally, they aimed to seize the airport thus denying the UN its strategic APOD (Air Point of Disembarkation) and base.

Therefore, UN command had to counter and a plan to implement the destruction of Katangese resistance in the Élisabethville area was hatched. What would become known as Operation Unokat was a brigade in attack with a further brigade encirclement; in effect a division-sized operation. The operation was to be carried out in two phases: Phase One would contain and keep pressure on the Katangese Gendarmeries and mercenaries, in the Tunnel area particularly, with mortar fire pre-H-Hour (the exact time for the attack to commence). Phase Two, the Indian and Ethiopian battalions would surround Élisabethville by cutting off and blocking key routes – effectively sealing the city – preparatory to the destruction of the Katangese Gendarmerie and mercenary resistance by the Irish and Swedish battalions. This second phase was itself made up of two parts, one for the Irish 36th Battalion, the second for the composite 12th/14th Swedish Battalion. The one brigade-sized manoeuvre involved two deliberate and deep battalion-in-attacks – one Irish, one Swedish – supported by Indian 120mm heavy mortars.

The specific mission for the Irish Battalion, out of the brigade operation order, was the vital task of seizing and holding the Tunnel and to exploit forward positions in order to secure the right flank of the Swedish attack on Camp Massart, the Gendarmerie base. The UN brigade-in-attack plan for this offensive operation had therefore to synchronise the efforts of a number of elements of different nationalities, to coordinate their moving parts with fire support, properly integrated to a precise timetable, in order to dominate the fluid tactical situation. In turn, the individual battalions prepared their own respective attack plans, integrating with the specific details of the brigade's mission and its coordinating instructions. Thus 'Operation Sarsfield' was brought into being, with A and B Companies launching the main attack on respective twin axes, mutually supported by C Company in reserve. The main effort of the entire brigade attack and overall divisional effort lay in the hands of the Irish, and as circumstances were to play out, hinged mostly on A Company's efforts to seize the Tunnel.

In addition to its significant tactical importance, the Tunnel's capture would have immense psychological value, smashing the Katangese grip on the city's access, and allowing the UN to retake control of its freedom of movement and the overall situation. In exerting its military force in support of its mandated stand, the UN was making a massive statement to the world that it was prepared to back its position militarily. The loss of this major junction was crucial in breaking the morale and will of the Gendarmerie and the mercenaries. This was high-stakes stuff, tactically and strategically, both militarily and politically. It would be heavily defended and not easily given up.

The importance of the plan, its clear communication and effective execution, was emphasised at the 'O' Group, where the commander imparts his plan to his subordinates through the issue of orders. These full formal verbal orders are the key to ensuring that commanders within the battalion clearly understand the part they have to play in the upcoming action; that all important aspects are covered; and a precise prescribed formatted sequence is followed. That the mission completion is paramount is emphasised and the mission itself stated unambiguously, then restated for effect. Questions are answered and no effort is spared to ensure everyone has a clear understanding of the coordinated action to conduct the operation is arrived at. More than that, the commander will impress his personality on the operation and motivate his commanders verbally. It is here that leadership, that unseen but immediately obvious quality, comes directly into play and the unit cohesiveness of action is built around the commander's intent, and Lieutenant Colonel Hogan's intent was very clear: the Tunnel was to be seized and held and A Company were to do it.

Code Word: 'Sarsfield'

On the afternoon of 15 December 1961, Lieutenant Colonel Michael Hogan, Officer Commanding, 36th Infantry Battalion, received orders for the UN offensive to commence early the following morning (16 December). He issued orders at 2100 hours and H-hour for the attack to commence on the Tunnel was fixed for 0400 hours. In the intervening

The Battle for the Tunnel (Élisabethville) | 71

hours, between receiving his mission and issuing his own orders, Lieutenant Colonel Hogan had to prepare his own plan of action and his unit for combat. In the circumstances, time was the number-one enemy and he had to know both what, and perhaps more importantly, how to think in order not to allow precious hours and minutes to slip by. Having been given his mission he now had to prepare his plan to achieve it, and these efforts would only culminate when – having estimated the situation he was tasked with – he would develop and impart this plan via his 'O' Group (orders group) and launch the troops of his battalion into the forthcoming fray as fully prepared as he possibly could make them.

To craft his plan he had to consider what the mission accomplishment tasked him with, both stated and inferred. What did he have available in terms of military assets to achieve it, did he need additional support, and how was he going to organise all of this to best effect? In the given circumstances he and his staff had to determine the risks associated with the various options in light of the successful accomplishment of the essential tasks required of him and decide which were acceptable. Military men do not gamble. They take risks, but they weigh the different degrees of risk between one course of action and another, mentally and methodically war-gaming and scoring each. When it comes to analysing the mission, the trained military mind set works backwards, so to speak. A reverse logic and mental process kicks in, beginning with the objective to be achieved then analysing the time and physical space available to achieve it, in order to establish the correctly sequenced chain of events to be set in motion. This then drove the schedule of activities that had to occur. Out of this process fell clarity, the more concise construct of the essential mission for the 36th Battalion plan. Its precise purposes and specific tasks.

There is an old army saying that 'time spent on reconnaissance is time well spent'. An initial 'map recce' is first conducted aided by any air photographs that are to hand. This informs the undertaking of the on-the-ground physical reconnaissance, important in the assessment of terrain and developing the various courses of action. The advantages and disadvantages of each course of action are considered and compared and a decision arrived at. In this case the maps were of limited use, there were no air photographs and physical reconnaissance was restricted so as not to give the game away to any observant Gendarme or mercenary. It was nonetheless useful in confirming the obstacles that would slow the advance, disrupt their movement and impede the manoeuvre towards the objective; the Tunnel. It was a built-up area, highly suited to defence. There were open spaces, good for the defender's observation and fields of fire, bad for the Irish troops' cover and concealment, and of course the Gendarmerie and mercenary defenders held the key terrain, which held key advantage and upon whose capture the entire mission hinged. Consideration of the defenders' situation would try to identify how they were physically positioned, on and near the objective, where were his strong points and of what strength and with what equipment. What were his capabilities, to avoid, and his weaknesses, to exploit? Lieutenant Colonel Hogan and his staff brainstormed the various options, seeking a preference. They asked themselves if tasked to defend the tunnel how they might organise it. Finally, Hogan gave consideration to his own troops. They were for the most part seasoned, sound, non-commissioned officers (corporals and sergeants) and young – many very young – privates, mostly inexperienced and certainly ill-prepared for what had confronted them thus far and what faced them now.

Still not recovered from the lengthy journey from Ireland, the apprehension of strange new surroundings was debilitating in itself, allied to the general air of nervousness, concern, tension and stress of the continued hostilities. The discomfort of having no beds and snatching a few hours sleep here and there all had a huge wearing-down effect on their physical and mental energy. However, all of them had been exposed to the almost non-stop series of incidents since their arrival and during the build-up of his plan Lieutenant Colonel Hogan knew that would make a difference, a big difference. Rather than attempting the undertaking without any experience they were well and truly 'blooded', some among them not gung-ho exactly, but after enduring for days the retaliatory mortar fire at Liege crossroads – some in storm drains with water up to chest height and with casualties suffered – they were keen to have a go.

The second battle of Katanga was well and truly under way and 5 December 1961 had marked a deadly new phase to the conflict. The UN had been stunned by the loss of life and now its on-the-ground lines of communications were being slowly strangled; its competence and commitment challenged; its operation's very existence threatened. Forcefully facing up to this adversity presented an opportunity for the UN to get on the front foot and Operation Unokat would close the net around Élisabethville. Operation Sarsfield would see the Irish, as part of Operation Unokat, go after the high value target that was the Tunnel, the immediately adjacent railroad and the hospital complexes. Operation Sarsfield was about to commence. They deployed expecting a fight, and a fight was what they were about to get.

A Company in Action

With live ammunition in their weapons, the minutes and seconds ticked down. With a real 'enemy' ahead of them, also waiting to fire live rounds at the Irish troops, A Company was poised to become involved in large-scale action. (See map on p. viii.) Elements of the Operation had already been set in motion, but the code word for the commencement of the Irish attack: 'Sarsfield', had yet to be transmitted by the battalion commander. The men of A and B Companies were to move across staggered start lines, their parallel axis of advance along the railway line and Avenue des Savoniers, respectively. A Company were to advance with Nos 1 and 2 Platoons' forward left and right, with Commandant Joe Fitzpatrick in the centre. No. 3 Platoon would advance rear right and the Company HQ, under Captain Kevin Page, rear left. Already ahead of them and forward left were B Company. C Company minus was moving behind in reserve. Both companies had already sustained casualties during the week since their arrival. The men were worn down, weary but not yet fully exhausted, and despite their tiredness were in good spirits. Nonetheless, when out beyond the point of no return, having crossed their start lines, understandably each would be contemplating the now inevitable fight and so were apprehensive – some terrified – yet all ready to face the difficulties ahead of them and enduring the strain. But all definitely on edge, their unease and concern palpable. Theirs was an ability to control this fear and suppress its effects, in a word, this was courage.

Commandant 'Bill' Callaghan (later Lieutenant General and Force Commander of UNIFIL 1981–86), then OC of B Company, explained:

> The night of the battalion orders – the evening before the attack on the tunnel – in the battalion headquarters at Leopold Farm, there was an evident tension and anxiety, and afterwards I remember saying to myself somewhat understatedly, 'I hope this goes well'. Nonetheless, there was also a feeling that we had been given a job and that job we were going to do. We had a shared objective, but different parallel axes of advance.

Interestingly, these axes were initially reversed to what transpired, as later the respective axes were changed to facilitate the thought-to-be easier approach to be given to A Company after their harrowing experience at Liege crossroads over the recent days. B Company was tasked to approach head-on along Avenue des Savoniers and up, forward of triangle FGD, with A Company right-flanking along the railway tracks. After the battalion orders, each company commander held his own 'O' Group to disseminate the battalion Plan of Attack, Commander's Intent and Scheme of Manoeuvre, and their specific part in its achievement. Second Lieutenant Peter Feely (later Colonel) was commander of No. 3 Platoon, A Company:

> The night before the attack on the tunnel I felt afraid, of course, but not an overwhelming sense of dread or anything like that. Since our arrival the weather, the new and strange surroundings [and] the unfamiliar noises at night had all generated a sort of nervousness, but over the eight or nine days and the episodes building up to the attack on the tunnel you quickly learned to recognise what was of immediate, obvious and urgent risk, and that was what became of concern to you. However, that night, 15 December, after the company commander's orders and briefing, prior to getting a few hours sleep I shared a can of Guinness with Lieutenant Paddy Riordan. Having opened it we both took a few small sips only, each leaving the majority of the can's content unconsumed, whereas ordinarily both would easily have accounted for it, so perhaps there was an unconscious concern and muted fear. Overall, however, I felt a definite overriding sense of relief. Relief that we were no longer, after the experiences of Liege crossroads, continuing to sit and get hit-up, rather going on the attack, getting up, moving and doing.

A Company fatalities homeward-bound.   Courtesy of the Military Archives, Dublin

Lieutenant (later Colonel) Sean Norton, Platoon Commander Number Two Platoon 'A' Company put it another way:

> On the 'start line' on 16 December, for the attack on the tunnel it was pitch black and the rain was bucketing down. If I didn't feel afraid I'd be afraid of myself. Every leader must have fear; it keeps a discipline in your thinking. For the most part, however, I was concentrating on what I had to do, getting on with the job in hand, my responsibilities took up my thoughts and my thinking.

During the form-up on the start line (SL) Nos 1 and 2 Platoons had to change places as they had got into each other's form-up positions by mistake. This was the second fateful readjustment that future circumstances would later play a tragic hand in. On the upside, the UN force now enjoyed air superiority, with most of the Katangese aircraft captured or destroyed. News of the successful UN air strike on Kolwezi airstrip on 5 December was greeted by a furious Tshombe, who had been in Paris. His enraged reaction expressed the unambiguous statement that this could now only mean 'real war'. Following the mercenary-led Gendarmerie actions ever since, real war was now the result in the sense that the Operation Unokat was a conventional-style military undertaking.

The weather was both a hindrance and a help; the torrential rain hindered control and movement of the Irish advance, but at the same time along with the pre-dawn darkness it helped to cover their movement. It was also a hindrance insofar as the advantage of air superiority was wiped out, UN planes unable to take to the air or safely identify their targets, a help in that it sheltered the approach of the Irish, adding to the cover already provided by the darkness. The synchronised pre-H-Hour mortar barrages had commenced with firing in advance of B Company's earlier crossing of their start line. The orchestration of this 'mortar music' was conducted by laid-down timings in the Brigade Fire Plan, its gradual but ever-building tempo rising to a cacophonous crescendo as the mortar fire engaged specific target areas concurrently ahead of the choreographed movement of the UN troops' advance.

The Indian 120mm heavy mortars provided 'lifting and shifting' fire, first in front, then to the rear of the Tunnel area. These adhered to the strict detail of the scheduled scheme of the laid-down fire plan, thereafter available 'on call'. A fire plan is the synchronised target-specific, time coordinated use of the artillery, mortar and air assets available to fix an enemy in position and/or force them to seek cover while ones' own troops advance (in relative safety). Such 'on call' battery was necessary to react to unanticipated situations arising, as difficulties and different circumstances developed, and their effects necessary to counter any mortar response from the Katangese and mercenaries. As more and more mortars rained fire down on the opposition positions, there was movement, much concurrent movement.

The UN, overcoming its difficulty in reorganising itself since Operation Morthor and having previously struggled to get a purchase on a peacefully negotiated political platform, refused to be bullied, and having traded punches with the Katangese was now taking a full-blown fire fight to the secessionists mercenary-led force. Keyed-up UN soldiers from the Indian and two Ethiopian battalions first moved to surround and seal the city before the Irish and Swedish stormed in.

This initial encirclement was to isolate the Katangese forces, the city's investment preventing them being reinforced, providing direct fire support for the UN forces and protecting the assaulting troops from counter-attack. Their adrenaline triumphant over trepidation, the Indian Gurkhas and Ethiopians moved out, commencing the 'surround and storm' objectives of Operation Unokat. The Indians moved east and north, the Ethiopians west at Lido. A number of clashes occurred with the Ethiopians fighting fiercely, losing fourteen dead and with four wounded while the Indian troops suffered one fatality. The battle had begun, the Indians and Ethiopians were playing their part; next up were the Irish.

The Battle for the Tunnel

'We were ready and "on" target for the tunnel. We had found our ranges beforehand the previous day, recorded them and also the line with two aiming posts. I knew what I had to do but had never done it before; firing overhead, with moving troops underneath, for real, was a big responsibility for someone with limited experience.' Sergeant Joe Scott, Sergeant Michael Butler and Corporal Paddy Guerin were A Company's main 'mortar men'. They, Private John Woolley, and others in support of the Platoon marshalled the gun line, consisting of three 81mm mortars. For his part, the underage Private Woolley had joined up the previous year for excitement, and with the possibility of UN service in Congo materialising had volunteered along with everyone else for the 33rd Battalion. He recalls his experience:

> I actually got picked but was dropped off the list because my mother wrote in to say I was underage. I was furious and disappointed. Private Joe Fitzpatrick replaced me. He was with those who were involved in the Niemba ambush, one of only two survivors of the eleven-man Irish patrol … would I have been [a survivor]? I went out with the next battalion, the 34th, which was an enjoyable experience for me, so I went out again with the 36th Battalion. Busy on arrival, we were firing day and night for seven days. Because it was the wet season in Africa there was a lot of mud around; inevitably, [and] no matter how careful we were sometimes some

of the mortar bombs got dirty and damaged. Also 'fouling' built up in the mortar barrel and occasionally mortar bombs got stuck in the mortar tube barrel. Once we spotted a mortar being set up by the Katangese and received orders to fire on it. First shot was reported back as 'near', second shot as 'nearer', third shot as 'hit'. So now 'on' for distance and direction we dropped a mortar bomb into the tube, it got stuck, we cleared it and dropped a second bomb in, it too got stuck. As this was happening, the 'enemy' mortar crew got up and ran away – they'll never know how lucky they were. In all, during that week prior to the attack on the tunnel, the outgoing number of mortar rounds we fired came close to a thousand. The crews used to put extra charges (relays) on the mortar fin, kept in place with rubber bands, to get extra range. Extensive use then of a weapon, the general attitude towards which, scarcely a week before, was that it was never going to be fired; after all, we were going on a peacekeeping mission.

Sergeant Michael Butler recalled:

When digging the mortar trench I was myself guilty of [doing] something that I so often before gave out to students on courses and soldiers on exercises for not doing: digging a 'sump' in the pit itself so in case it rained the water would flow off the bottom of the trench into it. On the early morning of 16 December it rained heavily and in the downpour we began, as per the fire plan, firing at [0230 hours], other firers had commenced at [0200 hours]. On the early morning of the 16 [December] there was a prolonged monsoon-type torrential downpour. The mortar trench became sodden very quickly, so when we fired the first 'warmer' round out of the mortar it got embedded in muck and we had to dig it out. The mortar fire plan tasked 36th Battalion mortars to commence, continue at a given rate of fire, then cease, at specific times and targets. The muck was making this difficult and at one stage Private John Woolley's mortar had gone so far down in the pit the sights were below the level where it was possible to use them. So he took the barrel off the base plate, threw sand-bags onto the base-plate and parts of his uniform, then placed the base plate from one of the other mortars on top, then the barrel and recommenced firing, maintaining the 'rate' of fires required. Once we were finished we were soaked with rain and filthy with mud, but the job was done, the Fire Plan completed.

Neither were the Irish the only ones adversely affected by the heavy rain because as B Company advanced along the Avenue des Savoniers – in full view of the Tunnel although some distance away – they encountered little resistance. Surprised, and needless to say relieved, as they progressed along they noticed a number of shallow trenches well-filled with rain. It occurred to them the Gendarmerie must not have taken too kindly to the weather and sought shelter in the railway carriages further back. Consequently, they were encountering no resistance and were not being held up. All the while heavy mortar fire overhead was suppressing and weakening the defences on the Tunnel itself and subsequently any defensive positions in depth (not linear or shallow, rather extending rearwards).

The overall plan of attack was dependent on the operation's tempo, the speed of activity of the UN force relative to that of the opposition aided by its audacity, the willingness of the attackers to take risks, and both rapidity and boldness – the weather conditions fortuitously favouring their delivery. But the Irish were well aware that whatever the weather the Gendarmerie and mercenaries were not going to simply give up the Tunnel. It would have to be seized from them. The Tunnel was the decisive point of their defence and so would be heavily defended. They could not ride on their luck forever and surprise alone would not carry the day. At some point the Irish knew it would take a dramatic and determined drive to wrestle it from them. The strong points would have to be stormed.

Ready to advance, A Company had to move forward on a very narrow frontage. The configuration of the urban man-made topography of the built-up environment meant that instead of the convenient, conventional, clear parallel axis for mutual support between their lead platoons in line, they were canalised, channelled and confined to moving on either side of the railway tracks in two columns each. Designated one behind the other on the left-hand side of the railway tracks, initially Nos 1 and 2 Platoons had found themselves formed up incorrectly in each other's place. This had to be rectified, with all the noise and clatter that two groups trading places, each of thirty-two men with all their equipment plus some attachments, would generate. Fortunately the downpour, the darkness, the visible movement and the distance covered the noise and commotion from carrying forward. Fifty years later, retired Colonel Sean Norton DSM, then a lieutenant and Platoon Commander of No. 2 Platoon, remains struck by the irony of what subsequently developed and led to what at the time seemed an innocuous, inconsequential, almost unnecessary correction. In the event he was not to dwell on it, because Commandant Joe Fitzpatrick, Officer Commanding A Company, ordered them across the start line.

A Company were now on the offensive, they moved out as one; sombre, serious and silent. The fighting not yet begun, inwardly each was already at war with himself, struggling with the situation and faced with the demands of upcoming combat, not knowing if he was a match for it. The advent of going into action has the strong, but at the same time strange, quality of being stomach-churningly tense while also presenting a heightened sense of excitement. They were under no glorified illusions, any misapprehensions had been shattered since arrival. To date, their short service in Katanga had been physically demanding and hugely stressful. In the attack proper they knew speed would be crucial, maintaining momentum and movement critical. Commandant Joe Fitzpatrick and each of his platoon commanders, Lieutenants Paddy Riordan, Sean Norton and Peter Feely, in charge of Nos 1, 2 and 3 Platoons, respectively, understood this. Looking for the muzzle-flash of any would-be snipers, anticipating ambush, negotiating and clearing obstacles, maintaining silence, ensuring no one got lost and coping with the weather and the darkness degraded their progress and prolonged the duration of their approach. Corporal Gerald Francis, point man for the advance, remembers:

> I guided the Section and so the Platoon and hence the entire Company right at Liege crossroads along Avenue Liege. Forward, left of us, B Company had already reached and secured the area known as triangle GFD where the roads Chaussée de Kasanga and Avenue des Savoniers met. The forward point or tip of this triangle faced the tunnel at a distance of some 200 to 300 yards which was directly in

front of them further along Chaussée de Kasanga. For my part, where Avenue Liege met the railway tracks at the level crossing, I opened the gate and the platoon, with the remainder of the Company following, swung left onto the railway tracks, which were parallel to Avenue des Savoniers. Completely dark and [in] lashing rain we advanced up along the railway tracks. The distance of the gap between the wooden railway sleepers underneath and supporting the railway tracks did not correspond to the length of a normal man's stride and so we walked, quietly along the side of the tracks, knowing this would lead us directly in onto the Tunnel from the right. All we had to do now was follow the tracks and not alert any sentries.

A penetration more than a flanking envelopment, the sheer boldness of the frontal manoeuvre hinged on stealth and getting as close to the Tunnel as possible before being spotted. A Company needed to be methodical and synchronised, clinical and determined, but first and foremost, forward and concentrated in order to achieve surprise. They knew their actions, reactions and presence of mind on 'contact' needed to result in the rupturing of the defenders' resolve to resist; they would have to be forced into giving up the tunnel. It was a clash of wits and wills, a battle of nerves as much a test of war-fighting skills. Crucially they first had to gain a foothold to launch the assault proper. Commandant Joe Fitzpatrick knew what had to occur to make this happen. But before this he also knew the time was surely nearing when they must come under hostile fire. There is a saying among the military that 'the best laid plans rarely survive contact with the enemy', a saying he was hoping on this occasion would not be true. Each step nearer the objective without contact was borrowed time. Prior to their departure to Congo, A Company had trained hard in the Glen of Imaal, County Wicklow, to be able to perform something well that they hoped they would not have to. Four weeks later they had crossed an actual start line and were advancing towards 'enemy' contact, for real.

First Contact

The concerted two-pronged approach was progressing well, and in the case of B Company a little too well. Lieutenant Tommy Dunne, commanding the point platoon of B Company, was out in front. He remembers: 'It was pouring rain and quite dark and I was aware only of going in the general direction of the Tunnel until suddenly we found ourselves in a dip in the roadway. Sergeant Enright, Platoon Sergeant, gasped audibly realising where we were, "Sir", he said, "the Tunnel, we're almost in it."'

The dip in the roadway was the gradual downward slope of the dual carriageway underpass beneath the railway line tunnel itself. Concurrently, on their right A Company were at their most exposed, approaching to within the last 100 metres or so of the Tunnel proper. Corporal Gerald Francis, Lead Section Commander, No. 1 Section, No. 1 Platoon A Company, recalls:

> We followed the tracks all the way along and it brought us to within fifty yards, almost on top of the Tunnel. We were so close we could hear the Gendarmerie talking. They had put on the Tunnel itself two railway carriages and had placed themselves in them along the parapet of the Tunnel. We stopped at an agreed point and it was here the Company was to get into – as much as space allowed – an 'arrow-head' formation. Lieutenant Riordan and his radioman, Private Andy Wickham, went forward beyond me. Suddenly a blast of gunfire, I think from one of the railway carriages on the tunnel, was directed our way. Lieutenant Riordan fell and didn't move. I kept looking at him to see if he would move but he didn't. I had to be sure he was dead. I was in a kind of disbelief. The survival instinct is a very strong one, however, and it took over. They were not firing at us as specific individual targets, they were blasting away in our general direction, aiming I would say on fixed lines impacting on the walls of the buildings behind us. Their ammunition was arranged in many of the weapons in use against us in a sequence of armoured piercing, ball and then tracer. So every third shot of the incoming rounds were tracer and such was their volume I remember seeing the luminous, glowing, melting phosphorous from these dripping down the walls around us. It was at these impacts that other firers now placed their aim. Our platoon had hit the ground, Nos 2 and 3 Platoons were strung out along the railway track behind us, moving immediately sideways off the railway tracks into cover.

Though inevitable, it was nonetheless sudden, sharp and shocking in its occurrence; an edgy, raw, alarming, menacing violence. Although braced for it, the contact when it came was unbelievably brutal, causing that involuntary individual full-body freeze frame, a shivering shudder, and then the momentary mental registering of the realisation that 'this was it', all occurring within a split second. The shots shattered the suspended atmosphere, projecting A Company into a whole other sphere of activity, one of urgent reaction. The bullets ripped through the darkness with a pulverising potency and tore into the night, shredding any illusions of an easy victory. The fire, not pinpoint accurate, nonetheless had a reckless intensity, an improbably heavy volume and a murderous intent. No 1 Platoon took the full ferocity of the first fearsome fusillade. Be it by design or chance, it was No. 1 Platoon's commander who was downed. Reasoned or random, Lieutenant Paddy Riordan fell, fatally wounded. The loss of its commander at this critical moment threw the platoon into disorder, a disarray further degraded by the ongoing pummelling being put out by the voracious defensive screen.

When fire was opened on them, No. 2 Platoon under Lieutenant Sean Norton went to ground on the left, taking cover in the welcome folds and undulations of an open space. They were pinned down by the ever-increasing rate of incoming fire from light, medium and heavy machine guns and an increasing, undetermined number of riflemen. When fired on in such volume at close quarters, the natural reaction is to go to ground and stay there. The most basic instinct is to remain as you are while the bullets whiz overhead and impact around you. The earth is your friend, shielding you from harm. It is entirely counterintuitive to want to move, you are safe where you are. Both conscious and unconscious reasoning compels you to stay stuck to the ground, that is until your platoon or section commander orders you to move. Even then your sixth sense – survival – pervades upon you not to budge one inch. For all the urgings of someone else, be they in command or not, there is a marked reluctance to move. In order to survive the ever increasing volume of incoming fire, Lieutenant Norton needed his platoon to move, and move now, though they felt they needed to stay.

Ahead of them, another scenario was developing on the railway tracks with No. 1 Platoon. There matters were more complicated and compounded without their platoon commander and the platoon was still in the immediate vicinity to the source of the firing, in the killing area. Cover was required, but cover from fire, not just cover from view. Lieutenant Norton knew he had to get something solid between his platoon and the enemy. The difficulty of control increased and the dangerous urgency of the moment became more apparent. For his part, before his platoon's reluctance to move became refusal, Lieutenant Norton resolved that he simply would not allow his men to remain where they were, and like a man possessed his drive drove them up, his 'get up and go' got them up and to the safety of a secure structure behind a disused, non-functioning hospital building.

Every infantryman knows the soldier's mantra when encountering effective enemy fire. The basic battle drill of fire, dash, down, crawl, cover, observe and fire is rehearsed time and time again in training. However, when heavy bursts of incoming fire are impacting close by 'for real' this can cause the collapse of your composure and can be a real challenge to your character. From a command and control perspective this can make things go fundamentally wrong. With No. 2 Platoon making for the safety of the hospital building, led by Lieutenant Norton, No. 3 Platoon took cover to the rear under the charge of Lieutenant Feely. Joe Fitzpatrick, OC A Company Commander, knew he needed to get to No. 1 Platoon in order to regain its shape, otherwise they could be ripped apart by the incoming fire – horrific in its intensity – and all too soon be in free-fall, powerless to resist and unable to address the momentum. To rectify these issues in the heat of battle requires a special kind of mind set.

Meanwhile at the forefront of B Company's advance, Lieutenant Tommy Dunne had halted his platoon and moved his two sections into buildings left and right of the road and the third into a shop they subsequently called 'Dunnes Stores' at the apex of the road junction FGD, facing the tunnel. While checking on his sections' locations with his platoon runner, Private Mick Daly, they came under fire from the Gendarmerie defenders along the Tunnel. As they ran for cover they accidentally tripped over an unexploded rocket shell, fired previously during the week from a UN jet fighter and embedded upright in the middle of the roadway. They landed one on top of the other in a helpless, hopeless, haphazard heap; a happy landing as it happened because had they not fallen where and when they did and had remained fully upright a savage burst of heavy machine gun fire would have cut them to pieces. The Irish were now well and truly about to become involved in a full-on fire fight.

Fire Fight

The quick-fire explosive barrage of bullets was like a whirlwind sweeping all before it. It was unrestrained ferocity with a decidedly mean streak of malevolence. This was a full-throttle hammering delivered by automatic weapons in the hands of people who knew how to sight and use them to great effect. The Irish advance was hurting and in trouble. They were under intense scrutiny and all their suppressed fear was coming to the surface. The defenders had their steam up and were surging ahead, pouring out a furious rate of fire that was full-on and fast; anything and anyone exposed would be blown to smithereens. Before the Irish will evaporated and they retreated in a rabble, their quest quickly quelled then quenched like the throwing of a switch, Commandant Joe Fitzpatrick knew he had to immediately reconfigure and restructure his shocked, stalled and stricken lead platoon.

Operation Sarsfield required the achievement of surprise followed by the winning of a short, sharp engagement. Putting this into effect, A Company had been on the cusp of completing almost total surprise when, once discovered, to their own surprise the resulting contact was so fierce that it had thrown its lead platoon into disorder. If such disarray was allowed to degenerate further it could completely dissolve the Company's momentum, disintegrating the attack's initiative completely. In being tasked to take the Tunnel, A Company now had a mountain to climb. Commandant Joe Fitzpatrick, with his lead Platoon stricken, his remaining platoons separated and his Company pinned down, found communication was made difficult by a lack of radio sets and their poor range and effectiveness. The initial contact had been costly in fatalities and injuries and heavy fire continued to pour in. Somehow he had to reignite the impetus of the advance. At that point in time, the mountain ahead seemed like Everest. Now the Company's primary battle was within themselves, each man having to find in himself that desire to succeed. He had to turn their individual doubt into a collective sense of self-belief. He had to make fighters of the frightened men.

To have a fighting chance, Lieutenant Norton knew they had to cause events to happen faster than the defenders could react to them. He knew the intent of his Company Commander's orders and in turn the goal of the Battalion commander's. This he felt was not going to happen by remaining still behind cover; instead he had to achieve this goal by dealing with what was happening right there in front of him. The consequence of the decentralised nature of how the advance had evolved granted him a freedom of independent action but also placed upon him an onus to identify and seize any opportunity presenting itself – or to make one happen. Suspending the reality of the shock of the situation they found themselves in, undoubtedly a very tight spot, he needed some clarity of thought. Further bursts of gunfire from the tunnel gave him his answer: simple things work best. They were going to blast their way back into the battle. If nothing else it would surely lift spirits. This stark, ruthless, cold-blooded resolve was to be the catalyst for their revival; they were going to win the fire fight and pave the way forward for a turnaround. They were going to stand up and fight. More correctly, kneel down and fight, with the 84mm anti-tank recoilless rifles perched on their shoulders.

Developed to be used in a defence setting in a conventional wartype scenario to cover a threat from tanks, in this case the anti-tank recoilless rifle was a versatile, multipurpose, direct fire resource under the command of the battalion commander. It had an identified offensive use: to secure the advancing battalion's assembly area, forming-up point and start line and later in the attack on the final assault against enemy armour and reorganisation against counter attack. Highly adaptable and flexible, the use of anti-tank recoilless rifles could be adjusted specifically to the task to be undertaken, and so it was organised to be given to the appropriate sub-unit, consistent with the particular role for which it was intended to be deployed. Hence A Company were given six anti-tank recoilless rifles, two per platoon with a view to their aggressive use, and so were placed well forward under close control of the platoon commanders. These proved lighter, more portable and quicker into action than the light 60mm mortar used by platoons. In any case, A Company only had one 60mm mortar and were similarly short of light machine guns.

In terms of support fire weapons available within the platoons, the anti-tank recoilless rifles were it, and it was up to the platoon commanders to make use and take full advantage of them. As far as Lieutenant Sean Norton was concerned they could well have a pronounced impact and be the answer to their stiffest test, causing the hunters in the tunnel to become the hunted. A Company were bloodied but unbowed, and put to proper use the resulting blast impacts on the tunnel's parapet could well have a deterrent effect on the Gendarmerie and mercenaries and a galvanising one of recovery and resurgence for the Irish, energising them, Lazarus-like. The shock of the Katangese response would have to be turned into the awe of an Irish reaction. The face of war may have changed dramatically but it is still the deadly primal collision of wills between opponents.

A Company had identified that the 'eighty-four' had the potential to grant a perceived and real edge if used correctly. They had trained and practised with it previously on 'the Glen', firing it repeatedly at traversing tank-shaped cardboard cut-out targets and had admired its effect. New to the Irish army, their predecessors in the 35th Battalion were the first to bring it into service overseas. A number of promising 'shots' had emerged and one such was now entrusted with the task of 'taking out' the firepower focussed against them.

The battle was set to be joined in close quarter combat as the Irish attackers and Katangese defenders were about to become aggressively engaged. The Gendarmerie and mercenaries had employed a judicious mix of machine guns and a high density of individual riflemen spread along the parapet of the tunnel's railway bridge, among railway buildings and inside carriages. The parapet of the railway bridge in particular provided ready-made, instant cover. Running across the entire width of the dual-carriageway underneath the railway bridge itself was a walled parapet set on its external edge, a ready-made concrete 'balcony' even in its original form, but both barricaded and fortified provided an ideal and strong point in itself. This key man-made feature was a structure affording excellent fields of fire and a hugely advantageous defensive position, except that is, for what Lieutenant Sean Norton had in mind.

There was some difficulty with their plan, however, as considerable risk was involved. A characteristic of firing the 'eighty-four' anti-tank weapon was its significant signature back blast of flame exiting from the rear of the gun, necessitating clearance of personnel behind the weapon when firing. Direct fire of this weapon using line of sight to the target required the firer and his number two to have to step out from behind the safety of the cover of the disused hospital building, remaining exposed to the heavy automatic fire. If the machine-gunners reacted quickly enough the firer would surely be mowed down even before he got his shot off. There had to be a readiness to face and endure this definite danger, to struggle to suppress one's fear, since there was a high liability and a distinct possibility of harm or death. This was a particular moment to put yourself in a perilous, precarious position and leave matters to providence. Pressed hard against the cover of the hospital building, intensely aware of the circumstances and all too conscious of the possible consequences, would you manage to step out, however momentarily, or not? It was will over wisdom and single-mindedness over sense. Was it to be payoff for those painstaking days, weeks, months of training and years of preparation? It had all come down to this.

Suddenly courage won over caution, fatalism over fear, as with a slight lull in the firing an Irish trooper stepped out, knelt down, placed the loaded 'eighty-four' on his shoulder and picked out a machine gun position along the parapet. Hands starting to shake, weapon wavering – steady, steady – he takes in gulps of air, oxygenates the brain, settles down, picks out his target again, squeezes the trigger and lets loose the anti-tank round. The roar of its ignition erupted and the brilliance of the flame from its back-blast dramatically lit up the still pre-dawn darkness, only to be superseded seconds later by the noise of the explosive detonation of its impact on target. The defenders had one less machine gun. The Irish had a foothold in the fire fight.

Platoons Under Fire

'The Irish were bruised, not broken' was the message delivered by the impacting 84mm anti-tank round as it smashed into the bridge; a sign that the thrust of the attack, though stalled, was not breached. At the same time, further stemming the tide, Corporal Gerald Francis, perilously perched at the point of the hapless lead platoon, readily risked exposure to rally those immediately around him and opened up returning fire into the left-hand railway carriage with his Gustav sub-machine gun. The firing from it stopped briefly, only to commence again and he instantly returned fire. This same exchange happened three more times, a burst of fire from Francis's Gustav and return fire from the carriage. Francis was aware that he was shaking, and taking stock made a deliberate effort to intentionally calm himself. In doing so he somehow remembered that the characteristic of the Gustav sub-machine gun is that when fired on automatic, with the finger constantly squeezing the trigger, the rounds arch upwards and to the right. Thinking it both curious and timely to recall this, he proceeded to fire single shots only, separately but in rapid fire, and used a full magazine of thirty-six rounds in this manner. The firing from the carriage ceased.

He then engaged the second railway carriage and Private Andy Wickham joined in, the pair of them joined a little later by Privates Gerry Kelly and Michael Searson. Being the furthest forward, the four Irish troopers tackled the defenders from the right, keeping up solid volleys of intensive return fire. All this took some time to unfold, and at the same time No. 2 Platoon, under Lieutenant Norton, were developing their own situation. Meanwhile further left, staring point-blank at the tunnel, Lieutenant Tommy Dunne's platoon were not idle.

Back on the railway tracks, Corporal Francis's small group were now fully and decisively engaged in an intense fire fight with the mercenary-led Katangese Gendarmerie. Despite the Irish troops' valiant efforts, the Katangese delivered a murderously heavy volley and Private Wickham fell injured. Charlie Connolly, the medic, managed to reach him, but despite his attention and persistent attempts to render first aid, Private Wickham's wounds proved fatal. Corporal Francis now called on his 84mm anti-tank team to attempt to respond and engage those ahead. He selected the left-hand railway carriage as the target and ordered the use of an anti-personnel round at minimum range aimed two metres above the roof. Realising that the group would all be within the danger area, in the heat of the moment Corporal Francis instructed them to do it anyway. It worked perfectly, the round exploding against the carriage and rendering the Katangese defence ineffective. Buoyed with their success they were instructed to repeat the shot. Further back, No. 3 Platoon, under Lieutenant Peter Feely, had manoeuvred into firing positions and when they spotted movement amongst the railway carriages they engaged. All of these mini-encounters were happening simultaneously within the fire fight. Back with Corporal Gerald Francis, his section had two 'Energas', an FN rifle modified with a fitting or attachment allowing it to fire Energa anti-tank rifle grenades. By inserting a special round it fired a projectile that looked like a rocket-shaped missile, the advantage being it would travel further than if thrown ordinarily, achieving a greater range. Loading his Energa, Corporal Francis fired, hitting the second railway carriage but the grenade failed to explode. Not put off by this he readied a second Energa and as it happened a Gendarme appeared with rifle raised so he fired directly at him; this one worked.

The Irish were beginning to hold their own, which was a definite improvement, but they were still not reaching their objective. As the intensity of the exchanges grew, Private Gerry Kelly sustained a serious gunshot wound to the groin, and other casualties were being taken. The fire fight was in the balance, there was enough edge and steel in this compelling clash that both sides believed they had the greater imperative

Members of B Company 35th Battalion on the Tunnel, Élisabethville, summer 1961.
Courtesy of the Military Archives, Dublin

to prevail; the Katangese defenders were in no mood to capitulate and the Irish were unrelenting in attack. One elemental force had to give. Defending with all their guile and know-how, if the Gendarmerie and mercenaries were able to sustain their rate of fire they could maintain dominance. Maintaining the status quo was not going to achieve the mission for the Irish, they could all too easily become forestalled and so had to force a change in their fortune. But how? Meanwhile Private Christy Lynch, a radioman to Lieutenant Sean Norton, heard more bad news over his radio: 'Two down at No. 1 Platoon.'

Fire for Effect

When the Katangese gunfire erupted, the Irish lost the initiative of their attack. Even though shots were being fired blindly at them through the darkness, the sheer volume was a considerable deterrent to movement and the Irish predicament was acute. Now well forward they were exposed and vulnerable. The attack had stalled, the onset of day was approaching and the tactical balance of the situation would further favour the defenders, as come daylight they would be better able to clearly see what they were shooting at. Frayed nerves, already raw and tense, could easily prove the Irish platoons' undoing.

As he looked anxiously out across the ground in front of the Tunnel, taking cover from the withering gunfire, Lieutenant Sean Norton knew the attack hung in the balance. A bad situation was getting steadily worse by the minute. He knew that when faced with a seriously deteriorating situation you have to do something about it and a capacity to invent ideas, to use every tool you have, to cause a process to begin was badly needed. Lieutenant Norton was determined the Katangese success would be short lived. The key to breaking a strong defensive position is to find a soft spot, then exploit it. Here there really wasn't any, but the success of letting loose the 84mm anti-tank round suggested to him that an increased concentration of this firepower at a crucial point could be decisive. Events needed to be dramatically influenced and Lieutenant Norton, encouraged by the firing and effect of the 84mm anti-tank round, knew that it warranted a repetition. Still, discouraged by the improbability of survival, he urged caution. Lieutenant Norton vividly recalls the moment:

Given that [the Irish trooper who had fired the first anti-tank round] had achieved success the first time, I felt a repeat of the same was in order. It was best under the circumstances to accompany him this time and so we both stood out together; he fired and found his target, two machine guns silenced. We ventured out seeking a third hit and found it. Three rounds in all, three hits. The intensity of their fires waned somewhat.

Tenacity won out over terror. Under the direction of Corporal Gerald Francis and from neighbouring B Company's forward position, under the direction of Lieutenant Tommy Dunne, simultaneous 84mm anti-tank rounds impacted onto the Tunnel parapet and into the railway carriages, all creating a critical moment – but only if seized upon. The battle itself was in the balance and this was the breakthrough moment for the assault on the Tunnel. Lieutenant Sean Norton recognised this immediately and trusting his instincts ran forward, as if possessed, into the unknown. His Platoon, no more knowledgeable about what exactly was out in front of them, followed, exploiting their opportunity and grasping it willingly, keen to reinforce success yet even keener to do whatever it took to stop being fired at.

Impact!

Along the tunnel's parapet, from inside the railway carriages and the railway yard's buildings, the Gendarmerie and mercenaries kept up an inferno of flying lead at the Irish. In the darkness, rain and noise they saw first the blinding flash of the 84mm anti-tank gun's back-blast then heard the roar of its ignition, overtaken seconds later by the thunderclap explosive detonation against the Tunnel's parapet. The strike's eruption had an instantaneous and abruptly shocking effect. The projectile's impact with the rim of the Tunnel took out one machine gun and caused the others to immediately fall silent.

The tunnel's defenders were shocked. Seconds later they were showered with clumps of charred concrete, choking in the billowing smoke, with the noise of the explosion still ringing in their ears. Their cessation was only momentary, however, and urged on by the mercenaries they resumed a ferocious, blistering rate of fire at the Irish.

That is until another 84mm anti-tank round resulted in a second hit, followed shortly by a third. Pandemonium followed as the air burst detonations from No. 1 Platoon's 'eighty-four' added to the chaos while the fire from B Company created a combined lethality from which they could not recover. The severity of the concentrated 84mm anti-tank fire was sustained, crippling and destructive and there was no viable response. The defenders were overwhelmed and overwrought, their resolve to resist rendered rapidly redundant. The persistence of the explosive collision of the anti-tank rounds smashing repeatedly against the parapet's concrete caused a massive maelstrom of mangled masonry which forced the defenders to flee.

Mistakes happen in war, and 'blue on blue' situations occur when you come under fire from friendly forces mistaking yours for the enemy, or vice versa. Among the doubt, fear, darkness, miscommunications, movement, strain, speed of events and confusion, errors during the 'fog of war' – often a combination of small individual mistakes occurring simultaneously – have consequences, sometimes fatal. A fired-up No. 2 Platoon, A Company, under Lieutenant Sean Norton, bouncing back from the brink of being seriously shot-up, were now reenergised and on the move. It had seemed like the Irish advance was going to collapse in the face of the sudden, severe and exceptionally heavy fire it was being subjected to, a moment for serious soldiers to stand up and be counted, and they did. Having survived the first 'unfriendly' fire, a horrendous, harrowing hostility, to now fall victim to 'friendly' fire would be tragic in the extreme, and all too easily could have happened when No. 2 Platoon, A Company emerged from the right, straight into B Company's arc of fire.

No. 2 Platoon's advance had taken them from behind the cover of the disused hospital building, down the embankment onto the dual carriageway and across Chaussée des Kasanga, and up the other side into the railway marshalling yard, taking fire all the time from the tunnel area. Private Pat Lally, born in Mellows Barracks, Renmore, Galway, and whose family before him had seen generations of soldiering with both the Irish and British armies, recounts the event:

> I was tall and lean, so maybe that was why I got the Bren gun (a light machine gun of Second World War vintage which fired .303

calibre ammunition. The LMG provides the main firepower for a section, of which there were three in a platoon). It, together with the magazine boxes of ammunition, were heavy to carry. Having been fired on, then taking cover behind the hospital and advancing towards the railway yard, we had first to cross the dual carriageway with the weapons, ammunition, backpack and poncho. Moving over a fence I fell head first, ending up with my feet pointing skywards, unable to move, up-ended. Someone behind me pushed my legs forward and I was able to gather myself. I remember, along with others, firing a number of bursts into the railway carriages where fire was being directed at us, and the firing stopped.

The shock effect of the 'eighty-four' blasts dislodged the Katangese defenders from their laterally arranged strongpoint. The Irish, having got in close by stealth, were upon them and their defence was shallow. When it came, however, the Katangese defenders' reaction was frantic and ferocious. Well set and well laid out support weapons fired along fixed lines into anticipated avenues of approach, made convergent and restrictive by the built-up area around the vicinity of the Tunnel. Forcing the fight into confined spaces, making their fire more lethal and deadly, the Katangese abruptly halted the Irish advance and turned its cohesion into confusion, the regaining of control further complicated by the darkness. Yet the Irish fightback had granted the opportunity of a possible purchase position as a basis for progressing the attack and Lieutenant Norton set about pressing home this possible advantage.

By this stage, Commandant Joe Fitzpatrick had drawn parallel to Corporal Gerald Francis and his half section, looking for a situation report and a casualty status. Pulling up a chain link fence they scrambled underneath to meet him, continuing to give covering fire all the while at those who were firing on them. By this time Corporal Francis had run out of ammunition, so as the two men spoke Corporal Francis reloaded two 36-round magazines. Commandant Fitzpatrick's concern was to get the remainder of No. 1 Platoon off the railway tracks and into proper cover. Enquiring of Commandant Fitzpatrick what he and the five others from No. 1 Platoon's lead section who were with him ought do now, Corporal Francis was instructed to join the advance with No. 2 Platoon. Corporal Francis was bleeding from his left ear lobe and Commandant Fitzpatrick was concerned for him, but as he was feeling no pain he did not feel like getting treatment at that stage. Commandant Fitzpatrick was keen to gain ground and have the Company move forward beyond the railway carriages in case the Katangese Gendarmeries and mercenaries were reforming for a counter attack, which they were. Corporal Francis calls the moment to mind:

> The Katangese Gendarmerie and mercenaries had withdrawn from the Tunnel's parapet but we were unsure – and it was dangerous to assume – that they had vacated the railway carriages on it. So Lieutenant Norton took his platoon down onto the dual carriageway and up the other side into the railway station's marshalling yard. Now we were aware there were three large companies of Katangese Gendarmerie in defence of the tunnel area (100 in each) and while we had bloodied them there must be plenty of others about. As it happened there were, and we were suddenly in amongst them.

Among the stationary engines and railway carriages there was darkness, shooting, shouting and confusion. The Irish attackers, hugely outnumbered, became intermingled with the Katangese defenders and it became a chaotic affair, a shapeless frenetic effort. The Irish suddenly flooded in on a collision course, uncertain who was friend or foe nor where they were. It was impossible to know what was happening beyond one's very immediate surroundings, a situation ripe for 'blue on blue' fire, survival an unpredictable outcome. After three or four minutes of mayhem and madness, the Katangese Gendarmerie panicked somewhat and withdrew. The instinct for survival dictates the Irish were not worried about those running away from them but far more concerned about anyone lingering, and that occupied their minds and actions. However, with the Tunnel in their hands the Irish 'tails were up', morale was high, emotion took over, and the platoon's advance was extended.

Corporal Dan Mannix and some others kept going, threatening to go beyond the safe distance of exploitation and risking running into the 'shifting' mortar fire from their own 81mm mortar section supporting the attack from Liege crossroads firing line. Checking themselves before they became victims of their own success, they returned to the railway carriages in the marshalling yard, which allowed them some respite until the Katangese started firing into them, whereupon they got out and went under the carriages, taking cover behind the steel wheels and returning fire. Lieutenant Norton described the advance:

> Three rounds, three hits, the intensity of the defenders fire waned momentarily, sufficient to push the platoon forward. The further we went, curiously, the less resistance we got, so I kept going, exploiting the situation. We moved forward rapidly under the covering fire of four more 'eighty-four' rounds, so much so I was afraid of over extending my advance and becoming cut off or isolated. In the event, we did become a little stretched.

However, the situation was much improved and the Tunnel was in Irish hands. However, things were a long way from secure.

Assault and Clearance

In charge of the defence of Élisabethville was the mercenary commander Colonel Roger (René) Faulques, an ex-French Foreign Legion paratrooper, veteran of Dien Bien Phu (Vietnam) and Algeria. From a sandbagged, camouflaged nerve centre in the centre of the city he directed defensive operations, commanding a necklace of key positions at vantage points all around the capital. These were a series of entrenchments, a ring of fortified structures manned by groups of Katangese Gendarmerie led by mercenaries equipped with support weapons – carefully sighted machine guns mostly – all backed up by on-call mortar fire. Scarred and walking with a slight limp, Colonel Faulques maintained command and control from his hidden headquarters, coordinating the main Katangese defensive effort. With a large bank of radio sets linked through individual frequencies to the front-line strong points and support elements, he received situation reports and incident updates, responding with instructions and orders. Ever more hard pressed, he was becoming increasingly concerned by the adversely developing situation at the Tunnel.

Lieutenant Norton's platoon, having penetrated hard, had fought fast to gain a forward foothold. The two other platoons, under Commandant Fitzpatrick's overall direction, were now following, also fighting forward in quick succession. Fire was still pouring in on them and the matter was not yet clear cut and much in the balance. There was plenty of fighting still left to do. Lieutenant Norton was keen to make the most of the opportunity presented to him but was fearful that where his advance paused it might remain, so he pressed the advantage while he had the upper hand, eventually stopping it himself before his platoon became too overstretched. They had progressed all the way from the cover of the hospital building down onto the dual carriageway and up the bank into the railway marshalling yards. Amid the momentary confusion in the marshalling yards his platoon progressed in pockets well along the railway tracks. Now they had to turn around, consolidate and clear the way ahead. Inevitably, small unit actions broke out as individual groups of reinforcing Gendarmerie inexplicably stumbled headlong in from the side. The first such approach was a group of four Gendarmerie in a taxi, with windows down and weapons protruding. Suddenly confronting a small group of unsuspecting Irish, each group was baffled, disbelieving at what they were seeing, both a split second away and a hair trigger between life and death. Whoever reacted quickest survived. Private Tom Foster's instincts were fastest, his wits keenest and his aim sharpest. Bringing his Bren gun into action, he brought a line of fire onto the vehicle and saved the day.

Having cleared the area in and around the big railway yard sheds, No. 2 Platoon turned their attention towards assaulting the railway station building proper. However, very heavy small arms fire began to be received from the PARC VT area (a commercial area adjacent to the railway yards); Colonel Faulques was not conceding the Tunnel just yet. One of the factors in the broader ongoing battle in the Élisabethville area was now directed to come into play: mobile fire bases. Under the direction of Colonel Faulques, these jeep-mounted mercenaries equipped with .3 or .5 calibre vehicle-borne Browning heavy machine guns, recoilless rifles and bazookas, raced to plug gaps, strengthen the resolve of wavering Gendarmerie positions and stiffen the opposition towards wherever the advancing UN most threatened their defences. Job done in one location, they would move speedily to where they were needed. One such mercenary jeep, loaded with a .5 HMG, arrived and engaged No. 2 Platoon, who responded unhesitatingly – hitting one occupant – and the vehicle roared out of sight behind the railway station building.

'Dropping a section' as a fire base, where ten Irish troops put down covering fire, the remaining two sections of ten men each manoeuvred left – flanking onto the railway station building. The firing from this area dwindled as the attack progressed. On reaching the building the Irish discovered the jeep had been driven away, and somehow they knew it wasn't coming back any time soon. The platoon was then ordered to secure the ground held and an 'eighty-four' anti-tank weapon team were told to return back along the railway yard to the Tunnel area to deal with an outbreak of firing emanating from railway carriages on the Tunnel itself. Two 84mm rounds shortly silenced the firing. Two Gendarmes hurriedly jumped down from the railway carriages and made off up the road towards the roundabout. In so doing they ran into the fire of No. 3 Platoon under Lieutenant Feely, who had been given responsibility to clear the area northwest of the Tunnel.

One month short of being promoted to full Lieutenant and getting his second 'bar' (or today a 'pip' – rank insignia), Peter Feely's No.3 Platoon was next ordered to clear the remaining unchecked railway carriages in the marshalling yard for hidden snipers and Gendarmerie gunmen. This he set about doing himself with the use of Mills 36 hand-grenades, lobbing them through the windows before, once they had exploded, entering the carriages to clear them with his Gustav sub machine fire. He describes it:

> Approaching the first railway carriage I lobbed a grenade towards the open window only it fell short, bounced off the window frame and dropped onto the railway tracks; there it remained, without exploding. This wasn't supposed to happen, you were to pull the pin, throw, and it exploded. Only I did but it didn't; now what? Wait. Wait for it to go off, but when? After a moment or so I lost patience and moved, I felt, in fact I knew, I had to. It didn't explode. Sequentially, systematically I cleared those railway carriages and the platoon moved on to clear the area.

In so doing, both from the railway carriages and the area in general, the Gendarmerie were flushed out and seen running off. Character and action held A Company in good stead, resulting in the pendulum of fortune swinging their way. The Tunnel was theirs.

Three Green Flares

Arm outstretched skywards, Commandant Joe Fitzpatrick, Officer Commanding A Company, had an important task to perform. He slid the first flare into the chamber of his Verey light pistol and holding it aloft squeezed the trigger. Up, upwards it went, momentarily disappearing into the darkened rain-sodden sky and swallowed by the grey murky bleakness, before suddenly, spectacularly exploding in a profusion of green. He quickly repeated this action twice more. The three green flares was the signal for 'Tunnel taken', mission accomplished. A hard ask and a tough task, it had taken assertiveness, well-trained troops and self-believing junior leaders to complete and achieve it. The plan had not survived contact with the enemy and unusual things had happened and kept on happening. The physicality and intensity of the close-in combat was full-on and the exchanges, unsurprisingly, had a significant edge. But there's a beauty in simplicity and the combativeness, competence and confidence of the Irish had a huge bearing on the outcome.

Irish troops operating a checkpoint on the captured Tunnel. Note the specially modified bayonet for the Gustav submachine gun (left). Courtesy of the Military Archives, Dublin

Contact with the Katangese enemy had begun badly, but the resultant anger had an energy and sustained by composure the Irish never wavered. With the wit and imagination to know they just had to make things work, they survived the withering fire of the opening onslaught and endured the nightmare of the sustained intensity of incoming fire before they thrived and came back. They knew they had to make a significant play and have the final say. This composure of collective effort, this refusal to lose, however, was every bit as much about a number of individual acts of bravery, courage, leadership and resourcefulness, which were significant in their execution and achievement in emotionally draining, physically dangerous, hugely difficult and dire circumstances.

A Company had just been through a sharp, intense, unforgiving fire fight whose outcome was unforeseeable and liable to be won or lost at any number of given moments, and it wasn't over yet. Colonel Roger Faulques, mercenary commander of Élisabethville's defence, was planning to make one more last desperate throw of the dice. At 0745 hours, one and a quarter hours after its seizure by the Irish, Colonel Faulques ordered a massive mortar barrage to fall all around the tunnel area. His forces threw everything they had at the Irish, and Faulques knew, like the combat veteran he was, that unless he could shift the Irish off the Tunnel, its loss could cause a momentous shift in the high-stakes battle for Katanga itself. The moment was now, the position here, and not only was this tactically vital but also strategically and symbolically significant as the Tunnel's loss to the UN would grant them a corridor from which they could dominate the capital and give the impression that the UN force had grown in stature, willing and able to give militarily to back itself politically. The Irish braced themselves as the Katangese mortars opened up to pound the newly-taken position, steadfastly refusing to be denied their victory and that of the UN. The battle for the Tunnel had been a battle within a battle. The three green flares symbolising victory, tactically, for the Irish battalion fortifying a belief in themselves, strategically for the UN which had galvanised their political efforts with military backing, and personally for the individual Irish participants, strengthened with a seam of submerged raw energy which came to the fore when it was asked of them.

The battle for the tunnel was the battle for Élisabethville, which was the battle for Katanga, which was the key to the battle for the Congo.

Reorganisation

Frederick the Great once said: 'He who defends everything, defends nothing.' On 16 December 1961, the 36th Battalion had taken and held the contested territory with two companies; A Company concentrated on the Tunnel and B Company linked nearby with the Swedish forces. While most UN units were spread thinly on the ground the Irish, who held the most important region, had the task of dominating their immediate area. It was one thing to seize the Tunnel, A Company now had to make sure they held onto it. To do so they kept their defence compact. The attackers had become defenders, and they had to ensure against any infiltration by the Katangese or attempted recapture of the cleared objective. A Company prepared a close-in all round defensive perimeter encircling the Tunnel with No.2 Platoon and half of No. 1 Platoon south, in the vicinity of the railway sheds, while No. 3 Platoon and the other half of No. 1 Platoon were to the north, in the area of the railway yard and hospital.

Defences set, the 're-org' was a consolidation of the seized objective involving the holding of ground around the area taken – for a while. Initially at least they had a chance to draw breath and ponder on what had just occurred. Any sense of victory however was severely tempered by the loss of Lieutenant Paddy Riordan and Private Andy Wickham. Lieutenant Norton states:

> There was no emotion evident, we were tasked to take ground, now to hold it; consequently there was a lot to attend to. We had two dead and some twenty or so wounded. Matters were businesslike; we were mostly wondering for how long we would have to be here. Curiously only then did it strike me, we had been in the same uniforms since arrival on the 6 [December], some ten days previously.

They had been in action straight off the plane. It had been high drama from their arrival and required a direct approach. They were presented with a very different kind of challenge than they had anticipated when boarding the Globemasters at Dublin airport. Different questions were asked of them than they thought would be the case, and all of this at speed. They controlled what they could and got on with matters, demonstrating a collective will not to come out second best, until finally they had to demonstrate sheer bloody-mindedness and become full of attacking intent. When put on the back foot in battle they found themselves involved in a titanic exchange but had the greater desire for the fight and the greater will to win. The Irish needed it more than the mercenaries wanted it.

It was routine during the reorganisation process for section and platoon commanders to drill check their personnel, individual ammunition requirements and their fitness for the future fight. This basic procedure was to throw up a number of interesting instances, evidencing the true exposure of the Irish to the deadly nature of the undertaking they had just come through. Corporal Sammy Gregan was to identify that his 'jaw felt sore' and upon examination it was discovered there was a bullet lodged in it. He was subsequently medically repatriated to Ireland and so missed serving out the remainder of his tour with the 36th Battalion. He returned to the Congo with the 37th Battalion and was the first off the plane to greet his homeward bound colleagues. On taking off his backpack Corporal Gerald Francis, already shot through the earlobe, discovered bullet holes in it; his tea-mug with a bullet hole clear through. Corporal John Power was to find that his Gustav sub-machine gun mechanism had become jammed and he was unable to pull the mechanism to the rear. Seeking assistance, an inspection showed his weapon had been hit and damaged by a bullet. The Irish had well and truly been in the line of fire and quite a few had narrow escapes, near misses and close calls.

Checking the Company's physical fitness ascertained they could only continue to fight if they had enough ammunition. Resupply is an essential task that should be undertaken early on in the reorganisation position and Captain Quartermaster Harry Crowley and his 'Q' team set to the task, Signalman Peter Fields among them:

> We set off in our resupply vehicle laden with ammunition boxes and ration packs. Shortly along Avenue des Savoniers, we unexpectedly

The Battle for the Tunnel (Élisabethville) | 103

came under fire so immediately pulled over to the side and ran into a house with a garage attached. I dived into the garage and looking out the window saw a number of Gendarmerie running between houses on the opposite side of the Avenue. We returned fire. There was no further firing in our direction so after a duration we resumed our journey. Not long after, but still short of the Tunnel, we were surprised to yet again come under fire. Stopping abruptly, we took cover on the side of the road and returned fire, round for round; the firing stopped. No further interruption was experienced.

We drove under the Tunnel and reported to Commandant Joe Fitzpatrick who was busily supervising the 'digging-in' consolidation process in anticipation of an imminent reaction from the mercenaries and Gendarmerie.

A Company didn't have to be told to dig deep and dig fast. Fortunate not to have suffered more casualties, they had little time to wallow in any 'what ifs' because now the real concern was to ready themselves for the inevitable incoming mortar bombardment, which soon arrived. It was quickly evident that the occupation of their hastily prepared defensive positions needed to be more dispersed and they redeployed. They quickly set about it and by mid-afternoon they were glad they had, as they had to withstand a second mortar barrage as intense as the first. The location of the firing was identified as being from the Union Minière complex and 36th Battalion mortars replied. In between the Katangese mortar bombardments, in fact shortly after the first, the Swedish battalion moved out across their start line and two hours later had breached the defences at Camp Massart. 'Storm-In' was completed.

Meanwhile, the Indian Gurkha battalion had completed their move along Avenue Churchill and reached Athene School. The two Ethiopian battalions, having cleared the Lido and Zoo area, moved towards Camp Massard to close the ring around the city. Operation Unokat was completed, and successfully so. There were eighteen UN dead and twenty-one seriously wounded, but the UN had taken the initiative and seized the opportunity, the second Battle of Katanga now going their way. The Katangese response was confined to indirect mortar fire, falling this time onto the Swedish camp. The following day, early morning, Indian heavy mortars were moved into B Company's area to bring the Katangese mortars within range. Threat countered they were moved further forward later in the day into the captured Camp Massard to quell incoming mortars landing there. Due to the disposition of the UN's 1st and 2nd Brigade troops around the city of Élisabethville, orders were issued for the strict control of mortar fire.

Matters remained unsettled throughout 18 December, with many mortar bombs falling on the Tunnel area and sniper firing continuing during the day, also into the 36th Battalion area. Notwithstanding, the Battalion Ordnance Officer commenced the disposal of unexploded mortar bombs, including one 4.2 inch bomb of British manufacture in the company lines and battalion headquarters area.

The UN force commander and Brigadier Raja visited the Irish lines, congratulating them on the seizure of the Tunnel. Meanwhile mopping up operations by the Ethiopians and Gurkhas continued in Élisabethville. There was a Baluba threat to move into the city from the refugee camp and those who succeeded in reaching the city engaged in some looting. The UN Brigade Headquarters set up a depot for the storage of confiscated loot. Finally, at last light the 36th Battalion was informed that the water system, which had been cut off along with light and electric power shortly after the Irish seizure of the Tunnel, had been poisoned. In any event, rainwater had been used for all purposes since the mains were turned off on the morning of 16 December. Not everything falling from the skies was necessarily bad.

Unsure exactly where the notion came from, Lieutenant Peter Feely found himself inspecting the depth of the impacts on the concrete parapet rim of the tunnel: 'As regards the penetrative effect of the fire of the 84mm anti-tank round on impact, it was said to be twenty-one inches on concrete and on measuring this after the attack it proved to be precisely correct. It was a good weapon to have and I was now glad to have it on the "re-org".'

While Lieutenant Feely was wondering about the depths of impact of the 84mm anti-tank gun, Lieutenant Sean Norton wanted to solve a riddle of his own. He walked to within a few metres or so of the rail carriages on the Tunnel and let loose a number of 9mm rounds from his Gustav sub-machine gun, only to see them bounce off the carriages' exterior. They had little or no penetrative effect, due to a combination of small calibre round and tough material used in the construction of the carriages. Meanwhile, Corporal Sammy Gregan, being stretchered away with the bullet still stuck in his jaw, was completely distracted from what was going on around him. All he wanted to know was if those who had shot him had been accounted for. Indeed they had, and reassured only then did he relax.

Aftermath

Straight into action from the off, the Company had a mix of very young soldiers, old soldiers and seasoned NCOs. These senior NCOs proved very steady and together with the old soldiers successfully settled the young privates in those early days. They all learned on the job, and once 'digging in' (digging trenches) had commenced they didn't have to be told twice to provide good overhead cover, even as the remainder of the trench was being dug. Mortar fire was very frightening, and even though direct small arms fire was also deadly – and you frequently heard rounds passing through the leaves on the trees – it just didn't have the same menace about as mortar fire. It bothered Captain Harry Crowley particularly, and he was not alone in this. He was not involved in the attack on the Tunnel proper, as his role was resupply, especially on the 're-org' and particularly of ammunition.

Commandant Joe Fitzpatrick, the Company Commander, was very steady and the Company soldiers liked him. He had worked them hard on 'the Glen' and when No. 1 Platoon was fired on and the attack's momentum stalled he was the one who got among them and moved them on, maintaining the impetus. Lieutenant Sean Norton, Platoon Commander No. 2 Platoon, was also really in the thick of the action from arrival to the Tunnel 're-org'.

There were others who displayed courageous actions, accurate fire, leadership, coolness and control and where disregard for personal safety was evident. In truth, A Company had distinguished themselves with honour, distinction and merit, yet they were tough, pragmatic and modest about it. They had been given a job to do and were determined to go about it. That the action was of the nature it became resulted directly from the drastic change in the UN mandate earlier in February, a more coercive resolution authorising the use of force in accordance with Chapter Seven of the UN Charter, a significant step up from its 'police role' of keeping the peace to which they now hoped to return. What was remarkable about their actions was their unpreparedness. The Company had no combat experience, were under-equipped and had no training of a continuous, comprehensive, collective nature – it was fifteen years since the 'Emergency' ended in 1946. An amazing action, all the more so because it had simply not been done before.

An action of this nature was unexpected, and certainly so when Ireland decided to face up to its responsibilities as a member of the UN, seeing participation as its obligation as a UN member state. Following on from the consensus of the UN Security Council Resolution authorising the mission in the Congo, and responding favourably when asked to participate, Ireland regarded it as an opportunity to demonstrate its identity as a truly neutral peacekeeper, keen to secure its reputation of being an ideal peacekeeping nation. A Company's action at the Battle of the Tunnel certainly contributed towards that. As did Irish pack rations.

The 36th Battalion took with them to the Congo Irish pack rations for twenty-one days. They were popular enough with the troops but more so with other contingents on the occasions when attached to the Irish for rations. They were superior to the American day rations, which were considered generally unpalatable, and the Irish pack rations were a Godsend during the period of hostilities. But the need to be supplemented by fresh rations – meat, vegetables, bread – always increased in the aftermath of hostilities. This is where and when Captain Harry Crowley came into his own, his target now the up-coming Christmas dinner.

Before that, however, there were matters requiring attention and Gendarmerie still had access to some portions of the city. It would be all too unfortunate should anything adverse happen now, especially after their precipitous induction to Katanga and the belligerence of the last ten days or so. All firing was suspended at 0715 hours on 19 December while the Katanga government, the Congolese central government and the United Nations were engaged in peace talks. Meetings were held with Red Cross personnel in order to facilitate the distribution of food in the 36th Battalion area. At this meeting the opportunity was taken to demonstrate that Irish troops did not loot private property and had sealed up to the best of their ability such houses as had been searched to reassure the Red Cross that Balubas were not allowed to loot or kill in any area controlled by the 36th Irish Battalion and to satisfy them that white refugees who were old and infirm had been housed and fed.

In the morning the post office was still occupied by Gendarmerie, who subsequently withdrew. The two Ethiopian battalions captured Union Minière after first light, though opposition was strong which necessitated a full frontal assault resulting in heavy casualties. The control of refugees and the apprehension of suspects continued and civilians began moving freely in and out of the city. Unexploded mortar bombs were disposed of by ordnance officers in the different Company localities over the following days and during one operation the 8th and 35th Ethiopian battalions were machine gunned and mortared for a considerable part of the day. The International Red Cross began organising the distribution of foodstuffs to the civilian population and the Baluba refugees. White residents in the Irish battalion area who had fled during the fighting were encouraged to visit their homes and remain. A Company remained 'dug in', securing the Tunnel. Lieutenant Sean Norton says of that time: 'During the aftermath of the action at the Tunnel there were those, myself included, whose speech was slurred, and we kept talking quickly, very loud for days, unceasingly. Another difficulty was an inability to sleep for some time afterwards. It was perhaps best described as a type of a high but one I would not want to experience again.'

Meanwhile Captain Harry Crowley was hard at work getting the best deals for scarce amounts of petrol, and securing the best cuts of meat from the Battalion ration store, to the detriment of the other companies. There was also the barter method – flour for sliced pans, coffee and cocoa for mincemeat, onions and milk for salami. It was a matter of getting the best from the rations. The unit history of the 36th Battalion records: 'Christmas Dinner was enjoyed by all.' They even had plum pudding, thanks to some liberated dried fruit.

C Company replaced A Company in the Tunnel on 28 December and although they were relieved, A Company were far from relaxed. Signalman Peter Fields remembers:

The month following 16 December was quite intense and stressful, the Tunnel and the railway line left and right of it had to be held, it was now precious to us having lost two on the day of the taking of it. While the Christmas dinner was enormously enjoyable the 'Q' and cooks had worked wonders with the food, but up to early January the tempo was still up, only gradually and incrementally did it decrease. We did not know what was going to happen, if anything. We knew there was a truce, but what is a truce, only a temporary cessation of war. We were kept on our toes, there was a lot going on.

PART II
LEBANON (1980)

CHAPTER 4

Attack on At-Tiri

Tug of War

'Hold the rope, hold the rope', came the encouraging cries of the respective coaches of the two inter-company tug-of-war teams as the 'second pull' had just begun in earnest. The strain on the rope was taken up by both sides and their competitive spirit was fierce. Pulling each other, at opposite ends of the rope, were Headquarters (HQ) and Reconnaissance (Recce) company teams respectively. Surprisingly, HQ Company had pulled Recce Company and both company teams were again 'on the rope' for the second pull. 'Heave!' roared the respective supporters, enjoying the spectacle, the application of both teams vigorous. Easter Sunday, 6 April 1980, had dawned bright and clear over South Lebanon. The religious rites of Easter having been duly celebrated, Irish battalion personnel had relaxed and entered enthusiastically into an enthralling afternoon of amusement at the Battalion sports day.

Taking place as the final noteworthy event before rotating home, a successful six-month tour of duty was entering its last few weeks and morale was high. The competition for the various, more serious, track and field events was nearly completed and the fun events had begun; the welly-throwing competition was ongoing next to the Total garage and a rutted, hard, dry pitch was the arena hosting the exertions of those involved in the tug-of-war competition. There was no denying the excitement, the efforts of the participants matched equally by the spirited exuberance of the supporters. In the tug of war, both sides sought to bring to bear an applied combination of technique, teamwork and tenaciousness. Each attempting to establish a physical superiority over the other sufficient to make them yield ground. Ribbons on the rope as markers, symmetrically placed and equidistant from the rope's centre, measured the distance designated to be pulled and would tell who won or lost. Victory would be achieved by a coordinated rearward rhythmic stepping movement, a unison of feet and heels, in step and in tempo, digging into the ground, desperately seeking purchase as a pivotal platform to 'pull' their opponents off their centre of gravity. The technique of dislodging your opposition took hours and hours of training, commitment, preparation and rehearsals. All that had come down to this. Now, on the second 'pull!' the victors of the first round, HQ Company, were looking to cause an upset and win outright. The vanquished, Recce Company looking to even the score and bring the matter to a third and deciding 'pull'.

The strain showing on their faces, arm muscles aching, neither team was prepared to yield. Suddenly, a frequent call was heard: 'Recce turn out, Recce turn out'. The rope was instantly dropped and team members and supporters alike ran scrambling onto and into their waiting armoured vehicles. Matters were made very clear, the available information stark, the De Facto Forces (DFF) militia had made a bold bid for At-Tiri. The Battalion Reserve, consisting of Recce Company and additional elements, were to move immediately to bolster C Company in situ. Inside twenty-five minutes, Recce Company vehicles were breaking the brow of Hill 880. Unknown to those inside them, the 'Battle of At-Tiri' had already begun and they were about to become involved in a serious struggle and a far more deadly 'tug of war'. At stake, tactically, the village of At-Tiri, operationally, the credibility of the UNIFIL mission; strategically, the will of the UN.

The 'Leb'

Like Ireland, Lebanon has had a troubled history and a turbulent past. Civil and foreign wars have been fought on its soil and it was home to thousands of Palestinian refugees who fled north into Lebanon and neighbouring Jordan after the creation of the state of Israel. Continuing waves of immigration had brought the Jewish population of Palestine to a sizeable minority, then following the Nazi's extermination of European Jews during the Holocaust, the aspiration emerged that Palestine would become the universal refuge for all Jews. Since 1948 the state of Israel, formally Palestine, has had a Jewish majority. The proclamation of the Jewish state under the termination of the British mandate for Palestine was followed by war between Israel and the neighbouring Arab states, ending in victory for Israel and the signing of separate armistice agreements. The old Palestinian boundaries with Lebanon and Syria on the north and east remained unchanged. Then, in June 1967 following the Six Day War with Egypt, Syria and Jordan, Israel occupied the Sinai Peninsula in Egypt, the Gaza Strip, the West Bank of the Jordan River, including the Old City of Jerusalem, and the Golan Heights region in south western Syria. The expulsion of militant Palestinians from Jordan in 'Black September' 1970 caused yet another influx of Palestinians into Lebanon, creating a 'state within a state'.

Following raids by Palestinian guerrillas from Lebanon into Israel, the Lebanese found themselves affected by large-scale Israeli retaliatory raids. Weakened by a civil war of their own, essentially between Muslim and Christian Arabs, the Lebanese made various failed attempts to control the Palestinians and Syrian forces had to intervene to prevent a Palestinian victory over the Muslim Lebanese. Matters were further confused by an Israeli Army invasion of the south of the country in

A lull in hostilities. Despite the severe pressure, morale in C Company remained high.   Courtesy of Comdt Ned Kelly (retd)

1978, launched to prevent Palestinian Liberation Organisation (PLO) guerrilla incursions southwards across the Lebanese border into Israel.

Into this turmoil and tempestuousness entered the United Nations Interim Force in Lebanon (UNIFIL), established and mandated on 19 March 1978 under UN Security Council Resolution 425 to:

> Confirm the withdrawal of Israeli forces from Lebanon.
>
> Restore international peace and security.
>
> Assist the government of Lebanon in ensuring the effective return of its authority in the area.
>
> Prevent the recurrence of fighting and ensure that its Area of Operations is not utilised for hostile activities of any kind.
>
> Protect and render humanitarian aid to the local population.

UNIFIL faced problems from the beginning and the undertaking was very much a foreign venture for the personnel of the six battalions comprising the UN force of nearly 6,000 peacekeepers. There were culture differences and other difficulties arising from going into a Middle-Eastern Arab culture with different behaviours and norms, and if that was not easy enough there were operational difficulties also on the ground.

The Israeli Defence Forces' (IDF) 'Operation Litani' forced the Palestinians to withdraw north of the Litani River and into the coastal city of Tyre. Israel subsequently made a partial withdrawal from South Lebanon but not before establishing an Israeli-controlled security zone immediately north of the border with Lebanon. When the Israeli army withdrew they left behind them this buffer zone in the south known as the Christian Enclave, ruled by a Proxy Force called the Christian Militia or De Facto Forces (DFF), The Irish found themselves sandwiched between the PLO and the DFF.

The DFF were led by a Major Haddad, who was a renegade major from the Lebanese Army. His original raison d'être in South Lebanon was to act as a counterbalance to the PLO and defend Christian interests there. The Israelis found Haddad a useful ally and saw the

DFF as a proxy force for their own particular policies, therefore they financed, trained, armed and supplied the DFF. UNIFIL, and the Irish in particular, were deployed against the DFF and had to operate in a highly charged atmosphere. After the Israeli Army's partial withdrawal, the Palestinian guerrillas regrouped. With much of their equipment intact, the situation in South Lebanon remained extremely tense and volatile. The UN force, which had entered Lebanon to separate Israeli and Palestinian forces, often found itself fired on by both sides.

The area assigned to the Irish battalion in the UNIFIL Area of Operations (AO) was in the shape of a triangle spreading at its base from the village of Rshaf to beyond the village of Barachit, a distance of approximately ten miles from east to west. The distance from the base line to the apex, north of As-Sultaniyah, is again approximately ten miles. The Dutch battalion and the Senegalese battalion were positioned to the west and east, respectively, with the Nigerian battalion to the north. Tebnine, in the centre of the area, is about 900 metres above sea level and approximately 30 km from the Mediterranean coastline. The entire area was hilly and undulating with three main towns of approximately the same size – Tebnine, Barachit and Haddata – and a number of smaller towns set in amongst the valleys. There were no rivers or streams in the area and the land was stony but nonetheless fertile. The roads were narrow, unbanked and for the most part teetering on the edge of steep inclines overlooking the deep villages, or wadis, which criss-crossed the area of operations. Winters were normally mild in the area, but the 1979–80 winter had been exceptional. From mid-December to March temperatures were down to zero for much of the time, with strong winds and heavy rain an everyday occurrence and the odd snowstorm from time to time.

The main form of employment for local people in the district was farming, using methods which had not differed greatly from those used in Biblical times. Ploughing was carried out with a light plough pulled by single or paired oxen, seeding and harvesting were all done by hand. There was little evidence of farm machinery aside from the odd tractor. Tebnine, population 3,500, was a trading and administrative centre for a large area of South Lebanon, being at the hub of the road system. This was where most of the produce for a wide area was marketed, particularly the main cash crop of tobacco.

To carry out its mission in line with its UN mandated role, the Irish battalion manned Observation Posts (OPs), Listening Posts (LPs), Checkpoints (CPs) and Patrol Bases (PBs) right across its Area of Operations, from Rshaf to Barachit to Duya Ntar as well as four Ops in the area controlled by DFF forces – Mhaibeb, Blida, Jabal As-Saff and al-Ras. A total of fifty-one posts initially, subsequently increased to fifty-three, were manned by the 46th Irish Battalion on a twenty-four-hour basis, throughout each day of its tour of duty. As it had been with the three previous Irish battalions in the area, these posts were the eyes and ears of UNIFIL, and ultimately of the UN Security Council through the Secretary General.

Rules of Engagement

The discipline of non-escalation, despite provocation, is the hallmark of peacekeeping and the Irish were among the best. Participation in peacekeeping operations has been the most significant development in the Defence Forces since its establishment. The emphasis on conventional military training within the Defence Forces has allowed it to integrate successfully into UN forces. Its internal security role, performed to aid the civil power, has rendered the Defence Forces especially suitable for peacekeeping. Its use of minimum force only, its application of the non-escalation principle and its disciplined restraint has seen the Defence Forces and Ireland make a significant contribution to peacekeeping and has increased the force's levels of training and morale. In addition, Irish soldiers have a natural talent to earn the trust and confidence of the people and parties in the mission areas they operate in, having demonstrated their ability to defuse potentially explosive situations by compromise, flexibility, tact, dialogue and humour. The Irish were impartial, and were clearly seen to be by those living in the Area of Operations.

There was, however, a growing resentment by the DFF, whose perception of the Irish battalion's firmness in its response to harassment was that it was detrimental to their attempts to push forward from the enclave. There was equally a misconception on behalf of the DFF that Irish efforts to make compromises were perceived as weakness. It is one of the dilemmas of peacekeepers to achieve their mandate when placed in a context where there is in fact no peace to be kept, where the parties concerned in the mission areas do not observe the taking of the necessary steps for compliance with the decisions of the UN Security Council and openly obstruct the fulfilment of the mandate. Often, the deployed peacekeeping force unfairly faces the blame for the non-resolution of a situation which is, in fact, beyond their ability to influence. UNIFIL was placed in southern Lebanon to keep the peace between two parties where there was no peace to be kept, between two parties – the Israelis and the Palestinians – and by extension the Syrian military forces inside Lebanon. UNIFIL was formed during the Cold War era, at a time when the US still supported UN peacekeeping as a means of avoiding overseas military commitments by its own forces which would risk a superpower confrontation.

The deployment of UNIFIL into southern Lebanon, it was believed in New York, would encourage the Israelis into leaving the south of the country. It wasn't believed that Israel would want to stay. Yet they did stay, and they wanted to be there. Because of this the UN, and subsequently the Irish, fulfilment of the mandate – indeed maintaining their very location – became a more challenging prospect than was first anticipated. Therein existed an undercurrent of tension inherent in simply undertaking the mission that was made more manifest by occupying the ground where you were placed, and so the Irish faced their share of confrontation. Those who serve in peacekeeping forces are equipped with light defensive weapons but are not authorised to use force except in self-defence. This right is exercised judiciously because of the obvious danger that if a UN force uses weapons its impartiality is, however unfairly, immediately called into question. This requirement sometimes demands exceptional restraint on the part of soldiers serving in peacekeeping forces. In common with all UN peacekeeping forces, UNIFIL only used force in self-defence. Normally other means were used first, such as blocking with physical obstacles, negotiation, liaison at higher command levels and the deployment of reinforcements to the scene, including the Force Mobile Reserve (FMR). The other parties in the area, the PLO and Israeli-backed DFF, knew full well the constraints under which Irish battalion operated in respect of the use of force and were not above exploiting that knowledge to their own advantage. Peacekeeping required well-disciplined, well-trained and well-led troops who stood firm when necessary in the face of provocation when the normal response of a soldier would necessarily be forceful.

Effective liaison is important at all levels and has to be exercised regularly and as required. When an incident occurs the value of regular liaison becomes readily apparent. Liaison with the locals at checkpoint level, through platoon-commander, company-commander and battalion HQ liaison results in the development of contacts among the other parties. These contacts were used in situations which developed between the Irish battalion personnel and the PLO and DFF at whatever level was required to defuse potentially dangerous 'stand-offs'. In very difficult situations, liaison between UNIFIL HQ staff with higher level contacts could be of greater assistance to the troops on the ground. Sometimes the intervention of the UN in New York (UNNY) was required. From the beginning of the Irish involvement in UNIFIL, there have been many dangerous incidents in which rounds and shells impacted on Irish battalion positions, and numerous tense stalemates were normally defused through established peacekeeping liaison techniques. At other times the operations assumed a very routine nature.

However, the At-Tiri break-in and seizure attempt had a more sinister intent. It was to illustrate the complexity of the problems facing the Irish battalion and the danger which is a constant companion of peacekeeping soldiers. The term 'peacekeeping operation' is not mentioned in the UN Charter, but since 1956 had evolved as a significant and essential part of the functions of the United Nations. Peacekeeping missions are manned by armed contingents from member states placed under the command of the UN. The Defence Forces made its first contribution to peacekeeping in 1958, when fifty officers were assigned to the United Nations Observer Group in Lebanon (UNOGIL), or observers along the Armistice Demarcation Line (ADL) between Lebanon and Israel. When their mission with UNOGIL was finished, some transferred to the UN Truce Supervision Organisation (UNTSO), established in 1948.

Peacekeeping has come to be defined as an operation involving military personnel, generally infantry units (unarmed or) lightly armed for self-defence, to maintain peace and international security and peacefully settle conflicts, normally with the consent of the conflicting parties. While peacekeeping operations involve the use of military personnel, they achieve their objectives without the use of arms, contrasting with later peace enforcement missions. The UN Mandate establishing a Peacekeeping Force makes provision for the use of arms for self-defence. The terms of reference for UNIFIL stated that self-defence includes action against attempts, by forceful means, to prevent UNIFIL from discharging its duties under the Mandate. It has been said of peacekeeping that it is not a job for soldiers, but it is only soldiers that can do it.

Behind the Lines, Behind the Scenes

The maintenance by UNIFIL of OPs outside its Area of Operations (AO) and inside the 'Enclave', the Israeli Controlled Area (ICA), did not reflect the military reality on the ground but instead encouraged a potential fulfilment of the mandate on the map. These OPs were not only a source of irritation to the Israelis and their ill-disciplined militia the DFF, but were also a source of huge concern to UNIFIL, as in the event of trouble these OPs, cut off from UNIFIL's AO, were acutely vulnerable in any confrontation. These 'Hostage Posts' had been the Achilles heel of the Irish peacekeeping forces since their arrival in South Lebanon. Now, the 46th Irish Battalion had to maintain four OPs; at al-Ras, Jabal As-Saff, Blida and Mhaibeb. To maintain these posts, rotate troops and resupply them meant having to make tactical compromises, since politics dictated deployment and deployment dictated tactics, and this situation was tactically disadvantageous.

On its arrival in 1978, UNIFIL had never taken full control of the area intended for its deployment. The Irish battalion headquarters (Irish Batt HQ) was in Tebnine, not where it ought to have been at Bint Jbeil, a village now deep inside Israeli-controlled South Lebanon. As the DFF resisted UNIFIL efforts to deploy into and patrol the whole area, antagonisms and tensions grew between the DFF and the Irish. Due to militia aggression, instead of gradually gaining ground the Irish had actually conceded territory to the DFF. However, to lose At-Tiri village and crossroads would be a serious political and military setback to UNIFIL, and the UN could not afford to lose control of or compromise on any further ground. The Irish were acutely aware that this was South Lebanon and it was all about territory.

There were wider appreciations, however, than on-ground tactical realities, and these were political. Then there was politics itself and how this would affect the on-ground realities. Earlier in 1980, the Irish president and Minister for Foreign Affairs made an official visit to Bahrain. At the end of this visit a joint communiqué was issued, the Bahrain Declaration, a paragraph of which stated: 'The two sides stressed that all parties including the PLO should play a full role in the negotiations for a comprehensive peace settlement. In this regard, Ireland recognises the role of the PLO in representing the Palestinian people.'

The effect of the communiqué in South Lebanon was to increase the tension between the DFF and the Irish UNIFIL troops. News of the statement soon reached Israel, where one newspaper's headline declared: 'Ireland recognises PLO. Is prepared to Host Arafat', and in South Lebanon Major Haddad threatened to use force to oust Irish troops. He demanded that they be withdrawn because of Ireland's attitude to the PLO. The DFF also resumed shelling of the Irish area and stepped up their policy of harassment.

Break-in

Alerted by Platoon Headquarter's rooftop sentry, the manner of the notification somehow forewarning alarm, 22-year-old Lieutenant Tom Aherne realised something very wrong was developing very quickly. Arriving on the rooftop, one glance towards the commotion at the East end checkpoint confirmed the seriousness at what was unfolding. A group of militia had arrived at checkpoint 6-15A and were breaking through: 'It was with disbelief I saw the alert was all too true,' he reported. Three DFF vehicles containing twenty-six militia members, one armoured half-track and two jeeps, had arrived at the sand-bagged checkpoint position. Stopping, they deployed and suddenly swarmed all over it. Ordinarily they would approach via the road from Kunin, slow down and maybe exchange a few words then proceed right towards the 'Brown Mound'. This time they turned left and made directly for At-Tiri village.

Using surprise, speed, numerical strength and the physical assistance of the half-track they succeeded in forcing their way through, despite the best efforts of the checkpoint personnel. Once through they moved with purpose, 300 metres into the village outskirts. Jumping from their vehicles they took up positions inside local houses on both sides of the road. They also commandeered a building close to the checkpoint, known as the Outhouse, and the half-track and one jeep blocked the end of the avenue leading to the Irish UN Platoon Headquarters. The second jeep continued to the west end of the village, and subsequently blocked the road there. Lieutenant Aherne recalls: 'My first thoughts were, how could this be happening? Why do I have to be the one in this place, on this day, when this is happening to me? I recall that clearly. In my head I was already going to go down in the annals as the officer who had lost the village.' The DFF had made the first move and an immediate Irish reaction was required.

Lieutenant Tom Aherne, Commander No. 5 Platoon, C Company, outwardly displayed calm but inwardly was searching for ideas. He picked up his Gustav sub-machine gun and strode purposefully towards the end of the avenue onto the roadway, where the progress of the DFF's half-track had been checked by the APC from the Platoon HQ which had moved forward to block it. As Lieutenant Aherne did so he noticed a group of DFF militiamen approaching him, their apparent leader with a pistol in his hand. Extending his hand downwards, still gripping the pistol, the militiaman fired three rounds into the ground, while bizarrely offering Lieutenant Aherne a cigar with the other. Both actions, one threatening, one not, jolted Lieutenant Aherne into taking full and immediate stock of the DFF action.

He quickly summarised the new reality; the DFF had broken into At-Tiri and all vehicle access inside the village was now controlled by them. His Platoon HQ (Post 6-15, nicknamed 'Wuthering Heights') was cut off from all vehicle movement and could only be reached by foot. The Outhouse, near the east end of the village, and the main checkpoint (CP 6-15A) was occupied by the DFF and the less prominent west end listening post (CP 6-15B) was cut off, but still in radio contact. But what to do? Lieutenant Aherne recalls:

> Report the situation as existed and secure that part of the village which was still in our own hands. I wish I could say I [had] thought of it, but instead it was one of the Platoon's corporals, Corporal

Gaffney I think, who thought to block the back road to Hill Eight, Eighty (880). I ordered the deployment of two 84mm anti-tank gun crews along it. The DFF had made a mistake, a serious one. Instead of securing the crossroads junction granting access to Hill 880 when they had the opportunity, they had gone straight for the village.

From a farming background in Stradbally, County Waterford, rural common sense came to bear and Lieutenant Aherne reasoned it was time to close the gate behind the DFF and reseal the checkpoint, reinforce it and add barbed-wire for good measure. He further secured the Platoon HQ by placing his men around it in an outer perimeter. The DFF had broken into At-Tiri and gained ground and the initiative, but the Irish had contained their incursion. In essence, the DFF had gained a foothold but No. 5 Platoon had not lost the village completely. The DFF had acted but the Irish had reacted. The result was an uneasy stand-off and now it was time to negotiate and rebalance the equilibrium before its momentum became a new fixed reality on the ground. Both sides were in a position to reinforce their personnel and neither side lost time in doing so. The Irish Battalion went into full alert.

Full Alert

The Irish 46th Battalion was being challenged and the unexpected situation asked searching questions of them. Their experience and understanding to date suggested this confrontation, albeit unimaginable, would reflect the reality of similar incursions that had happened before and its resolution, as in the past, would be found through negotiation. Despite the extreme provocation, patience and persistence would, it was thought, prevail, even within the heightened atmosphere.

Trouble, danger, fear and uncertainty are all best faced, if possible, with the odds evened. Parity or superiority of manpower and firepower, even as peacekeepers, will always strengthen your position and reinforcement will grant any negotiation credibility, giving you an on-the-ground power of persuasion. Within half an hour, reserves from Haddata, under the Company second-in-command, had arrived. Captain Ned Kelly immediately took an APC along a perimeter route to support the isolated Irish at the west end of the village. Captain Dan Murphy, Weapons Platoon Commander, and Captain Liam Murphy, Platoon Commander Rshaf, remained in Haddata and became the 'link' between Commandant Dave Taylor in At-Tiri and the Battalion Commander in Tebnine, passing on conversations in which Irish was frequently used.

Commandant Dave Taylor, Commander C Company, was at the Battalion sports day near the Total garage when he was alerted by his second-in-command of the events unfolding in At-Tiri, who in turn was responding to the receipt of Lieutenant Aherne's reporting of the DFF break-in. When he arrived in At-Tiri he took mission command, using call sign 'Three Niner' (3, 9), and set up a tactical Company HQ at the At-Tiri platoon headquarters, where it was to remain until hostilities ceased. Ten minutes later the Battalion Reserve arrived, including the 'Recce Company' tug-of-war team and its supporters, some forty personnel in all. Commandant Larry Coughlan, Company Commander 'Recce Company', referred to as 'Ironside', call sign 4, 1, and Captain Adrian Ainsworth, Forward Observation Officer (FOO) with the Heavy Mortar Troop, were deployed in the vicinity of the east end checkpoint (6-15A) and given responsibility for the surrounding area. Within the hour, a further platoon of some thirty personnel from Battalion Headquarters in Tebnine, under second-in-command Captain Tony Gilleran, Headquarters Company, added to those already arrived to bolster the strength of C Company. With the subsequent arrival of more reinforcements from C Company, by 1530 hours – two hours after the DFF break-in – some 120 Irish personnel of all ranks were in the village. However, they weren't the only reinforcements as the DFF proceeded to reinforce the Outhouse with a half-track, a mortar crew and twenty personnel. DFF reinforcements were also arriving on foot, outflanking the Irish positions. At the east end checkpoint, the village's main checkpoint, another DFF half-track positioned itself in an anticipated attempt to ram the Irish APC blocking the road, but at the last moment it backed away and turned off its engine. An estimate put some sixty or so DFF militiamen in the village, with over thirty in the vicinity of the east end crossroads checkpoint.

All along the ridge line north of At-Tiri, the Irish posts and checkpoints – the respective responsibilities of 46th Battalion A, B, and

C Companies – also went to full alert. Concurrently, at Irish Battalion Headquarters in Tebnine a request to UNIFIL operations was made for UNIFIL Force Mobile Reserve assets and acceded to. A Dutch APC platoon and a Fijian mortar platoon subsequently arrived at Haddata (Post 6-11) and held there. Later, a Ghanaian APC platoon materialised and was kept at Tebnine (Post 6-9). None were yet committed but the shock DFF break in at At-Tiri had led to a quickly escalating situation. The aggressive action of the DFF had required an appropriate and proportionate UNIFIL reaction, but what about their further counter reaction? A tense and potentially highly confrontational situation was quickly developing, circumstances not for the faint-hearted. As Lieutenant Aherne recalls:

> It [was] with wholesale relief that I saw the Company Reserve come over the hill within the hour after the break in and it was with even further relief that I saw the Company Commander, Commandant Taylor arriving with the Battalion Reserve a short time after that. We were there all night but do you think I remembered to implement some sort of platoon routine? I did not. We were all up all night, wondering what was going to happen the next day.

Negotiation

Through fate and timing, Commandant Dave Taylor C Company, call sign Three-Niner, was suddenly responsible for dealing with a situation whose circumstances were liable to change quickly and unpredictably, which, in terms of volatility, was potentially volcanic. For now it was a chaotic scene, with no perceptible front line. The DFF were in the village, amongst and in between the Irish personnel, and it was confusing and unsettling. Worse, it was highly dangerous. Commandant Taylor was a 'father figure' to C Company and a role model for its officers. A serious and quiet man, but with a friendly disposition, he exuded a certainty of purpose and what he said happened.

While there had always been a tension along the Enclave line and a number of flashpoints had occurred during the Irish tour of duty leading up to this incident, they had not been especially tumultuous. The three previous Irish battalions had been probed but nothing nearly as severe or quite so untoward had occurred as the raid into At-Tiri. There had been prior issues at the 'Black Hole' and 'Bayt Yahun', but the placement of a 'ground ninety' (90mm anti-tank gun) and an AML 90 armoured car, respectively, had addressed these matters and the Irish largely held the line. These incidents had not been too dissimilar to border experience at home and so was within the competence and compass of C Company members. This was not the only familiarity with which the Irish troops, especially those from the west could identify. The Area of Operations nestled among the stony hills of South Lebanon bore a geographical similarity to that of Connemara and the west of Ireland generally, and as in Ireland the rural villages were small and poor. By local standards At-Tiri, with a population of around 300 exclusively Shiite Muslim, was quite a large village. Tobacco farming was their main occupation and except for its location it would have been largely unremarkable.

Occupation of At-Tiri aided access to Hill 880, and that's where Major Haddad wanted to be. That he wasn't displeased him, and he had a temper. In fact he had a psychotic personality that would swing sharply between awful anger and boundless bonhomie, which resulted in the Irish troops being harassed one day and not the next. The hand of those who armed, trained, supplied and uniformed the DFF was invariably never too far from this volatility. Israeli's proxy force had its own chain of command and it was some of Major Haddad's lieutenants, now in At-Tiri, that were to negotiate with Commandant Taylor and his lieutenants.

Previous confrontations had taught the Irish personnel how to navigate such incidents, though this incursion's inherent intent, and their blatant use of force, while not altogether new, had a raw recklessness to it that singled it as being out of the ordinary. For Commandant Dave Taylor, the on-ground commander, it was a hard reality that he was not to shy away from and he knew exactly where to begin. He made contact with the local DFF leaders who were known to be in the village, Abu Omar and Abu Askander, through local liaison with the Post Commander, Lieutenant Aherne.

The meeting was held in the house of the village mukhtar (the head man) and the atmosphere was strained. The prevailing tension was palpable and the likely expectation of success low. The two sides talked directly to one another, with no smiling or idle banter. The DFF claimed they had been invited into the village by its inhabitants and demanded to be permitted to establish a permanent command post in the village and carry out patrols at their convenience. In response Commandant Taylor employed and demonstrated a measured calmness. He informed the DFF that they should withdraw from the village and return At-Tiri to the status it had existed in before their incursion. With the two sides so intractable the meeting quickly concluded without resolution, to no one's surprise. Walking back from the mukhtar's house, the issue unresolved, confirmed Commandant Taylor's feeling beforehand that the matter was not going to be resolved around the negotiating table. Neither had it and it was more evident now that the situation was not going to improve any time soon. A conclusion made apparent almost immediately by the DFF escalating the situation by adopting firing positions and inviting the local population to riot in their support. While this received little response, it certainly increased the tension in the village.

Then a situation report ('sit rep') was received from 'Ironside', Commandant Larry Coughlan, that a serious confrontational situation was developing at the village's east end, near the main checkpoint (CP 6-15A) and there was the likelihood of a fire fight erupting. The DFF understood checkpoint 6-15A was the hinge on which access to Hill 880 depended upon, and they wanted total control of it. Pushing and shoving developed into a fist fight and the militiamen's proposed progress was only prevented by pure Irish physicality. Threats were issued, weapons cocked and firing positions adopted. A fire fight looked increasingly likely but did not occur, and the impasse continued. Pressure was ongoing and building and a sense that the situation was not going to improve dawned early. It was all a prelude to the development of a desperate struggle.

Confrontation

(Sunday evening, 6 April 1980)
Hill 880's significance as critical terrain, a feature granting its occupier a distinct advantage, had been recognised seven weeks prior to the events at At-Tiri by Lieutenant Colonel Jack Kissane, Officer Commanding

46th Battalion, and he ordered it to be occupied by the Irish (Post 6-15C). Major Haddad wanted At-Tiri village as a springboard from which to take this strategically important terrain, with its commanding views along the ridge granting the observer dominant fields of fire into the entire Irish battalion AO. His plans to seize At-Tiri by surprise had been frustrated and his militias' attempted break in only partially successful. Nevertheless, he now had a foothold in which he could escalate matters to achieve his objective. The negotiations had told him that this time the Irish were less likely to accept compromise and were more determined than ever not to be bullied. It was time to test that resolve and increase the intensity on the Irish.

As a large crowd of anxious villagers gathered near the CP, a burst of twenty rounds from a Kalashnikov AK-47 small arms rifle was fired by the DFF in the vicinity of the checkpoint. Hearing the shooting, the DFF personnel at the west end joined in and opened fire and half an hour later two 60mm mortar rounds impacted on waste ground 200 metres north west of At-Tiri. There was a further heightening of tensions with the firing of a tank round by the DFF in Bayt Yahun which impacted within twenty metres of Post 6-15C on Hill 880, followed shortly by eight rounds of heavy machine gun fire, all designed to accelerate the situation. As well as harassing fire, the Irish began to receive physical harassment on the ground. Captain Ned Kelly's APC and crew, sent to the west end of the village to pick up the stranded Listening Post (LP) personnel, was isolated and cut off after it had picked up the patrol.

A further Irish APC was ordered to move to the village's west end to help extract the stranded APC, crew and occupants. This APC moved via the ring route to the North of the village on the 'North Circular Road', and as the would-be rescuing APC made its way into the west end it encountered the DFF at a crossroads known as the 'Junction'. As dusk approached the rescuing APC started to inch its way forward, blinding the DFF with its searchlight, and scuffling broke out. The DFF were markedly aggressive and rather than exacerbate an already awkward situation the APC was ordered to set up a checkpoint at the Junction, which was given the designation 6-15D.

The previous negotiations had not led to a resolution of matters and further liaison was necessary. The officer commanding the Irish battalion sent a strong protest to Lieutenant Colonel Gary Gal, the

Israeli Defence Force (IDF) Liaison Officer (LO), regarding the DFF actions at At-Tiri. Inside an hour, UNIFIL operations in Naqoura, on the shores of the Mediterranean within the Israeli-controlled Enclave, received a message from Major Haddad:

> At-Tiri village is Lebanese and so are its inhabitants. The meeting between the Lebanese forces and the Lebanese inhabitants of that village has been arranged. No foreign force will prevent such meetings henceforth in the whole of Lebanon. In any case, if Irish Batt dislike the situation and they are interested in combat, it is suggested they should go and participate in their fight in Belfast. After they liberate Belfast, we shall find another mission to keep them busy. In any case, not in the Middle East.

Major Haddad took stock of the situation. The DFF had achieved surprise but his initial momentum had been stalled. He was hoping the Irish peacekeepers would, as in the past, adopt the 'softly, softly' approach to the DFF and he would press his advantage. Tomorrow would tell.

Long Day's Night

For Lieutenant Tom Aherne, Sergeant Billy Hutton, Corporal Paddy Gaffney and the men of No. 5 Platoon C Company, 46th Irish Battalion, the day ended a long way from where it had begun. Although geographically unchanged, the command structure and disposition of troops in and around At-Tiri had changed immeasurably. The situation had gone from stable to decidedly tense and a huge number of events had been compressed and distilled into a short amount of time, an underlying unease readily apparent. More immediately, a distinct overt threat had to be countered and an on-ground command structure was improvised to address this. (See map on p. viii.)

Officer Commanding (OC) C Company, Commandant Dave Taylor, in overall command on the ground, set up his tactical HQ in Post 6-15, the At-Tiri Platoon HQ (Platoon Commander, Lieutenant Tom Aherne, continued in command of Platoon HQ and its perimeter). OC 'Recce' Company Commander, Larry Coughlan, took up responsibility for the east end village checkpoint, 6-15A, and its surrounding area while Second in Command 'Recce' Company, Captain Noel Byrne, was in the west end of the village at the 'Junction' (6-15D) and was responsible for any matters developing there.

The disposition of the UNIFIL Force Mobile Reserve had been requested and was converging on At-Tiri, the majority being held uncommitted inside the immediate area around Irish battalion AO. For those already deployed on the ground at At-Tiri, the world was what was in front of them. Already the shape of the defence of At-Tiri, if unsettled, was compartmentalised, concentrating itself into three distinct but overlapping areas: the main checkpoint area CP 6-15A at the east end of the village, which controlled the road network; centrally around the Platoon HQ at Post 6-15; and the west end 'Junction' at CP 6-15D.

After the day's surprising events, Captains Adrian Ainsworth and Tony Gilleran, accompanying 'Ironside' Commandant Larry Coughlan around the 6-15A checkpoint area at the eastern end of the village, wondered between themselves what the following day would bring. It was unknown and uncertain, and also quite unnerving. In fact they laughed between themselves, a soldier's sense of comedy and black humour coming to the fore as they peered into the darkness of the night's sky, joking that they could actually trace the outline of a question mark in the stars above them. Concurrently, at the western end of the village, a wedding reception was unbelievably taking place in the mukhtar's house to which, on the spur of the moment, some Irish in the vicinity were invited. Captain Noel Byrne recalls:

> Despite many cups of tea (shi) and the multitude of cigarettes, the most welcome aspect of the occasion was the opportunity to have a wash. To the vast amusement of the local ladies the soldiers gleefully washed in their helmets and then danced and sang in the courtyard. The reception itself was a sombre affair, despite the best efforts of the Irish to enliven the proceedings.

No star-gazing or attempted merry-making was being indulged in at the centrally located tactical company headquarters, however, instead attention was turned to concentrating on formulating a plan to assist

Captain Ned Kelly and his crew, still trapped in the stranded APC with the troops from checkpoint LP 6-15B. To gain more information a reconnaissance patrol was ordered and while the DFF were engaged in conversation, a foot patrol slipped quietly into the darkness to gather intelligence.

Force Mobile Reserve

Pre-dawn, Monday, 7 April 1980

Following the request by Irish Battalion HQ Operations Cell to UNIFIL HQ Operations in Naqoura, the Force Mobile Reserve (FMR) went on immediate standby to assist. The Irish were also located among the UNIFIL HQ Staff officers and formed part of the unit known as UNIFIL HQ Camp Compound, administering and running the headquarters. Comprising of a mixed multinational company plus (Coy+) strength, deployable to shore up any one individual national UNIFIL contingent when hostilities along pressure points flared up, this was an important military tactical innovation but had also a crucial strategic political and diplomatic dimension. It was not just an individual battalion nation's diplomats voicing concerns and formal protests, but those of the collective contributing countries constituting the UNIFIL force. Mobilising the FMR put reinforcements on the ground where they needed to be but automatically raised the combined force of international opinion. For the Irish battalion it was now the FMR's on-ground immediate tactical effect that was required first and foremost. Consisting of soldiers from Fiji, Senegal and Nigeria, they were to be placed under the operational control of the Irish battalion and to rendezvous at Tebnine in the early hours. Arriving at staggered intervals throughout the night they were joined by the recently-arrived reinforcements from the Dutch and Ghanaian battalions.

The DFF break-in and gain of the initiative put into play a number of strategies. The DFF believed they could maintain the momentum, but the response of the Irish battalion so far was not exactly as they had anticipated, as was revealed during the brief negotiation. The DFF had learned the Irish stance was straightforward and to the point; there would be no acceptance of DFF pressure in or around the village and they were to withdraw completely. However, the DFF, bolstered by their successful surprise entry, knew two things: the Irish as peacekeepers had always done their utmost to ensure there was no escalation of violence during periods of intense harassment; and that they were very aware of the vulnerability of their so-called 'hostage posts' inside the Enclave. Determined to develop the situation, the DFF were planning to set about tightening their grip on At-Tiri. At the same time, plans were being hatched by the Irish to recover the 'at risk', stranded APC, crew and occupants at the western end of the village. Though it was still dark, day two had begun.

The stillness of the pre-dawn darkness was suddenly shattered by the simultaneous starting and revving of Irish vehicle engines at the east end of the village. This was a deception, and a signal of the commencement of the plan to rescue the APC and move forward at the west end of the village. The plan was for one of the two APCs at the west end junction to move forward and link up with the stranded APC, the second one holding the 'Junction' crossroads. This would be achieved by distracting the DFF with the ruse of the deafening engine noises. However, there had been a small prior problem. Earlier, a DFF jeep had blocked the narrow route to the stranded APC and it had to be moved. But how? It was decided to ask the opposing DFF personnel at the contested Junction for coffee. They readily agreed, perhaps glad to grab the opportunity to be allowed to pass through the Irish checkpoint, but once allowed through in their jeep they were not allowed back – until the rescue operation was commenced and completed.

With the plan's commencement, the rescuing APC moved forward and immediately the DFF came into the alley and stood in front of the vehicle. The driver was instructed to continue driving slowly ahead and the DFF militiamen were brushed to either side of the APC and opened fire with their AK-47 rifles. The APC moved into a small square and immediately came under fire from another DFF patrol. Directions were passed to the stranded APC to help it negotiate its way along the twisting lanes. Meanwhile the DFF attempted to immobilise the rescuing APC by putting cement blocks and large stones in its path to interfere with and block its movement. It overcame this by maintaining motion, both forward and backward, though joined by the stranded APC both encountered difficulties due to the restricted confines of the narrow lanes. However, they both arrived safely back at the west end 'Junction', twenty-two minutes after they commenced. This was a small success but an important one.

The Irish erected concertina wire at 6-15D, the 'Junction', reinforcing its physical defences in time to greet the arrival of the DFF, now in an extremely angry mood. In the midst of the ensuing negotiations and scuffles, the DFF attached a jeep to a strand of the concertina wire and pulled it away. Then it was time for some invention of their own, claiming one of their men had been seriously injured by the APC moving down the narrow alley. The Irish countered by claiming he was the man seen running after the APC firing his weapon from his shoulder. On the advice and the urgings of another DFF militiaman, the man in question suddenly lay on the ground and complained he was unable to walk or move his shoulder. The DFF carried him away on a stretcher and subsequently claimed he had suffered a fracture of the thigh and shoulder. Later still they were to claim he had died from loss of blood. The stand-off continued, with cocked weapons aimed at the Irish, and the escalation only eased when the DFF, still promising problems, realised the Irish were not for standing down.

A Fijian platoon from the FMR was deployed into At-Tiri village and came under the operational control of the local commander. The Fijian troops were distributed throughout the ranks of the beleaguered Irish, their main task to reinforce checkpoint 6-15A. Whatever anyone thought about the mythical medical accusations of the 'injured' DFF militiaman at the west end of the village, there was no denying the all too stark reality of the approach of a DFF Sherman tank, menacingly on the move towards checkpoint 6-15A. Together with five Mercedes cars, fully laden with militiamen, the enemy was incoming.

'Contact'

Monday, 7 April 1980

As the tensions increased, so did the firepower. Perhaps emboldened by the arrival of the tank, which stopped just short of checkpoint 6-15A at the eastern end of the village, single rounds of small arms fire began to be discharged indiscriminately by the DFF from all of their positions.

The tank itself took up a firing position, with its barrel pointed towards the Irish AML 90 armoured car. Permission to engage it was sought but refused. Car Commander and C Company, Recce Section Commander, 23-year-old Lieutenant Tony Bracken recalls:

> Having successfully snatched a few hours' sleep overnight in the upright position, inside the AML 90, imagine our surprise; Corporal Cyril Henry, Trooper Paddy Moore and I making up the crew, when a Sherman tank trundled up the road from Kunin crossroads and took post a barrel's length from our vehicle. The noise of its approach, and its resting place directly in front of us, made for a somewhat surreal experience. This bizarreness continued as I told Corporal Cyril Henry to lay the battle-range on the tank at the turret-race. This is where the turret is fixed to the hull and it represents the only vulnerable area that a front-on tank exposes to the enemy. I then, almost dream-like, found myself selecting a 90mm HEAT (high explosive anti-tank) round from the ammunition racks and loaded it into the point of breach closure. We exchanged a wry look and I can only imagine what must have been going through Trooper Paddy Moore's mind as he sat in the cramped seat of the driver's compartment with the hatch closed and this large relic of World War Two parked twenty metres or so from his feet.

Sporadic small arms fire was being loosely directed at the scattered UNIFIL positions within the village, when suddenly an accelerated and dramatic surge in firepower was perceptible in terms of rate and calibre. This indiscriminate fire grew steadily and all UN vehicles in the area were being hit. Distinctive among the 'dings' peppering the vehicles was the sound of a .5' HMG (point five inch heavy machine gun), a high calibre weapon with great penetrative power. Extremely effective, an up-scaled version of the .3' machine gun which first saw service in 1917, its original version was introduced by the American army in 1927. Further modified in the intervening decades, but largely remaining unchanged, different versions existed called the M2, M2HB and M3, but it is much more commonly known as the 'point five' produced in the USA by Fabrique Nationale (FN) of Belgium. In

1984, four years after the At-Tiri incident, it was introduced into the armoury of the Irish Defence Force. The effective planning range for the weapon is 2,000 metres, but service ammunition will travel over three times that distance. In addition to its use against troops, its armour piercing incendiary hard core (APIHC) ammunition gave the point five the ability to take on lightly armoured vehicles out to a range of 600 metres.

The first thing the Irish associated with the point five was a healthy respect for its fire power, the second was that the DFF had it and the Irish didn't. The Irish were, however, all too familiar with its distinctive firing sound, a sound that had reverberated around the hills of South Lebanon since their arrival. Its deep, rhythmic, almost sluggish sound, once heard, is hard to forget, all the more so when you are on its receiving end. Formidable in the provision of large volumes of close supporting fire brought to bear on any target, it was a highly valuable weapon and an immensely desirable asset to have. The DFF mounted theirs on half-track vehicles and the close confines of the village environment exaggerated its already highly offensive fire, making it more menacing than it already was.

Withstanding this sharply numbing experience was now the grim reality for the Irish in At-Tiri. The ferociousness of the initial foray of fire, unexpectedly employed by the DFF using both HMGs and their collective small arms at close range, was a shock. Its suddenness matched only by its severity and the abruptness of the transition of the situation from calm to hostile was wholly unnerving.

The extraordinary actuality for peacekeepers in 'contact', enduring incoming fire from any armed elements, flies in the face of their normal training as soldiers. The peacekeeping role requires that fire is not fought with fire, but rather responded to with restraint. The peacekeeper absorbs the aggression, rather than reacting in like manner, to de-escalate instead of accelerate the confrontation. This role in such circumstances creates its own inner tensions, giving rise to a mental and emotional strain caused by these two directly competing forces, worse, working in direct opposition. For each Irish peacekeeper a quiet storm was raging within; troubled externally, in turmoil internally. In tandem, and also hugely unsettling, was the all too immediate exposure to harm, all the more so as the danger wasn't near, it was *here*. And

Attack on At-Tiri | 135

with it fear, of the effects of unfriendly fire; executed in good volume, accurately delivered and steadily maintained.

The unexpectedness of the experience, the tension, the danger, the fraught and fearful atmosphere, and the uncertainty, all stretched the aggravated state of anxiousness of the Irish into a taut, destructive and confused heart-pounding inner pandemonium. Next a crisis, when the incoming indiscriminate fire, sustained and saturating, materialised in one murderous moment when Private Stephen Griffin was shot in the head. Severely wounded, he required urgent 'casevac' (casualty evacuation) and it would have to be done under fire. This swift and precipitous slide past the point of passive peacekeeping was subsequently to dramatically change matters, but for now the withholding of return fire was maintained. The tempo of events that had so electrifyingly kicked-off was continuing to happen too fast for further negotiation to take effect.

A young Corporal from the composite Battalion HQ reinforcing platoon, himself having been shot in the hand, knew this and further accurately understood that once the situation had progressed past the point of confrontation, fire must be defended and defeated by return fire. The afraid man wants to do nothing, but while the Corporal was not unafraid of the escalating events, his greater fear was to allow the situation to further deteriorate by continuing to hold fire. Driven out of cover to courageously seek the section radioman, the section Corporal managed to sprint to the radio operator located about fifteen metres from his position. He contacted the command vehicle, call sign '4-1', reported the situation and requested permission to return fire. Waiting on a response the Corporal realised that in his efforts to get to the radio operator he had been hit a second time, however the round had not penetrated the flak jacket he was wearing. In the event the reply was to 'wait out'.

The disciplined denial of soldierly impulse and instinct intensified the peacekeepers' feeling of isolation. The reaction was to become mystified about the particular circumstances of this suddenly occurring situation and feel a crippling sense of helplessness and a dwindling of confidence. Matters were to deteriorate further, as it happened, when a DFF assault was launched. The nature of the extraordinarily disadvantageous situation caught the section unawares and took its toll on their resolve. They found themselves in an unenviable dilemma, wishing to defend themselves but as yet restricted from doing so, a wholly unnatural state of being not only as soldiers but also as individuals, as the natural survival instinct is strong. A large-scale attack on their highly exposed position saw them overrun by approximately forty armed DFF. They were quickly disarmed and forced to move to an area in front of a large stone wall out of sight of the UN post. Their flak jackets were forcibly removed and the nine Irishmen instructed to line up against the wall. Their captors lined up facing them, their weapons pointed menacingly at the peacekeepers with what appeared to be deadly intent. A DFF commander then ordered them into a truck and they were driven into an Enclave town and incarcerated in the upper floor of a building under armed guard.

'Man Down'

Hit in the head and critically wounded, 21-year-old Private Stephen Griffin was in need of urgent casualty evacuation (casevac) and medical attention. Originally from Galway, a member of the first field Engineer Company based in Collins Barracks Cork, he had been part of the reconstituted reserve sent to At-Tiri to reinforce the Irish peacekeepers. Alerted to Private Griffin's injury by the second AML 90 armoured car commander, Lieutenant Johnny Molloy, Captain Adrian Ainsworth immediately decided to render assistance, which required unavoidable exposure to the ongoing heavy fire across open ground. It had to be done, and in like circumstances he would have expected the same to be done for him, Captain Ainsworth, together with medic Private John Daly, unhesitatingly broke cover by jumping over a stone wall and began making their way towards the wounded Private Griffin.

Surprised by the drop on the far side of the wall, they nonetheless gathered themselves and staying low, very low – initially hunched down, then crawling, then hugging the ground – they moved forward while firing was continuing around them. Having covered a distance of about 200 metres they successfully reached Private Griffin and began the evacuation. Trying to carry Private Griffin proved difficult, as although not especially large, he was heavy and the gunfire was unceasing. Captain Ainsworth constructed an improvised stretcher using two FN rifles from Private Griffin's GPMG comrades joined with fixed web belts and they placed the injured man onto this loose frame. It worked but the arrangement necessitated staying largely upright to carry him back and they presented a better target to those firing. However, they kept moving and made sufficient progress over the open ground to reach the shelter of the stone wall unscathed. In a position where they could be moved by road, Private Griffin and his GPMG team were loaded into the rear of a Land Rover and together with medic Private Michael Daly, still under fire, they headed for the helicopter pad to be medically evacuated (*medevaced*) to the Norwegian Medical Company Hospital at UNIFIL HQ in Naqoura.

Because of the severity of his injuries Private Griffin was transferred onto Rambam Hospital in Haifa, Israel. Lieutenant Colonel Frank Whyte, Camp Command UNIFIL HQ, tasked the camp Quartermaster Captain George Kerton, a Cavalry Corps Officer from the 1st Armoured Squadron Curragh Camp, to go to Jerusalem and find Father Sean Conlon, one of two 46th Irish Battalion chaplains who was there on a sixty-hour pass. Checking with Father Adam, a priest from Sierra Leone and manager of the Vatican-owned Notre Dame Hotel, he met Father Conlon emerging from the Old City. Arriving at Rambam Hospital, they found the Intensive Care Ward on the seventh floor of this nine-storey hospital, a large open-plan ward with between sixty to eighty patients, all on low cots and festooned with a vast array of constantly moving and noisy medical apparatus. The neurosurgeon was from Eastern Europe, and spoke no English, but he was accompanied by an American nurse. The nurse, translating, began to cry. The bullet was lodged in Private Griffin's brain but the issue was beyond one of recovery, rather it was seeking permission to switch off the life-support machine. This sanction was forthcoming a number of days later by Private Griffin's sister and brother, who travelled from Ireland out to Haifa. The following day the *Jerusalem Post* newspaper contained an article on how two of his organs had been donated, one to an Israeli Arab and one to an Israeli Jew.

Conflict

For Commandant (later Brigadier General) Johnny Vize, Battalion Operations Officer at the Irish Battalion HQ Operations cell in

Tebnine, though physically removed from the At-Tiri hostilities he was at the same time fully immersed in all aspects of it, and indeed he was essential to the action itself. For him, and Irish Battalion HQ, a week without incident was rare:

> There was always something. Incidents were ongoing all the time: incoming shelling from Saff-Al-Hawa; tank fires from Brown Mound; prior attempted incursions into Bayt Yahun, Rshaf and At-Tiri. Confrontation was nothing unusual. UNIFIL was not yet a well-established mission. Tensions from within, but especially along the fault line that was the Enclave, could have escalated at any time. For us, At-Tiri was how they manifested themselves unprecedentedly and at their most menacing. [At first], the outbreak was assumed to be yet another short-lived incident in the making, instead it was one that developed fast, became fluid, then deteriorated rapidly. There was a realisation this could become a protracted situation.
>
> Our Battalion National Day was due during the coming week and I had prepared a detailed map board, inclusive of fine contours, highlighting the critical high ground relief features throughout our AO. Instead of this being the backdrop for our National Day, it became a battle board. We divided the duty officers into two teams with twelve-hour shifts, while the Battalion staff would be on the go for twenty-four hours each. This was done because the sense of seriousness was ratcheted [up] dramatically after the shooting, and what would prove to be critical wounding, of Private Stephen Griffin.
>
> This was a watershed, firings close we were used to, now this was a direct hit and so different. [It] made us realise matters were either going to get better very quickly, or become very much worse. The hope was that they, the DFF, would recognise they had gone too far and would take a step back. Instead, if they persisted with their aggressions the situation was not going to go away. There followed a second quick realisation [that] for it to go away we were going to have to get stuck in and what that meant [was] we didn't clearly know as to where this was going or might end, or where it would lead us to before then.

Attack on At-Tiri | 139

Perhaps the [starkest] of the sudden set of realisations was while this was an international affair, there was a strong sense amongst us that in the first instance it was very much an Irish matter. As far as we were concerned we were very much on our own to drive the determination of the outcome. It would be up to us to see this through, toe-to-toe on the ground with a violent aggressor hell bent on forcing their will with mounting firepower. The international dimension was diminished for us as it was we who were cheek by jowl with an adversary seeking to gain ground, and advance his position not advance peace. Our attitude and actions would be pivotal to the outcome. It would be up to us to find and command sure and certain answers to the changing and challenging uncertainties. It was up to us to stand firm.

Reacting to the initial break in at At-Tiri, Irish Battalion HQ Operations Section had activated and dispatched the Battalion Reserve and requested from UNIFIL Operations the deployment of elements of the UNIFIL Force Mobile Reserve, the dispatching of a further infantry platoon to reinforce the Battalion Reserve, the effecting of the medevac for Private Griffin, and maintaining command and control of all the moving parts now on full alert reacting to circumstances as they arose. Irish Battalion Operations Cell was a conduit for arranging communications, maintaining a two-way information flow with Irish Defence Forces Headquarters, UNIFIL Headquarters and of course the Irish Battalion Company Headquarters, especially C Company HQ, the sub-unit in contact.

Most of all, this sharp-end situation required command. While the experience of the three previous battalions told us to expect volatility, we never expected, as peacekeepers, to join battle with belligerents as such. It was an acute journey into the unknown. A bizarre situation, one requiring leadership. We were faced with aggressors with murderous intent, provoking the situation. With the tension tangible there was a palpable sense of determination on our part also, to achieve what we were there to [do] … to hold the line and effect their eviction from the village.

An Irish life was likely lost [and] we weren't [going to lose any] more. We were peacekeepers who chose negotiation over confrontation, always seeking ways and means of defusing the tension. This confrontation had moved into high gear. Often previously fired at this time we had been attacked; this time we had a critical casualty.

If this latest attempted encroachment into At-Tiri had been a miscalculation on the DFF's part, it was a mistake made far more serious by their blatant belligerence and use of violent assault. Their opening of indiscriminate sustained fire resulted in the Irish Defence Forces losing Private Stephen Griffin, its first man lost in action in Lebanon. This same incident had seen others being wounded, with many narrow escapes and others suffering shock. Confrontation had become 'contact' and 'contact' had become conflict. The shooting of Private Griffin could well have been the beginning of the DFF losing the confrontation. Irish soldiers had arrived in Lebanon to be UNIFIL peacekeepers and now to be credible peacekeepers they had to employ soldiering skills. To preserve peace they would have to fight for it. It was time to meet force with force.

'Calm but Tense'

Tuesday, 8 April 1980
The first two bizarre days over, the uncertainty of the events continued into a third. As dawn broke, the Irish found themselves in a situation filled with vagueness and ambiguity. Give a soldier a mission, however difficult, and the means to achieve it and you give him clarity. The current circumstances dictated they could not feel anything other than being disturbed and troubled. Their unease was not helped by the lack of a defined front line. The militiamen were in and around the village and among the Irish. The battle lines were imprecise, indistinct and ill-defined, both physically and procedurally. The Irish knew all too well that this in-exactitude and lack of precision was fertile ground for blurred thinking and doubtful decision making. They were in unknown territory and had to put logic into the matter, give a shape and form to their structure. This involved a compartmentalisation of flash point areas within the village: at the east end checkpoint; the 'HQ House'; and the west end 'Junction'. Lieutenant Tom Aherne established a defensive perimeter around the HQ House and, having not implemented any

sort of routine during the first night with all his platoon remaining needlessly awake throughout the duration of darkness into the following Monday morning, put a routine into place with conscious attention paid to weapons cleaning, personal washing, feeding, resting and duty rotation of his platoon. Curiously, throughout the tour and unaffected by the ongoing incident, was the listening of music on huge personal 'ghetto-blasters'. Albums popular at the time were *Rumours* by Fleetwood Mac, *Another Brick in The Wall* by Pink Floyd, *Breakfast in America* by Supertramp, and songs by Blondie and Donna Summer. Sleeping bags were distributed, with half his platoon sleeping at any one time and the remainder on alert. The only place to sleep was 'on the job', either on a rooftop, the roadway, or in an APC. Until a day-and-a-half ago it had not been an especially tumultuous tour of duty, but it had suddenly turned tempestuous, then turbulent, and now looked to continue troubled.

An early-morning meeting between Abu Askander and Commandant Dave Taylor resulted in the release of three of the nine Irish peacekeepers held captive by the DFF. The remaining six continued to be held in Saff al-Hawa. All three were in good shape and had been treated well. Their handover occurred at the east end checkpoint of the village (6-15A), where the Sherman tank had become the constant preoccupation and companion of Lieutenant Tony Bracken and the crew in the Irish AML 90 armoured car.

A ludicrous situation prevailed, for if either vehicle had fired its main weapon against the other, so close were they to each other, it was doubtful that the round fired would have had the chance to arm and would not impact explosively. Instead the unexploding shell would hit its target hard and the ensuing headaches of the crew would have been considerable and long-lasting. The surreal situation of one armoured vehicle within twenty metres of another required the Irish AML 90 crew to constantly check what direction the tank was facing. Was the main armament still pointing in their faces? Did anyone appear in the turret? Was there anybody in it at all? It became the first thing to check on in the morning and the last shadow over their position at night. Curiously it all began to seem normal.

Nevertheless, throughout At-Tiri Irish nerves were being stretched tight, the tension causing a mental and emotional strain. It was all swirling around in their heads: the hurt, the anger, the shock, the uncertainty. These feelings of anxiety were exacerbated when small arms fire inflamed and made worse those already wound tight, the crack of gunfire playing on their frayed nerves. These feelings were, however, juxtaposed with a strong sense that if these militiamen wanted a fight, then they could have one. Their restraint in not returning fire was further tested when the Irish resupply APC coming over Hill 880 from Haddata was fired on by the DFF.

The 'Gravy Train', as it was to become known, was the provider of real-life support in the form of hot meals, water, sleeping bags, cigarettes and other necessary supplies. These essentials were crucial to the maintenance in the field of the At-Tiri reinforcement effort. Captain Kevin Heery, Assistant Battalion Logistics Officer, and his staff kept this essential lifeline going. Meanwhile, the small kitchen in the HQ House was simply swamped, overwhelmed by the nearly ten-fold increase in numbers. Hence bringing fire to bear on this lifeline was striking a raw nerve in all. Not least because the Herculean efforts of C Company HQ's cook, Corporal Johnny Gill, and equally that of Private John Long, No. 5 Platoon's cook, were highly appreciated.

Further firing occurred, this time into the checkpoint area. To be precise the DFF were shooting at the Irish AML 90, though no casualties resulted. A few minutes later the tank at Bayt Yahun turned its main gun towards the hilltop Observation Post (OP, 6-15C) on Hill 880 itself. And then it happened. At the west end crossroads a confrontation erupted. Initially there was scuffling, pushing and shoving, which quickly became bad-tempered then heavy and very physical. An attempted infiltration by Abu Emile and a party of DFF militiamen, with suspected Israeli Defence Forces (IDF) among them, was eventually halted by a head-on, no-holds-barred, determined combination of fisticuffs and Irish rifle butts. Matters deteriorated further and quickly so, when the bruised militiamen brought rocket-propelled grenade launchers (RPGs) to bear. If they did so, Captain Noel Byrne remembers: 'Our lads were proficient and skilled, their reaction to this situation was automatic; they were doing all the right things without being told. The 84mm anti-tank guns were produced and loaded in quick time in reply. In short, they performed.' With the DFF aggression matched by Irish determination, the situation deadlocked and there a fragile stand-off commenced. After some discussion the situation was defused, but all positions in At-Tiri remained very tense.

Barely had matters settled when back at the east end checkpoint, the DFF half-track, which had earlier fired on Corporal Johnny Gill's 'Gravy Train', now opened up on a soft-skinned Land Rover, driven by Trooper Gerry Mitten, taking Private McCarthy to hospital with an ankle injury sustained earlier at the west end. When the half-track ceased firing the Land Rover ceased moving. Lieutenant Tony Bracken witnessed the incident:

> I decided I [had] better go out and see and to do so I walked out. Accompanying me was Corporal Michael Jones. Reaching the Land Rover there was no one in it so I called out. Trooper Mitten responded from a field some thirty or so metres in from the track. He had been wounded by shrapnel in his left thigh and calf. A unit colleague of mine from Longford, I asked him for his first field dressing (a bandage carried individually by all) only he did not have his. In mock annoyance at having to use mine on him, the joke employed to ease the nervousness of the situation, I bound his wounds and stopped the flow of blood. We were aware of rounds continuing to be fired but matter-of-factly persisted with what needed to be done. It was important to get him back to the checkpoint, but with the Land Rover immobilised all four [of us] began to hobble, stumble [and] stagger back. But not before Trooper Mitten insisted I collect his rifle from the Land Rover, he not wanting it left behind.

As happened the previous day with the casevac of Private Stephen Griffin, so too was Trooper Gerry Mitten fired upon as his evacuation continued, and so took longer to execute. While this was ongoing there was further DFF fire into all areas of At-Tiri, including the HQ House. This increased, then ceased, only to intensify a few moments later. Under cover of this firing, the DFF launched an attack up the avenue towards the HQ House, using houses on either side as protection, firing as they advanced. This was a full-blown attempt to overrun the HQ House and seize control of the village. The DFF were making a serious move and if they succeeded the village was lost. This was a critical moment.

Lieutenant Tom Aherne was with his Company Commander, Commandant Dave Taylor, on the flat roof of the HQ House. Commandant Taylor gave orders to the Platoon Commander to prepare to return fire and that HQ House, Post 6-15, was to be defended. Simultaneously, Officer Commanding B Company, Commandant Seán Hurley, was informed to warn the Irish in the Enclave posts of the situation and to give orders to return fire, if necessary, in self-defence. For the next ten minutes the DFF militia fired upon the HQ House, fire which intensified even further as their advance continued. If this assault was to be halted it had to be done so now. Commandant Taylor unhesitatingly ordered Lieutenant Aherne to return fire:

> I was ordered to return fire, but what was I actually to do to give effect to this. Was I to return fire or was I to order someone else to return fire? Again, all the fire orders I had learned in Cadet School were going through my mind, but do you think I could remember the correct sequence (group, range, indication, target, fire). What was I going to do? Who was I going to shoot at? Thankfully I had the good sense to turn to my good Platoon Sergeant, Billy Hutton, and say: 'You fire, and I'll fire', and we fired ten rounds of controlled fire each. While doing so Commandant Dave Taylor informed the Battalion Commander, Lieutenant Colonel Jack Kissane: 'returning controlled fire'. All militia movement towards the HQ House stopped and their firing ceased. We learned two lessons from that: One was the DFF did not like being shot at; and second, once they had forced us to fire back they had lost, because the gloves were off. We were not going to be restrained by their aggressions anymore.

With the assault on Post 6-15, the HQ House, halted the UNIFIL troops were finally forced into a situation where they had to return fire. In some respects, Tuesday, 8 April 1980 was a significant day in the history of Irish service with UNIFIL inasmuch as this was the day the Irish demonstrated that though they were peacekeepers under the UN flag, they were Irish soldiers who would fight when authorised to do so. When fire was returned it was aimed, restrained and in self-defence. After the incident Commandant Dave Taylor met with Abu

Askander, though the meeting was inconclusive. Shortly afterwards, Lieutenant Colonel Jack Kissane sent a message to Commandant Taylor: 'All negotiations with DFF from now on will be on the basis that they leave the village. When fired on, Irish Batt will return fire, and not only from the locality fired on.' Within five minutes the DFF in At-Tiri opened small arms fire on UNIFIL positions. Fire was returned and two minutes later the DFF firing ceased, yet the situation continued to remain very tense. Unexpectedly, within the hour the six remaining Irish peacekeepers held captive at Bayt Yahun were released. This, of course, followed ongoing high-level international intervention, pressure and liaison to which the on-ground peacekeepers were unaware of, critically engaged as they were in countering hostilities, tensions and developments. Local liaison continued with Commandant Taylor and Major Klein (UNTSO OGL) meeting Abu Askander, Abu Emile and Abu Omar in an attempt to end the deadlock, but without conclusion.

Later that evening Major Haddad sent a message to UNIFIL OPS: 'As a one-way positive gesture to show goodwill to bring a solution to the problem at At-Tiri, I have given instructions to move the tank from the village to Bint Jbeil. I am sure that this will bring a positive solution to the whole problem at At-Tiri.' It did move, but it didn't bring a solution to the problem because without the DFF moving from the village, the problem remained. The day that had begun 'calm but tense' was to end 'tense but calm'.

'Tense but Calm'

Wednesday, 9 April 1980

Calm and calming were the mellifluous tones of the Fijians singing night prayers from their dug-outs around At-Tiri village, their melodious, dulcet voices drifting gently through the darkness of the Lebanese night. It was suggestive of the more harmonious, serene and mellow aspects of human existence and belied the contention and tension of the enduring reality of the circumstances in which they found themselves. Tuesday night gave way to Wednesday morning, but not before Lieutenant Tom Aherne went about his night rounds checking his platoon positions, where:

We had one man sleeping, one man alert, when suddenly three rounds impacted very close to where I was moving. As it turned out these rounds were fired by one of my young privates. When I got to him he was shaking like a leaf. He said: 'I thought you were one of the DFF, sir'. We had to take him out [of the field] there and then. He was one of five that had to be taken out before Saturday due to the impact of shock. There it was manifesting in front of my eyes and I didn't really know what I was dealing with.

For Lieutenant Tom Aherne, shock came as a shock to him. Not everything can be explained by logic, why some peacekeepers can deal with the mental and emotional distress, upset and otherwise adverse effects of the pressure, tension and confusion of the circumstances they faced in At-Tiri while others, side by side with them, struggled but coped, and others still became overwhelmed. The exposure to uncertainty and anxiety was unsettling, and the suddenness, intensity and duration of those sometimes extreme events caused vulnerability to become apparent. Those noticeably impacted by the close firing of small arms fire, near misses by HMG rounds and other would-be abnormal stressors, were removed from the field to avoid additional strain being placed upon them before they became further dazed, disorganised, disorientated and ultimately dysfunctional.

The night remained quiet. Just after midnight the Sherman tank at the east end checkpoint (6-15A) started up and moved back towards Kunin and those UNIFIL troops awake continued to make improvements to their defensive positions. Piling stone upon stone, some of the structures began to take on a beehive hut-like shape. Others were equally elaborate in form as a general enlargement of positions occurred. Worryingly, intensive movement of IDF personnel was detected, moving from Saff al-Hawa towards Kunin. Four M113 armoured personnel carriers and five half-tracks were observed with an estimated eighty personnel accompanying them. These were subsequently seen preparing defensive positions to the north east and west of Kunin. The vehicles were used to cover these troops while they worked and these positions were reinforced throughout Wednesday. To date no IDF formations had taken a direct part in the UNIFIL/DFF confrontation, and as a result of their presence the tense situation in At-Tiri became increasingly fragile.

Later in the morning a message was relayed from Major Haddad to Irish Battalion via UNIFIL Operations: 'To quieten the area, I took my tank out of At-Tiri yesterday. The right-of-way, for my men is still blocked. You promised to give me some answers and none were given yet. I want my answers immediately.' An immediate reply was quickly forthcoming: 'Reference your message regarding right-of-way for your men, the way will be open for your withdrawal.'

An hour later Commandant Dave Taylor and Abu Askander met in At-Tiri. Commandant Taylor was informed that a high-level DFF meeting has been held the previous night and the At-Tiri incident and general DFF/Irish Battalion relationship was discussed. Commandant Taylor asked if the DFF were pulling out of At-Tiri and Abu Askander replied that would be a political matter. Half an hour later, Abu Askander, Abu Emile and an IDF officer, Major Chaim, were identified at the DFF tank position in Bayt Yahun observing Hill 880. Shortly after, Major Haddad was allowed into At-Tiri for a meeting with Commandant Taylor. Positions remained deadlocked and Major Haddad departed.

Then it was the DFF's turn to strengthen their defensive positions in At-Tiri. Just before dusk, the Irish battalion's Operations Officer, Commandant Johnny Vize, sent a Warning Order to 'prepare to illuminate targets during hours of darkness as required'. This order was particularly intended for the 120mm Heavy Mortar Troop in 'the Glen' in Ayta az Zutt. Captain Conor O'Boyle had previously directed their firing in a prior illumination exercise. Not long afterwards, UNIFIL OPS sent a message to all stations (all UNIFIL Battalions): 'Important that all forward OPs are instructed to maintain a very high state of alert. Any information on troop or vehicle movement in their area to be reported instantly.'

The IDF presence in the Enclave was a major concern. There was much apprehension as to their possible intentions and suddenly there was considerable movement by the DFF. The southern hillside opposite At-Tiri village was being 'recced' by a number of personnel in uniform and it appeared that positions were being selected. A number of tanks and half-tracks were observed digging-in. Unknown to those in At-Tiri at the time, while the confrontation between the DFF and UNIFIL was taking place there the PLO had launched a successful attack on a settlement in northern Israel. The attack on the Misgav Am kibbutz again brought criticism of UNIFIL from Israel. In this instance Israel responded by sending over 250 heavily armed and supported troops into South Lebanon. These troops established positions in and adjoining the UNIFIL area of deployment. At the time it was not clear what the IDF intended to do, it was a large-scale incursion and could have been the preliminary stage of another operation similar to 'Operation Litani', events surrounding which had set the whole UNIFIL peacekeeping operation in motion. Alternatively, it could have been to support, directly or indirectly, the DFF attempted takeover of At-Tiri. In any event it had a profound effect on the morale of UNIFIL troops defending At-Tiri and was also seen to make the DFF more aggressive and less flexible in their negotiations. These factors had to be taken into account by the military commander at At-Tiri when assessing what the appropriate response to the DFF incursion should be.

In the criticisms of UNIFIL's failure to prevent the infiltration and attack on Misgav Am, few commentators made any reference to the attack on the Irish position in At-Tiri by the DFF. While this was underway, and UNIFIL attention was focussed on At-Tiri, the PLO attacked the settlement. This was one of the occasions when the Irish Battalion and other elements from UNIFIL were almost exclusively involved in resolving problems created by Major Haddad's militia. In this regard they were seriously hampered in preventing armed infiltrations through their Area of Operations and the DFF themselves committed men and resources to harassing UNIFIL instead of preventing infiltrations through the area under their control. The Israelis claimed the PLO had infiltrated through the Irish and Nigerian battalion areas yet produced no proof to this effect. UNIFIL denied these allegations and the situation was aptly summarised by one media commentator at the time: 'If the five terrorists did pass through UNIFIL lines, they also passed through Haddad-land and Israel's own defence system. By what logic, it is asked, do the Israelis expect under-strength, multinational peacekeepers to be more efficient and highly motivated than the Israelis themselves.'

The real and deeply felt misgivings of a distinct IDF presence getting into position near Saff al-Hawa and the making ready of prepared defensive sites further forward near Kunin were considerable. An anxious day was spent observing and reporting, though there were no confrontations. In the afternoon Major Haddad arrived at nearby Bayt Yahun accompanied by four IDF Land Rovers. But apart from this, the now 'normal' routine of both sides' sentry rotations and ration replenishment took up their attention. The evening and night passed very quietly with no activity to be reported on either side. All that was well and good on one level, but on another less visible one, Commandant Dave Taylor knew there was much to be done to allay the new level of unease and counter the obvious disquiet caused by the newly arrived IDF presence and build-up.

Round for Round

Thursday, 10 April 1980

At first light on day five a completely new and unexpected sound echoed around the village of At-Tiri. A member of Lieutenant Tom Aherne's platoon, in full dress regalia, was standing on the roof of HQ House, 'Wuthering Heights' (Post 6-15), proudly and loudly playing the bagpipes for all and sundry to hear. The reaction was immediate and overwhelming, as all of the platoon members, the additional Irish and the other Fijian and Dutch UNIFIL reinforcements cheered and clapped enthusiastically, their spirits lifted. It was just one of those moments you could not script, but one that was entirely appropriate and in many ways unbelievable. Yet here it was, happening for all to see and hear. A huge and appropriate tonic that was invigorating and restorative for all of those within earshot and an encouragement for the peacekeepers to do what was required of them. Enthralled at the performance, Lieutenant Aherne's appreciation for the musician made him realise that the episode, if slightly surreal – almost eccentric – was in fact a manifestation of the coming together of his platoon into a cohesive unit in response to the situation they found themselves in. They understood what 'coming under fire' actually meant, an initiation without equivalent in any other walk of life. They understood what returning fire meant, an occurrence not everyone in uniform is called upon to perform, and they understood, having suffered much aggravation, the relief of finally being able to meet fire with fire. Lastly, they understood the importance of supporting each other.

The wails of the bagpipes had barely subsided when thirteen IDF APCs were spotted on the move from Saff al-Hawa to Kunin, and there was some concern as to their proposed purpose. The sight of so many M113s drawing closer was a distinct cause for trepidation and reinforced the seriousness of the situation. Direct IDF involvement would be a strikingly dramatic escalation. Still some way off, they drew ever nearer and it was with some relief when they were seen to stop near the village of Kunin and site themselves in the previously prepared positions.

Suddenly, a UN convoy was spotted breaking the brow of Hill 880. When the DFF saw the convoy the militia half-track near the Outhouse immediately opened fire on it, causing the occupants to quickly seek cover. Negotiations eventually allowed the convoy to continue on its way. Around midday, information was received that Major Haddad had entered the village across country from the south. He stayed for a while then left through the east end checkpoint and made his way to Saff al-Hawa. Up to now, Major Haddad had been permitted entry to At-Tiri by UNIFIL from time to time, for negotiations and to visit his men. This arrangement had an unsettling effect on the Irish and today the decision to adopt a tougher policy was taken.

Early in the afternoon, Major Haddad once again arrived at the east end checkpoint seeking to gain entry into At-Tiri. Arriving in a small open-topped jeep, with a second as escort and with Israeli soldiers in his retinue, he boldly demanded entry through the checkpoint to the village. He claimed to be intending to visit the village mukhtar, a now unfortunate and beleaguered man. Having prevented from the outset any sort of DFF vehicular access through the checkpoint, the demand rang hollow. Moving past the barbed wire at the checkpoint, Lieutenant Tony Bracken, on instructions from Commandant Larry Coughlan, informed him he could not enter the village to which Major Haddad, his sense of self-importance suddenly undermined, replied in dramatic – even melodramatic fashion – something to the effect of: 'Your battalion commander has made a wrong decision by denying [me] entry to At-Tiri. Does he realise the danger in which he is placing you, his troops!' Affirming his faith in his commander and the soldiers who stood with him, Lieutenant Bracken informed Major Haddad he would obey his commander's orders without fail. Major Haddad and his crew sullenly returned to Kunin.

Planning the attack on 'the Tunnel'. The Offensive Scheme of Manoeuvre used in taking 'the Tunnel', Élisabethville, Congo, December 1961.   Courtesy of the Defence Forces Printing Press

View of Checkpoint 6-15 A from the roof of the Platoon HQ House 6-15, the point of the Christian Militia break-in to At-Tiri, Lebanon.   Courtesy of Comdt Ned Kelly (retd)

Hole in UN Post 5-16 Platoon HQ at At-Tiri, Lebanon, from a solid shot tank round. Had it been a high explosive, fatalities would likely have resulted. Courtesy of Comdt Ned Kelly (retd)

Destroyed Christian militia half-track at entrance to UN Post 6-15 Platoon HQ at At-Tiri, Lebanon, April 1980. Courtesy of Comdt Ned Kelly (retd)

A happy and relieved Capt Noel Byrne during the immediate aftermath to the 'move in' to retake At-Tiri. Courtesy of Comdt Ned Kelly (retd)

A KFOR Convoy with Irish vehicles at the head presents a strong posture in Kosovo. Courtesy of *An Cosantoir*

Typical refugees from Darfur, whom EUFOR Chad were sent to central Africa to protect from Janjaweed bandits. Courtesy of French Military Combat Camera Team

A EUFOR Chad/RCA Logistical Convoy deploying into Eastern Chad, April 2008. Courtesy of Defence Forces Press Office

Irish soldiers dismounting from the rear of a MOWAG APC and going into action to protect IDP camp in Goz Beïda, Chad, June 2008. Courtesy of the Defence Forces Printing Press

Irish Battalion MOWAG Armoured Personnel Carrier during clashes between Chadian government troops and Chadian rebel forces near Goz Beïda, Chad, June 2008. Courtesy of *An Cosantoir*

Dutch troops under Irish command contain Chadian rebels in Goz Beïda, Chad, June 2008. Courtesy of Defence Force Press Office

Irish Engineers conduct de-mining operation along a route near the Golan Heights in Syria, April 2014.   Courtesy of *An Cosantoir*

Irish dismounted element conducts a foot patrol while accompanying a MOWAG APC to ensure overwatch security along the Syrian–Israeli border, May 2014.   Courtesy of *An Cosantoir*

Irish troops with the United Nations mission in East Timor (July 1999–May 2004), conducting a patrol in arduous terrain, temperatures and conditions, pass through a local village. Courtesy of Defence Forces Press Office

Irish troops with the Quick Reaction Force of the United Nations Military in Liberia, November 2003–May 2007, prepare for a 'Heli-Lift' prior to conducting a patrol. Courtesy of Defence Forces Press Office

As a result of the refusal to allow Major Haddad to enter the village, retaliation was expected and tensions in At-Tiri increased greatly during the day. Predictably, the DFF stepped up their harassment. Two tanks from Saff al-Hawa manoeuvred forward of the Brown Mound. All through the afternoon the tanks were heard moving behind the ridge south of the village and eventually they adopted hull-down positions from where they could engage UNIFIL positions. Then the mortaring began, six rounds falling into the nearby town areas of Tebnine and Barachit, though thankfully no casualties were reported. The DFF then started using the loudspeakers on the mosque to incite the villagers 'to rise up against UNIFIL'. The villagers did not respond but tensions increased further in and around the village.

In the early evening, as darkness descended, a local villager passing through the west end 'Junction' with a can of petrol (kerosene) was stopped by the DFF. They took the can from him and emptied the contents onto the road. Waiting until the liquid started to flow under the Irish APC at the checkpoint (6-15D), the militiamen used a hand flare to ignite it. The Irish were quick in their response and spread sand over the approaching flames to extinguish them, thus preventing a major incident. Their attempt thwarted, the DFF retreated behind cover and opened up with small arms fire. The Irish put three flares in the air, illuminating the scene, and returned fire, round for round. The crack of gunfire reverberated around the village, echoing and adding to the sound as more rounds were fired. With the last of the gunfire ringing in the Irish troops' ears, the DFF disappeared into the night. However, the situation remained tense and retaliation was expected at any moment.

One hour later, eight of the IDF M113s were observed preparing to move. Was this it, had the time come? When they did move it was laterally, to the east of Kunin, as the Israelis started to withdraw their troops under cover of darkness. It turned out that this was after discussions between UNIFIL Force Commander and the Israeli Chief of Staff. More significantly, the Israelis had also come under weighty political pressure from the US to end their violation of Lebanese sovereignty. Premier Begin was due to meet President Carter in Washington in mid-April and the Israeli incursion would not have been conducive to a successful meeting. Hence the Lebanese government had decided to bring the matter before the UN Security Council for an urgent debate. The US did not support the Israeli action and its anticipated attitude in any UN Security Council debate on the subject could be embarrassing to Israel and detrimental to its relations with the Carter administration. Unfortunately, however, US pressure upon Israel did not extend to – or was not strong enough – to prevent the DFF attempts to take over the village of At-Tiri. Once again UNIFIL was left largely to its own devices in its endeavours to implement the UN mandate with the Irish at the sharp end.

Over the past few days the DFF antagonists had pushed hard, and in their determination had in fact pushed too far. Their aggression had been eventually responded to with forceful defence and now they faced gunfire rather than compromise. The Irish had stood firm and continued to show resolve, even at great risk to their own personnel, persuasive proof for the DFF that the Irish battalion had little intention of simply handing them control of At-Tiri village. This tangible transformation had to be respected and the deteriorating operational situation had changed the dynamic. Oddly it was a dynamic from which the Irish had found strength, both subtly and overtly. The Irish were good at compromise, but they did not like their predisposition and ability to reach agreements and forge settlements to be seen as a weakness. The effective Irish tactic of returning controlled fire, round for round, was now established. This was to lead directly to a situation where the DFF would soon have to make a decision, either to leave At-Tiri or to try to make one last push to dislodge the Irish.

Build-Up

Friday, 11 April 1980

The initial brazenness of the DFF break-in at At-Tiri had stunned everyone but at first had elicited no armed response. This was not surprising, since the overall initial intent of the UNIFIL operation was one of containment, negotiation and persuasion, which it hoped would see the DFF leave the area. Incursions, however, had been happening in the Irish battalion's Area of Operations for over a year, starting with the 44th Battalion. These DFF operations resulted in the establishment of some permanent posts across the key terrain occupied by the Irish.

The question for the 46th Battalion was whether or not At-Tiri would now be added to this DFF list of successes. Another possibility was that the status quo following their break-in might stagnate, thereby resulting in a scenario where the incident might be handed over to the 46th Battalion's successors.

There was some belief that had the DFF adopted a less reckless and more measured and conciliatory approach, that scenario could have unfolded and it may well have fallen to another formation to sort out the problem. After all, apart from the indignation of it, thinking strictly strategically how important was the actual village of At-Tiri itself to the tactical posture of the Irish? It would have been far more damaging to the Battalion's defence if Abu Omar and his band of DFF had headed straight for Hill 880 at the outset. The 46th Battalion may well have settled down to a long wait had the DFF not raised the stakes as the week progressed. The UN position at Bayt Yahun had previously been partially compromised by the DFF, an event they were now trying to repeat in At-Tiri, and they had managed to circumvent another Irish position the previous year and successfully seized a key element of the terrain before being halted. On its seizure they promptly placed a Sherman Main Battle Tank (MBT) there with a garrison of some ten to fifteen personnel. From this vantage point they had often sent harassing fire thundering down the valley towards Ayta az Zutt and Tebnine itself. They also operated an illegal checkpoint controlling entry into the Enclave at Bayt Yahun crossroads. They sometimes rejoiced in starting up the Sherman and moving it around the compound, just to gauge the reaction of the Irish platoon and the speed in which they would assume the blocking positions required. Similarly, they had succeeded in placing a Super Sherman tank into their position known as the Cuckoo's Nest at Rshaf.

From Lieutenant Colonel Jack Kissane's point of view, as Commanding Officer 46th Irish Battalion, At-Tiri was one aspect of a wider concern. For him 'sticking diligently to the mission' was important:

> I had to maintain an overview and control other areas concurrently. While At-Tiri was a huge concern, the entirety of the Battalion Area of Operations could not be left vulnerable. We knew it was a DFF tactic to get in as near as possible to their opposition. I was

also conscious of it becoming a protracted operation, concerned that we had to maintain our ongoing ability to continue. The rotation of supplies and internal maintenance of company and platoon routines, allowing for rest, being particularly important.

Lieutenant Colonel Kissane's concerns about rations and rest demonstrated that he had not only the specific situations to worry about but had also to take the wide and the long view as well. As for his command style: 'I was a consensus-seeker. Before making a decision I would take soundings and considerations from others. Everyone had a contribution to make.'

The situation was becoming protracted and it might have been that this stand-off would be handed over to the soon to arrive 47th Irish Battalion. The critical wounding of Private Stephen Griffin had occurred on the morning of the second day, when the Irish were not yet in returning fire mode. It had occurred so quickly and so early on in the week, unprovoked and a dramatically significant escalation, that it was a huge shock to the Irish forces, though not one that led to Irish retaliatory fire. The persistent DFF presence inside the village and their aggressive pursuit of enlarging their hold on At-Tiri led to an attempt to capture the HQ House, Post 6-15. With this assault a tipping point had been reached and the Irish were forced to return aimed controlled fire or be totally overrun. Still, the DFF persisted with their pressure tactics and continued with harassing fire, tactics of intimidation and threatening behaviour that was countered round for round by the Irish.

Early on Friday, day six of the confrontation, DFF tanks south of At-Tiri opened up with HMG fire on UNIFIL positions in the village. Fire was returned by the Irish and all firing ceased within a few minutes. Shortly after, DFF militiamen in the half-track at the Outhouse near the east end checkpoint opened up with HMG fire on an Irish resupply convoy. UNIFIL troops in At-Tiri returned fire and a fire fight ensued. The Irish had decided that further firing by that half-track would no longer be tolerated. A sequence of well-placed bursts of 7.62mm fire from the AML 90 armoured car's coaxially mounted MAG 80 machine gun took effect. First a burst above the half-track with tracer, then a burst at the track of the half-track and finally a burst at the HMG machine gun itself, the source of the DFF's hostile fire. Lieutenant Tony Bracken followed the impact of his aimed rounds:

> After the third burst, I saw a flash in the area of what I knew to be the top cover of the half-track's HMG machine gun. The gunner leaped off the back of the half-track in haste. The half-track at the Outhouse had harassed our convoys for the last time. Our firing had succeeded when all manner of negotiation and entreaty had failed. This lesson, gradually absorbed by the Irish and UNIFIL troops since the beginning of the week-long incident, was now fully assimilated.

Later that morning, another UN convoy containing Officer Commanding (OC) Irish Battalion and a UNIFIL HQ VIP party including General Nilsen, UNIFIL Deputy Force Commander, visited At-Tiri. At the village west end, while on a rooftop receiving an on-site up-to-date briefing, the Deputy Force Commander (DFC) of UNIFIL also received the unwelcome attention of a house-proud local woman, who charged at him with a sweeping brush, annoyed that where she had just swept may become untidy again. It was the DFC's turn to come under attack! There was also continued IDF vehicle movement on the road between Kunin and Saff al-Hawa. However it appeared they were moving rearwards and their withdrawal was completed by late afternoon. This good news was countered just as quickly with bad news when radio contact was lost with three Enclave OP's (Observation Posts) and the fourth post in Mhiabeg was surrounded by the militia and DFF small arms fire was reported. UNIFIL (Irish) troops at the Enclave post at Mhiabeg were taken prisoner by the DFF but later released. While news of this was unfolding, competing reports of the DFF starting to harass Irish troops at Bayt Yahun was also being received.

Within the hour this confrontation had developed into a serious riot. Children aged between 12 and 16 years old were incited to stone UNIFIL troops and during the riot small arms fire was directed at UNIFIL positions by approximately thirty DFF personnel. Under cover of the small arms fire and the stone-throwing rioters, an APC from the Ghanaian battalion was overrun and set on fire, having had petrol poured around and into it. The Irish UNIFIL troops successfully advanced and retook the burning APC and managed to remove the ammunition from inside it. There were no casualties but considerable damage was caused to the APC. Meanwhile, in At-Tiri Major Haddad arrived at the east end checkpoint but was refused entry and departed while further west one of the DFF Super Sherman tanks at the Cuckoo's Nest changed its location to join the two tanks already situated to the south of At-Tiri, leaving the Irish wondering how to interpret this action.

In the early afternoon, the local villagers reported that there was going to be shelling and they were taking cover. The shelling did not take place and in mid-afternoon young villagers, children and teenagers mostly, were led outside the UN area by the DFF to the Outhouse beyond the east end checkpoint where Major Haddad gave an interview to the Israeli media. In the meantime, Irish foot patrols recommenced in the west end, a development that aimed to show the UN was reasserting its influence on the village. During the patrol there was no contact with the DFF but the reaction of the villagers was one of delight. The DFF were not happy when they heard about this occurrence and they assaulted the village mukhtar for allowing the UN to patrol. The DFF, however, did not attempt to encounter the UN patrols themselves. For some two hours before midnight there was some sporadic small arms fire from DFF positions in At-Tiri, aimed at unknown targets, thereafter both sides settled down for an uneasy night after another unsettling day. Meanwhile, matters inside the Enclave continued to be eventful.

Extraction

The Enclave, Friday, 11 April 1980

The manning and resupply of the Enclave posts was the responsibility of the Irish Battalion Company based in As-Sultaniyah, and in April 1980 this responsibility had rotated to B Company. Situated between the Israeli border and beyond the limit to which UNIFIL was allowed to deploy, their isolation and vulnerability within the Enclave led to them being commonly referred to as 'hostage posts' though repeated requests to have them closed down had been denied. Tactically they did not afford any military advantage, rather the opposite, but politically their occupation demonstrated a UNIFIL presence in that part of the Israeli/ DFF controlled enclave. Access to these posts, four in all, Observation Post (OP) Ras, Blida (Post 6-24), Mhaibeb (Post 6-25) and Jabel As-Saff (Post 6-26) was controlled by the DFF and permitted only on Mondays, Wednesdays, Thursdays and Fridays. Frequently this already limited access was denied and the posts could be without relief for periods of up to fourteen days or more. Troops supplying the posts were often the subject of hijackings, harassment, intimidation, robbery and abuse. Use of force was governed by UNIFIL Standard Operating Procedures (SOPs) and was also conditioned by an overwhelming Israeli-controlled DFF presence in the area.

His own start of tour deployment delayed by a week due to the birth of his firstborn, Captain Declan Lawlor's arrival in South Lebanon was straight into an active confrontation in Bayt Yahun. For the 29-year-old Weapons Platoon Commander, B Company, from Portarlington, it was to set the tone for his tour and he was to experience frequent incidents of shootings and close fire:

> The PLO were always trying to infiltrate and this would create a response from the DFF. We frequently captured [PLO infiltrators], disarmed them and took them back to the Tyre pocket. There were of course periods of calm and quiet and I struck up an on-ground relationship with a DFF aide to Major Haddad, a Lieutenant Barracat. After two months there the Company rotated to Haddata and my platoon and I were located in At-Tiri. The village was subjected to mortar fire from time to time and one night when I was in Company Headquarters in Haddata the shelling became quite intense. Returning to be with my platoon in At-Tiri, the shells were landing on the track in front of us as we were going over Hill 880.
>
> In March the Company rotated to As-Sultaniyah and the Company's platoons took it in turn to man the OP's in the Enclave. I and my platoon found ourselves there in early April, as the At-Tiri incident erupted. Prior to this matters with the DFF were a bit like chess, we'd stop their incursions into our AO and they'd stop our resupply of the OPs in the Enclave. They were in fact token posts, UNIFIL not being allowed to deploy right up to the

Israeli border [and] were an albatross around our necks, tactically disadvantageous. Sighted in a non-tactical way they were undefendable and undermanned. There wasn't much we could do to affect our own safety. Mhaibeb was the platoon headquarters post, with eight or nine personnel, a prefab and tents. Each of the three remaining OPs had a complement of five.

Some weeks previously I had been tasked to devise an emergency evacuation plan from the posts, to effect a covert overland self-extraction. I was not to use the road network out of the enclave and my route had to link up with company APC's transport in close proximity to Barachit village. This plan had to work, so the best way to ensure this possibility was to actually test its feasibility. I selected a route from a 'map recce' of the contours along the steep valley floors (wadis) to safety. Where these wadi floors intersected at junctions I chose Rendezvous Points (RV points) for those from Blinda and Jabal As-Saff. However, OP Ras was too far off. The OP Post personnel, now joined up, would be formed into two teams, leapfrogging in bounds, each over-watching the other. I tried it [and] it worked and we adopted it as a feasible contingency. Having conducted a map and ground recce [and] rehearsed it myself, I nonetheless wondered how the plan would be executed for real. In the event it needed to be [and] three weeks later I was to find out.

Towards week's end, with the situation in At-Tiri becoming increasingly more tense, discernible from monitoring the radio traffic on our communications network ... and ever conscious that there wasn't much we could do to affect our own security and safety, we were becoming anxious. The best we could do was to build up fire positions around our perimeter. For my own part I started sleeping with my pistol under my pillow.

Friday morning early, while in the post prefab eating breakfast, I was looking out the window towards the perimeter gate, essentially barbed wire, listening to Joan Baez singing 'The Night They Drove Old Dixie Down' when a number of DFF half-tracks and DFF personnel approached the post and fanned out around it. I jumped up and ran to the perimeter opening where our sentry was. I met two DFF. Extremely anxious, I nonetheless exchanged the usual greetings after which they said to me: 'Captain, you must come with us.' I firmly but friendly told them I could not leave my post whereupon they grabbed me, each taking hold of one of my shoulders. I wrestled myself free of their grip by pushing them forwards and stepping backwards, leaving them holding my uniform pullover in their hands. I then grabbed our sentry's rifle and swung it at them. One of them fired at me, narrowly missing me, instead hitting a barrel next to me. His shot alerted the remainder of the DFF and they responded by opening up at point-blank range for five or six seconds of sustained fire. At that point, I put my hands up and together with the post's occupants was bundled into the back of a half-track.

I felt more embarrassed at being caught out than fearful, and as soon as we were taken out of the half-track at a nearby village I protested their actions strenuously. Inexplicably, within a half-hour we were told to remount the half-track and were driven back to our OP. Nothing was taken in the interval [and] all was as we left it, including [the] pistol under my pillow. However, there was also a line of bullet holes across my tent in line with my bed space where I would have been lying. I lost no time reporting the matter on the radio, pointing out our continued vulnerability and recommended withdrawal, enforcement, or rearmament with 84mm anti-tank and GPMG's. The Company Commander, Commandant Sean Hurley, proactively sought permission for our withdrawal.

While waiting on a reply we had to anxiously remain in situ. He later, along with a large Irish patrol, came out to visit us. We felt great to have such reassuring numbers in situ with us. As it happened, the DFF chose this moment to return to recapture us [and] a tense stand-off ensued. The DFF withdrew [and] the Irish patrol departed back to Company HQ. Glad to be still liberated and enjoying the moment it was all to fleeting, as shortly after my platoon personnel at OP Saff As-Jabal were seeking permission to be withdrawn. While talking on the radio with them their radio suddenly went eerily silent at their end. Ominous, it could well mean they were taken. They were. Then we received news that permission was granted for our withdrawal. I had clearance to get my men out of the Enclave, only without being noticed. It had come time to give effect to my covert self-evacuation plan, for real.

Their future freedom, maybe their lives, depended on it: 'The responsibility nullified my fear. I was simply too preoccupied to be afraid.' That Captain Lawlor had a plan, which in essence was straightforward and one he knew could work, was a sign of sound military planning. Now all he had to do is show it would actually work. This was a planned withdrawal under DFF pressure, conducted to avoid conflict in an unfavourable tactical situation. They had to remove themselves from a tactically untenable context in confused and rapidly changing conditions prior to an anticipated DFF bid to overrun them. Put another way, this was an authorised self-evacuation to avoid captivity.

Their move out was to be effected without an over-watch force to hold off the DFF until they were out of danger. They had to rely on speed, silence and stealth, but first to do nothing to signal their intent to withdraw to the DFF. They had to be careful to maintain a normal pattern of behaviour until nightfall to conceal their intentions. Darkness was going to be their ally, making detection difficult. Captain Lawlor intended to exploit the conditions, keeping the execution of his prudent abandonment plan simple. However, as simple as it was and with the advantages of both surprise and the cover of darkness, it would take very little for matters to go wrong. Their withdrawal would be hampered by reduced visibility, as navigation is made much more difficult in darkness, sound travels further and it can be difficult to identify friend from foe. The odds were what they were and were still better than remaining, but in leading them out who knew where this attempt would take them?

Darkness fell and the occupants of Post 6-25 (OP Mhaibeb) moved out quietly, cautiously and slowly, but happy to be heading out of the Enclave and away from the clutches of the DFF. Moving stealthily to the rendezvous point (RV), the designated meeting point at the appointed wadi junction, an easily recognisable terrain feature, they successfully linked up with the occupants of the Post 6-24 (OP Blinda). One misunderstanding, miscommunication or mistiming about the RV and there would have been difficulties from the beginning. Not so, and so far so good. With the absence of the occupants of Post 6-23 (Jabal As-Saff), who were believed captured, they were smaller in number, so instead of two groups leapfrogging one another all the way out, instead Captain Lawlor simplified matters and they progressed together, as one group.

At night movement is slower, and if intercepted by the DFF ('bumped') the ensuing engagement would take place at a shorter range. Responding to Captain Lawlor's encouragement and his clear and effective control measures they moved forward, stimulated by his calm, visible leadership. Moving well, but still with a long way to go, the possibility of discovery still existed, as did an off-chance encounter with a coincidental PLO infiltration or concurrently bumping into a DFF ambush party. Armed parties moving unknown to each other, unrecognisable in the darkness of night and in a heightened and tense atmosphere, was all part of the possible danger and uncertainty inherent in the extraction attempt. The risk of these variables did not detract from the benefit of avoiding captivity. The drama was unfolding successfully inside the Enclave beyond the village of At-Tiri, a fractured piece in the overall mosaic of a fragile situation.

With Captain Lawlor and his group not yet fully clear of the Enclave, those inside At-Tiri settled down for the night. As Captain Lawlor successfully led his group through the potential perils of a covert self-extraction, Sergeant John Power, under threat at OP Ras and being provoked with harassment and frequent fire, was steadfastly refusing to surrender. Isolated along with his small cadre, with meagre supplies of food and water, he continued to hold out with great courage and efficiency. Could it be that the Irish in At-Tiri could hold out even for another day? Now clear of the Enclave proper, Captain Lawlor and his group were looking to link up with their APCs in the environs of Barachit village, that is if both groups were in the right place at the right time. To his immense relief, and those of his men, they were. It had been an extraordinary extraction.

Move In

Saturday, 12 April 1980

In heightened circumstances it is not so much that peacekeepers rise to the occasion but rather they realise the level of their training. In terms of preparing soldiers to experience such engagements, it is difficult to properly close the gap between training and live incidents. The fear, chance, uncertainty and misunderstanding of these chaotic, dangerous and adrenaline-pumped moments is challenging to replicate and gaps in training can become all too evident in reality. Earlier in the week, after Lieutenant Tom Aherne and his platoon had established a perimeter defence around HQ house, where the Company HQ was now located, he decided to issue grenades. A few minutes after he had done so a private came up to him and expressed his unfamiliarity with grenades, and as it turned out a number of his platoon were uncertain about their precise use. There was, however, no gap in everyone's understanding regarding the use of force.

The return of fire was a big issue, as was the discipline of non-escalation. Coming from an Ireland of the late 1970s, at a time when 'The Troubles' along the border with Northern Ireland and their spill-over into the Republic occupied the Irish Defence Forces in Aid-to-the-Civil-Power duties in support to the Irish police (Gardaí), an understanding of the graduated use of force was very much the order of the day. It was hammered home that if you used force you had to know what you were doing, why you were doing it and be able to justify your behaviour in the circumstances. That had a major impact on how the Irish forces conducted themselves and this discipline of non-escalation at home translated into highly disciplined restraint overseas. This conscious subcultural ethos had kept situations from escalating out of hand and in At-Tiri the Irish return fire had been controlled aimed warning shots in response to the reckless and indiscriminate firing of the DFF. A less prudent use of fire, as if in war, would have resulted in any number of DFF killed. As it was, the Irish suppressing fire had taken lumps out of the walls, door jams and window frames of the buildings occupied by the DFF. However, the margin left between its continuance and a shift in the DFF tactics in 'upping the ante' was becoming increasingly narrow. Irish lives, and those who had come to reinforce them, were at stake and the situation was becoming ever more edgy and tense.

Escalating matters to effect a breakthrough was exactly what Major Saad Haddad had in mind. The status quo was not going to achieve his intent to gain control of At-Tiri and ultimately Hill 880. He needed one more desperate effort, one final push to end the deadlock, so he had set about orchestrating an injurious initiative involving the inhuman use of unarmed civilians to riot. Herded towards the Irish positions, the DFF were ominously seeking to manipulate a clash between the UNIFIL Irish and this hapless group. A reluctant rabble they may have been but they presented a difficult and dangerous dilemma for the Irish. Of course, this cynical ploy was precisely what Major Haddad had planned to cower the Irish and set them off balance; confrontation with a fear-filled, terrified throng of unarmed civilians. His manoeuvrings had begun earlier in the morning, when tank fire was directed into Tebnine, mortar fire into Barachit, and sporadic small arms and HMG fire into At-Tiri. Abu Askander had arrived in Bayt Yahun and informed the Post Commander, Captain Billie Campbell, that he had five Irish personnel, captured previously from one of the Enclave posts, as hostages. He threatened that in the event of any DFF militiaman or civilian in the At-Tiri area being injured he would take appropriate revenge against the Irish prisoners. 'One for One' was his starkly stated intention. Neither was this the end of his attempted browbeating and bullying, declaring that the earlier tank, mortar and small arms fire into the villages of Tebnine, Barachit and At-Tiri had been a warning only, and that these villages could and would be fired on if he went unheeded.

The confrontation was as much a battle of wits as it was of wills. However, the Irish will was unfaltering and their determination undiminished. Still, the main focus of their worry was where this latest pressure tactic was going to end. Designed to make the Irish 'go into themselves' and then exploit their momentary uncertainty, the DFF hoped to overrun their positions using a human battering ram. Youths, brought on trucks from Tebnine and other surrounding villages, were approaching in waves and throwing stones, bricks and bottles at the UN forces. Behind them, the DFF were intimidating and inciting the civilians by shooting into the air over their heads and into the sides of the road beside them. The villagers were being forced to advance on both Irish positions simultaneously, towards the Irish AML 90 armoured car in the village centre and towards the east end checkpoint. The DFF ploy was to engineer an armed response from the Irish to shoot into the crowd, whereupon it was considered likely that the DFF would also fire into the crowd, inflicting casualties among them and blaming the Irish. The situation demanded an immediate reaction but not an armed one, and the Irish were instructed not to fire. They could clearly see the reluctant villagers being intimidated by the DFF, and at the east end checkpoint Captain Adrian Ainsworth's answer was to intimidate the intimidators, specifically one local DFF leader, 'Captain George'. Within an arm's length of 'Captain George', with only a strand of barbed wire separating them, Captain Ainsworth withdrew his Browning Automatic Pistol (BAP), pointed it at the militiaman and persuaded him to cease the intimidation of the villagers.

Meanwhile, inside the village the DFF were attempting more menacing efforts using burning tyres as a tactic. Pouring petrol into tyres, then lighting and rolling them down the hill towards the Irish, they sought to set their vehicles alight, especially the AML 90 Armoured fighting vehicle. The Irish could not give ground and a number of well-aimed warning and containing shots dispersed the crowd and their intimidators. Surprised that their attempt was all too short-lived, the DFF were put further on the back foot when the occasion was suddenly seized upon by the Irish to put a pre-planned contingency into effect to retake the village. Enough was enough and Commandant Dave Taylor gave orders to move in and re-secure the village. Preparations were made to advance into the village centre from the west and HQ House simultaneously, in what was to be a synchronised two-pronged pincer assault.

This phase coincided with an increase in the level of DFF fire from within the village on both Irish checkpoints and on HQ House itself. Although much of this firing was wild and reckless, it became evident that a DFF sniper was at work. Moving from position to position, Captain Adrian Ainsworth settled his reinforcements and passed the word that the retaking of the village was imminent and they should get ready to move. He noticed a certain calmness descend over his troops, a quiet determination and an undeclared resolve. The only noise apart from the DFF firing was of men preparing their equipment and themselves. Among them he noticed an older Fijian who had fought in the Second World War, arranging his kit while periodically glancing at a photograph, no doubt of his loved ones, then in his own silent isolation he noticed him praying.

Continuing to move from platoon member to platoon member, giving them instructions, ammunition and the timing to move, Captain Ainsworth came under fire. Pausing for a few moments he moved again and once more drew fire; he had drawn the DFF sniper's attention. Just then there was the sudden eruption of HMG fire onto the HQ House and intensive DFF small arms fire onto all Irish positions. The militia, clearly annoyed that their ploy at press ganging the reluctant villagers to riot and overrun the Irish positions had failed, were now using them instead as human shields, from behind which they were attempting to re-engage the Irish. Shouting to all within earshot, Captain Ainsworth warned everyone to stay well under cover until the order to move was given. He himself moved again, this time to his machine gun group, also Fijians. He spoke with Private Seveti 'Sorro' Sornaivalav, telling him what arc of responsibility he is to give covering fire into. 'Sorro', smiling happy with his orders, moved to kneel closer to Captain Ainsworth and suddenly a shot is heard:

> I hear a 'crack' sound, then a small thud, like a knife going through an apple. Suddenly, shockingly, I am wet with blood. I am shot, I think to myself. I wait for the pain and the numbness. 'Sorro' and I seem to fall against each other and both together [we] fall into a deep hollow in the ground. I am pinned down by him on [top of] me. I cannot move. What is wrong? I feel the ground but no pain. I try to move. I free my arm. His head is resting against me. Lying there I realise I am not shot, ['Sorro'] is. I whisper a short prayer in his ear. A great sadness descends on me [and] I call the medics for assistance.

After some time a calm descends on the Irish position as the medics carry out their task, Private 'Sorro' Sornaivalav was immediately medevaced, under fire, but died later. Fire was returned by UNIFIL troops and the crowd disperses, the DFF gunfire waning momentarily and the situation beginning to calm. The DFF Super Sherman tanks south of the village fire three rounds into At-Tiri. The HQ House takes a direct hit and suffers damage to an outer wall but no casualties.

The sounds in conflict are as many and varied as the feelings caused by their reality, when suddenly a new sound is heard, a new reality, and a new fear. This is an unfamiliar sound and it brings an unfamiliar unease. With confusion and strain on overworked senses already struggling with trepidation and tautness, the Irish listen as the noise gets louder. The Irish and Fijian troops brace themselves and wait but the noise passes overhead. Immediately relieved they realise that the Dutch on Hill 880 have opened up with their tube-launched, optically-tracked, wire-guided (TOW) missile. UNIFIL reinforcements under Irish command were responding to the tank fire. They waited for an impact explosion but none came. The missile had fallen short, it was a warning shot.

Suspense and uncertainty was the shared experience of all in At-Tiri during that week. Like most of the Irish there, for 26-year-old Limerick man, Lieutenant Johnny Molloy, Troop Commander Armoured Car Section, 'Recce' Company, based in the village of Haddata and rushed to the village of At-Tiri, the week was to have a number of turning points. One of the biggest was what had happened the previous day in Bayt Yahun:

> A huge turning point for me, one which affected my attitude considerably, was the DFF's use of civilians to riot and the tactic of employing fire to cause damage to vehicles. I realised they could, and most likely would, use that ploy here. They had revealed their game plan to me [and] I was ready. I was certain of one thing, and that was I was not going to give up my armoured car. The rioters came in waves, ushered forwarded by the DFF in an attempt to flood our positions. Concertina wire and overhead bursts of fire from us contained them. I remember at one stage seeing amongst the mob, mostly a mix of teenage and young adult males, an elderly woman extending a stick with a burning rag on its tip in the vain attempted hope of setting our armoured car alight. They had to be deterred from continuing. I took out my sidearm, a 9mm Browning automatic pistol, and fired a number of rounds into the air. The crowd retreated, withdrawing out of sight around a corner. Forced back out by the DFF, one of the first such was a young male carrying a jerry can of petrol. To discourage him and the others from progressing further I ordered containing fire to be placed into a nearby wall. It worked and we achieved the desired effect of causing them to make another hasty retreat out of sight again. In so doing, the jerry can of petrol was knocked out of the hands of the young male. Remaining on the road, it presented an ideal target, but before we could switch our fires onto it, it was swiftly retrieved.

The game was still on and was only set to become more serious and deadly. It was in one of those moments that Private Seveti Sornaivalav had fallen victim to the DFF sniper. DFF firing within the village escalated and tank rounds impacted inside At-Tiri. The HMG fire from the half-track on the roadway below the HQ House was becoming increasingly menacing and a distinct close-in hazard. All too aware that both it and the half-track near the east end checkpoint had caused serious problems all week, it had been Lieutenant Molloy's mission to mark and if necessary neutralise this threat should it display signs of being used in a life-threatening manner. It just had:

> It was time to neutralise it. I had received prior permission to do so from 'Recce' Company Commander, Commandant Larry Coughlan, he in turn previously from Commandant Dave Taylor, and while a pre-considered wholly-justified act it was every bit as much part of the momentum of the moment. It was a premeditated life-saving preventative reaction; well war-gamed by Commandant Dave Taylor in advance. Having been fired on for days, suffering fatalities and wounded, enduring week-long ongoing harassment; and witnessing the cowardly abuse of civilians, put in harm's way [by the DFF] for their own ends, the burden of being unable to react finally [was] now removed, resulted in a huge release of energy from this frustration. We experienced an overwhelming feeling of emancipation from our exasperation. This dangerous escalation removed the impediment of non-reaction. We were no longer hampered and finally, finally, able to match like with like, to meet action with reaction, to resolve their recklessness with the required response of our own. We were, at last, able to fight for peace, because if we didn't, there wouldn't be any. We had shown considerable constraint, remained resolved, now, finally, had come the time to restore control of At-Tiri.

An axiom in military circles is the plan frequently does not survive its first engagement. This did and the Irish hit hard and directly. After a direct and purposeful advance up the road towards the half-track, the Irish AML 90 armoured car and crew, supported by a section of troops under Captain Tony Gilleran, swiftly inflicted immobilising damage on the DFF armoured vehicle by firing two rounds into it then promptly withdrew. This sudden, sharp and crisply executed manoeuvre took the DFF by surprise and caused a temporary lull in the exchange. Lieutenant Johnny Molloy took advantage of the pause to assess damage to his AML 90 armoured car. He and his crew were concerned by the multiple impacts received on route to and from the half-track. However anxious the crew were, they became more so when Lieutenant Molloy suddenly began laughing. At the beginning of the week, during the initial rush to get into At-Tiri, Lieutenant Molloy had grabbed whatever equipment and few personal effects were to hand in the short time available. In his haste he had mistakenly taken the uniform jumper of his colleague, Lieutenant Ger Ahern, 'Recce' Company's anti-tank platoon commander. When involved earlier in the riot situation, he had placed the jumper behind the grill on the front of the armoured car and there it had stayed during the subsequent events involving the half-track. As a consequence, on their advance towards the half-track it was shot almost to shreds. Nonetheless was a sorry sight and on discovering this Lieutenant Molloy was imagining his friend's face when he returned the jumper to him, in tatters, as a joke.

Commandant Dave Taylor knew that attack is about momentum and once you build it up it's hard to stop. He interpreted the initiative had begun to swing the way of the Irish with the damage to the DFF's centre of gravity in the village – their half-track. He knew for his plan of attack to be decisive it must be developed according to the distribution of those opposing him. Having ascertained where their heart was located he arranged his actions accordingly. He knew how to think and this told him what to think, which gave him command of the situation rather than permitting the situation to command him. To rule by actions instead of acting by rules, his ability to anticipate and improvise were now a premium for the Irish. Determined to retake control of the village, Commandant Taylor had fashioned his plan accordingly. The events unfolding as they had now afforded him the opportunity to put it into effect. Sharing the circumstances of the unfolding situation with those on the spot, he judged the most favourable time for his improvised company-in-attack plan to be mounted.

There were no formal orders group ('O' Group), which all those with responsibility for their separate tasks to succeed in gaining the objective would attend. Instead, in the intervening days since the break in by the DFF he had patiently waited to put the elements of his plan in place for its possible but unpredictable occurrence. Suggesting its existence, he now imparted the plan individually to his men with the minimum of communication. 'He was that kind of leader, constantly visible to everyone throughout the week. We knew he knew what to do, he had only to tell us and it would be done. He was the quintessential leader of substance,' was how Sergeant Billy Hutton described Commandant Taylor. 'Everything we did came from him, he was calm and deliberate, his controlled, unexcitable nature was infectious.'

Private Padraigh Cloherty agreed with Sergeant Hutton's estimation but explained it differently:

> They (the DFF) wanted our (HQ) House, it dominated the east end checkpoint. Commandant Taylor reassured us [and] we trusted him, he wasn't sitting hiding in a corner, he was everywhere. We were lucky we had a very good man. He could see things happening, see things coming. It was as if he had experienced it all before. He was thinking way ahead. I think they (the DFF) thought we'd fold. We were afraid, we were young [but] Commandant Taylor knew we'd win and good leadership combats the fear. And we had a good platoon commander in Lieutenant Aherne and a good Company Commander in him.

The taking out of the half-track was important but it was not yet fully taken out, it still had the 'point-five' HMG intact as a viable weapon. Lieutenant Molloy knew what had to be done. He also knew, as did his crew, that confronting the half-track this time, without the element of surprise, would be a very different proposition – and it had been no joke the first time, they had taken a lot of fire. He also knew that the situation was not going to resolve itself:

> They were wise to us now, worse, we had seen extra DFF with Rocket Propelled Grenades (RPGs) amongst the houses, and those who were there the first time had not gone away either, and were waiting. The repeat task was unnerving and the prospect of advancing up the road again held a lot more anxiety than before.

Support fires were called for [so] I contacted Commandant Dave Taylor and requested covering fire, the intention being as we drove forward he'd direct suppressing fire in front of us. As we moved, the fire support base on top of the roof of the HQ House would constantly 'lift and shift' their hail of fire forward of us. This 'fire and movement' was made difficult by trees blocking their line of sight from Commandant Taylor's firebase on the flat rooftop of the HQ House … of our line of advance up the road. Deciding an increased volume of fire would compensate for the obscured view, we settled on the matter.

Irish fire opened from the rooftop as if a pressure valve was being released. Their pent-up collective compressed will was finally finding its freedom. The roar of the gunfire announced an Irish fight-back was on and it was time to suffocate the self-belief of the DFF:

Energised by the sheer amount of suppressing fire being laid down in front of us, for us, we headed up the road towards the already half stricken half-track. The hail of fire was so extensive all I remember was impact smoke rising off the road and walls in front of us. This continuous voluminous volley allowed us [to] put our armoured car in position to strike. We moved up and put two more rounds into it, giving it a blast of machine gun fire for good measure before we moved back.

For Trooper Thomas 'TC' Martin, driver of the AML 90, Saturday, 12 April was already a noteworthy day, it being his twenty-second birthday. However, it would be all the more memorable because of his direct involvement in the dramatically unfolding events. As the rioting crowd had gathered it could only have been ominous for the Irish:

Looking out of the episcope from inside our armoured car I noticed they were mostly teenage kids, and reluctant ones too. They were only involved because of the DFF coercion, who fired at their heels to get them to move and become involved in stone throwing and the rolling down the hill of burning tyres towards us. These, they hoped, would get in underneath our vehicle in particular and set it alight. That matter satisfactorily dealt with, I heard the order come over the radio, move up and take out the half-track. 'Oh, here we go,' I said and had now to become 100 per cent fully switched on to what was happening.

Captain Ainsworth (right) and Corporal Mac Seoin receiving the Military Medal for Gallantry for their actions in relation to the At-Tiri incident.
Courtesy of *An Cosantoir*

To concentrate properly was difficult, trying to keep my ears open to hear the orders being relayed while doing what needed to be done, driving-wise. The cackle on the radio headset [and] the noise of surrounding gunfire both Irish and DFF, but particularly distracting, not to mention disturbing, were the incoming rounds impacting heavily on the armoured car's turret. The noise was like having a tin hat on your head with people hitting it with a hammer.

As we drove towards the half-track we were being hit with a lot of stuff. The firing was so intense and concentrated it knocked the middle episcope actually inside onto the floor of the turret and I was afraid the bullets would enter through the open space, only I was forgetting there was a layer of armoured protection cover still between me and outside, the episcope being a periscope-like L-shape. The heat inside the armoured car was immense. We fire. Smoke filled the interior. The noise, the heat, the smoke, the excitement, the uncertainty, the combination of it all was all too precarious. We didn't know what was going to happen next?

Body heat rising, chest tightening, heart thumping, breath quickening, vision widening, palms pulsing with sweat, anxiety so extreme it felt inescapable, nausea unfolding. 'We were all too aware of the Super Sherman tanks standing off to the South of the village to our left,' recalls Trooper Martin. 'We felt sure they would take a specific interest in us now. I remember saying to myself, if we get out of this unscathed and alright I'll light twelve candles in a church when I get home.'

Trooper Tom 'Deno' Jones, the gunner in the crew, fired the fourth and final round. Trooper Thomas 'TC' Martin continues:

We hear the roar of the explosion, [see] more smoke. Job done. We gave the half-track a final blast of fire from our machine gun for good measure. It was then [that] Lieutenant Molloy, Car Commander, reported over the radio: 'I'm finished firing, and he's finished moving.' The sweat was pouring out of me, it was difficult to breath. We were now a target for sure.

In a covering Panhard APC, Corporal Charlie Mott used his coaxial twin machine guns to support our withdrawal focusing his efforts particularly on the other half-track forcing it to move behind the Outhouse. We made use of whatever cover was available, driving between the village houses with our turret swinging constantly in the direction of the Super Sherman tanks, to reply immediately in the event they opened up on us. I remember contemplating the idea of actually driving into a house for cover if the circumstances warranted it. They didn't [and] we reached relative safety down the road around a corner. I'll forever remember the armoured car door opening and someone mercifully pouring an entire bottle of welcome cold water over my head. Once recovered I noted the very many black sulphur marks all over the front of the armoured car from where the bullets hit us.

Having largely stood sentinel in the face of DFF aggression and intimidation, now the time was ripe to launch an attack on militia positions in the village and the time had come to drive the DFF out. As soon as the Irish commenced suppressing covering fire with clarity and precision, events began evolving rapidly. From the west end of the village Captain Noel Byrne and Lieutenant Peter Marron marshalled their rapid Dutch and Irish APC-borne advance into the village centre to secure it. Simultaneously, from the east end Captain Adrian Ainsworth got his Irish and Fijian reinforcements up and going, firing as they moved. This concerted rush forward was further complemented by a northwards push from the Irish HQ House towards the Outhouse area.

These efforts to retake the village were met with hostile fire, and a lot of it. The Irish responded and at this stage anything could happen. The Irish, having achieved surprise by the sudden neutralising of the half-track, complemented now by this sudden collective surge and mutually supported by an increased and well directed volume of fire, began to have an effect. One DFF militiaman was killed and a number wounded. 'We were going in and were determined to do it', is how Captain Noel Byrne described the moment. Simultaneously to the combined inward push into the village centre was a complementary outward sweeping expansion cascading beyond the village's eastern and western exteriors. Several moving parts of the plan to retake the village were in motion, each individually employing fire and movement as they manoeuvred forward tactically. The overall advance was covered by overarching fire from the rooftop of HQ House. A swift and clinical rout of the DFF was in progress and the assault proved too much for the militia. The immense pressure had shattered their now suddenly brittle confidence and what was a militia force suddenly became a scattering of individuals. All organised unity vanished and unable to re-establish control the DFF disintegrated, retreating into the surrounding wadis dragging their wounded with them.

A house clearance operation began in earnest to ensure that no DFF were hiding or attempting to regroup. Every room, loft and outhouse was searched and cleared. Suddenly a burst of gunfire signified that not all resistance was quelled when DFF gunmen were located and a mini shoot-out ensued. Surrounded and outgunned they quickly surrendered and the two disarmed DFF prisoners were handed over to the HQ House platoon. As suddenly as it had begun the heavy fire fight was over. Seven days after their break-in, their week-long stand-off filled with harassment and intimidation, the DFF challenge had been answered. With this victory the Irish had regained At-Tiri, UNIFIL its credibility and the UN its will. The Irish, under Commandant Dave Taylor, had moved-in and At-Tiri was once again in Irish hands.

Reaction and Retort

It had been an abrupt assault, an abrasive action and an able and assertive attack. The simplicity of the conduct of Commandant Dave Taylor's contingency plan to retake the village had a beauty about it. He knew that in order to have the final say the Irish needed to make a significant play. The sudden, sharp sortie against the half-track, followed by a fast and fierce fire fight covering the direct and determined drive into the centre of At-Tiri, all stemmed from a week long refusal to lose the village. Big events often revolve around small moments and in At-Tiri the fighting space too had become compartmentalised. Inevitably, small sub-unit actions broke out. Sometimes their outcomes came down to a single moment or hinged on the individual act of one person. This is a consequence of the decentralised nature of how matters evolve once bullets start flying. You can only deal with what is in front of you and for sub-unit commanders it places an onus of responsibility to seek, cause or seize on any opportunity presenting itself, but it also grants the freedom for independent action and any one such action can be a turning point.

Commandant Taylor had caused events to happen faster than the DFF could react to them. In the end there was a composure in the collective effort of the Irish and their UN allies but it was every bit as much about those individual acts of bravery, courage, leadership and resourcefulness. These were significant in their actions and achievement in emotionally draining, physically dangerous and difficult circumstances. The Irish had retaken the village but knew this wasn't the end of the matter. They quickly and consciously readied themselves for the likely DFF reaction and it wasn't long in coming.

The retaliation first manifested itself with incoming 82mm mortar rounds. They slammed into the village, impacting heavily into and among the Irish positions. The ground shook with their blast, shrapnel scattering and the hot molten metal menacingly seeking its prey, indiscriminately spreading out in search of victims, eager to arbitrarily maim and kill. Being caught on the wrong side of a mortar barrage is a savage, raw and violent exposure to dread, destruction and death. One mortar round landed within twenty metres of Captain Ned Kelly, C Company's second-in-command, a distance guaranteed to deliver his demise. Waiting for it to explode he recalled what had happened to bring him to this juncture, this particular point in time, in the development of events. He had been in At-Tiri from early in the week, in fact he was leading the first reinforcements to arrive:

> Initially, on the Sunday, 6 April, I was Orderly Officer in C Company Headquarters, Haddata, and had received the dramatic landline call from Lieutenant Tom Aherne to report [that] the DFF had broken into At-Tiri. I immediately informed the Company Commander, Commandant Dave Taylor, who was … at the Battalion Sports Day. He ordered me to get to At-Tiri without delay with whatever number of reinforcements I could muster. Driving our APC was Trooper McDonagh and while en route it was deemed advisable to proceed directly to relieve the vulnerable Listening Post 6-15B at the exposed west end of the village.
>
> Blocked by the DFF, a militiaman pointed his AK-47 at Trooper McDonagh's head to dissuade him. I ordered him to steadily

'drive-on' and he bravely complied. We reached the two occupants of the listening post, much to their relief, whereupon we were all immediately surrounded. The DFF toyed with us, taking the pins out of their grenades [and] throwing rocks at the APC pretending them to be the actual grenades. We stood our ground until successfully rescued the following morning by a relieving ruse of our own, employing the distracting revving of vehicle engines at the villages' east end.

As Company Second-in-Command I was largely confined to the Company Headquarters. It being a 'Winter trip' (October to April), my responsibilities for the smooth running of the company had included 'Winterisation' duties, keeping accommodations waterproof and clothes dry, ensuring adequate supplies of rations, water, gas for the M59 cookers, kerosene for the heaters and generally seeing to whatever needed to be done, and there was always matters to be attended to in support of the Company and the Company Commander.

During the week Commandant Taylor had never become flustered by the DFF, he showed them no emotion, was stern and stark [and] gave nothing away. We had been backed into a position, we had been patient all week, [and] something decisive had to be done. The riot and the firing of tank shells was the moment for action and the fire fight ensued. With our retaking of the village, the firing had ceased and the DFF were allowed to withdraw, dragging their wounded with them. Commandant Taylor then ordered Lieutenant Tom Aherne and me into the village with a ten-man section each to clear it, sweeping westwards.

Kicking in doors we piled into houses afraid we'd be met with bullets coming out. We steadily worked our way westwards and when finished found ourselves in open ground on the west end outskirts of the village. Mortars started falling around us and we took cover immediately behind a wall. The barrage was ongoing for some minutes when one, and it only takes one, mortar bomb landed uncomfortably close to me. Instinctively I knew I was within its killing radius, despite being behind a wall. It would have an effect, perhaps an adversely dramatic one, I was too near it was as simple as that. I waited. I continued to wait, thankfully it did not explode.

Major Haddad had earlier been reported to have been seen at the DFF tank positions at the Brown Mound south of the village, so it was no surprise when the mortar rounds became increasingly interspersed with sporadic tank fire. The DFF's reaction to their ejection from At-Tiri had been swift and the might and menace of their direct fire tank rounds and indirect fire mortar bombs began to arrive with greater frequency and accuracy. The mortar bombs now began falling all around HQ House, peppering it but not impacting directly upon it though one round did hit against its side wall. Next, however, unlocking the padlock on their patience, the DFF released a salvo of direct fire tank rounds, scoring a direct hit on HQ House. A 75mm shell penetrated the front wall of the house and spliced through several inner walls before burying itself nose first in the mosaic-tiled floor of an interior room, occupied at the time. In the centre of the house, ten weary troops trying to get some rest suddenly weren't, and for the most shocking of reasons.

Sergeant Billy Hutton was among those on the house's rooftop when the tank round struck and was the first to react:

> The tank round impacted hard. As I ran down the stairs from the roof I was imaging what I might find. Not knowing what I was going to discover I fully prepared myself for encountering casualties, wounded, or worse! On entry, the room, the beds, the occupants, were all covered in plaster dust and stone fragments. I had to look hard to take in the scene. Then, had to look again to recheck my first impression. Disbelievingly, I confirmed to myself, with amazement and relief, that no one was hurt. The totality of the injuries was, extraordinarily, a superficial cut above one occupant's eye. The tank round was solid-shot, not high explosive, if it had been, I would have encountered an entirely different scene.

With the platoon 'HQ house' taking direct fire, Lieutenant Peter Marron and fellow cavalry officer Lieutenant Tony Bracken found themselves caught in the open in the vicinity of the destroyed half-track. Scrambling for cover they both took refuge in an empty Irish Panhard APC that was conveniently in the middle of the road. It had been driven there from the front of HQ House following the destruction of the half-track. Sitting relieved in the relative safety of the APC and somewhat buoyed by the recent success, each no doubt spurred on by an increase in adrenalin, they both observed at the same time, that the driver's hatch was open. Given the barrage of fire still ongoing, the hatch was promptly closed. That it would have little bearing in the event of a direct hit on the vehicle meant little in the situation in which they found themselves, but the survival instinct is strong. And the Irish were fighting for theirs now.

In response, a second TOW missile was launched from the Dutch on Hill 880, again targeted to fall short and it succeeded in silencing the tanks. However, the threat was still far from over when more sinister and uncertain news was received. A report to Irish Battalion from UNIFIL OPS gave information that intense DFF and IDF vehicle movement had been detected, followed fifteen minutes later by a second report of ten IDF vehicles observed by Post 6-24 in the Enclave crossing the Israeli–Lebanese border and advancing towards Saff al-Hawa. For now these reports were on the periphery of their predicament, there were more immediate problems. The DFF had looked to create a spark to swing the momentum back their way. But it hadn't happened and the militia had failed to deliver the knockout punch with the direct hit on HQ House. They continued the stand-off and increased their indirect mortar and direct HMG fire on the Irish positions.

Despite the difficulties this and the previous bombardments had posed regarding maintenance of command and control, the Irish remained coherent, their resilience unrelenting. The bombardment continued with both an intermittent intensity and a mix of sporadically spaced rounds. This persisted throughout the remainder of the afternoon and into the early evening. But worryingly was the ever-increasing notion that a DFF ground counter-offensive was brewing. There was a continued increase in vehicle activity at Saff al-Hawa and the pace of events was again accelerating. Did the DFF plan to do something deep? If so surely their tanks must re-engage. Check with the Dutch, were they ready to counter this threat, yet again? With darkness descending the Dutch TOW missiles had no night firing capability!

A problem requires a solution so an immediate substitute was sought. The Irish had their 84mm anti-tank recoilless rifles. Developed to be used in a defence setting in a conventional war-type scenario to cover the main tank threat, the anti-tank recoilless rifle was a versatile, multipurpose, direct fire resource. Its identified offensive use was to secure an advancing battalions assembly area, form-up point and start lines, then later in the attack take a final assault line against enemy armour and finally in occupying a reorganising position against counter attack. Highly adaptable and flexible, its use could be adjusted specifically to the task to be undertaken and it was in this particular role that it would be deployed now. Only it too needed night sights and these were urgently sought in nearby Tebnine. The Dutch were requested to source their equivalent, the Light Anti-Armour Weapon (LAW) and issue these to their TOW missile crews. The possibility of firing supporting 120mm mortar illumination rounds to light up the tanks, then for them to be engaged by the TOW missile crew was also examined and permission sought. Meanwhile batteries were needed for the Panhard AML 90s and APCs. Between monitoring ongoing DFF vehicle movements and making necessary arrangements for defending against a counter attack, news was received that a Dutch soldier was missing, last seen on patrol in At-Tiri with the Irish. It took an hour and a half to locate him and so the madness continued; the noise of gunfire ongoing, small arms bullets whizzed by, 'point five' HMG rounds interspersed with tracer flying in and the blast impacts of mortars exploding.

It became a vivid sound and light show, made all the more graphic and brilliant against the fading evening light. Tasked to place a UN flag on a small hilltop beyond the east end checkpoint, Captain Adrian Ainsworth and a section plus, some fourteen Irish in all, complied. Exposed to the lethality of the continuing cocktail of combustion, it was not long before fire was shifted and a creeping barrage moved towards the hilltop and those occupying it. Captain Ainsworth, an artillery officer, admired the accuracy of the barrage's 'Fall of Shot' even though he knew that he and those with him were the intended targets. Flag planted, job done, the artillery and creeping mortar barrage came ever closer and with no cover available, he sought permission to move off the hill. After what seemed an eternity permission to move was granted. Relieved, they lost no time in re-joining their main body at the east end checkpoint area.

Now dark, the South Lebanese twilight is not one that lingers, Captain Ainsworth distributed night vision equipment among his reinforcements. Suddenly he hears an incoming round arriving and they all dive for cover. It explodes in the field beside him but some distance off: 'It was a tremendous eruption, but also one with a difference. I look over the wall, a phosphorus round. The bastards, I think to myself as I watched the fireball burning brightly, an incendiary glowing in the night.' Then he hears another one in the air, and drops immediately onto the roadway. The round is on its own trajectory and its landing arbitrary. His life relying on random chance and circumstance, proximity to the round's killing radius is the intermediary between life and death. The next few seconds uncertain, the outcome would be decided by fluke or fate. Lying face down on the roadway it passes overhead and explodes 100 metres away in a suddenly burning blast of energy, an instantaneous flash of orange-red flame giving way to a continuous glaring blaze of brightness. Then a lull, the relative silence broken only by the sound of small arms fire. He gets up, lets out a huge sigh of relief and appreciates the narrow line between reassuring reality and awful oblivion. This ease is only fleeting however as he hears another incoming round:

> Exasperated and panic stricken. I jump off the road. The noise grows louder. I land on the ground, possessed by fear. I think this time I am a goner. I try to move but my legs are stuck. I feel pain. I bend down and feel barbed wire. I realise I have jumped into all the wire I got my troops to lay five days earlier. The noise of the incoming mortar round gets louder. I feel helpless. After all I have seen and gone through during the week, to be now stuck in wire, not able to move, nowhere to go, just to wait. I lean back and feel the wall. I wait. The round lands and explodes. I'm not hit. I'm lucky again. I looked out into the darkness of the wadi facing me, it was pitch black, a lull envelopes the village. I leant back on to the wall and wondered for a moment when will this nightmare cease. I am tired, disoriented, gripped by the cold water of fear. Day seven, what more can happen, what next? [After] what felt like ages, I eventually free myself and in the darkness I stumble along parallel to the wall. Total silence, surreal, [just] me and myself locked in a moment in time. Then I hear a human voice calling out my name. I say 'yes', snapped back to reality again [as] a hand grasps out to me in the darkness and pulls me up onto the road at Checkpoint 6-15A. Back into the safety of the Irish sandbagged position

amongst friends. Safe once again my pal Lieutenant Johnny Molloy hands me a cigarette.

For Captain Adrian Ainsworth and all those at At-Tiri, the week had presented a rainbow of realities, and it wasn't just for those in the village. News was received that Sergeant John Power and his crew in OP Ras within the Enclave were continuing to come under small arms and HMG fire. News next of a message received from UNIFIL Ops to the Irish battalion from Major Haddad: 'Four Irish Batt soldiers detained by villagers of Aynata and because Irish Batt fired on women and children I (Haddad) will be unable to prevent villagers from taking revenge. Prisoners held by Irish Batt must be returned at Saff al-Hawa by 1900 hours.' Then the mortaring ceased.

Was this the moment for the DFF counterattack? Reinforcements arrived from Irish Battalion and were deployed into new positions reinforcing the perimeter around the environs of the village in order to defend against any DFF incursions during the night. The UNIFIL Force Mobile Reserve, reinforced throughout the day, had redeployed into the Irish battalion area and the Force Commander had arrived in Haddata. It had been an extraordinary day for the Irish, for UNIFIL and for the UN. How was it to end?

Nightmare at Naqoura

Saturday, 12 April 1980

With At-Tiri lost and the DFF pushed out and defeated, reprisal shelling started immediately with a militia mortar bombardment launched upon the village. Concurrently the coastal village of Naqoura, forty kilometres or so away where UNIFIL HQ was located, was also selected for mortar and small arms attack. Isolated from the rest of the peacekeeping force, Naqoura was within the Israeli-controlled Enclave on the shores of the Mediterranean. UNIFIL HQ was built around a former Lebanese customs and immigration post for movements between Israel and Lebanon and the DFF maintained a number of strongpoints on high ground and on the nearby roads around the UN headquarters. As a result they were capable of cutting off access to the camp and could confine the personnel there as virtual hostages. The main IDF/DFF positions were at the Israeli border (the Armistice Demarcation Line of 1949) at Rosh Hanikra and at the checkpoint on the road to Tyre known as the Charlie Swing gates. During the Irish tour of duty these two positions were frequently closed, cutting off freedom of movement and isolating personnel at UNIFIL HQ.

The ill-disciplined DFF proved volatile and unpredictable, and this led to a constant undercurrent of tension between the militia and UNIFIL. With the ongoing confrontation in At-Tiri, this tension had increased considerably during the course of the past week and on 12 April 1980 the DFF launched a continuous and indiscriminate mortar and small arms attack on UNIFIL HQ. This lengthy revenge attack for the loss of At-Tiri commenced mid-afternoon and continued for four and a half hours. One prefabricated accommodation block was completely burnt out and the Irish HQ Camp Commandants Office and Orderly Room, as well as the neighbouring Post Exchange (PX, the base shopping centre), were damaged beyond repair by additional mortar fire. Twenty-one other prefabricated buildings were hit by small arms fire or shrapnel, and mortar rounds impacted and penetrated the concrete roof of the logistics stores in the HQ Compound. UNIFIL's medevac capability, often used to assist Lebanese locals, was lost when three of the four Italair Bell helicopters were damaged by small arms fire and rendered unserviceable. Stores, spare parts and communications equipment were damaged and the plumbing and electrical infrastructure were hit.

Ten vehicles, including a fire fighting truck, were destroyed and the Norwegian doctors, nurses and medical staff had to move their patients, some of whom had been wounded in At-Tiri during the week, into shelters where they continued to treat them throughout the shelling. Although the possibility of adding to the list of wounded was high, no other significant injuries were suffered. French Lieutenant Colonel De La Forge, from UNIFIL HQ Logistics Branch, was hit in the forehead by shrapnel and he was carried, bleeding profusely, to safety by Irish Captain Paddy Gore, who gave him first aid. However, with the remainder of the contingent's personnel taking to the bunkers, and as the attack occurred on a Saturday, when few civilian UN staff members were present in Naqoura, casualties were light. As Captain Gore recalls:

> While [we were] eating lunch, heavy gunfire blew away the side of the cookhouse. We made a hasty retreat out through the door and window and sought shelter down on the beach. From here we could see and hear heavy gunfire and mortar bombs hitting the water some 100 metres away, zeroing in on the UNIFIL HQ Compound and old custom house. We started to move up the beach towards the shelter using movement drills, as there were a lot of openings onto the beach down from the hills [and] we were not armed. On reaching the shelter it was packed to capacity. When the firing ceased and things seemed safer we moved out of the bunker. There was considerable damage. A while later further shooting rained down on our location, hitting the Assistant Chief Logistics Officer, a French Lieutenant Colonel De La Forge. He was hit, as far as I can remember, on the side of his head and fell near me. He was bleeding heavily [so] I gave him a fireman's lift and brought him into the duty room to administer basic first aid. It turned out not to be a serious wound. After that things began to quieten down and we began to assess the damage and fallout.

This was a cowardly attack by the DFF since UNIFIL HQ was not a location where operational troops, manoeuvrable platoons or quick reaction forces were located, rather the mission's headquarters contained command and control staffs, administrative offices and logistical support facilities and had only a small defence platoon for local protection.

Irish personnel and members of the International (UNIFIL) Military Police Company assisted the Ghanaian defence platoon and took up defence of the UNIFIL HQ compound and nearby Camp Tara while the French Logistic Battalion secured their own area. Irish Captain Dermot Sherrif, with the International (UNIFIL) Military Police Company, remembers:

> Once the initial sniping started we noticed the few local workers who were in on the Saturday began leaving the Compound and so we suspected something was up. This was confirmed soon after when the mortars started coming in. They were falling perfectly sequentially, in an ordered creeping barrage, their impacts moving steadily up along the compound in an almost perfect pattern. We

watched the fall of shot and later went out to mark the 'blinds', those that failed to explode, for demolition afterwards. We went out among the buildings to make sure what was being left undamaged was secure. I remember we found $1,500 in the cash register of the international canteen and secured it.

During the barrage it was decided not to call in the 120mm rifled heavy mortars from the Dutch Battalion because of the possibility of some of the mortar shells falling wide and impacting on innocent civilians in the villages of Naqoura and Alma Achaab.

Over the following days the Irish personnel in the UNIFIL HQ contingent and those from other Battalions in Naqoura became involved in a clean-up operation, making damaged buildings habitable and reinforcing defensive positions and shelters. Word was received that further attacks would be launched and a number of days later an Irish sandbagging party at Camp Tara, within UNIFIL HQ, came under fire. No one was injured and work continued under cover and concealment. Thereafter work in exposed areas was carried out during the hours of darkness.

De-escalation

The DFF had been pushed out of At-Tiri and they were not happy about it. Their response had been immediate and widespread with At-Tiri village subjected to a violent bombardment and UNIFIL HQ, some forty kilometres to the south, coming under sustained attack for four and a half hours. An apparent build up for a possible ground counter attack on At-Tiri was also in the offing so elements of the FMR, redeployed to the far side of Hill 880, remained there on stand-by to meet this threat. The situation was once again finely poised and very tense. Shortly before midnight on 12 April 1980, the Irish Battalion radio network sprang to life with an all stations message: 'All stations, all stations, this is zero, a cease fire has been agreed.'

High-level liaison had succeeded in bringing an end to hostilities and it was now important to remove from the scenario as much of the military means as possible. Throughout the early-morning hours both sides withdrew their reinforcements in response and on completion the way was clear for an agreed exchange of prisoners. This was effected with the involvement of United Nations Truce Supervision Organisation, Observer Group Lebanon (UNTSO OGL) personnel and supervised amidst a throng of media. The stricken DFF half-track was also handed back. The guns had fallen silent. Almost. Within the hour, and for over thirty minutes, some 250 militia HMG rounds were reported fired into the general area of At-Tiri, targets unknown. Post 6-24 (OP Ras), which was still holding out, similarly reported the firing of almost 100 HMG rounds in their vicinity, targets unknown. After that, with no further rounds being fired, the situation in At-Tiri was restored to that existing a week before. At first light Officer Commanding C Company, Commandant Dave Taylor, along with the C Company reserve withdrew from At-Tiri over Hill 880 back to Haddata. Calm was restored to the area once more.

When news of the cease fire reached the Irish battalion it was met with huge relief, a release from anxiety and a deliverance from tension. The occasion did not excite euphoria or triumphalism, nor was there any exuberant delight as such. Rather there was a shared sense that the Irish had delivered on their mission. The taking back of At-Tiri was extraordinary and there was pride in this and how it was achieved. In the end the Irish action was direct, dramatically so, but not before they had turned the other cheek and given suitable warnings. The Irish peacekeepers had shown the utmost restraint and they had fired well-aimed containing shots along walls that were being used for cover by the DFF, though there was the occasional splintering of a door post or window frame. When it came to the final fire fight, they showed utmost control. Little did the DFF realise that among the Irish troops were some of the best shots with open iron sights in the Defence Forces. Most were members of An Chéad Chathlán Coisithe, 1st Battalion, the Irish language speaking unit from Mellow Barracks Renmore Galway. Many of Lieutenant Tom Aherne's platoon were successful competition shots, and of course there was Captain Eamon 'Ned' Kelly, revered then and for a long while after in Defence Forces shooting circles as one of the greats of his era with the FN rifle, the Gustav sub-machine gun and Browning automatic pistol.

With the village now returned to full Irish control and reinforcements from both sides removed, At-Tiri became once again relatively quiet.

But success has a price, and this included threats of acts of reprisals from Major Haddad. There was also an unusual report that a court of inquiry was being called for by the UNIFIL Force Commander, General Erskine. It was to be presided over by a Canadian officer from the UN Disengagement Observer Force (UNDOF) in the Golan, but it was also suggested that Major Saad Haddad would also serve on the board of inquiry. Lieutenant Colonel Jack Kissane, Officer Commanding 46th Battalion, immediately stated that no member of the Irish battalion would ever take part in such an inquiry. There was none.

With the adrenaline rush of a chaotic week over and mixed feelings of relief and pride notwithstanding, for Lieutenant Tom Aherne there was a strong sensation of once again being alone and a sudden stark awareness of isolation descended on him. He was now facing a different challenge altogether, one of an unexpectedly pronounced desolation:

> This was the most difficult time for me as I was left on my own in the village and I knew it could start all over again. I met the local mukhtar, who told me the villagers were having a problem getting kerosene as the DFF were stopping them from going to the next village. He also matter-of-factly told me, [somewhat] forebodingly, [that] they had been offered (by the DFF) a huge sum of money for the body of an Irish soldier!

In Cold Blood

18 April 1980

Revenge, the thirst for the settling of human scores through blood-for-blood retaliation, eye-for-an-eye reprisal and a tooth-for-a-tooth retribution, was a highly held and much believed in tenet of the cultural credo in the Middle East, one that had suddenly become personal to Mahmoud Bazzi from Blinda. A week earlier his brother, Massoud Bazzi, was the militiaman killed in an exchange of gunfire between the DFF and the Irish during the wrangle for At-Tiri. Bazzi, himself from within the DFF, believed in this tradition of '*sulha*', the traditional Arab form of conflict resolution by exacting a penalty of death for a killing or the payment of money without further loss of life. Bazzi, however, sought satisfaction to this so-called 'blood feud' with the Irish through murderous means.

Still holding out against the DFF without relief, the Irish personnel at OP Ras needed evacuation. Around mid-day on 18 April 1980, a prearranged convoy, 'Team Zulu', led by the United Nations Observer Group in Lebanon (UNOGL) headed into the Enclave to effect this. The unarmed UN officers from UNOGL were Major Harry Klein of the US Army and the French officer, Captain Patrick Vincent. They were accompanied by American Press reporter Steve Hindy and Lebanese photographer Zavan Vartam. Three Irish battalion drivers were required and Privates John O'Mahoney, Derek Smallhorne and Thomas Barrett were made available.

Organised by UNIFIL HQ and coordinated with UNOGL and IDF/DFF contacts, this liaison was necessary and important in respect of any UN attempted activities in the Enclave, the Israeli Controlled Area (ICA) of South Lebanon. Effective liaison was paramount, especially with respect to the specific and significant nature of this kind of precise undertaking about to be attempted. These very necessary contacts, communications, understandings, agreements and coordinated arrangements would need to be very firm, and the people identified to carry them out needed to be responsible.

From the off, the first scheduled rendezvous (RV) did not materialise as prearranged and the DFF escort was not at the designated meeting place. Abu Askander did not show up at the Bayt Yahun crossroads checkpoint and it was also ominous that no sentries were present. The UN convoy waited for a DFF escort to arrive and when none did, Major Harry Klein's fateful decision to proceed set in train a tragic sequence of events. He decided that the UN convoy ought to continue unescorted towards Saff al-Hawa, and unaccompanied they progressed deeper into the Enclave. The further the UN convoy progressed, the deeper into difficulty they were getting. Arriving at the DFF checkpoint near Saff al-Hawa gave further cause for unease. Usually a well-manned checkpoint, which would frequently host a DFF half-track, on this occasion there was only one sentry, who waved them through unhindered.

Beyond Saff al-Hawa, a blue Peugeot car was seen approaching the convoy from ahead. At the wheel was a moustached man with a noticeable patch of white in the middle of a head of black, slicked back hair. This was Mahmoud Bazzi. Driving initially in the opposite direction to the convoy, once he had passed by Bazzi did a U-turn in the road and followed them from behind. Close to the village of Ras, a group of young men armed with Kalashnikov AK-47 rifles suddenly appeared on the road in front of the convoy. The trap was sprung and the convoy halted, surrounded. The occupants were ordered out, captured and driven away, they had been out-gunned, out-numbered and out-manoeuvred. The three Irish drivers only had two weapons between them, an FN rifle and a Gustav sub-machine gun, which were also seized by the DFF.

The convoy personnel were taken to a bombed-out school in the village of Ras where the Irish troops were singled out and led away towards stairs leading to a basement. Bazzi, wearing a black undershirt symbolising 'death', picked up Private Tom Barrett's sub-machine gun and opened fire, wounding Private John O'Mahoney who fell, but missing the other two drivers. Wounded and lying on the staircase, Private John O'Mahoney was again fired on by Bazzi and hit once more. Meanwhile, Privates Derek Smallhorne and Thomas Barrett fled downstairs to escape Bazzi and his band of belligerents. They did not get far, and recaptured outside they were quickly bundled back into the blue Peugeot and driven off to be murdered in cold blood.

Meanwhile, Private O'Mahoney, assisted by the non-Irish convoy personnel, was helped up the stairs and put into a local Mercedes which took him back to Bayt Yahun. He was quickly transferred to the UN helicopter pad inside the Norwegian Maintenance Company (NorMain Coy) in Tebnine, opposite the Irish battalion HQ, Camp Shamrock, and flown to the newly-repaired Norwegian Field Hospital in Naqoura where he was treated and survived.

With all access to the AO closed off after the events at At-Tiri, rendering collection and delivery of food and stores impossible, Captain Paddy Gore, based at UNIFIL HQ in Naqoura, was dispatched by the Chief Logistics Officer to go through Syria to Beirut to organise deliveries of food from Lebanon. Four days later, having successfully put a workable alternative in place, he was returning down the coast road from Beirut and nearing Naqoura was stopped by a DFF patrol. As they did not speak English and his Irish shoulder flash insignia having broken off some days earlier they were unaware of his nationality.

Among the militiamen a young teenager pressed his AK-47 rifle against Captain Gore's neck for some five minutes. Employed as a local worker in Captain Gore's office in Naqoura, the teenager recognised him but said nothing and the patrol let him go. On arriving back in Naqoura, Captain Gore met Lieutenant Billy Harrington who wanted to know where he had been. He then informed Captain Gore that three Irish peacekeepers had been shot that day in 'the hills'.

Being soldiers as well as peacekeepers and being human as well as being soldiers, a man remained a man even after he puts on a uniform and the murders of their comrades provoked a strong reaction amongst the Irish. 'With their packs on, weapons in hand, they fall in, prepared, ready, waiting, wanting, to go back over the Hill (880) and when held in check from doing so, couldn't see why not.' Captain Noel Byrne's experience in 'Recce' Company echoed such thoughts, occupying the minds of many Irish soldiers that night but none were publicly expressed. In response to a message from the UN Force Commander, General Erskine, asking that the Irish Battalion should not retaliate, Lieutenant Colonel Jack Kissane replied: 'We are a disciplined and professional army, and we will behave like one.'

The manner of the deaths of the two Irish soldiers at the hands of the DFF, and the wounding of Private O'Mahoney, shocked Irish and international opinion. The Secretary General of the UN, Dr Kurt Waldheim, immediately expressed his 'shock and outrage' at their 'murder in cold blood ... by DFF' and Irish/Israeli relations, already tense, reached an all-time low. The murders focussed attention on the difficult role UNIFIL was being asked to perform and the Irish government launched a diplomatic offensive to press Israel to withdraw support from the DFF. An emergency meeting of the Irish government to discuss the situation in Lebanon ruled out any possibility of withdrawing Irish troops from UNIFIL. A statement said that a precipitous withdrawal could have consequences at a time of heightened international tension. The statement also supported the Security Council decision that the peacekeeping force should take immediate and total control of its Area of Operations.

The Israelis denied that they were in any way responsible for the murders and attributed blame on the so-called 'blood feud'. The Israeli Defence Forces even went to the trouble of organising a special news conference in Bint Jbeil, Major Haddad's stronghold in South Lebanon. The murder of the two Irish soldiers had demonstrated to the world the ill-disciplined and criminal nature of Major Haddad's militia. Nevertheless, the Israelis made it clear that they would continue to support the DFF, a position that was considered 'highly irresponsible' by the Irish Ambassador to Lebanon at that time. Although not referring to the Israelis by name, he was also reported as having said: 'Those who build up the Frankenstein monster and then say they cannot control it, cannot run away from the consequences.'

The murder of Privates Smallhorne and Barrett was also strongly criticised by the US administration and the argument by the Israelis and Major Haddad that this was the outcome of a traditional blood feud involving members of the local population was not accepted in Washington. Prior to the murders, Major Haddad had demanded a ransom of 40,000 Lebanese Pounds or the corpses of two Irish soldiers from the local population. This was to be compensation for the killing of one of his men during the At-Tiri incident and Major Haddad could not now claim he was not responsible for what happened. The Irish government asked the US to put pressure upon Israel to stop supporting the DFF and curb their activities and it was reported that the Taoiseach had written personally to President Carter on the matter. The government also sought the support of the European Community in its campaign to place UNIFIL in full control of its AO, right up to the international frontier with Israeli. The non-Community members also issued a statement condemning recent developments and supporting the call for UNIFIL to take control of all its intended area.

In New York, the UN Secretary General had kept the members of the Security Council informed of the unfolding events in Lebanon and a strong statement (S/13900) was issued on 18 April 1980 after the murder of the two Irish soldiers. Although the statement did not mention Israel by name its message was, nonetheless, clear and unambiguous: 'The Security Council strongly condemns all those who share in the responsibility for this outrageous act. The Council reaffirms its intention to take such determined action as the situation calls for to enable UNIFIL to take immediate and total control of its entire area of operations up to the internationally recognized boundaries.'

Harnessing this world-wide political reaction, an Irish diplomatic initiative was launched. The Irish government held a special meeting on 20 April 1980 and issued a statement which made specific reference to the Security Council's intention to take the necessary action to enable UNIFIL take control of its entire area. The Irish government now looked to the Security Council for this action. It did not want the peacekeeping force to adopt a more aggressive stance, which would be more appropriate to a peace enforcement mission, but the action required under the circumstances had to be of a political and diplomatic nature. It required the cessation of the harassment and attacks on UNIFIL by Major Haddad's DFF and to achieve this the militia had to be deprived of all outside support. The government also sought to arrange an early meeting at Ministerial level with the other troop-contributing countries. The purpose of the meeting was to consider the adequacy of the measures taken by the UN Security Council in ensuring the effectiveness of the force and the safety of its personnel. Determined Irish soldiers had made a brave stand for peace at At-Tiri, now determined Irish politicians and diplomats were making a brave stand for the peacekeepers of UNIFIL.

An Uneasy Peace

Sad and sorrowful, funerals are always distressing. Mourners mark the end of a life and the poignant passing of an individual's physical existence on this earth. Heartbroken family, friends and comrades are left struggling to deal with the shock, the heartfelt emotion and deep grief; the bewilderment of a premature farewell. Loss is uppermost, all the more incomprehensible when unexpected, those left behind coping with the disbelief of the sudden finality. The formality and protocol of a military funeral, with the ceremonial participation of the military band, the uniformed bearer party, the military police pall bearers and the march past, adds to the solemnity of the occasion. With the gravity of the 'last post' sounded by the buglers and the sharp, sudden starkness of the 'shots over the grave' by the firing party, Privates Stephen Griffin, Thomas Barrett and Derek Smallhorne were laid to rest in Galway, Cork and Dublin. There was also mourning by the Sornaivalav family in Fiji and lamentations too for the Christian–Lebanese Bazzi family bemoaning and bewailing their bereavement in Bint Jbeil. After the series of events and incidents, there was a deeply felt sadness throughout the fifty-three Irish battalion posts in the hills of South Lebanon for the casualties they had suffered.

In New York, in the course of the Security Council debate, two draft resolutions were introduced. In both instances the US let it be known that if put to a vote they would have no option but to veto. A third and final draft, adopted as Resolution 467 (1980), was introduced on 24 April 1980, though the US abstained on the voting, along with the USSR and the German Democratic Republic. The Resolution was significant in several respects, it commended the Force for its great restraint in very adverse circumstances and called attention to the provisions of the Mandate that would allow the Force to use its right to self-defence. This was a very significant provision and was the first time the Security Council found it necessary to make direct reference in this way to the Force's right of self-defence. In essence it was a retrospective approval of the action taken at At-Tiri and supported the use of force by the Irish troops in defence of themselves and their positions. In this regard it was also a reminder to all of the parties concerned, and the Force itself, that this was the appropriate action in the circumstances.

The Resolution also condemned all actions necessary contrary to the provisions of earlier Resolutions on South Lebanon. In particular it strongly deplored 'Israel's military intervention into Lebanon' and the 'provision of military assistance to the so-called "de-facto forces"'. The US abstention on the adoption of Resolution 467 exemplified its policy and attitude to the problem of South Lebanon at the UN. In his memoir, *Keeping Faith*, President Carter later admitted that since direct American interest was primarily concerned with, 'a concerted effort to find a permanent solution to the continuing Lebanese tragedy' no such effort had ever been mounted by the United States. The US continuously sought what it perceived to be a balanced perspective in the resolutions adopted by the Security Council and in this regard it was echoing similar Israeli demands. The US Permanent Representative stated that his country had abstained from voting because the Resolution did not deal with the problem in a balanced or comprehensive way. In this particular instance, the US insisted, the emphasis was on condemnation rather than constructive proposals and it made no reference to the PLO attack on the Misgav Am Kibbutz in northern Israel nor other Palestinian attempts to infiltrate the UNIFIL AO. This was consistent with previous American statements relating to the Middle East question and the UN, and the then view of the US Administration was that parties were also involved in what it termed a 'cycle of violence' and to attribute blame or responsibility to one party reflected an imbalanced and unfair approach. Why should the encroachments by the DFF warrant special attention while the activities of the Palestinians in Lebanon go unmentioned?

It can be argued that the US administration's point of view was justified on certain occasions. In this instance, however, it was not. The DFF had instigated an unprovoked and unwarranted attack on UNIFIL troops in At-Tiri, while the attack on Misgav Am, to which the US administration wanted to refer to and condemn, did not take place until after the militia attack. It had no direct relationship with the events surrounding the At-Tiri incident, which could have precipitated the withdrawal of the Force, and the DFF could not have carried out the attack without the support of Israel. A member of the UN, Israel had chosen to totally disregard the authority of the organisation and was protected in its actions by the US administration. If the threat of the American veto had not existed, the Security Council could have taken action against Israel to ensure compliance with its resolutions. This US policy of the time did not give the peacekeeping force the support it deserved and denied the Security Council the opportunity to do likewise.

After the At-Tiri incident and the 'enclave murders' of the two Irish soldiers, the Irish government called for a ministerial level meeting of UNIFIL troop-contributing countries, at which eleven attended. It was proposed that the meeting be held in Dublin to discuss and assess the situation, but had to keep in mind that there was no formal role for this group in the UN framework, neither executive nor consultative. The lack of a constitutional base meant that they had limited power as a group to influence matters. Prior to the meeting, the Minister for Foreign Affairs announced that Ireland intended to rely on a diplomatic presence to persuade the Israelis to cease supporting Major Haddad's militia. This approach was confirmed when the agreed communiqué was released after the meeting. After the determined stand at At-Tiri and the passing of Resolution 467 (1980), the troops of the Force wanted to see an endorsement of the firm policy adopted by the Security Council. However, the conference's significance fell short of this expectation as no major decisions were taken and any suggestion that the peacekeeping role of UNIFIL be changed to a peace-enforcing one was ruled out. In the words of Ireland's Foreign Minister, there was 'absolutely unanimity on peacekeeping'. There was also a thinly veiled threat to withdraw the troops if the situation did not improve. The actual text of the communiqué on this point stated that 'unless rapid progress is made in the creation of conditions in which the Force can operate more safely and effectively, including adequate international protection and immunity for its personnel, its continued viability may be brought into question'.

This threat could not be taken lightly, though at the same time it was not an ideal means of putting pressure on the Israelis and the DFF and in certain instances it could be counter-productive. Major Haddad had often expressed his desire to get the Irish, and UNIFIL in general, out of South Lebanon and if he considered that putting more pressure on the Force could precipitate a withdrawal then he was likely to do just that. Despite this obvious danger, the ministers saw it as their only effective means of putting real pressure on the Israelis to curb the activities of the DFF. Although the Israelis were often critical of the Force, they were also pragmatists. They realised that there were more benefits than disadvantages from UNIFIL's presence in Lebanon. The danger in this premise was that once they changed their minds and decided otherwise, diplomatic pressure and threats to withdraw would mean nothing. There was also evidence within Israel that the diplomatic offensive and bad publicity as a result of the At-Tiri incident was causing some Israelis to question the official government policy on Major Haddad and Lebanon. Soon afterwards the intentions of the Israeli government were made clear when a Foreign Ministry official stated that 'we will use our own influence to alleviate tension between Haddad and the UN Forces but we cannot see our way to removing support for him'.

Despite this, the defence of At-Tiri was a watershed in relations between UNIFIL and the De Facto Forces. The initial refrain from returning fire was not a continuation of the 'kid-gloves' compromise approach but an awareness by the Irish commander on-ground that it was not appropriate to do so until his troops were in reasonable positions from which they could return fire and when it became evident there would not be a negotiated solution to the impasse. Then restrained small arms fire was resorted to in self-defence and this only escalated to the use of heavy weapons on the order of the local Irish commander. The restrained and firm reaction to the incursion proved to the DFF that UNIFIL was committed to the defence of its AO and helped achieve an uneasy peace for a short period between UNIFIL and those forces. An official 'understanding' was arrived at, that the peacekeeping force was prepared to use the necessary means to defend itself and carry out its duties. It also focussed attention on the predicament of the peacekeeping Force and Israel's continued support of the DFF.

The At-Tiri incident brought about the consequent adoption of Resolution 467 (1980) which made specific reference to UNIFIL's right to use force in self-defence. Matched with political consensus and will, the subsequent potential to provide UNIFIL with sufficient authority to adopt a firmer stance toward the DFF and armed elements was a distinct possibility. That this was beyond the political considerations and circumstances UNIFIL found itself in was not a reflection on the peacekeeping force. In his report on UNIFIL for the first six months of 1980, the UN Secretary General went on to state: 'A peacekeeping operation must achieve its major objectives through means other than the use of force, and this consideration certainly applies to UNIFIL ... I believe that the main road to full implementation of the UNIFIL mandate lies in a political and diplomatic effort.'

In the latter part of 1980, the DFF continued to resist further deployment of UNIFIL and continued their attempts at encroaching upon their Area of Operations. Despite the events of the year and the continuous requests by the Secretary General, co-operation between the parties concerned was not forthcoming. The Secretary General's policy regarding UNIFIL was the only one feasible under the circumstances. UNIFIL's effectiveness as a peacekeeping force depended primarily on gaining co-operation, while its survival depended on its remaining impartial and uninvolved in Lebanon's factional wars. In a situation as volatile as South Lebanon, the continued existence of the peacekeeping force reflected the realism and political astuteness of the Secretary General and the military commanders charged with implementing the mandate on the ground.

In the early years, UNIFIL was never allowed to completely exercise its mandate and was harassed on an ongoing basis by Palestinian armed groups and by the Israeli-sponsored DFF militia. The meeting in Dublin of representatives of the troop-contributing nations after the At-Tiri incident and the killing of three Irish soldiers acted as a wake-up call to the UN in this regard and better procedures for liaison between it and the troop-contributing nations were put in place. Ireland, a small nation on a big UN-backed stage had made its mark yet again. The At-Tiri incident was further testament to Ireland's commitment to the United Nations and to the cause of international peace. It is a record, one involving sacrifice, of which the Irish nation can be justifiably proud.

Battalion Second-in-Command Commandant Michael Minehane, later Major General and Force Commander UNIFICYP (April 1992–August 1994), summed up matters as follows:

> When we arrived to Lebanon in November 1979 we knew of the possibilities of trouble. We had been aware of the difficulties experienced by our predecessors. We little thought that we would be tested in the way we were by the Israelis and their agent Haddad, to the point of losing lives. That we were was greatly regretted by all at the Battalion HQ. At great cost we disabused a heavily armed opponent of any suggestion that we were a soft touch. We put some backbone into a UN peacekeeping force that had been pushed around by the Israelis since 1978.

Strange Soldiering

The 'At-Tiri Incident', or as it was initially referred to later the 'Battle of At-Tiri', had violently erupted into open hostility when the 'strange soldiering' of peacekeeping had to incrementally transform into no-holds-barred 'solid soldiering' needed to preserve the peace. The Irish soldier serving as peacekeeper appreciates that it is the dogged perseverance of the impartially-applied policy of 'Patience, Persistence, Persuasion' that is the essence of peacekeeping. The Irish peacekeeper – professional, disciplined, experienced, even-handed and friendly – had sometimes suffered criticism by observers for their approach to peacekeeping in South Lebanon in that their policy of negotiation and persuasion could be misinterpreted as a weak 'kid-glove' approach by certain parties. However, this was more a reflection that the promised co-operation with UNIFIL from parties to the conflict was not forthcoming.

The 'Battle of At-Tiri' was an important early incident during the Irish battalion's long and continuing UNIFIL chapter. The determined Irish-led reaction to the attack on At-Tiri village was a crucial moment in UNIFIL's history, and a particularly salient one within the Defence Forces overseas story to date. The explanation and illumination of its causes, course and consequences epitomises the sometimes dramatic dilemmas faced by Irish peacekeepers and the often onerous nature of peacekeeping in its performance. At the time, At-Tiri and its loss could have caused a momentous shift in the high-stakes struggle for stability throughout South Lebanon itself. Not only was the victory tactically vital, but it was hugely strategically and symbolically significant also. It granted the view that the UN force had grown in stature and was willing and able to give militarily to back itself politically. The initial Irish disciplined restraint at At-Tiri, then a strong show of force and a determined stand, marked a significant change in their policy towards DFF incursions and encroachments and led directly to the UN Security Council adopting Resolution 467 (1980).

The Irish Battalion AO has always been one of UNIFIL's most active and difficult. Its policy of 'Patience, Persistence, Persuasion' was important in maintaining an impartial role on its patch of mountainous Middle Eastern terrain. Interposed between the warring parties in 'the hills' of South Lebanon, parties whose activities had such an adverse effect on the normal lives of the local people, the Irish battalion had sometimes to cope with intimidation and coercion from either or both sides that on occasion resulted in tense stand-offs, troublesome stalemates and dangerous confrontations.

Lieutenant Tony Bracken, serving twelve years later in the autumn and winter of 1992 with UNIFIL's Force Mobile Reserve, met among the constituent Fijian platoon also deployed there a Sergeant named Ben Cati. He had been a young private in 1980 and was a member of the Fijian mortar platoon at At-Tiri. The surprise and coincidence of meeting another national who had shared the experience was in itself unique and pleasing, but when he told Lieutenant Bracken of the importance of the incident to the Fijian Army and its lore, he was flabbergasted.

So proud are they of their association with the Irish during the 'At-Tiri Incident' that by 1992 the Warrant Officer commanding the mortar platoon had achieved iconic status, been promoted to the rank of Major and posted to their Military Academy. The Fijians had also written a battle song to mark their participation in the incident. The context and importance of such a composition in the Fijian Army is quite different to other military forces because they are such wonderful singers, both individually and chorally. Any such commemorative songs would be widely known and performed regularly across the service.

Lieutenant Johnny Molloy didn't have the heart to return the borrowed, bullet-riddled, jumper to Lieutenant Ger Ahern and still has it, something he continues to smile about. On arrival back to Ireland, Trooper 'TC' Martin, the AML 90 armoured car driver, stopped off in Kill Church, County Kildare, while making his way home from Dublin Airport. There he lit the twelve candles, as he had promised, not telling his accompanying parents exactly why for a number of years afterwards.

Afterword

In June 1982, the Israeli Minister for Defence, Ariel Sharon, directed the Israeli army to mount 'Operation Peace for Galilee', the second invasion of Lebanon. Its stated objective was the destruction of all Palestinian guerrilla bases in South Lebanon. Its less obvious purpose, however, called 'Operation Snowball', had a twofold aim: to set up a right-wing pro-Israeli government in Beirut, and to break the will of the Palestinians in the West Bank by dispersing the PLO leadership. Although this full-scale invasion forced most of Arafat's Palestinian guerrillas out of Lebanon, it resulted in Israel's prolonged military occupation of the country. Inevitably, come time for the Israeli army's withdrawal, made under pressure, roadside bombs and suicide bomb attacks became the standard reaction from the emergent Lebanese Shia Amal and Hezbollah activists. As the Israeli army withdrew southwards in the spring of 1985, these activities moved with them.

It was five years and ten Irish battalions later, and now the 56th Irish Battalion had to contend with the newly developing situation. There were indicators that the Israelis wished to establish a new Enclave line forward of the existing one, and the question was where exactly would it be placed, as clearly the existing line was now tactically unsound in many areas. This question also had ominous implications for the Irish battalion, since its area contained many of the key villages and terrain on which Israeli military and surveillance positions could be sited. Emphasis was placed on the need for even greater security and readiness, as it was evident that tensions would rise in the wake of the Israeli army's close concentration on the villages and hilltop features adjacent but forward of the current Enclave line. A significantly changed military scenario to that five years previously now prevailed: the tactical situation was fluid not fixed and the Israeli army was inside the UNIFIL AO in South Lebanon, beyond the Litani river and operating up to and inside Beirut. In short, they were in occupation of Lebanon.

It was also now a situation characterised by movement. The Israeli army and its security services carried out searches and snatched suspect persons, surrounded villages and removed suspect youths and men for interrogation and blew up houses of those suspected of involvement. There was also movement southwards of massive Israeli army columns, beginning the withdrawal of war-weary soldiers back to Israel and the Israeli-controlled area. There is nothing more vulnerable or vicious than an army in retreat. Within their own AO the 56th Irish Battalion were active, checking many of these dubious Israeli actions, and some inevitable confrontation followed. Behind both the present and the potentially new Enclave lines, the Israeli army did not want impartial European troops watching their behaviour, monitoring their movements and trying to establish the sovereignty of the Lebanese government in an area in which the Israeli army wanted their own militias to hold sway. Thus firing on Irish troops became a near nightly occurrence.

As the Israeli army's phased withdrawal had gathered considerable momentum, the question for the Irish Battalion was which of the dominated 'high places', or which ridge of hills, would be chosen by the Israelis as key terrain? Would it be the one inclusive of Tebnine where the Crusader castle, Toron, was already in use as an observation post, or that with Hill 880 and six one-niner Charlie (619C)? For the Israelis, this militarily stronger and extended Enclave line must surely encompass both hilltop positions. Debate on the issue ended when in mid-April 1985, a massive Israeli bulldozer and M113 armoured personnel carriers moved onto Hill 880. They were subsequently joined by the Irish and a tense stand-off began, ending only when instructions to cease contention were received from UNIFIL HQ. Hill 880 was now in Israeli hands and 619C would be next. The new Enclave line was being established and another new and different phase for UNIFIL to negotiate was about to begin.

There would be other challenging phases, dilemmas and dramas as the operational situation ebbed and flowed and otherwise evolved over the years. The common sense approach of forty-seven successive Irish battalions over twenty-three years continued. Their sensitive integration and their consistent adaptation to the evolving operational environment meant they were able to provide a valuable contribution to UNIFIL's stabilising presence in the midst of the various militias, upheavals, uncertainties and tensions. Forty-four Irish soldiers died in Lebanon, one, Private Kevin Joyce, remains missing. In November 2001, the 89th Irish Battalion, their tour over, withdrew with dignity, and with their departure the Irish involvement in UNIFIL ceased. Individual members of the 46th Battalion were to return to serve within other Irish UNIFIL battalions, each different from the previous. Warfare is as old as history, while peacekeeping is a modern phenomenon. The UNIFIL mission was difficult and showed that in order to keep the peace you must have it first, and the parties to the conflict must contribute to achieving that state of affairs. This was largely absent in Lebanon and UNIFIL was never to completely exercise its mandate, being harassed on an ongoing basis by armed groups and Israeli-sponsored militias.

The UN force in South Lebanon was often criticised for not achieving anything, yet UNIFIL was neither a combat nor a diplomatic agency. Instead it could be best described as a conflict-control presence whose strength was in holding ground and negotiating and the Irish had been particularly good at it. Their success may be best measured by imagining what would have happened if they weren't there, if they hadn't maintained impartiality and been even-handed. This stabilising contribution by UNIFIL positively influenced the situation, with Irish Battalion providing a degree of normalisation for the people in their area. Realising this meant that many Irish soldiers continued to return there to serve as peacekeepers. In short, they saved lives.

The Irish packed up their equipment and effected their withdrawal as part of the reduction of the overall UNIFIL force, which took place because of the Israeli government's decision in May 2002 to unilaterally withdraw its army from the buffer zone along its northern border inside Lebanon. The withdrawal followed a bloody conflict with the Lebanese Amal and later Hezbollah guerrilla forces. Hezbollah's military wing, the Islamic Resistance, had become increasingly efficient at attacking the Israeli Defence Forces and its new local surrogate militia, the South Lebanon Army (SLA). The increasingly deadly Hezbollah actions in the late 1990s on the IDF earthen-banked compound fortresses dotted along the ridge lines on the buffer zone, including Hill 880, created pressure within Israel for a withdrawal. That was finally agreed to under the leadership of Israeli Prime Minister, Ehud Barak, who was also a former Chief of Staff of the IDF.

The withdrawal from Lebanon was a politically risky move for Barak's government, but it took place alongside the peace agreement with the Palestinian leadership of Yasser Arafat and amid hopes for a permanent peace settlement in the Middle East. Barak, one of the most decorated soldiers in the Israeli military, knew personally of the horror and tragedy in Lebanon. He had served in the thick of the Israeli invasion and bloody warfare of the early 1980s, eventually withdrawing to their expanded border 'security zone'. The UN Security Council in New York passed resolutions calling for a complete Israeli withdrawal. Israel, until Barak, had consistently ignored resolutions asking it to withdraw and the security zone remained in place for more than fifteen years.

Typically, Hezbollah or Amal would launch surprise attacks on Israeli or SLA positions and compounds, striking fiercely then withdrawing quickly into the deeply ravined terrain. The Israelis would then respond with artillery barrages and aerial bombing. In the centre of these often stood UNIFIL and the Irish battalions. Hezbollah rocket attacks on northern Israeli towns had on two occasions precipitated massive retaliatory bombardments of the South Lebanese countryside, and 'Operation Accountability' (1993) and 'Operation Grapes of Wrath' (1996) were launched in an effort to drive out Hezbollah fighters who were becoming increasingly effective in their attacks against SLA compounds and IDF patrols. These huge savage and sustained artillery and aerial bombardments delivered death and destruction and sent upwards of 300,000 people to seek refuge from the havoc.

Those suddenly and shockingly displaced gradually returned and when it came four years later, after a prolonged and intense campaign of harassment witnessed by increasingly deadly and sophisticated Islamic Resistance onslaughts, the final, complete and total Israeli withdrawal was sudden and with little bloodshed. Hezbollah had pre-negotiated the return of the Lebanese displaced from the Security Zone and these mainly elderly men and women returned to their villages and homes for the first time in more than twenty years. Among them were grandchildren who had never seen their ancestral homes, At-Tiri included. That there was an At-Tiri to return to at all was only because the few old people who had stayed clung on, despite repeated hassle and harassment, but did so because they were fed, helped and largely protected by successive Irish battalions.

There is a memory, among those old folks, of Irish battalion deliveries of oil and blankets, of Irish bloodshed among the barren hills, the tobacco fields, the orchards and olive groves for a peace that finally saw UNIFIL fulfil its purpose. Advancing the situation politically and diplomatically is for the politicians and the diplomats. Their failure to do so becomes a matter for the warrior and subsequently the peacekeeper. Too often confrontation is employed instead of common sense; agendas instead of accordance, vested interests instead of mutual interests. It has been, and remains, the sad fate of Lebanon and the Lebanese to be the battleground for the region's belligerents. Foreign involvement made local issues more confused and complicated, more intractable and difficult. In withdrawing their forces back across the border, Israel's eventual compliance with UN Resolutions 425 and 426 meant UNIFIL, under command at the time of Acting Force Commander, Brigadier General Jim Sreenan, later Chief of Staff of the Irish Defence Forces, became heavily involved in the establishment of the 'Blue Line', the dividing line between the two countries based on an internationally recognised border. UNIFIL contingents also moved forward, establishing new positions inside the former Israeli Controlled Area (ICA) and patrolling the Blue Line. A major reorganisation of the UN force also took place that saw a reduction in the number of troops and contingents serving with UNIFIL.

And so ended a major era in the history of the Irish Defence Forces' participation in UN peacekeeping operations. In the future there would be no more involvement in open-ended missions with vague or unenforceable mandates. UNIFIL confirmed Ireland's position as a major player in UN peacekeeping and the experiences gained on that mission were to be drawn on again and again in years to come. A whole generation of Irish soldiers were influenced by their service in Lebanon and a deep bond lasted for many years between them and the people of South Lebanon, with whom they shared many hardships. Throughout the years, while little could be done militarily due to the mandate and the structure of UNIFIL, Irish troops did what they could to protect the ordinary people of South Lebanon and to help them to survive. Service in Lebanon has left its mark, with many still dealing with the pain caused by the deaths of comrades. These memories will take time to heal and the hurt to evaporate.

Peacekeeping is a repetitive business and all too frequently international peacekeeping forces are required to return to the areas in which they previously intervened. While UNIFIL remained after the cessation of the Irish involvement in 2001, it was an involvement renewed in 2006 after the previous year's outbreak of hostilities and the events of that year were similar to those of 1978. Having left Lebanon in 2000, Israel invaded again after Hezbollah carried out a cross-border raid, during which they succeeded in kidnapping two Israeli soldiers. The confrontation escalated and UNIFIL expanded, the cycle was starting all over again. This time the Irish were not lingering and limited their involvement to one year. More recently, since mid-2011, they have become involved for a third time, and at the time of writing (February 2017) are still currently deployed.

Ironically, South Lebanon is the quietest it's ever been for the entire duration of the Irish experience. This is so only because Hezbollah has such a tight grip and with the hostilities in Syria they have enough to deal with elsewhere. Lebanon overall is highly precarious and the situation highly volatile. Sectarian tensions are brimming between Sunni and Shia, though both sides are working hard to keep a lid on the situation before matters reach a tipping point that cannot be rolled back from. As for matters with the Israelis, no one really saw the events of July 2006 coming and essentially it was an incident that went too far and developed into a thirty-four day conflict with Hezbollah. But it is likely there will be another such conflict and both sides are ready for it, though neither want it right now. When the fighting is done the peacekeepers will return, no doubt the Irish amongst them.

In terms of longevity and commitment, UNIFIL is by far the most important overseas mission ever undertaken by the Irish Defence Force: 'UNIFIL I' (1978–2001; twenty-three years in duration with over 30,000 individual tours of duty and 47 lives lost); 'UNIFIL II' (2006–07); and 'UNIFIL III' (2011 to the present day). 'UNIFIL I', 'UNIFIL II' and 'UNIFIL III' are terms by which the Irish Defence Forces refer to their individual durations of participation, and while the UNIFIL mission has been ongoing continuously since 1978, Irish Defence Forces participation in peacekeeping in this area has been ongoing for far longer. On 28 June 1958, the first Irish Peacekeepers led by Lieutenant Colonel Justin McCarthy took up duty on the Lebanese–Syrian border assigned as part of the United Nations Observer Group in Lebanon (UNOGIL).

Since then, not a single day has passed without an Irish soldier manning his or her post, standing guard, observing or patrolling somewhere within the world's most dangerous places. A unique record, it is a noble role and individual members of the Irish Defence Forces are proud of their peacekeeping participation and proud to serve in the role of peacekeeper, one to which the Irish personality is well suited. On the cessation of a tour of duty there are mixed feelings upon leaving Lebanon, with a sense of satisfaction tinged with sadness. This provision of protection, contributing towards building the foundation of normality and stability from the ruins of trouble and turmoil, is a worthy achievement tempered by leaving people with whom you have formed a bond. The task of a peacekeeper is particularly demanding because peacekeeping operations are, by definition, established in areas of conflict where acts of violence and breaches of international and local agreements are daily occurrences.

Peacekeeping is soldiering with a difference and the Irish are good at it. Ireland has established a hard-earned and much envied tradition of being soldiers for peace, one of the cornerstones of which was the At-Tiri action. Upon such incidents, and others before it in the Congo and since in Chad and the Golan, the everyday professional conduct of routine peacekeeping duties over the last sixty years is how a reputation was earned and is maintained. This pursuit has exacted a high price and much sacrifice that must never be forgotten.

PART III
KOSOVO (2004)

CHAPTER 5

Blocking Position

Menacing and determined, the riotous Albanian crowd had emerged from Kosovo's capital, Pristina, and headed south on the highway towards the Serb-populated town of Čaglavica. Energised by exasperation and underpinned by fear and frustration, the crowd had assembled in Pristina and their mood whipped up in a whirlwind of hatred and hysteria. United Nations peacekeepers from Kosovo Force (KFOR), Irish peacekeepers central among them, were hastily deployed to face down the rampaging mob. The crowd's raw anger all too frighteningly evident, pandemonium was about to break loose. The mob hit the KFOR line with formidable energy, an unstoppable force propelled against an immovable object, and a highly fractious clash erupted, a close-quarter, fanatically fought confrontation. Once fighting began it escalated rapidly, with full-on physical contact, heads split, arms broken and no quarter shown. Although they were battered and bruised the Irish line held firm, but for how long could they keep up a controlled peacekeeping response against a sharp upsurge of ethnic violence, tipping a precarious situation, and the Irish with it, deeper into chaos.

The United Nations in Kosovo

Kosovo has been the subject of a territorial dispute between the Republic of Serbia and the self-proclaimed Republic of Kosovo since it declared independence on 17 February 2008. While Serbia still claims it as a part of its own sovereign territory, Kosovo's independence is currently recognised by 114 countries and since the Brussels Agreement of 2013 it has accepted the legitimacy of Kosovo's institutions.

Kosovo is directly translatable into 'the land of blackbirds', and standing in the UN-mandated North Atlantic Treaty Organisation (NATO) Kosovo Force Headquarters (KFOR HQ) in Film City overlooking the capital Pristina, it is easy to understand why. With the early onset of dusk in the autumn and winter afternoons, the black birds come to roost in the trees on the site of the headquarters – thousands of them. Strictly speaking, the black birds you see in Kosovo are crows, rooks and jackdaws, but gathering slowly at first, then ever-increasingly, soon a rippling sea of black birds almost menacingly manifests into an incoherent infinite flock. Swirling, swooping and spiralling haphazardly in disorganised, almost deranged, aerial antics, thousands of black birds dramatically dance and dart across the skyline. Without direction, first one way, then the next, each appears not to know which way is which but none of them want to be left behind. The hugely impressive sight of their frenzied flight is only surpassed by the ear-splitting shrillness of their cacophonous cackle, their penetrating cries a mix of sudden, rapid-fire raucousness.

Equally unsettling is their surprising near silence as they momentarily settle, en masse, on trees, rooftops or along telephone wires. You cannot but wonder what they are thinking as they stare down at you, a hard stare, a kind of all-knowing stare, and if perchance you need to move from one building to another it's easy to feel as if you are running the gauntlet as thousands of black eyes watch you. Then just as suddenly they quickly fly off again, circling and dipping exuberantly in a dizzy, giddy, frantic, frenzied madness before finally coming to roost for the evening among the trees. The hysterical pandemonium to be performed all over again the following morning as they fly off for the day, only to return to repeat their ever-recurring pantomime.

Within line of sight of KFOR HQ, the Gazimestan memorial monument located on Kosovo Polje, literally 'Kosovo Field' or 'Blackbird Field', commemorates the most famous battle in Serbian history, the Battle of Kosovo in 1389. On 28 June 1989, exactly 600 years later in a town of the same name nearest to this 'field of blackbirds', Slobodan Milošević, the power hungry president of Serbia and Chairman of the League of Communists, stirred up memories of this battle, the most seminal moment of Serbian history, using emotive rhetoric. During his speech Milošević deliberately misrepresented the significance of the battle of Kosovo, and based more on myth than reality manufactured a symbolism of 'Serbia for the Serbians'. 'We will not let you be beaten again', Milošević told the Serbian masses, 'we will defend you', and

Irish troops rehearse riot control drills in Kosovo. Courtesy of *An Cosantoir*

the Serbian media further massaged this message, propelling it more powerfully into the mainstream. By presenting Serbian victimisation as the result of poor political leadership, Milošević was seeking power in Serbia by championing Serbs in Kosovo.

There is a long history of conflict between Serbs and Albanians, especially in Kosovo, with ethnic differences in mutually incomprehensible language and lineage at the root of the conflict, which also included differences in religion and tradition. The name, 'Yugoslavia', in itself means 'the Slavs of the South' and the Albanians are not Slavs. The lost Battle of Kosovo of 1389 was fought by an alliance of Serbs and Albanians against the Ottoman Turks. Its subsequent symbolism, however, has a significance other than the factual event upon which it is based. Altogether there has been as much ink used to describe the actual, albeit thoroughly disputed, versions of Kosovo history as blood spilled fighting over it. To understand the historical roots to the conflict in Kosovo you will often have to contend with contradictory, certainly contested, competing and complex Serbian and Kosovar Albanian versions of rival histories, and though they significantly differ in detail, each is deeply believed.

The International Community Intervenes

For a number of years beforehand, informed observers of the Balkans had been warning of a potential conflict in Kosovo. It was in Kosovo that the break-up of Yugoslavia would come into sharp focus, some suggesting the likelihood of a bloodbath. After the First World War, Kosovo became part of the new kingdom of Yugoslavia, then after the Second World War General Josip Tito's communist rule saw it become a province of Serbia. A republic within the federal system, Kosovo enjoyed a degree of autonomy, but in the break-up after the death of Tito ethnic tensions that had for long been kept in check were clinically manipulated and exploited emotionally by Slobodan Milošević in his grab for power. Serb nationalism confronted the 'Albanianisation' of Kosovo, a land considered by Serbs to be the homeland of their nation and on which many of their medieval Orthodox monasteries are located.

The Kosovar Albanians wished to preserve the autonomy that the province had been used to as part of Tito's Yugoslav federal system. However, in 1998 war in Kosovo between the Kosovo Liberation Army (KLA), a guerrilla force formed in the mid-1990s in opposition to Serb rule, and Slobodan Milošević's Yugoslav National Army continued to escalate as his Serbian forces, in a grim and very violent struggle, sought to destroy the KLA and regain control of the province. Bloody and brutal, late 1998 and early 1999 saw a dramatic deterioration and an escalation of the situation with retaliatory expulsion of Kosovar Albanian women and children from their homes in hamlets, villages and towns across the region. There was much looting, house burning, rape of women and the executions of adult males and older boys. In the face of these mass killings, and with a worsening humanitarian situation that saw nearly half a million people internally displaced by the fighting, it became clear that decisive action by the international community, complemented with credible determination to use force to end the killings and abuses being committed, was necessary.

Confronted by widespread ethnic cleansing of Kosovar Albanians by Serbian security forces, an international response not to permit the kind of mass murder of Kosovar Albanian civilians that had previously occurred to civilian Muslims in Bosnia (Srebrenica, 1995) and Croats in Croatia, a 78-day NATO air campaign, 'Allied Force', was launched against the Federal Republic of Yugoslavia (FRY). From 24 March to 12 June 1999, the NATO air campaign inflicted serious damage to Serbia's infrastructure. This led to the signing of the Military Technical Agreement between NATO and the Federal Republic of Yugoslavia on 9 June 1999, whereby Serbian military and paramilitary forces withdrew from Kosovo and NATO forces, along with their Partnership for Peace (PfP) allies, were allowed to enter.

Fighting and peace-making over, it was time for peace enforcement and support operations to begin. On 10 June 1999, United Nations Security Council Resolution 1244 was adopted and two days later the Kosovo Force (KFOR) in 'Operation Joint Guardian' was deployed as the withdrawing Serbian forces returned to Serbia. KFOR was a strong force of 46,000 troops provided by 19 NATO and 19 (non-NATO) contributing nations, including Russia. The Russian contingent of 250 soldiers from the Stabilisation Force (SFOR) in Bosnia surprised everyone with their sudden overland arrival ahead of the main KFOR advance to Slatina Air Base located at Pristina International Airport. KFOR Commander, British Major General Michael Jackson, was to challenge his superior officer, American General Wesley Clark, Supreme Allied Commander Europe (SACEUR), over how to handle the situation.

Fearing that an unnecessarily insensitive confrontation with the Russians might escalate, Major General Jackson famously told General Clark that he was not going to start World War Three for him. As it happened, the Russian interest may well have stemmed not from what lay within Kosovo but underneath it. Although there were no visible telltale signs to suggest it, Slatina Air Base played host to the second-largest underground military aircraft hangar complex of the former Yugoslavia. During the 78-day NATO bombing campaign, before the Yugoslav military withdrawal, this impressive underground hangar facility kept safe and serviced two MiG jet fighter squadrons. There was evidence that NATO had targeted the tunnel entrance, attempting to bomb one of the massive steel doors protecting the 431 metre tunnel, though no significant damage resulted and it was still possible for aircraft to taxi in and out. The squadrons of MiG-21bis and Mig-21UM aircraft suffered no losses, every aircraft remaining intact. Hugely expensive to build, the underground hangar complex was part of General Tito's formidable defence network. The hardware which the complex may have contained was never fully ascertained and has remained the subject of much unresolved speculation ever since.

Meanwhile, KFOR got on with playing its crucial role in contributing towards Kosovo's reconstruction, and the Irish Defence Forces contributed a transport Company to the effort. The responsibilities of this international security presence included deterring renewed hostilities, demilitarising the KLA, establishing a safe and secure environment, ensuring public safety and order, supervising de-mining, supporting and coordinating closely with the work of the international civil presence, conducting border monitoring duties as required, and ensuring the protection and freedom of movement for itself, the international civil presence, and other international organisations. One year after the deployment of KFOR, 1.3 million refugees and displaced persons had returned to their homes, 50,000 houses had been rebuilt, about 1,000 schools had been cleared of mines and ordnance, and the KLA had been demobilised and engaged in a reintegration programme.

One-third the size of Belgium, half the size of Northern Ireland and only slightly larger than Lebanon, Kosovo is a small region less than 11,000 square kilometres or 6,875 square miles. Located on the south east corner of the unstable Balkans, where war has raged every fifty years or so, on its southern border is Macedonia (Former Yugoslavia Republic of Macedonia, or FYROM) which is immediately north of Greece, while a Grecian, Bulgarian and Romanian territorial wraparound on its far southern and eastern frontiers removes Kosovo from the periphery of Europe, placing it more central geographically. Being where it is grants Kosovo geopolitical significance and the international community is regularly tested and actively engaged in preventing ethnically-motivated incidents, both perceived and real, from spiralling into broader tensions in its own back yard. A crucible for crisis, Kosovo has potential for a regional spill over that Europe does not want (centrally) within itself, a region returning to war with resultant refugees pouring across borders.

Though an international peacekeeping presence is permanently fixed there, it is still an eternal source of criminally involved illegal migrants.

Despite its multi-ethnic character, Kosovo is, however, predominately Albanian Muslim, governed in complete separation from Serbia. On the intervention of KFOR, Kosovo was an unfinished, still-fragile tiny state far from ready to stand on its own feet, financially or otherwise. The international community has been attempting to move Kosovo towards a normal state within the European perspective in a gradual and careful manner. But it has to do so in a complex environment, externally and internally. The Kosovar Albanian population first welcomed KFOR as liberators, however this changed somewhat as the purpose of the international presence was revealed to be not only to maintain a safe and secure environment but to shape that environment so that the proper practice of law and order was maintained and guarantee the safety of the remaining Serb minority.

In Kosovo there is a diversity of communities, both ethnic and religious, with 92 per cent of the population being ethnic Albanians with a moderate Muslim orientation. They have an identity as Albanians living in a country called Kosovo, or 'Kosova', as they say in Albanian. Moreover, they share a common Yugoslav and Ottoman history with neighbouring states. Besides Albanians, Serbs are the second most numerous ethnic group (5.3 per cent) and they perceive themselves as Serbs and consider Kosovo as part of Serbia, although, especially in the south, many had to grow to accept the new reality of living in a state in which Albanians constitute a majority. Albanians in Kosovo do not share the sense that they are northern Albanians but rather Kosovar. Kosovo is an historical name and today's borders were only defined in the 1950s and not based on any previous historical border or ethnic lines. Besides Albanians and Serbs, the 1.7 million population comprises Turks, Romas, Bosniaks and Ashkalis (2.7 per cent).

Economically, Kosovo was poor and generated little output. Poverty was widespread, in places chronic, and prosperity has proved to be elusive, with little signs of improvement. Living standards were well below those in neighbouring countries and unemployment was high, the labour market dangerously depressed with between 40–50 per cent without jobs. Traditionally sustained by remittance from its diaspora abroad, foreign donor aid contributed to rebuilding Kosovo's destroyed infrastructure and houses, both sources of income set to decline, with cement, scrap metal, agriculture and some mining the main activities. Kosovo exports little, imports much, and has a small domestic market. Income from taxes is pitifully inadequate. This feeble ongoing, fledgling state of affairs means Kosovo has still a long way to go economically before it can consider itself self-sustaining. Before that it had to be self-governing, and neither was it ready for that, so UNMIK (United Nations Mission in Kosovo), an UN-administered supervision apparatus, oversaw the region's governance. Worryingly, demographics also presented a huge challenge. With a large young population, 50 per cent were under twenty-five and 70 per cent under thirty, Kosovo's bleak economic position allied with its inherent instability could potentially threaten its political and actual existence. Being largely contested, with a requirement for much inward investment, foreign assistance was crucial.

The Irish Deploy

The Irish Defence Forces deployed to Kosovo as part of the 46,000-strong KFOR peacekeeping force was a military logistics company consisting of a fleet of articulated demountable rack offload and pickup systems (DROPS), 4x4s, and ancillary vehicles. This unit was a theatre-level asset under the control of KFOR headquarters and their mission was to provide for the transport of equipment and materials to KFOR military units and humanitarian organisations working with the UN. This frequently involved long-haul journeys from KFOR's Sea Port of Disembarkation (SPOD) in Thessalonica in Greece to a multitude of KFOR and humanitarian locations across Kosovo.

In October 2004, the Irish Defence Forces' involvement in KFOR was expanded with the replacement of the 8th Irish Transport Company with an Armoured Personnel Carrier (APC) mounted infantry company, the 27th Infantry Group, which was largely drawn from troops serving with the 2nd Infantry Battalion based in Cathal Brugha Barracks, Rathmines, Dublin. Commanded by Commandant Larry McKeown, it consisted of three separate infantry platoons, each with thirty-four personnel. On arrival it too was based in Camp Clarke in Lipljan, 15 km south of Pristina. Coverage of the Irish company's

190 square km Area of Responsibility (AOR) was carried out through active patrolling and projecting a strong presence while becoming familiar with the area and what was going on in it. At times it was also necessary for the peacekeepers to be available for specialist tasks. There were a small number of minor incidents that were quickly responded to and appropriately dealt with, and matters within their AOR and KFOR-wide slowly began to settle.

Remaining aware of the situation and responding to the lowering threat levels, this posture towards security softened after a while permitting the use of soft-skinned vehicles as the norm. Still, in its early years the safety of both the local populations and KFOR could not be taken for granted as the inter-ethnic divide leading to tensions was bubbling under the surface.

Tinderbox: Events at the Austerlitz Bridge

In the centre of Mitrovica, eighty kilometres north of Pristina, the Austerlitz Bridge, also known as the 'New Bridge', spans the Ibar River dividing the Serb north of the city from Albanian south. It was here, early on 17 March 2004, that Albanians protesting the believed drowning of three Albanian boys, following the drive-by shooting of a Serbian teen, clashed with Serbs. KFOR troops, UNMIK police and Kosovo Police Service (KPS) members interposed themselves between the marauding mobs and kept them apart until machine gun fire and grenades began to be used by both sides. In the ensuing riots eight people, two Albanians and six Serbs were killed with some 300 or so more wounded including eleven French KFOR peacekeepers, two seriously.

Blocking Position

The sudden eruption of inter-ethnic violence swiftly ignited thirty-three riots in two days involving over 50,000 people across Kosovo. (See map on p. ix.) KFOR and the international community had not seen it coming and were caught largely unawares, though an overall imperfect response saw KFOR troops face down the difficulties and restore peace. This was maintained by the rapid deployment of an additional 2,500 peacekeepers to speedily reinforce the existing 17,500 KFOR troops.

Before it ended, however, there were 19 fatalities, 900 injuries, 700 minority (Serb, Ashkali and Roma) houses were damaged or destroyed, 30 Serbian churches and 2 monasteries were vandalised or wrecked, and approximately 4,500 people displaced. There was a lead-up to the disturbance, but when it happened it was huge.

Scheduled protests from KLA veterans' associations and trade unions were expected and planned for, and even a 'worst case' scenario was anticipated. However, what occurred was far worse than that and the violence was not even on a scale of what was imagined. The interethnic violence was to reach its highest level since the war in Kosovo had concluded in 1999, four and a half years earlier. The ignition was spontaneous, rather than organised, but once the riots commenced they were quickly seized upon by extremists, criminals and other groups who gave vent to a pent-up, deeply-felt exasperation, underpinned by fear and frustration, at a lack of perceived progress towards the realisation of the Albanian populations' aspirations for Kosovo. Isolated incidents incited events and violent situations presented themselves faster than KFOR could react.

With a momentum for demonstration already building against a background of KLA veterans grievances and trade union demands, the potential for unrest was exponentially added to by Kosovo Serb anger at the shooting of a Serb youth in Čaglavica on the evening of 15 March 2004 and Kosovo Albanian counter-anger at the Serbs subsequently blocking the main highway south of Pristina in protest. The following day, 16 March 2004, the Serbs in nearby Gračanica blocked their road in solidarity, effectively cutting off Kosovo's capital from the south of Kosovo. The already pervading atmosphere of demonstration and protest, added to by grievance and anger on both sides, only needed a spark to set off the powder keg and the lit fuse was not long in coming. During the evening of 16 March on RTK, Kosovo's public television channel, news began to be broadcast of reports of the drowning of three Albanian children in the Ibar River in the village of Cabra, near the Serb community of the Zubin Potok valley. Subsequently unproven, reports by Kosovar media outlets alleged the children were chased into the river by Serbs with dogs in revenge for the previous days' shooting. A deeply troubled Kosovo was set to explode, and explode it did.

Throughout the afternoon an estimated crowd of up to 3,000 Kosovar Albanians moved from Pristina in the direction of Čaglavica, and there they were opposed by two platoons of Finnish peacekeepers from SISU Company on the left (minus the Irish platoon who were further north along the highway [Route Hawk], concurrently holding the containing line), a full Company from the Swedish battalion in the centre, and on the right Setanta Company comprising two Irish platoons and a Finnish platoon. UNMIK Police, UNMIK Special Police and Kosovar Police Service units were in support. Quickly escalating, its ferocity resembling a modern-day medieval pitched battle with sheer brute force against stubborn will. The rioters engaged the KFOR peacekeepers; iron bars against batons; stones against shields; Molotov cocktails against tear gas; rocks against rubber bullets; burning petrol-drenched rags on long poles against stun-grenades; and bottles against pepper spray. The crowds' physical weight of numbers pressed against KFOR's disciplined public order formation. SISU Company attempted to prevent the crowd moving into the village from the main road and there were clashes resulting in minor injuries to a small number of soldiers and some damage to KFOR vehicles. Similarly, the Swedish Company and Setanta Company encountered like clashes also resulting in minor injuries and damage to vehicles (broken windows).

The earlier news and rumours of inter-ethnic clashes at Mitrovica having reached Pristina, the roadblock mounted by Serb villagers just three kilometres south of the city was a ready-made focus for the attention of the huge number of angry and determined Kosovar Albanian demonstrators. The Containing Position (CP) at road junction Red 52, manned by Lieutenant Ed Holland with his platoon and assorted police units, succeeded in slowing the flow of demonstrators, thereby buying time to put in place more KFOR and police units and allowing them to position themselves in a Blocking Position (BP) where the ground was falling away to the left and a large construction site to the right. This area favoured a defence and it was there that KFOR made its stand. It was, however, on the very edge of the village of Čaglavica itself and the confrontation was to last from early afternoon to late evening. The ad hoc mixture of Irish, Finnish, Czech and Swedish KFOR peacekeepers, together with UNMIK Police and Kosovo Police, faced a tough situation. The KFOR peacekeepers were strong, well trained and with good equipment and what faced them to begin with were mostly youths and students, though as matters developed they were supported by a more organised and apparently coordinated mix of hardliners and extremists, a criminal element among them.

The rioters were supplied with water, sandwiches and Molotov cocktails, and makeshift first-aid points sprang up. Some had weapons while many equipped themselves with materials from the construction site and used them against KFOR. Particularly effective was the rioters' use of steel rod reinforcement bars during close-quarter man-to-man exchanges, as the situation rapidly deteriorated into near open battle. The stakes were high and the assault sustained, and any momentary malfunction in the defensive system could be seized on in the moment by the mob and break through. It quickly became an additional obstacle and it was very much a case of 'all hands to the pumps' for KFOR. After a period of tough hand-to-hand exchanges, the sheer weight of numbers began to force KFOR back. Sensing an opportunity, the mob hit the KFOR defensive wall and pushed it back. Some houses were set alight and shots were fired by the Serbs thinking that KFOR was unable to respond. These were replied to by the Albanians and an exchange of firing commenced. In reply, the Swedish fired several warning bursts from a 12.7mm HMG and the firing on both sides eased off. Taking advantage of this lull in the physical engagement with the rioters, and grateful for the respite, KFOR regained its position and the fighting resumed.

Notwithstanding the imbalance in numbers, and with the resumption of the barrage of missiles, the KFOR line remained intact, principally because of the KFOR leadership at all levels. The section commanders were in the same line as the troops and the platoon commanders were only five metres behind, placing their hands on the backs of the soldiers and encouraging them. Behind them the company commanders in turn heartened and motivated the KFOR forces. However, the physicality was taking its toll and Norwegian reinforcements were called for. It would be a while before they arrived and they had to go west from their base around Slatina Airport as the roadblocks remained in place in Pristina. At 1830 hours Lieutenant Holland and his platoon, having withdrawn from the CP at R52, now arrived to the Battle Group's tactical HQ in a SISU APC in Čaglavica. While he went to receive a quick briefing he informed his troops to dismount and fall in to their public order formation. He was ordered to move his platoon forward to the front line and assist the Swedish and Norwegians on the right-hand side of the highway, as they were under immense pressure. With determined faces, staring through the Plexiglas shields, and with batons held ready the solid mass of the platoon marched forward, smacking the side of their shields in unison, the smart soldier-like beat encapsulating the energy and emotion of the encounter. With adrenaline pumping they joined the line.

All along the KFOR line, the impact and physicality of the situation was immense. Matters were severe and the tension was rising, the already antagonistic atmosphere becoming increasingly combative and the immediate prospect uncompromising. The first thing to greet the newly arrived Irish Platoon to the right flank was a hail of missiles from the mob in front of them. Propelled through the air was every kind of debris from the construction site imaginable, all too conveniently located beside the crowd. Not satisfied with this bountiful supply, the carcasses of dead animals were added to their armoury and the crowd even set chickens from the overrun Serb outhouses on fire and threw them at the KFOR troops. In reply the Swedish discharged stun grenades, the Norwegians fired rubber bullets, and UNMIK Police used tear gas to contain the crowd. All the while sporadic overhead firing was ongoing between the besieged Serbs and Albanian attackers.

Shouts, roars, screams, bangs, cracks, thuds, curses and threats could all be heard and added to the melodrama of the melee. Here and there a KFOR soldier could be seen raising a gloved hand to rub disbelief and exhaustion from his face. Communication and a common understanding of the importance of not allowing the collapse of the line were crucial, training and equipment essential. In the moment, mental and physical resolve needed to be to the fore as the situation came down to who had the greater will. This was raw hostility and the crowd was looking to create a kink in the KFOR line and exploit it. Lieutenant Holland's platoon, inserted into the lines right flank, now had their portion to defend – a smaller frontage than before – and were able to adopt close formation with each man's shield along the front rank interlinked with that of the man beside him and the second line putting theirs overhead. Yet the heavy onslaught continued, with everything thrown at them, especially petrol bombs, and the mob fought against the front rank of long shields.

Suddenly a demonstrator was killed, a victim of the ongoing shooting, which infuriated another demonstrator – believed to be his brother – who jump-started a truck from the construction site and drove it menacingly at the KFOR line, as it happened directly at members of the Norwegian Task Force, KFOR reserves. Two of them opened fire, killing the truck driver, but it was in low gear and kept going. The Norwegians jumped into the cab and directed it into the low ground to the left, the truck crashing off Route Hawk and coming to an abrupt stop. This inflamed the crowd further and their ferocity intensified as they attempted to break through, throwing slates, rocks and iron bars while others were hammering at the shields with wooden stakes and poles. The two platoons of Irish C Company on the left flank, under Commandant Larry McKeown, like those of their Swedish, Finnish, Czech and Norwegian counterparts all along the KFOR line, matched this intensity and casualties on both sides were running into the dozens. It was then that KFOR communications went down, the result of too many phones and radios being in one place at one time. As it became dark and difficult to see illumination was used and the lights on the vehicles turned on, though many were shot out. It was 2000 hours and KFOR had been in the fight for six hours without food or water. Having to perform extreme physical exertions, some began to faint from dehydration and sheer exhaustion and it began to get cold. The estimation of the situation turned to how many casualties could KFOR sustain?

Seizing the initiative, a KFOR water cannon was employed as were two Finnish APCs on the left and two Swedish APCs in the centre. These provided good cover as the entire KFOR line, right, left and centre, advanced in unison and succeeded in pushing the crowd back despite their aggression and a massive hail of missiles. UNMIK police fired tear gas without warning and this caused control problems for the Irish as they struggled to fit their respirators while simultaneously holding the line of advance. Once their respirators were fitted they were in a better position to advance and maintained the pace. In fact they outstripped those in the centre, the Swedish coming under such an intense barrage that they could not advance at the same speed as the rest of the advancing KFOR line. A coordinated retreat to a defensive line was organised and during this period a Swedish APC broke down due to a mechanical fault. Due to pressure from the rioters, the Swedish troops briefly abandoned the APC and its crew and withdrew. The crew, adopting the correct procedure, locked themselves inside but now needed rescuing. Advancing on the APC, the crowd set fire to its tyres and shortly it would become engulfed in flames. Realising the danger to the peacekeepers inside the APC, the KFOR line moved forward in an attempt to rescue the crew and fight their way beyond them. The manoeuvre successful, the crew were rescued but KFOR were unable to recover the vehicle as it could not be moved. Under renewed pressure from the rioters, the KFOR line withdrew and the crowd torched the APC and destroyed it.

The burning of the Swedish APC proved a great mental fillip for the crowd and buoyed by this success they surged forward with renewed vigour, further intensifying their efforts to break through. The results were fairly brutal and the fighting fiercely focussed. The crowd flung themselves at the defensive line with all their might as wave after wave of Molotov cocktails come pouring down on the Irish. Then someone remembered: 'It's Corporal Kelly's birthday today', and amidst the pressure, the danger and the thoroughly fraught atmosphere, with a firm grip on their riot shields and with rocks and bricks, blows and kicks bouncing off them, the Irish start singing 'Happy Birthday'! This vivaciousness and spirit epitomised the teak-tough defensive grit and resilience that came from a deep pride in the huge effort they had sustained all day, and if they had to stay all night they were going to do so.

In the event, the following two hours were to prove their toughest as they faced the crowds unrelenting determination to force a way in, the determination of all those in the KFOR Line to keep them out, no less so. For two hours, the repositioning of the defensive line ebbed and flowed as the crowd pushed forward and KFOR pushed them back, the line never moving further than 100 metres either way. A US company arrived, seeking to get through to Mitrovica along Route Hawk. However, with no Crowd Riot Control (CRC) equipment they could not assist in contributing to the defensive efforts, but they did have supplies of illumination and gas. These were put to good use and it all suddenly stopped as the crowd disengaged, their energy dissipated. It was over, the mob were finally exhausted and they dispersed back north to Pristina. An inevitable few lingered but KFOR had held the line for twelve hours. They had defended Čaglavica and did so using proportionate force. But they might well have to do it all again the next day so a plan was formulated for KFOR to move forward to road junction Red 52 (R 52), clearing the route as they went. The Norwegians were central on the road, with the Swedish to the right and the Irish, with their three platoons once again reunited, on the left flank. The move forward did not pose any problems and it was now 0100 hours.

On successfully clearing the route as far as R52, the convoy on the MSR Route Hawk, the US Company among them, cleared into Pristina. Now KFOR was able to pick its ground and set up a defensive plan where the terrain offered the best advantage. Three defensive points were prepared for the next day, the Norwegian Task Force established a new Blocking Position (BP) on Veternik Ridge, the Swedish set up a strong vehicle checkpoint on Route Hawk, south of the Norwegian BP, and the Irish further south in the vicinity of a road junction north of Čaglavica. The Irish were the third and final defensive line and nothing was to be let past them. KFOR were ready, and in the event it was just as well.

Evacuation from the YU Flats

Just before midnight that same night, 17 March 2004, Captain David Hathaway was present in the Operations Room at HQ MNB (C) when an urgent request was received from UNMIK Liaison Officer to evacuate a Serb family from the YU flats in Pristina. It was reported that they were under attack by a mob in excess of 200 Kosovar Albanians who had surrounded their flat, had set numerous cars on fire and were in the process of breaking into the flats and attacking the inhabitants. At this point there were no UNMIK-Police or KFOR assets available to assist in the evacuation and this was relayed back by Operations Second-in-Command, Irish Captain 'Chuck' Berry, to the call sign requesting assistance. At this point the requesting UNMIK-P call sign became quite distressed and stated that this was a matter of life and death and if these people were not rescued they would certainly be killed. Once again the UNMIK-Police Liaison Officer appealed to Captain Berry to send in KFOR troops, but all reserves were committed elsewhere.

Captain Hathaway spoke directly to Captain Berry and stated that if he could get volunteers from the Irish troops in Camp Slim Lines in Pristina he would go there and take out the family. He gave a quick outline of his plan to the Chief of Operations and he agreed that they could take on the task. Two Swedish Headquarters members volunteered to drive the Swedish minibus. They quickly gathered six volunteers among the Irish troops: Corporals McTiernan and Doyle, Troopers Curran and Deere, Private Nugent and Gunner Mullins, and a Serbian language interpreter. Captain Hathaway gave a quick brief on the situation as he knew it, the rules of engagement and the plan of action. The emphasis was placed on speed and aggression to disperse the Kosovar Albanian mob, retrieve the family and withdraw before the mob could react. They were to use one Irish KFOR 4x4 jeep, the Minibus and a second Irish 4x4 jeep.

The Irish party departed Slim Lines and headed towards the centre of Pristina. When at speed they entered Nënë Tereza (Mother Teresa Street), they spotted a group of Kosovar Albanians but they made no attempt to obstruct the Irish entry to the YU flats complex. The road off Mother Teresa Street to the YU flats extended for over 400 metres, with many tight turns and bottlenecks. After negotiating this road without difficulty, they drove aggressively into the car park immediately in front of the flats. There were over twenty cars burning, their petrol tanks randomly exploding, resulting in the car park being smothered in a pall of black smoke. There was a mob of Kosovar Albanians immediately in front of the flats, but they took flight when the small KFOR group ran at them with rifles raised shouting 'KFOR! Get back, get back!' They established a perimeter among the surrounding buildings from which they could contain the crowd with aggressive posturing and shouted warnings. Although contained, the crowd started hurling stones and bottles and surged forward at intervals. With the assistance of the interpreter they located the flats in question where they expected the family to be located. At this stage there were a lot of screams for help and crying coming from the windows of other adjoining flats, and the interpreter translated that they were all going to be killed and needed help. It became obvious that the numbers needing extraction were not a single Serb family but dozens of Serbs and some international families, mainly UNMIK.

Captain Hathaway made the decision to take only the children with their mothers at this point, who were absolutely terrified and sobbing uncontrollably. They needed considerable encouragement to run to the relative safety of the minibus, which was positioned between the flats and the mob being held back by the troops positioned twenty metres beyond it. He promised those left behind that they would return and collect them all and gave them his mobile phone number. With fourteen women and children loaded in the minibus they collapsed the perimeter, mounted up and drove off at speed, the mob surging forward and attacking the vehicles with stones as they passed by. In an effort to block them in, the crowd had barricaded the roadway out of the flats and the drivers were forced to drive down a sloped verge in order to escape.

On their return to Slim Lines, the women and children were transferred to the national welfare huts and were given bedding, food and drink. Captain Hathaway reported to the Operations room and stated that if they were to return back to the YU flats it could only be done in armoured vehicles. At this point Lieutenant Colonel (later Brigadier General) Ger Ahern and Captain Ronan Dillon were present. Calls were coming in from the remaining Kosovar Serbs, who were by now very distressed, that the Kosovar Albanians had broken into the flats and were killing the Kosovar Serbs and that grenades had exploded and shooting was taking place. Permission was received from Chief of Operations to use the Commanders' two SISU Force Command Post vehicles. Two SISU crews were readied and the troops were briefed once again to return. Captain Dillon took command of the second SISU and they returned to the flats to repeat the exercise. They entered the flats complex at speed and drove into the centre of the mob, which scattered and took flight. Troops in both of the SISUs dismounted and established a perimeter in the same manner as before.

With a relatively secure perimeter in place, Captain Hathaway and Captain Dillon split up, taking an interpreter each. The cars were still burning fiercely and their petrol tanks were occasionally exploding, and close proximity gunfire was clearly audible, but the Irish believed they did not come under deliberately aimed fire. Contact was made with the Kosovar Serbs needing evacuation and the process began of loading them into the SISUs. Most of them were old, with many invalided and some showing signs of severe beating, and they were all terrified and crying. A wounded Czech UNMIK-Policeman who had been shot in the leg was also recovered by the troops and brought to the rear where he was medevaced out. It was reported that there was a Kosovar Serb male dying from wounds on the fourth floor of one of the flats and a trail of blood led from the ground to the fourth floor. At the scene the Kosovar Serb male was found to have a number of wounds and was suffering from substantial blood loss. Captain Dillon and Trooper Deere evacuated him and carried him down the stairs. They stabilised him as best they could and lifted him into the SISU.

The two SISUs were now very overcrowded but to the best of the knowledge of the residents there were no more Kosovar Serbs remaining in the flats, nor were there any evident. As before they collapsed the perimeter, mounted up and drove off at speed with the mob surging forward. This time the mob had constructed a reinforced barricade with cars and metal rubbish bins full of masonry and debris. The first SISU burst through the barricade, driving over the cars and throwing the bins out of the way, closely followed by the second SISU in the same manner.

On return to Slim Lines the civilians were again transferred to welfare care assisted by the medical cell and the British National Support Cell. At this point, Lieutenant Colonel Ahern briefed them that he was getting reports that there were still many Kosovar Serbs hiding in the flats and that the flats were now on fire. Captain Berry advised from Operations that from reports being received Kosovar Albanians were again in the flats attacking the Kosovar Serbs and they had set the flats on fire with the inhabitants inside. A short oral fragmentary order was issued to the troops and again the SISUs headed towards Mother Teresa Street. Upon entering the YU flats complex they discovered they could not drive into the car park area as the route had been obstructed with a barricade of over six cars blocking the road. The two SISUs were forced to stop short and the troops deployed forward to engage and turn back the rampaging mobs. The flats nearest the SISUs were evacuated first, in the same manner as before, and soon both SISUs were full.

At this stage UNMIK-Police Section Six arrived in strength with armoured trucks and stopped in cover 100 metres short of their position. Captain Hathaway liaised with their commander and stressed that as they now possessed numbers capable of securing the flats indefinitely they should stay until the evacuation of all Kosovar Serbs and Internationals was complete. He stressed that the command and control would be himself alone and that UNMIK-Police would act under his command through their leader on the ground. UNMIK-Police then deployed forward to the KFOR line and fired substantial amounts of tear gas into the crowd. The Kosovar Serbs in the SISUs were transferred under cover to the UNMIK armoured trucks to allow the SISUs to go forward and collect the remainder still in flats. With the help of UNMIK, the cars were pulled out of the way and the SISUs drove at speed to the extreme furthest block of flats, which were on fire with Kosovar Serbs still inside on the upper floors.

KFOR and UNMIK-Police repeatedly entered the buildings in turn to retrieve old people and invalids. The greatest difficulty in moving around was the thick pall of smoke in the stair wells of the flats as a result of fires in the Kosovar Serbs flats only, UNMIK and Albanian flats were untouched. When they were completely satisfied that all Kosovar Serbs were evacuated, the convoy of KFOR and UNMIK-Police returned to Slim Lines. In total, the Irish-led action evacuated 122 Kosovar Serb and Internationals that night.

Post-Blocking Position

On two fronts, in Čaglavica and at the YU flats, the Irish peacekeeping actions were considered a job well done, but the situation was far from settled. The region was still in turmoil and death and destruction continued to be visited upon communities Kosovo-wide. Circumstances in Pristina still needed urgent attention, and unrest was still fermenting and would shortly be given violent expression. The crowds were to come again. However, overnight KFOR had planned, prepared and put into position a triple line of defences: the Norwegians on the 'Ridge'; the Swedish at 'Red 52'; and the Irish at Čaglavica. The Irish Setanta Company were also to constitute the Brigade Reserve and were placed on five minutes 'Notice to Move' (NTM). Throughout the morning there was regular contact between all three lines, the Irish confident they would receive advance warning from the lines of defence in front of them.

On Veternik Ridge, the Norwegian KFOR troops had chosen their ground well and drawn a strong cordon across the highway with razor wire backed by troops and armoured personnel carriers. Here the highway cut into the hilltop, the raised banks on either side forming elaborate shoulders. This high ground position both protected the flanks of the KFOR blocking position and channelled any would-be rioters into a confined frontage, restricted to the width of the two sides of the highway. The conduct of any necessary defence would be a more focussed one, its command and control greatly facilitated, and it allowed for the effects of defence assets and resources to be more concentrated. Advance warning of trouble was not long in coming, when a Kosovar Albanian protest with a crowd of approximately 1,500 people commenced in Pristina at around noon. The question being would they advance out of Pristina and head up the highway ('Route Hawk') seeking confrontation? As it turns out, they did and they were.

A burst of gunfire in the early afternoon was the first indication that the Norwegian BP on Veternik Ridge was receiving strong opposition and some violence from the crowd of Kosovar Albanians attempting to break through their position. Numerous other bursts of gunfire from the Norwegian APCs, and the mild effects from the tear gas the Norwegians were firing at the crowd being felt, informed the Irish that a confrontation had begun and was continuing. The crowd were never likely to succeed in coming close to crossing the strong defensive line, but they were certainly going to make an attempt. With a platoon of Irish remaining throughout the afternoon at the third line of defence, Setanta Company, the Brigade Reserve on five minutes NTM, were ordered mid-afternoon to be prepared to counter a crowd of approximately 250 Kosovar Albanians assembling in Lipljan, suspected of being intent on burning the Kosovar Serb church in the town.

An hour later the situation eased somewhat, when the crowd had reduced to 100, only to swell to in excess of 1,000 two hours later. One platoon from the Brigade reserve was dispatched to reinforce about sixty members of the Finnish/Irish Brigade Group already in position protecting the Serb Church and Serb enclave in the town. By now the crowd at Veternik Ridge was beginning to disperse, with the Norwegians having resisted all their attempts to break through using tear gas, other non-lethal agents and the firing of containing shots to prevent the crowd from spreading and outflanking them. A determined KFOR presence at Lipljan was enough to see off the assembled crowd there and they too began to disperse. A later call out to the mixed village of Rabovce, where earlier approximately 350 Serbs had left to be accommodated in other Serb villages, saw C Company engage in constant patrolling, and negotiations with Kosovar Albanians in the village prevented any damage being caused to the Kosovar Serb houses which had been evacuated. There was one instance of an attempt to set a house on fire, but C company personnel succeed in extinguishing it before the fire caught hold.

The following day, C Company escorted 100 Kosovar Serb males back to the village while the woman and children remained in four other Serb villages. These were escorted back the following day. Before that, however, the Irish were ordered to deploy to Kosovo Polje in order to restore public order and establish a safe and secure environment there, as no KFOR troops had been in the town since 17 March. Establishing a Tactical Headquarters in the outlying Serb village of Ugljarevo, they commenced extensive mobile and foot patrols in and around Kosovo Polje. This high visibility operation reduced the tension within the town, especially in the Serb enclaves where the school, hospital and ninety-four houses had been burned. Some hours later they conducted a 'relief in place' with the newly arrived British company, the Royal Gloucestershire, Berkshire and Wiltshire Regiment.

The next few days saw a continuation of this high visibility presence, patrolling both mobile and on foot, escorting the returning Kosovar Serbs back to their villages and maintaining the three-line defence along Route Hawk on the highway south from Pristina to Čaglavica. All in all, these KFOR security measures contributed to restoring calm to the overall situation.

Aftermath

Kosovo's 'Mid-March Riots' occurred over several days, resulting in death, destruction and displacement. The international community, KFOR included, received criticism for not doing more to prevent the disturbances and react to them more quickly. However, the Irish were acknowledged to have contributed significantly towards defusing the rioting and to have held their resolve in the face of inter-ethnic aggression. Their actions earned a number of Irish soldiers' letters of commendation from the commander of Multi-National Brigade Centre, Brigadier General Anders Brannstrom. Major General Michael Finn, Chief of Staff United Nations Troop Supervisory Organisation (UNTSO), then a Lieutenant Colonel and Officer Commanding 27th Infantry Group, is humble when questioned on the citations and acclaim his unit received for their actions: 'The unit were widely praised for their involvement and while commendations were handed out to a number of personalities, it must be highlighted that all of the Irish troops present played a huge part and worked extremely hard to resolve the impasse.' In April 2010, Mr Peter Feith, then EU Special Representative to Kosovo, spoke of his admiration for the Irish Defence Forces and their contribution to peace and security in Kosovo when addressing the Institute of International and European Affairs in Dublin:

> a word of gratitude for the enormous contribution made by the men and women of Ireland for Kosovo's growth and European perspective. On 20 April, 220 Irish soldiers will leave their base in Pristina to return home. They have assumed duties at mission headquarters, in areas as diverse as patrolling and intelligence gathering, and in helping build so many areas of civil society.

Eighteen years after the beginning of the KFOR mission, thirteen years since the 'Mid-March Riots', and nine years since the institutions in Kosovo declared independence, many challenges remain. The open antagonism witnessed in earlier times between Pristina and Belgrade has been replaced by dialogue and attempts by both governments to focus on the improvement of the daily lives of everyone living in Kosovo. However, although hostilities have ceased discord remains, especially with regard to the northern part of Kosovo where the overwhelming majority of the population remains reluctant to accept an administration directed by Kosovan institutions. Clearly the operational theatre has changed significantly since the forces of the Federal Republic of Yugoslavia (FRY) were forced to withdraw from Kosovo by NATO's

78-day air campaign, Operation Allied Force (23 March–10 June 1999). Nearly 50,000 NATO troops entered Kosovo simultaneously as the Serbs pulled out. This synchronised deployment of KFOR and the departure of the Yugoslav forces was in accordance with the Kumanovo Military Technical Agreement (MTA) concluded between NATO and FRY on 9 June 1999. The following day, the NATO-led KFOR authority to act was mandated by United Nations Security Council Resolution 1244. Two days later, on 12 June 1999, KFOR entered Kosovo and Operation Joint Guardian had begun.

With a continuously improving security situation throughout Kosovo, KFOR has gradually downsized to currently approximately 10 per cent of its original strength. These continuous reductions should not be viewed as an engine of success in themselves, rather as a consequence of it. However successfully achieved, it was not without problems. The sudden and unforeseen eruption of inter-ethnic violence in March 2004 led to the reconfiguration of KFOR into Multinational Task Forces with greater flexibility and physically reduced areas of responsibility to ensure a more rapid response. Additionally, a large number of national caveats were removed when in June 2006 KFOR completed its transition from four Multinational Brigades (MNB East, Centre, Northeast and Southeast) to five Multinational Task Forces (MNTF Centre, North, East, South and West). Also included were the Multinational Specialised Unit (MSU), a Portuguese battalion serving as KFOR tactical Reserve Manoeuvre Battalion (KTM), and a headquarters support group (HSG).

By February 2008, efforts by both the UN Special Envoy for Kosovo, former president of Finland Martti Ahtisaari, and subsequently representatives from the European Union (EU), the United States and the Russian Federation – the Troika – proved unsuccessful in bringing the parties to agreement on Kosovo's status, an issue being left open by UNSC Resolution 1244. Even after its Assembly's declaration on 17 February 2008, not all EU, NATO and UN member states recognise Kosovo's independence. Two months later KFOR agreed to commence implementation of additional tasks in Kosovo, namely to assist in the standing down of the Kosovo Protection Corps (KPC) and the standing up of the Kosovo Security Force (KSF). Based on the improved security situation and the prevailing calm in Kosovo, KFOR was further reduced in strength and restructured. On its implementation in late January 2010, KFOR's strength was reduced to 10,200 and the Multinational Task Forces were restructured into five Multinational Battle Groups (MNBGs). KFOR was now to operate a 'deterrent presence'.

In light of the performance of the Kosovak Police (KP) and the support to law enforcement by the European Rule of Law Mission (EULEX), KFOR saw a further troop reduction to 6,200 by March 2011 as well as yet another restructuring. The five Multinational Battle Groups were reduced to two: Multinational Battle Group East (MNBG-E) based at Camp Bondsteel near Ferizaj in the eastern part of Kosovo, and Multinational Battle Group-West (MNBG-W) based at Camp 'Villaggio Italia' located near Pecj in the western part of Kosovo. A quickly deployable, on-call over the horizon Operational Reserve Force (ORF) remains available to support KFOR if necessary. Liaison and Monitoring (LMT) elements now operate in five separate Joint Regional Detachments (JDRs). These are the forward sensors of KFOR, with its soldiers meeting daily with the population of Kosovo. This important interaction allows the LMTs to gain a timely appreciation of their feeling regarding issues on the ground, and the overall reorganisation and new structure only became possible as the institutions in Kosovo assumed more and more responsibilities and tasks formerly executed by KFOR. At the same time the Force retained the capability and flexibility to respond to any potential crisis.

One example of the tasks taken by the institutions in Kosovo was the policing of borders with the former Yugoslav Republic of Macedonia, Albania and Montenegro. Tensions erupted in late July 2011 when unknown individuals attacked police officers attempting to enforce customs policies at two control posts along the Administrative Boundary Line with Serbia. One police officer was shot dead and the Jarinje crossing point (Gate 1) was burned down by a violent group. Roads throughout northern Kosovo were blocked with trucks, trailers, logs and car tyres. KFOR, tasked to ensure freedom of movement and contribute to a safe and secure environment, took over responsibility for both authorised crossing points, Gate 1 and Dog 31, until EULEX, Kosovo Police and Kosovo Customs reinstalled their presence in mid-

September 2011. Major tensions were to follow, with KFOR confronted by roadblocks and road blockers, many of whom were women, children and the elderly. KFOR succeeded in taking control of some of these barricades using surprise and swiftness. However, serious clashes did occur when small groups of individuals reacted using violence, including firearms and grenades. KFOR's response was one of resolve and a series of roadblock removal and bypass blocking operations proved successful while the focus at all times was not to cause casualties.

KFOR's unchanging and full commitment to its mandate and mission moved from 'facing the barricades' to 'promoting progress'. In October 2012, the EU-mediated high-level dialogue to 'normalise relations' constituted a strategic shift leading to a new and challenging phase for KFOR. With circumstances allowing the successful redeployment of the Operational Reserve Force at the end of 2012, a more comprehensive strategy was employed to contribute to progress. KFOR developed its 'KFOR Security Outreach North' concept as the guiding principle for its operations. At the time of writing, activities under its four pillars, 'KFOR Security Dialogue', 'KFOR's Own Operations', 'KFOR Support to EULEX Operations', and 'KFOR's Information Campaign' are ongoing. There are currently twelve Irish soldiers participating in staff appointments at KFOR HQ.

PART IV
CHAD (2008)

CHAPTER 6

The Dead Heart of Africa

Devils on Horseback

Darfur, Western Sudan, 2003

The sun had not yet risen and the night was pitch black. The sound of approaching hoofs went unheard by the villagers, still fast asleep and unknowing that they would soon be violently awoken to a nightmare – projected from tranquillity to turmoil in a split second. Terror, torture and torment was about to be unleashed by the sadistic marauding militiamen riding hard over the arid red compacted sands and through the rocks and scrubland of the sub-Saharan Sahel Savanna of West Darfur, intent as they were on murder, mutilation and rape. As the horsemen rode into the village the sound of gunshots, shouting, screaming and shrieking of terror-stricken traumatised women and children echoed around the dilapidated buildings. A cacophony of chaos, a maelstrom of madness, of suffering, anguish and of hell that seemed like it would never end.

Two young girls who hadn't managed to make it out of the village and were hiding in a hut in the midst of the mayhem caught the focus of the militiamen's attention. The Janjaweed attackers, the 'Devils on Horseback', circled the hut on their mounts, laughing, jeering and enjoying their amusement. Unable to bear the baiting any longer, the elder of the distraught girls made a desperate dash for freedom and attempted to draw off their tormentors. Wrong-footed by her agility, her speed and will succeeded in getting her through the crude cordon and driven by terror and the innate instinct to survive and protect her younger sibling she sped off into the darkness. Recovering from his surprise, the leader of the raiding party spurred his mount into action with his heels and gave chase. The pursuit was on; her quickness and agility against his horse's speed. It was life or death and she knew it – she had spotted a chance and taken it. The rider overtook her, then turning his mount around he swept her up at a gallop and returned to the village, dumping her down the village well to the roar of approval from the turbaned riders of his marauding mob. The younger girl, transfixed by the chase now took her chance, but she was too late and paid dearly for her hesitation. They burned her alive. This was the type of incident at the root of the crisis that the EU was working to address in eastern Chad as terrorised villagers streamed across its border from Darfur into Chad, further destabilising an already unstable country.

Threat Assessment: The Darfur Complex

The internal Chadian political and security crisis had been exacerbated by the Darfur Complex of eastern Chad, the north eastern Central African Republic (CAR) and Darfur itself, which was at the heart of the EU decision to participate in the multi-dimensional intervention in the region. The massive influx of refugees from Darfur and the large-scale internal displacement had been at the centre of the EU intervention, but the EU force was not mandated to deal directly with the root causes of the various crises, as was expected by many actors on the ground and at times by the Chadian government itself, nor to intervene against the rebel groups. Instead it had to walk the tightrope of impartiality and the EU adopted a comprehensive approach in its strategy. As a first phase it contributed to alleviating the worst consequences of the conflict, but to improve the political, economic and social conditions required a long-term perspective. A short-term military contribution could only help to redress some of the worst effects for the distressed population.

The European Union Force (EUFOR) had to deploy into and adapt to an environment with increased potential for violence in political, social and economic relations as well as ethnic tensions. EUFOR's military operation in Chad was one leg of a three-legged stool. EUFOR's leg was security, and the comprehensive approach of the entire mission could not hope to move forward unless military security was provided for the other two legs, the second of which was governance. Good governance included the effective rule of law and human rights. The third leg was economic development and all three of them had to work together if the crisis was to be resolved. At the time none worked in Chad, so the military leg was an absolute requirement to facilitate the environment in which the other two could operate. In what was a multi-layered conflict environment, EUFOR's military planners had to have a sense of realism in its limited role against any grand political expectations.

The twelve months prior to EUFOR's deployment had been of no small concern for Africa. Despite advances in some areas of the continent, the situation in Sudan remained troubling with intensified conflicts in neighbouring Chad and CAR. The conflict in Darfur had spilled over and threatened to destabilise an already troubled and turbulent Chad and there were other real and potential sources of turmoil. Chad and Sudan were fighting a 'proxy' war through various rebel groups and there was deep-rooted ethnic conflict and tensions between nomadic and settled communities as well as out and out blatant banditry. In this kind of fragile environment even a slight deterioration in the security situation had the potential to set off a 'domino effect', first causing the deterioration of the security situation in the border areas and ultimately leading to the destabilisation of the whole region.

There was a persistent multi-dimensional context in the EUFOR area of interest where three levels of conflict could be identified: regional, national and local. At a regional level the main driver was the ongoing so called proxy war between Chad and Sudan, which was mainly being fought through each country supporting the rebellion and rebel forces in the other, then there was a religious dimension in that the Sudanese regime represented a more extreme Muslim posture compared to the more secular approach of Chad. At the national level, rebels were fighting with arms against the governments in Chad and Sudan, aiming to seize power or at least a share of the wealth from the plentiful national resources for the population they represented. This level of conflict had both a political and an armed dimension that were difficult to separate from each other in Sudan and CAR but were strictly separated from each other in Chad. At the local level of conflict the struggle was often caused by ethnic, tribal and clan rivalry, or simply by the basic need for land and food. At this level criminality was flourishing and local conflicts were fuelled by the continuous ongoing conflicts at regional and national levels, creating fear and feelings of general insecurity.

The cause for the displacement of local people, known as Internally Displaced People (IDP), was mainly down to the local level conflicts, as the rebels rarely attacked the local populations. These tribal fights were between Arab and African tribes, internal Chadian clans and between nomads and sedentary, often agricultural, people. Land, watering holes and grazing rights were at the core of age-old disputes between nomadic Arabs and black 'African' farmers and increasingly drought and desertification caused tensions to rise even higher. If there's a tangible connection between the earth and human beings it was here in the Sahel, the transitional zone at the edge of the Sahara along Africa's harsh frontier between desert and forest. It was here also that the many levels of conflict had hardened and fragmented. Widespread fighting, civilian displacement and overlapping conflicts destabilised the whole region.

Tragically, the torching of villages by Janjaweed bandits, endemic gang rape, wholesale killing and the millions of people fleeing the terror in Darfur continued to make front-page headlines. Typically, the Janjaweed would ride in on horses and camels, their faces obscured with scarves, and when they opened fire it was to shoot at anything that moved. Mostly they came at dawn and when they left in the late afternoon dozens would be dead. The Sudanese government had mobilised and unleashed a scorched-earth campaign and the Janjaweed had become notorious for the sadistic way they laid waste to entire communities, slaughtering the men, raping the women and looting everything of value before torching the villages. In February 2003, Darfurian rebels, frustrated by years of neglect by the Sudanese government, took up arms against Khartoum to claim better power and wealth sharing. Two rebel movements – the Justice and Equality Movement (JEM) and the Sudan Liberation Army/Movement (SLA/M) – were to the forefront and an attack was launched on a military base in the town of El Geneina in West Darfur.

In retaliation, the official government response was both brutal and swift. Countless targeted reprisal attacks were made across the region against settlements regarded as sympathetic and supportive to the rebels, containing for the most part women and children. The ensuing struggle for control of the region involved large-scale ethnic cleansing of indigenous African tribes by Arab militias. The devastation visited upon these villages was delivered by a combination of Sudanese bombing attacks and raids by ruthless Arab paramilitaries, armed, trained and mobilised in the services of Khartoum – the so-called

'Janjaweed'. The UN Secretary General, Kofi Anan, raised the alarm with the permanent members of the Security Council and demanded the escalating humanitarian crisis be given top priority. Throughout the next year the UN unsuccessfully pressurised Sudan to accept its help to protect the civilians and the US Secretary of State, Colin Powell, publicly described the killings as genocide.

An African Union Mission in Sudan (AMIS) was deployed to Darfur but failed to stop the attacks and the conflict spread, threatening to spill over into neighbouring countries. In 2005, the UN accused the Sudanese government and Arab militias of human rights abuses but not genocide, and the Security Council agreed to refer those accused of war crimes to the International Criminal Court (ICC). The following year the Darfur Peace Agreement was signed between the government and the SLA/M but emerging smaller rebel groups rejected the accord and continued fighting. Meanwhile, the Sudanese government rebuffed increasing international calls for a UN force to deploy to the region and expelled the UN's top official, Johannes 'Jan' Pronk, from the country. Attacks on civilians and aid workers intensified and the fighting proliferated between rebel splinter groups and warring factions of Arab, non-Arab, tribal ethnic and government forces. Eventually, in 2007 Khartoum was faced with international sanctions and capitulated to an African-dominated UN presence and the United Nations African Mission in Darfur (UNAMID) replaced AMIS at the year's end.

More than four years after the start of the conflict, the Sudanese government continued its harsh response to the emergence of the Darfurian rebels. Its brutal and repeated reprisals and retaliations and appalling atrocities on countless settlements and villages provided the real spark to the flame that escalated the Darfur crisis into a major humanitarian disaster. Violence on the ground in Darfur, and especially its marked progressive deterioration, continued to drive civilians from their homes and the continued cycle of violence and human misery in Darfur underscored the UN estimates of 300,000 dead, most of these as a result of government neglect, starvation and disease. Many of the survivors had all too vivid memories of the widespread atrocities and two and a half million sought refuge, mostly inside Darfur itself but also in Chad and CAR. Recurrent fighting maintained a steady influx of refugees into these camps and it was estimated there were nearly

250,000 Sudanese refugees in Chad and 15,000 in CAR. For many what they witnessed still haunts them and what they endured still terrifies them. What they suffered still strikes fear, so much so that when children hear a plane approaching they run and hide, its roar reminding them of the Sudanese bombing raids on their village ... most of all they cannot forget, and will never forget, the fearsome Janjaweed.

There was no shortage of problems in these ill-controlled territories of the Darfur Complex, the 'wild west' of Sudan, and the distinct but intertwined dynamics between the Khartoum and N'Djamena governments and their respective rebel rivals and those emanating from their own internal and volatile domestic environments. Robust and functional Rules of Engagement became critical to the successful mind set for the EUFOR tactical commanders, conscious of the menace, capacity for mayhem and murderous intent of any number of potential would-be attackers. There wasn't one threat in Chad, there were many.

Peace-enforcement is tough peacekeeping and Chad was going to require tough peace-enforcement. If you intervene militarily in a country, even on a mercy mission, you must hold your nerve throughout. If force is required it must be used with enough will to make it work. If engaged with deadly force with hostile intent, you must be the ones determined to prevail. This is not military machismo, it is an unavoidable and essential matter of credibility and it is credibility that gives you success. If EUFOR was fortunate, this credibility might lead to success without a shot being fired. However, EUFOR could not input luck into its planning and the likelihood was the force would be tested sooner or later. Planning for the EUFOR mission in Darfur had to be undertaken with an ability to comprehend the on-ground reality of a brutal conflict, of death, displacement and despair. The answer was capability and character, with the military means available and the military mentality, intent and willpower to use them. The reluctance to take life was a major factor, but EUFOR had to be prepared for full-blown combat.

The situation in the Darfur Complex was constantly changing but mainly deteriorating, and turning threat to trust, savagery to security, strife to stability was no quick fix. In recent decades the populations there had seen armies, rebels and militias intervening with different motives and goals and EUFOR knew that this was a very troubled time

Irish Chief of Staff Lt Gen. Dermot Earley (left) and Minister for Defence Willie O'Dea being briefed by EUFOR Chad/RCA Operation Commander Lt Gen. Pat Nash (centre) in the OHQ, Mount Valerian, Paris. Courtesy of *An Cosantoir*

for Africa. The innocent were often caught in the crossfire of fighting, resulting in immense human suffering, and civilians were also the direct target of aggression. EUFOR did not underestimate the challenges of making a positive impact in such an environment, as its success was intimately linked to the level of trust it could achieve. EUFOR would not have the manpower to be a ground holding force and to fully secure its area of operations. It would have to operate during a period of high internal tension and continued threats from both inside and outside its eastern borders.

The 'Cowboy of the Sands'

Chad's president, Idriss Déby, was known as the 'Cowboy of the Sands' because of his courage, unquestionable fighting qualities and capacity for survival, all attributes much admired in the military society that was Chad. He was head of an army made up of clans and led by tribal leaders drawn from a society of warriors. Not only brave, he was also a tried and tested tactician and had earned an enviable reputation for being militarily able, having first led a series of victories against Libyan forces in the mid-eighties and later during that decade against rebel attacks. He had periodically undertaken military training with the French Army, attending military courses in the École de Guerre (Joint War School) in Paris, and in the mid-70s trained in France where he obtained his professional pilot's licence.

The son of a herder of the Bideyat clan, from the Zaghawa ethnic group, Déby was born in 1952 in Fada, north-eastern Chad. After attending officer school in N'Djamena, he served loyally with the army of President Félix Malloum. However, with the central authority disintegrating, Déby aligned himself with Hissène Habré, one of the chief Chadian warlords of the time, who subsequently seized power early in July 1982. Habré rewarded Déby for his loyalty by making him Commander-in-Chief of the army and later military adviser to the Presidency. Seven years later, however, Déby fell out with Habré when the latter accused Déby of preparing to plot a coup d'etat against him by attempting to increase the power of the Presidential Guard. Seeking refuge first in Libya, and then Sudan, Déby returned in December 1990 and effected a decisive attack into Chad, marching unopposed at the head of his troops, the insurgent group The Patriotic Salvation Movement, into the capital, N'Djamena.

Displaying both shrewdness and stubbornness he became known to the French as 'The Fox and the Mule'. He consolidated power through authoritarian means and favoured the Bideyat clan to the detriment of the Kobe clan, both of the Zaghawa tribe, which in its entirety was only representative of between two and three per cent of the population. In 2006, 'Chad' unilaterally reneged on an agreement with the World Bank, which obliged it to reserve some of its petroleum revenues for long-term development projects. Instead, Déby used the money to buy arms. Chad ranks near the bottom of almost every world league table, has 75 per cent illiteracy and almost half of its population is under fifteen years of age. Notwithstanding being poor, corrupted and lawless, Chad was not a failed state as such, but its government is a phantom one. Déby is both warlord and overlord, with a record of changing the rules of the political game, and the trigger to the current rebellions in Chad was his decision in 2004 to amend the constitution to allow him to run for a third time. His monopolisation and manipulation of power fuels the contesting of his political credibility, a credibility whose legitimacy is widely contested in the country and more importantly in the clan.

The key to understanding the then current context of the internal politics in Chad lay in the war in Darfur. When it broke out in February 2003, the leader of the rebellion in Sudan was a Chadian by the name of Abbaka, who was killed in 2004. He was also from the Zaghawa, the semi-nomadic people who lived on each side of the border between the two countries, and was sympathetic to his oppressed fellow Zaghawa in Sudan. Déby was acutely aware that the conflict in Darfur had the potential to destabilise his country, since the rebellion he had led some twenty years previously against then president Hissène Habré had been launched from Darfur, so in 2003 he was quick to back Khartoum in putting down the uprising. But this meant fighting his own tribal ethnic group and led to the erosion of popular support for his regime. In May 2005, the Zaghawa contingent of the Chadian National Army insisted that Déby replace the Chief of Staff and the head of the security forces with Zaghawas' sympathetic to the rebellion in Darfur. These changes led to Chad switching allegiance and supporting the rebels in Darfur, which provoked a reaction from Khartoum in late 2005. Déby's regime looked increasingly unstable since it was highly dependent on the Zaghawa who were themselves split over their support for the Darfur rebels. Regime maintenance and clan before country was the cancer that undermined Chad, the fratricidal struggle for power, for its own sake, its repeated tragedy.

Since gaining independence from France in 1960, decades of corruption, conflict, coups d'états and civil war have rendered Chad chronically unstable, undemocratic and underdeveloped. The various 'governmental regimes' based on clan ethnicity, despite a wealth of natural resources, had failed to responsibly distribute the proceeds equitably and provide even the basic needs for the population. Chadian politics was militarised and it was all about power and rebellion; seizing power by rebellion and maintaining power by resisting rebellion. Power had not changed hands peacefully in Chad since its transition from France nearly fifty years previously and each president since used to be a former warlord. There was an ingrained notion that power could only be achieved by violent means. Under Déby there was an increased concentration of power in the Presidency, whose authoritarian style was facilitated by the new oil wealth and the intervention of external powers. There was no Chadian state as such providing legislation, leadership and livelihoods for the ten million population, instead the State was one group's dominance over all others, and this dangerous domestic dynamic continues to endure.

The Events Leading up to Intervention

N'Djamena (Western Chad), late February 2008

There are different types of conflict, different styles of combat and different degrees of fighting, and in Chad the fighting is fast, furious and frontal. Distinctly direct, it is uniquely raw, primitive and crude. Theirs is a martial mentality which has not changed over the centuries. Chadians are warriors not workers and they are proud and eager to engage in the fight, their courage almost suicidal and their endurance legendary. Opposing columns can sometimes be between 1,000 and 1,500 in strength and they are often mounted on more than 100 vehicles, mostly converted Japanese pick-ups called 'Technicals', each containing up to twelve well-armed rebels.

When reconciled to fight, each column tries to outmanoeuvre the other to place their column perpendicular to the enemy's line of advance thus creating a 'T', like Nelson at the Battle of Trafalgar in 1805. This allows the concentration of firepower to be directed on the opposition's front and rear elements, yet presents the enemy's broadside with only a very limited target. Thereafter the opposition can be cut to pieces and destroyed by interweaving, interlinking and overlapping movements while all the time firing. Accuracy of fire, however, is sacrificed for volume of firepower, with large amounts of ammunition being expended during the fighting. The use of direct and indirect fire support weapons is not part of their military tradition, so there is often only limited and incorrect use of the Toyota-mounted support weaponry.

Indispensable, however, is the role of the Commanders, these 'lion leaders' standing tall, impressively brave and heroic at the front of their troops. Opposition commanders will openly challenge each other on their mobile phones and lead the Toyota charge like camel charges of old to within metres of each other, gambling everything on the fall of shot. It absolutely does not coincide with how western armies engage in war-fighting but it wasn't for western troops to judge, but to be aware of. Foreign also, and a complete antithesis for western troops, was the inclusion of 'child soldiers', often teenagers or younger. In Saharan tribes, puberty is when a boy becomes an adult and a warrior and is able to carry a weapon. For the west it is the brutalisation of the innocent, but through African eyes the tribal view is that if he stays in his village he runs the risk of dying of disease or an attack from the Janjaweed. It is better to die on the battlefield and there are no shortage of battlefields in Chad.

A Chadian saying is, 'when the rains stop, war resumes' and in November 2007 confrontations had already recommenced in the outlying regions of eastern Chad. By February 2008, the often disunited rebel groups had a new-found determination and unity of purpose in their opposition to Chadian president Idriss Déby. In addition, it may well have been the case, such was the timing and location of the fighting to come – matching closely as it did with EUFOR's intended early deployment plan – that the Sudanese government's own intent was to unleash chaos in the form of those same Chadian rebels whom Déby always claimed Sudan supported. The rebel's so-called 'State of War' declaration against French and other foreign armies was not a vague warning to the Europeans, they openly declared EUFOR a legitimate target.

On the first Saturday morning of February 2008, two hours before his marriage to Carla Bruni at the Élysée Palace in Paris, French president Nicolas Sarkozy phoned Chadian president Idriss Déby to offer him the opportunity to leave the country. French Special Forces, in a well-rehearsed operation, were standing by with helicopter engines running and rotary blades spinning to effect the order. Fierce fighting had erupted in the Chadian capital, N'Djamena, and in the Chadian presidential palace backing onto the Chari River, Déby took the call curtly, replying: 'I am the Chief, I am strong, I will win' and abruptly hung up. Two hours later, as Carla Bruni and Nicolas Sarkozy said 'Yes' to each other, Idriss Déby was saying a defiant 'No' to the rebels, and Irish General Pat Nash, EU Operational Commander, could not know what to say if asked the outcome, or even if the European Military

Operation to Chad was already defunct before it could commence. He strongly suspected it might be.

After four months of painstaking planning, of moulding and directing his multinational staff to his way of thinking and doing, of overcoming complex difficulties to get his force together and equipped, it was now looking increasingly likely that his Operational Headquarters' 'Battle Rhythm' might have to stop beating, abruptly and permanently. As the weekend progressed, open hostilities raged across the city and the fight for the Chadian capital was ferocious. There was little concrete information since telephone lines were down, State radio and television were off the air, and mobile phones were blocked. It was difficult to verify the reports of international media and thousands of the capital's inhabitants were fleeing to neighbouring Cameroon – crossing the Chari River using N'Djamena's Chagouda Bridge and primitive canoes. The French military were preparing to evacuate some 1,600 expatriates, diplomats and their families and fly them to Libreville in Gabon, where for now they were flying in French troop reinforcements. The lead elements of EUFOR, about twenty personnel, a mix of French, Irish and Austrians, were effectively spectators but importantly, together with the Force Commander, did their best to keep the OHQ updated. The rebels, having executed a rapid advance, initially avoided contact with Chadian forces and when conflict inevitably came were undeterred and so were now poised to overrun the capital.

In truth, despite their earnest intent and unwavering determination, the rebels were surprised to find themselves at N'Djamena. That they had done so was due to their avoidance of surveillance from French Air Force Mirage F1 and Atlantique reconnaissance observation planes. To remain undetected they had used a tactic known as the 'fan' as they moved. Their four-wheel drive vehicles gathered together only to refill fuel tanks, if possible under cover of vegetation, and then spread into small groups in the direction of their line of advance. They took the shape of a wide triangle formation with the base foremost, facing the enemy. They drove, insofar as possible, on the dry beds of the rivers where the sand was harder and reduced the risk of sinking. They crossed open spaces in small groups, travelling in tandem like a combat group negotiating an obstacle; one section covering while the other crossed then vice versa. In the larger open spaces speed was substituted for stealth and they moved quickly, a guide leading the column.

The Chadian army were also not idle in seeking out the rebel columns' advance on the ground. Assisted by six Mirages, two Atlantiques and one twin-engine Transall military transport aircraft, all equipped with thermic cameras, the squadron flew around the clock throughout the crisis. As quickly as they landed the film was developed and analysed at the headquarters of 'Opération Épervier' (Sparrowhawk) the site of the French military's presence in Chad, and within thirty minutes the information transmitted to the Chadian president. Finally an Atlantique 2 (ATL2) from Fleet 25F located the rebel column only 350 km east of the capital and images taken by a Mirage F1CT from 33 Wing highlighted the size and significance of the rebel force, with some 280–300 vehicles.

The Chadian forces moved to intercept, deploying in Ngoura to confront them, and a second Chadian Army detachment moved from Abéché to trap the rebels in a pincer movement. However, fearing they might be ambushed near Ati, the capital of the region of Batha, they hesitated and progressed tentatively in a very un-Chadian like manner. The rebels took advantage of their over cautiousness and bypassed the Chadian deployment by again adopting the 'fan' tactic. By surprise, speed and stealth the rebels successfully progressed to within 200 km of the Chadian capital. However, avoiding confrontation was becoming less and less likely as they neared their objective and their line of advance brought them inevitably to Massaguet, some 90 km from the capital. Déby knew only too well that the rebel advance had to be stopped here, because in 1990 he drove the same way at the head of his own column of rebels from Darfur in Sudan to N'Djamena to seize power from Hissène Habré who in turn did the same from Goukouni Oueddei in 1979.

A little less than 100 km east of N'Djamena, the surprise, speed and stealth that had brought the rebels that far was then substituted by strength. But Déby too was strong and at 0900 hours on Friday, 1 February 2008, at the head of 350 pickups, Chadian president Idriss Déby found and fought the rebels in Massakory. The opposing columns threw themselves at each other and the battle spread some 10 km along an axis on the Ati to N'Djamena route. Hundreds of four by four Toyota pickups pitched themselves against each other at full speed, furiously firing RPG rockets and with bursts of heavy machine gun fire. On contact the vehicles circled each other, firing wildly at point-blank range in a whirlwind of dust with black smoke bellowing from the fires of the first vehicles set ablaze in the bloody and confused combat. If the rebels had strength they also had a secret. Suddenly about twenty pickups from the Chadian army defected and went over to the rebel side, the advantage momentarily swinging towards the rebels. In the midst of the melee and coming to terms with this development, Déby was suddenly aware that the rebels seemed alert to his manoeuvrings and he realised the rebels had a second secret; they knew his radio frequencies.

Amid the hailstorm of bullets and explosions of vehicle-mounted recoilless cannons and RPG rocket-propelled grenades, Déby's four by four vehicle was suddenly surrounded. Concurrently some of his own Chadian army refused to fight and turned away, further treachery. At this moment, and defying sound tactical principles, one of Déby's Mil Mi-24 large helicopter gunships appeared overhead and maintaining a mid-air stationary position engaged the rebels with all its weapons, diverting the fire and attention of Déby's would-be attackers and allowing him to escape from the battlefield. Despite his withdrawal, no clear-cut outright winner emerged from the confrontation and Déby disengaged and returned to N'Djamena to mobilise the Zaghawa's of his ethnic clan, the loyal men of his Presidential Guard. On the journey back he narrowly avoided a rebel ambush.

By mid-afternoon, having settled with the rebels the location for the next confrontation, like medieval knights of old, the rebels and Déby's column both reached Massaguet, 90 km north east of N'Djamena. Déby had returned with seventy pickups, the rest destroyed or deserted, to be used essentially as a delay tactic, trading time for space, to slow down and wear down the rebel advance. An unbalanced contest commenced and this time the outcome was more clear-cut. Over several square miles, the desert of Massaguet took on the appearance of a giant graveyard filled with burnt vehicles, twisted ordnance and weaponry, strewn ammunition boxes, and amulets worn around the neck supposedly to protect against the enemy's bullets. Everywhere was the stench of death, once sensed never forgotten, and this time Déby was not the victor. But had his purpose been served? He withdrew to the capital and as darkness descended the rebels were now only 30 km away, the road to N'Djamena lay open. The rebel move was audacious and intelligent, both bold and brilliant. The timing of the offensive anticipated that the French would not protect Déby without the EU force in place, and if the French did act militarily, the arriving EU force would have been discredited before it even deployed. At the Élysée Palace in Paris, a midnight crisis meeting came to the decision to evacuate 1,600 expatriates and Opération Chari-Baguirmi was launched.

As darkness descended, from his palace in N'Djamena President Déby was busy organising the defence of his capital. Shaken by the rebels in the desert, he was preparing a static defence of the capital, though foremost in his mind he wondered if there would be any more rebel surprises. The perceived wisdom was that his situation was hopeless, but did he have a surprise or two of his own? The following morning, while President Nicolas Sarkozy was taking Carla Bruni for his third wife and EU operation commander General Pat Nash was taking his third cup of coffee at a Trocadero café, President Idriss Déby was taking stock of preparations for his third action against the rebels. He had not come out too well from the previous two and now he was fighting for his life. While wedding bells were ringing in the Élysée Palace, tank shells were ringing in N'Djamena. The centre of the Chadian capital was a hell of non-stop firing as the rebels attacked from all sides and Déby responded with all of his weapons. Earlier that morning the rebels had approached the capital from the north but then divided up, entering the city from three different directions and launching a disciplined coordinated and determined attack.

Too vast a city to defend in its entirety, instead Déby chose to concentrate his efforts around the presidential palace. To his rear he relied on the River Chari, his left flank was substantially secured by the airport where the French 'Épervier' (Sparrowhawk) force were deployed, firmly defending this strategic asset. Déby set out his defensive assets in 1 km long half circle arcs, known as a 'hedgehog' defence, within a 13 square km area containing a number of key roundabouts. Each axis from these granted a straight line of fire by any of his twelve Russian T-55 tanks, 1950s in origin but solid with forty tons of steel protection and each armed with a powerful 155mm cannon. The three-pronged rebel attack began from the east skirting the airport, in the centre straight towards the presidency, and from the west on the bypass towards the radio station where they intended to announce that Déby's regime was over. The rebels were operating an extended line of supply, far away from their bases inside Sudan, and they needed a quick victory. The rebels threw everything they had into the battle, a confrontation like this is won or lost in a day, two at most.

The onslaught had begun and the response from the T-55s was immediate. They concentrated their fire along the big avenues down which the rebel vehicles had to advance. The noise was deafening as tanks fired their 155mm cannons, the blast of their shells ripping through trees and walls and hitting their target, the explosions and fireballs of the 200 litre fuel drums on the back of the rebel pickups igniting. The response from the rebels was rocket-propelled grenades and heavy machine gun fire – cleverly maintaining mobility as they refusing to be fixed to any one spot and be destroyed – better to stay a moving target than a stationary one. With small arms exchanges between the rebels and Déby's dismounted 'infantry' protecting the T-55 tanks, the confrontations between rival columns moved along parallel roads, playing a deadly game of 'cat and mouse' and firing at and chasing each other. The rebels pushed hard and made gains and the continuing confrontation caused attrition on both sides. Who would last longer, which side could inflict more damage on the other, of the two forces which could endure more, on and on it went. Despite themselves, would the French have to intervene? Would the rebels make a go for the airport? If they could gain control of the airport, even a portion, they could access approaches from which to seize and control some of the key roundabouts and progress further towards the presidential palace.

Some furtive rebel fire was directed towards the French who responded in kind, but with more conviction, and the half-hearted rebel test firing tapered quickly off. Elsewhere, sections of French soldiers were caught in the crossfire as they assisted expatriates to evacuate on eighteen flights but none became decisively engaged. By early afternoon, fire fights were taking place everywhere; around the presidential palace perimeter near the central hospital, in front of the American Embassy and the radio station. The noise of the gunfire, with its sharp cracks, loud roars and thuds on impact, hastened non-combatants to take cover and seek protective shelter. For all of their efforts the rebels couldn't penetrate the tank cordon, yet Déby's forces seemed unable to stop them trying. Something had to give, one side had to blink, but neither did until the intervention by Déby of his four Mi-17 and Mi-24 attack helicopters which swayed the issue, strafing and rocketing the rebels. Their rocket pods systematically emptied, with each overpass inflicting deadly damage, the rebels were brought to heel and for now there was a stalemate as the rebels disengaged. After the day's fighting the centre of the city was filled with corpses. It was into this turmoil that the Irish Rangers would have flown. They were on their way to Dublin airport when they were told that the airport in the Chadian capital had been closed because rebel forces were getting near. They were given a last-minute order to return to McKee Barracks on Dublin's Northside and await developments.

What had developed in N'Djamena was not what the rebels had expected. They had not counted on this level of resolve from Déby and believed the fighting would all take place in open terrain and that on entry to the capital the president would flee. Street fighting, or fighting in built-up areas, is a different type of fighting. It requires different skills, training and techniques. It is heavier in casualties and much more demanding in quantities of ammunition. It literally goes from street-to-street, house-to-house, sometimes man-to-man in hand-to-hand fighting. Fighting tanks in the desert was one thing, but assaulting tanks in the streets – unable to attack them from the sides or behind – was another. Apart from a question of tactics it was also one of supply and time; food, fuel and ammunition were not available in infinite quantities. However, they had got this far, had supplies left and the French had not intervened. They retreated to the north east of the city to make preparations and plans for the next day's fighting. They knew it would be decisive.

There was rumour, counter-rumour, information, misinformation, claim and counter-claim all in abundance: 'The Chadian army had gone over to the rebels ... Déby's forces had deserted and fled across the Chagouda bridge with the thousands of N'Djamena's inhabitants ... the rebels had completely overrun the city ... Déby had fled to Cameroon ... the Chadian army had everything under control.' The media reporting was speculative and suggested Déby was doomed. Had the Chadian war chief, 'the Cowboy of the Sands', regained the initiative by not being defeated and was time running out for the rebels? Could the rebel chiefs Mahamat Nouri, Timane Erdimi and Abdelwahid Aboud Mackaye agree a course of action to break through to the presidential Palace? Could one true agreed leader emerge from among them and gain the supremacy and authority to maintain the initiative and keep the unity of the rebel alliance intact, or would it wilt under the strain? The dawn would shed its light on more than the coming day.

At the break of dawn the rebels launched a concerted attack focussed on a single axis, their objective the radio station building. Such was the collective intensity of the massed attack, allied to the defenders running out of ammunition, that the rebels succeeded in capturing the building – but not before the withdrawing Chadian troops had set the transmitters on fire and rendered them unserviceable. Spurred on by their victory, the rebels advanced across the Union roundabout and were again engaged some hundreds of metres further on, the Chadian army prepared to yield no further. The fighting became focussed near the central hospital then moved near the grand mosque. Firepower and will power fully in evidence, both sides were in deadlock. Fearful of becoming stuck in one place, the rebels looked to bypass the Chadian troops and sought a way through the city's 'big market'. They were now only 250 metres away from the presidential palace. Déby again employed his attack helicopters, taking off from the airport they were quickly spotted, and attacked the rebels – their firing setting the market ablaze. Angered by the use of the airport, the rebels threatened to fire on it so for safety and security the six French Mirage jets took off for Libreville in Gabon. Encouraged by the helicopters, Déby's forces hung on and then launched a counter attack. Slowly the rebels, lacking direction and with supplies dwindling, relinquished their momentum and were gradually pushed eastwards away from the presidential palace. By late afternoon the firing had stopped.

At dawn on the brink of defeat, Déby snatched victory throughout the morning where others would readily have conceded. Lacking unity of command and on the brink of victory, the rebel chiefs withdrew from the city, defeated where others could readily have succeeded. *C'est Afrique* – that's Africa. Hundreds had been killed, thousands were wounded, and property had been looted and destroyed – in essence, mayhem. Thirty-six hours of raging combat that was to become euphemistically referred to as 'the events'. The obvious danger for Déby was that there could well be a 'next event', because the rebels had managed to withdraw from the capital in an orderly manner, thereby ensuring that the power struggle within the country would continue.

So Much, so Far, so Fast: A Logistical Everest
'... and that, Sir, is why it cannot be done.' The briefing officer from Logistic Section stood away from the podium confident in the conclusive delivery of his presentation. He was now ready for questions, his entire demeanour suggesting he'd welcome and devour them. An experienced 'air-mover', his expertise, his computer-assisted analysis combined with no-nonsense logic and straight-talking manner, left him no reason to doubt his evaluation. He had brought along hard copy printouts as additional documentary proof of his detailed scrutiny. The movement cell of Logistic Section had been tasked with performing a study on the 'Strategic Air Transportation Logistic Deployment Possibilities' of personnel and equipment into Chad within new revised timelines. The briefing officer's in-depth examination was impressively detailed on a high-tech 'PowerPoint' presentation which was appropriate for the highly-charged atmosphere of the briefing and which suited the modern sophistication of the state-of-the-art Joint Operations Centre (JOC) of the OHQ. He pulled no punches, but neither did the Operational Commander in response: 'Do it anyway ... drive on.' There were no questions, the session was over.

It was the largest logistical move ever undertaken into Africa by the EU and the Irish Defence Forces. The logistic operation would see thousands of tons of vital cargo and essential, high value and sensitive equipment transported thousands of miles by ship, air, rail, and road into an impoverished war-torn Chad. It was to be the longest and largest autonomous EU military operation into Africa yet conducted and in terms of geography alone it could hardly have been tougher or more challenging. The demands of the military response required to address the operational complexities on the ground necessitated a suitably sized force to contend with the crisis presenting itself. This force had to be provided for in an uncompromising environment with extremes of climate in a race against time. The logistical pipeline was going to be the operation's lifeline and in the first instance EUFOR identified infrastructure as being key. The deployment phase, getting the troops on the ground, was the period in which EUFOR had to plan and deploy the capabilities in theatre necessary to conduct operations and maintain a robust, highly visible presence, whilst sustaining itself logistically and with medical support throughout its twelve-month mandate. EUFOR feared and faced considerable planning and logistical challenges during this phase, given the remote, vast and inhospitable area into which it had to deploy.

The host nation support that Chad and the Central African Republic could provide to the deployment was extremely limited. Chad had only two paved runways, one in N'Djamena capable of handling one strategic air transport aircraft at a time, and one at Abéché only capable of handling smaller tactical air transport (TAT) aircraft. The runways in eastern Chad were all unpaved gravel airstrips that were only able to handle smaller tactical and light aircraft. The airport runways were not long enough nor were their parking aprons large enough, and Africa did not have the quantities of concrete necessary to make them such. EUFOR immediately set about contracting major construction works, using concrete sourced in Portugal, to improve and develop airport runways and parking aprons for both N'Djamena and Abéché in order to facilitate deployment while not hindering the inflow of aid by humanitarian agencies.

Chad also had a very limited number of paved roads, mostly centred around N'Djamena, with the entire road network in the rest of the country consisting of unpaved dirt tracks that were passable only in good weather. In other theatres, at other times, EU forces on deployment were able to convert factories or school buildings or similar complexes into bases and camps. They were able to adapt, improvise and improve upon that which already existed. The simple and complex difficulty in Chad was that nothing existed, not even the infrastructure necessary to bring in the individual components of everything needed to start from scratch. EUFOR in Chad had to initiate everything for themselves in a country where there was nothing for anyone. They began with the infrastructure.

The establishment of land lines of communication through Cameroon to Chad and an air bridge from Europe to N'Djamena were crucial to the successful accomplishment of the simply enormous logistical undertaking. Described as a 'logistical Everest', it was more accurately a logistical nightmare. As is normal with military operations under the European Security and Defence Policy, the responsibility for deployment of personnel and equipment to theatre rested with the individual troop-contributing nations, of which Ireland was to be the second largest. Each developed a logistic plan for deployment by sea and air into Chad. Logistic Planning Conferences in Brussels and Paris ensured that the deployment of all troop-contributing nations' personnel and equipment was planned and conducted in a coordinated manner.

The Irish area of operations in eastern Chad was located at the outer reach of sustainable military range. Ireland being a small country, many other more powerful European forces would have been surprised if the Irish had successfully managed to deploy in theatre unaided and on time. But lessons had been learned from deployments into Lebanon, Liberia, Eritrea and Somalia. Invaluable experience had been gained and the Irish had benefitted hugely from these. This was a defining moment for the Defence Forces and there were not going to be any ad hoc Irish solutions to the enormous African problems. Ireland was up in lights, the European Force for the first time had an Irish operational Commander. Never before in its history did the Irish have so senior an international military appointment holder. The Irish had held individual Force Commander appointments with EU and UN missions before but this was at an entirely different level.

High, too, was the profile of this international response to the crisis in the Darfur Complex. Sudden, unexpected and definitely outside its normal comfort zone, nonetheless there was a realisation that this was both achievable and an opportunity to demonstrate the Defence Forces as credible, capable and competent enough to operate far away under difficult, enduring conditions. The people with the power to make this happen were already exercised. At the strategic military level, General Nash and his multinational staff were driving the planning and coordination necessary in relation to the revised timelines brought about by the delays arising from the lengthy Force Generation Process and the Battle of N'Djamena in February 2008. On the Irish political level, Minister of Defence Willie O'Dea was stoutly defending the level of resources made available, and on the Defence Force Headquarters level the logistical planners under Colonel Paul Pakenham, linking with their Operations counterparts, were engaged in the mechanics of the details of the preparation for the move.

The distances and timescale of the logistic operation were huge and short respectively – a tough combination. It was 4,000 kilometres and 15 days by ship from Ireland to Douala seaport in Cameroon, from Douala seaport to the Chadian capital N'Djamena was a further 2,000 kilometres and 25 days by rail and road. Finally from N'Djamena to the area of operations in eastern Chad was an additional 900 kilometres and up to 10 days by road, a total distance of nearly 5,000 kilometres and 50 days … at least. Overall EUFOR, including the MV Zeren cargo ship leased by the Irish, had to make nine sea lift transportations from Europe to Douala in Cameroon with twenty-one subsequent rail convoys and 140 road convoys along the Cameroon corridor to N'Djamena. In all, more than 2,400 units, containers of equipment and vehicles went through Cameroon during the deployment phase. The air bridge from Europe to Chad enabled strategic air transport aircraft such as the Antonov An-124 and Lockheed C-130 Hercules to unload equipment and personnel directly at N'Djamena airport. A total of 540 strategic air transportation flights from Europe, including seventeen from Ireland, were subsequently conducted into N'Djamena airport.

Chad did not possess the facilities required to house the force's headquarters in N'Djamena and Abéché, nor camps for deployment throughout the AO in eastern Chad. Construction of operational camps on brownfield sites involved a huge programme of engineering and building. Overall six camps, including four with a capacity for 600 personnel and Star Camp in Abéché, with a capacity for 2,000 personnel, enabled EUFOR to establish and maintain a permanent footprint within its area of operations. In addition to accommodating EUFOR troops, the camps provided facilities for the United Nations Mission in Central African Republic and Chad (MINURCAT), who worked side-by-side with EUFOR. The rear headquarters, at Europa Camp in N'Djamena, provided the force with an essential logistics and support base at the main point of entry into Chad. The location selected was an old prison compound near the international airport, within which EUFOR built accommodation for over 600 personnel. Europa Camp was the focal point for the coordination of strategic air transport to and from Europe, and for land convoys from Cameroon, and was a central hub in the supply chain to the area of operations. Star Camp in Abéché, 880 kilometres further east, was designated as the forward Force Headquarters (FHQ) and acted as a staging post for onward supply movement.

At Star Camp, EUFOR constructed two large aprons to handle the forces' multinational army aviation battalion assets with a capacity for handling up to twenty medium-sized helicopters and three tactical aircraft simultaneously. In the race against time to establish these new aprons in N'Djamena and Abéché and to construct the forward battalion camp sites, the Operation Commander accepted considerable risk. In late November 2007, some two months before the Political and Security Committee (PSC, a permanent body within the European Union dealing with Common Foreign and Security Policy issues) decision to launch the operation in late January 2008, or the formal approval of the operation budget by Athena's Special Committee, a working body of the EU Council which addresses issues related to the financing of EU military operations, he committed nearly €72 million for construction of these projects.

This decision, and the deviation from stringent EU procurement rules, was critical as it was central to facilitating the timely provision of the infrastructure necessary for the deployment and sustainment of the EU force. This was real-time decision making and it was not everyone who would have the character to make the call. Sites close to existing airstrips were chosen for three forward operating bases in eastern Chad: in Iriba the Multinational Battalion North was posted, consisting of Polish troops with a Croatian detachment; in Farchana was Multinational Battalion Centre, French troops with a Slovenian detachment; and in Goz Beïda was Multinational Battalion South, Irish troops with a Dutch Company. A French Company was also stationed at Birao in the Central African Republic.

Manpower and materials, time and deadlines, work priorities, concurrency of effort, excessive heat, no frills, no beer and no whinging. For the advance party of the 97th Battalion, under Commandant Gary 'Tex' McKeon, while speed was important, safety was essential and already they were a man short. On arrival, a scorpion bite while acclimatising in Camp Europa N'Djamena was a salient introductory lesson for one trooper. Although treated and stabilised immediately in a nearby French military hospital, further medical treatment was required and medical repatriation home. Whenever there's a new mission overseas there's a saying that you shouldn't go until the volley ball courts are built … but someone has to build them – and the rest of the camp while they're at it. With the site chosen and the manpower available it was just a matter of materials. EUFOR subcontractors had completed the horizontal works – those up to ground level – levelled the site, prepared security banks known as 'berm' – a low earthen wall with a dry moat surround – and dug out the sewage requirements for all the sites chosen. The individual nations had then to complete their own vertical build. Camp construction was preceded by site markings and confirmation that the various measurements would be the plumb for the build. The remainder of the advance group were flown down on successive flights and given a warm welcome by the Rangers as well as camel back spiders the size of your hand, black and white scorpions, snakes and an incredible variety of insect life.

Constructing Camp Ciara, the main Irish military camp near Goz-Beïda, began in earnest the following morning under the protective eye of the Ranger wing security party. Erecting the tents, ablutions and other life support facilities, workshop and office structure development continued at pace over the following weeks, work often interrupted by the arrival of convoys carrying containers, vehicles and MOWAG armoured personnel carriers on flatbed trucks, and fuel containers. The benefits of the Irish Defence Forces 'decade of change', a process begun in 2000 'to enable the Defence Forces to meet the requirements of Government in the changing national and international spheres' were being reaped. A series of consultant's reports, barrack closures and downsizing had led to the reinvestment of funds into new equipment and an increased emphasis on training becoming more field oriented and less garrisoned had paid off. The Defence Forces were involved in more exercises with more people involved and mistakes were welcomed as lessons were learned.

Over time it was evident that there were fewer mistakes being made while others were being identified. Personnel didn't have to be told what to do all the time and this ongoing training combined with continued overseas deployment to new mission areas meant a new level of competence and confidence was achieved. The Defence Forces were leaner, better equipped, prepared and more professional than ever before and it was all manifesting itself in Chad. That the Irish were prepared to go where and when needed didn't go unnoticed by other nationalities either. This operation was primarily about safeguarding the environment for the refugees and internally displaced people (IDPs), but you had to have a capability to do so and from the beginning the Irish had demonstrated theirs. They had to, for six weeks later would see the arrival of the Irish battalion proper.

The amount of planning that went into the comprehensive logistic Chadian endeavour was staggering. The development of an Irish logistic capacity regarding preparation, outsourcing and execution was essential alongside the synchronisation of strategic levels in tandem with operational and tactical levels. This was not about chance, individual initiative or luck, it couldn't be, it was too big for that. The task, in effect, was to build a small Irish village in the middle of Africa. In Chad, if you didn't have it you couldn't get it, therefore sequencing was key. Ensuring the right materials arrived in the most logistically correct order possible became the task for Commandant Earnan Naughton, Quartermaster of the 97th Battalion. This meant prioritising containers for the progressive use of their contents on arrival, to avoid what was needed first arriving last and vice versa, which in turn meant ensuring the work on the ground was planned well in advance, the containers packed accordingly and their transportation sequenced properly. Preparation was everything and detail was paramount, time, distance and circumstances demanded it. Inevitably, however, there were many such priorities and the decision was how to prioritise between them, to manage the balance between construction materials and force protection – weapons, explosives, armour and ammunition – and avoid getting bogged down. Because it was always a race against time, only now more so.

The delay caused by the elongated force generation process, compounded by the rebel attack on N'Djamena, all narrowed the window of opportunity considerably and the rains were already coming in from the south. There was only so much strategic lift capacity available worldwide and Ireland was not the only country in the market for it, nor Chad the only destination. At Douala port in Cameroon, EUFOR's sea port of disembarkation (SPOD) was where a rear station for onward movement office was established to receive the vital cargoes arriving by ship, having already travelled the 4,000 kilometres in 15 days, and break them down onto available road and rail transport. The cargo was then moved along the Cameroon corridor logistical pipeline, a 2,000 km overland journey taking 25 days to complete. Here again coordination between the troop-contributing nations was necessary, mindful of avoiding, curtailing or impinging upon the humanitarian agencies' capacities to move their own crucial food cargoes. N'Djamena was also EUFOR's airport of disembarkation (APOD), where strategic airlift flights arrived. Flight schedules, road and rail timetables, early arrivals, late arrivals, non-arrivals, containers and vehicles, personnel and vehicles, and essential equipment of all types had to be sorted, reprioritised and moved onto eastern Chad and the building of camps relied on it.

Commandant Enda De Bruin had the unenviable task of matching the material to the available means and modes of transport. It was vital to maintain the onward momentum as all too easily the heroic efforts of the logistics teams could come unstuck, the planning and preparation undone and mix ups in the scheduled sequencing manifest themselves. Millions of euros worth of equipment was arriving into an impoverished country and the temptations were great. The trains from Douala were quicker than the roads, supposedly, and plans made accordingly. However, they were becoming susceptible to strikes, derailments and even rioting. Knowing what had arrived, what was due, what was delayed and what was currently unaccounted for and getting it all onto tactical air transport or road convoys – there was no rail network beyond N'Djamena – was no small task. The indigenous transport comprised of old flatbed trailers, many pre-1970, with their flatbed areas not coinciding exactly with modern containers. Sometimes these consisted of two trailers welded together, and on the journeys eastward many broke down or became bogged down, their loads subsequently being picked up by the next passing convoy. Detailed manifesting, literally knowing what was in which container and where at any one point in time was crucial. For Commandant McKeon and the Irish Advance Work Party waiting in Goz Beïda, the following day's work was contingent on whatever arrived the previous day. But it all happened, it was made to. EUFOR and the Irish were 'into Africa' and the challenge was really just beginning.

Rangers and Rebels

Burnt by a ceaseless sun from a clear blue sky, the African desert manifests itself in many ways and assumes many appearances. In eastern Chad it did not correspond to the romantic notion of mile after mile of shifting sand dunes endlessly trodden by heartbroken French Foreign Legionnaires trying to forget an unrequited lover, but rather a rugged, scorched, rock-strewn landscape of undulating plains of compacted dirt and sand. Deserts are dangerous and Chad's was amongst the harshest on earth. The heat and hardness were unrelenting enough, but there was a less obvious hidden hell in its vastness. Lurking amongst its enormity was a monotony, a sterility of sameness. Hundreds of miles of immense wilderness: open plains, acacia trees and thorn bushes, the continuum broken only by low ridges, rocky outcrops and dry rutted river beds. All of this would challenge your consciousness to remain alert, but you had to be aware because there was death in the desert and it didn't differentiate between its victims.

The Irish Army Ranger patrols knew this all too well as they encountered isolated villages in desolate places on their long-range reconnaissance patrols. They were part of EUFOR's elite spearhead 'Initial Entry Forces', some 450 special forces from five participant countries, and would spend anything up to eight days at a time – sometimes longer – conducting one of the most high-risk operations ever undertaken by an EU force. Sent to lead the way, the Rangers conducted vital reconnaissance into the unknown, to find *who* was out there and whether they were friendly or not, *what* was out there, *where* exactly it was and *what* was going on. They paved the way for the eventual incremental deployment of the main force and the risks were very real. The area of eastern Chad was beset by many mobile militias, rebels and bandits, all armed to the teeth … and it was *their* home turf. Volatile was the new norm and the entire region was on a knife-edge. Eastern Chad was no place for people who didn't know what they were doing.

On arrival, the Rangers had used their time to good effect, acclimatising to the heat, scrub and bush conditions, orienting themselves and fine tuning their weapons and equipment. Now they were geared up and ready to put their lives on the line to face the wild and unpredictable under inhospitable conditions, thousands of miles from home. With the confidence and skills, teamwork and tenacity needed to face the unknown in such circumstances, they were the first ones in. To conquer uncertainty is the product of a selection and training regime that produces the toughest and best-trained soldiers, mentally and physically. To be there in the first place they had to prove themselves individually, and now they had to tackle arduous conditions and circumstances that most couldn't or wouldn't have been able to. Chad was a whole new chapter and the Rangers were depended upon to deliver.

Unusually for Special Forces soldiers they were being used overtly, not covertly, and they were there as much to be seen as to see. It was their job to let people know who they were as they in turn learned about the people, to give information as much as to get information and to let people know that this was a *European* force not simply another French one. Route reconnaissance, how to get where and which routes best suited what type of vehicles – most routes didn't suite vehicles at all – air strip verification, liaison with village elders, humanitarian aid agencies and MINURCAT were all part of their duties. The Rangers were ready for those whose welcome might be inclined more towards hostility and they had full authorisation, as would the entire force under the UN Chapter 7 Peace Enforcement terms of EUFOR's mission to Chad and CAR, to engage in combat – if necessary – with any armed elements in order to prevent criminal acts against refugees, IDPs, non-governmental organisations (NGOs) or indeed attacks on Irish or other EUFOR personnel.

Well equipped for their task in Chad, the overall Ranger detachment of fifty-plus members was split into a number of smaller teams. Each team was heavily armed with individual weapons such as the state-of-the-art Heckler and Koch assault rifle and machine guns. Each special forces team had heavy support weapons, such as the AT4 SRAAW short-range anti-armour weapons, M203 grenade launchers and other short-range missile systems, as well as the 7.62mm FN general purpose machine gun, with a rate of fire of 750 rounds per minute always available for support fire in the 'sustained fire' mode, or short 'killing bursts' of fifty rounds. A section level weapon, the Rangers had theirs vehicle-mounted on Ford F350 special reconnaissance vehicles (SRVs) along with Browning M2 .50 calibre HMGs. The choice of personal weapon was a matter for individual tastes, but in general it was the Steyr AUG A3, a variant of the standard Steyr AUG 5.56mm rifle on issue throughout the Defence Forces, which allowed the mounting of extras such as the M203 under-slung grenade launcher, capable of firing a grenade beyond normally thrown distances. In terms of available firepower, the Rangers weren't lacking any and had more besides. Crucially on call was air reinforcement in the form of Caracal or Gazelle attack helicopters fitted with anti-armour missiles.

The Rangers had analysed the rebel incursion into N'Djamena and assessed them to be better organised, trained and led than previously believed, concentrating their minds more so than heretofore. They had to have a predisposition, posture and preparedness to react to anything and to have the presence of mind to be ready for anything and to be able to respond appropriately and be flexible. They had learned this to good effect on a previous deployment in Liberia, some four years earlier, when a twenty-strong heliborne patrol had received word of local villagers being held captive in a metal container in extreme heat and reportedly being pulled out one by one, raped and tortured by renegade militia forces. Deviating from their route they had swooped in using speed and surprise, affecting the successful release of the villagers and detaining the renegade commander, known as 'The Prince', during the raid. Now called into action again, they found themselves once more in the so-called zone of maximum danger, or 'red zone', patrolling eastwards towards the border with Darfur in Sudan. In essence to gather intelligence on likely threats from any hostile or other de facto militia groups, but also to liaise with local leaders and assess their disposition towards EUFOR and particularly its Irish contingent.

One particular Ranger patrol, operating east of the village of Ade in the vicinity of Modoya, halted to further investigate this isolated village. Sending forward one element of the thirty-strong patrol in their SRV to check it out, the rest of the patrol took the opportunity to relax, while remaining circumspect to the circumstances and leaving one other SRV and crew to cover the cautious approach of their village-bound comrades. With their Kevlar helmets to hand, the Rangers loosened their shemaghs, a type of Arab scarf that provides protection from sunburn, dust and sand during the day and warmth during the cold desert night, and pulled them loose off their faces. Goggles with different coloured lenses – yellow and orange were favoured to increase contrast and make target spotting simpler – were worn to keep dust out of their eyes and Nomex fire-resistant gloves kept their hands warm in cold conditions and – especially here in the desert heat of Chad – stopped sweat from loosening their grip when handling weapons. In an unpredictable environment that was important.

Where unpredictability ends and surprise begins was where the covering party suddenly found themselves. The Ranger sentry manning the Browning M2 .50 calibre HMG threw a disbelieving glance at his companion in the front seat of the SRV. Up to then he was casually pointing his GPMG, mounted on a swinging arm attached to the side of the SRV, in the general direction of the village with the unconcerned but confident manner of someone expertly familiar and comfortable with it. Both again stared in the direction of the village to confirm what they believed they had seen in the first instance. One minute there was a small, isolated, simple little Chadian village, the next minute it was a small, isolated simple little Chadian village with 200 armed rebels emerging from folds in the surrounding landscape. One moment they weren't there, and then they were, to the disbelief of the observers looking on. It was the first time EUFOR had 'bumped' into any of the rebel groups and the numbers were not favouring the Rangers. Sent to establish a threat assessment, it wasn't going to be clearer than this and the situation was tense, dramatically so. The next few moments, how each side reacted to one another, were crucial. Could the Rangers control the moment or would the first of these confrontations take on a momentum all of its own. Could they afford the luxury of 'wait and see' or were they losing the initiative by the millisecond … and it was all going to be determined in that one moment.

There was a fleeting fatefulness, a series of split-second instants of indecision and uncertainty, a hair-trigger between life and death. The covering Rangers, alerted to the developing situation, initially considered it best to maintain observation from a distance before reacting, since the wrong decision could make a bad situation much worse and escalate a simple encounter into an engagement. A readiness to respond did not rule out being patient, and the small Ranger squad in the village were perfectly capable of defending themselves if necessary. They were equipped with an FN Minimi support weapon – a rapid-fire machine gun with an incredible rate of fire – that was more than sufficient to punch a hole in the rebel perimeter. Not yet fired upon, the Rangers instead decided to stand their ground, employing will power instead of firepower and discipline instead of fight or flight. They would exchange words instead of bullets and surrounded, surprised and seriously outnumbered it was appropriate that they bring into play their best weapons: brains and wit. They would attempt to talk themselves out of trouble and do what generations of Irish peacekeepers had done worldwide for six decades whenever they found themselves in tight corners and defuse what might otherwise become a difficult situation.

The group of heavily armed rebels were among those who had played a major role in the attack on N'Djamena some weeks before, almost succeeding in taking the capital. The lightning strike had put the region back into the forefront of the world's consciousness and almost succeeded in achieving regime change in Chad, and also its objective of delaying or stopping the arrival of the EU troops. However, the rapidly changing situation on the ground indicated some form of stability had been restored and two weeks after their schedule EUFOR recommenced its deployment of pathfinder troops in advance of the main body. Now they had come face-to-face on the ground, Rangers and rebels, and it was no time for hysteria. The deployment of European troops was one of the bravest and most important steps yet and showed the world that the European Union was capable of projecting force in an achievable manner for a completely altruistic end. But did these particular rebels understand and appreciate this?

Once fully deployed, EUFOR would be equipped with both the moral mandate and physical hardware to give potential attackers a bloody nose, but at this point EUFOR was very far from being fully deployed. It was impartial, but did these rebels believe this? Trust is built over time and through reciprocity. The manner of this message was being relayed by EUFOR's Initial Entry Force, the Rangers among them, and was part of building that process. Had there been enough time for this message to reach this particular rebel group, or were the next moments going to confirm that the rebels viewed the Rangers and hence EUFOR as belligerents and set about giving them a bloody nose by embroiling them in a fierce fire fight? Would the Rangers blink in the face of aggression? Both groups knew how to fight and were good at it, so would this random encounter end in shooting or serenity, bloodshed or benevolence, death or discussion? Would the 'warrior' rebels and the 'warrior' Rangers go head-to-head or would the Ranger's pragmatism pay off?

The encounter was fast approaching its tension-filled finale and the single decisive moment would suddenly be upon them. Just as suddenly it passed and neither side had blinked but nor had they opened up. As it happened these rebels were commanded by a one-time member of Déby's government who had an educated view of the world. He recognised the Irish flag badge on the Rangers' uniforms and having no rancour towards them agreed to speak through the patrol's interpreters. It was the first time EUFOR's international troops had established contact with one of the rebel groups and during the course of the hour-long conversation which ensued, and as apprehensions became inevitably less fraught, the soldiers chatted and posed for photographs, one such image subsequently being used a number of days later as a visual supplement to a briefing on the incident. A subsequent query from the Chadian authorities in relation to both the matter of the encounter and the photograph raised concerns that it could be used as propaganda against the Irish and EUFOR. The Operation Commander stressed the importance of maintaining freedom of movement for EUFOR personnel and their impartiality; that EUFOR was free to speak with all actors in theatre as it was not siding with any one party or parties, nor concerned with the internal politics of Chad. The incident highlighted and reinforced the significance that staying true to your mandate is a great strength.

War on the Move – The Rebels Return

Eastern Chad, June 2008

'Stand-to! Stand-to! No duff (this is for real), no duff!' Those in Camp Ciara, home of the newly arrived Irish EUFOR battalion and a detachment of eighty Dutch marines, couldn't hear more of the repeated message over the camp's public address system as the noise of impact explosions in the nearby town of Goz Beïda drowned them out. They were on their feet within seconds, helmets, flak jackets and weapons in hand as they ran for the perimeter defence positions, mortar-pits and weapon bays. 'Rebels to the right, rebels on the runway, rebels to the left, rebels on the runway. RPGs, repeat RPGs'. The camp itself was being threatened by a rebel approach from the airstrip. Suddenly a 'contact-report' on the radio: 'Hello zero, hello zero, this is seven zero. Contact report, over', as an Irish mobile observation patrol positioned on a hill overlooking Goz Beïda had just received incoming mortar fire. The urgency in the voice of the radio operator told the battalion operations room staff all they needed to know.

Meanwhile, an area immediately in the vicinity of D'Jabal refugee camp, which had been engulfed by the rebel's main effort, now became the scene of a serious onslaught and an ongoing intensive fire fight between Chadian government forces and the rebel attackers. The Irish, doing what they came to do, interposed and placed themselves in seven fully manned MOWAG armoured personnel carriers between the refugee camp and the fighting to shield and protect the refugees from the belligerents and were now themselves dangerously close to becoming caught in the conflict's crossfire. Three fast-moving situations were taking place almost simultaneously, each different and all dangerous, which required quick but reasoned reactions and fast but considered decisions – getting it wrong could cost lives.

Lieutenant Colonel Paddy McDaniel, the officer commanding the Irish 97th Battalion, had to judge the situation correctly with urgency but without emotion. For the rebels this was not about positions, it was war on the move, and for the Irish commander the fewer moving parts out there the better. The important thing for the Chadian National Army was to check this movement, part of a wider rebel incursion. For the Irish battalion, with a lot going on and a lot at stake, good communication links were vital and it was then that they failed. The nature of the high terrain that surrounded the area adversely affected communications and there was nothing else for it but to send the balance of the remaining armoured personnel carriers at best speed to reinforce the area, re-establish communications and extract the besieged under-fire observation patrol. For the time being the Dutch marines were kept in reserve.

Having been sent out earlier to monitor the movements associated with the rebel incursion into the Goz Beïda area, Commandant Tom McGuinness and his APC Company noticed that Chadian National Army elements had taken up a defensive line along the eastern side of the town of Goz Beïda. It wasn't long before the inevitable violent clash between the Chadian army and the rebels erupted, the noise of the engagement carrying all the way back to Camp Ciara. His communications still down, but knowing his commander's intent, Commandant McGuinness ordered his APCs to make for a position on the north eastern slopes of the hill occupied by the D'Jabal refugee camp – their job was to defend those refugees and that's what they were going to do. The rebels hit hard, striking speedily and firing furiously then quickly disappearing behind cover, only to re-emerge and hit again, each time fighting fiercely. The Chadian army responded and thick black smoke rose over the town. The fuel store of a German aid agency was ablaze, and unintentional fire from both sides rained down on APC Company – their MOWAGs' taking hits. Within the hour the forceful rebel foray proved too much for the Chadian army and they disengaged and melted away, surrendering the town to the rebels. The rebels went to ground to regroup and reorganise, choosing a location in dead ground – an unobservable fold in the undulating terrain – and blocked from the view of the Irish by three massive World Food Programme warehouses.

Now the Irish position was to wait, watch, wonder and try to preempt whatever move the rebels would make next. At whatever level, clarity of thought is crucial for a commander so as to inform his or her judgement. The pace of events, the confusion, communications – or lack of same – the terrain, supplies, most of all priorities are all part of the decision-making mix and are all important. Vital for the APC Company was to assess what the rebels were going to do next. Unlikely to withdraw, they could either go left or right. Left would take them on a direct collision course with the Irish, in which case the Irish would be forced to open fire, right would take them to Goz Beïda, where they would not. Mind made up, Commandant McGuinness knew what he had to do. The use of force was not an issue to be entered into lightly, but he was fully able to justify his considered intended actions. If the rebels came left they would have to get through the Irish position

MOWAG Armoured Personnel Carrier (APC) of the Irish Battalion's APC Company in position to protect the Internal Displaced Personnel Camp at Goz Beïda.
Courtesy of An Cosantoir

protecting the refugees. Given that they may have to open fire, the Irish determined to do so first. As soon as the rebels put their noses around the left-hand edge of the sheds they were going to be engaged with heavy and sustained fire.

Nor was there any uncertainty in the mind of Lieutenant Colonel Paddy McDaniel back in the operations room at Battalion HQ in Camp Ciara. He had an OP (observation patrol) under direct heavy fire, an APC Company taking indirect incidental fire and poor communications. An ongoing rebel–Chad National Army engagement with a serious threat to the refugees was all too real. The stakes were alarmingly high and getting it wrong could mean the difference between personnel living or dying where they stood. Blinded by silence due to the communications failure it was time to mobilise the balance of Reconnaissance Company (Recce Coy) and re-establish communications, reinforce the APC Coy and extract the OP patrol. No easy task and matters were certainly heating up under Chad's searing mid-day sun.

Commandant Mark Brownen was not one to shun a challenge, and this particular challenge may well include having to fight his way out past his own camp's front entrance. It was time to assess the threat from the rebels positioned on the adjacent airstrip. What had developed there was a tense face-off, rebels with RPGs (rocket-propelled grenades) and Irish with SRAAWs (short-range anti-armour weapons), each pointing nervously at the other. The Irish were behind the camp's earthen bank perimeter with its dry moat surround, razor wire and watch towers on top. They had cover from fire afforded by the prepared positions, heavy weapons and most importantly were resolute – an uneven contest and the situation was containable. It was now time to get Recce Coy's APCs out – moving and doing. As this group entered Goz Beïda, hearing and seeing firing all around them, they made their way towards Commandant McGuinness at D'Jabal refugee camp. Along the way communications were re-established with the OP, who reported they were taking even heavier fire than before, from both mortars and HMG, with at least one rocket-propelled grenade fired into the area that they were occupying. Extraction from the OP area was not possible at that time and they were instructed to continue with their evasive actions and move to an area below their present location, which afforded them some cover from fire.

On arrival at D'Jabal, Commandant Brownen's Recce Coy located Commandant McGuinness's APC Coy, and having received an update sent a situation report on his radio back to Battalion HQ. With the news that Commandant McGuinness's APC Company was intact, Lieutenant Colonel Paddy McDaniel ordered Commandant Brownen's recce company to move to extract the OP patrol. Moving his APCs forward until the OP patrol was visible to him, Commandant Brownen picked out a route which would afford the OP team cover from the firing and bring them towards him. That the incoming fire had become less intense was not altogether incidental. Captain John Tynan, officer-in-charge of the OP patrol, had two close reconnaissance vehicles – a cavalry variant of the MOWAG APC – with a Kreuzlingen remote weapons platform on top directed by a sophisticated guidance system from within, enabling the vehicle's heavy machine guns and 40mm grenade machine gun to be fired with hatches closed and hull-down. Military analysts consider it superior to those used by American troops in Iraq and Afghanistan, where exposed turret gunners regularly fall victim to sniper attacks. Made aware during the previous twenty-four hours that 2,000 rebels were making their way towards Goz Beïda, of which 800 had arrived, the Irish readied themselves and waited.

Although the rebel's modus operandi suggested they would make their move at dawn they didn't, then suddenly sprang a surprise attack at mid-day. The two reconnaissance vehicles, and a dismountable element within, took up position on a saddle feature on a hill at the eastern side of the main Goz Beïda–Abéché road. Their task was to observe eastwards in particular but also to seek an overarching watch of the area. Somebody didn't want them to be there and had opened fire on the position. The Irish weren't to be deterred lightly, though the impact of incoming fire creates an impression all of its own – unlike anything else – and there is nothing quite so unnerving. It is an experience set to fairly test anyone's ability under pressure.

For those who have not experienced the sensation, it is an initiation both welcomed and unwelcome at once, because then you know that the wondering of what it is like to be under fire is over. This is quickly overtaken by fear, uncertainty and a gripping sense of alarm that the next moments are unscripted and totally undetermined. Curiously, the realisation is both exactly as you might have expected and yet completely new and daunting. Most of all, to come under fire is bloodcurdling, knowing its initiation has come from someone with menace and intent, something real and surreal, bizarre, humbling and outrageously infuriating. Competing effects and emotions notwithstanding, the reaction is remote and automatic as years of training kicks in, presence of mind prevails and control takes over. Thus encouraged you get on with it. Awareness is heightened and with heart pounding, even in the heat your extremities can go cold, you take in a wider field of vision.

As the patrol moved evasively, they soon realised that the firing was following them which meant that somcone somewhere was acting as a spotter – calling in corrections to the fall of shot and bringing the aggressive line of fire back onto target, only they were the target. First they had to locate the spotter and once they had been found they had to be deterred. From being fired upon it was time for the Irish to return fire and they brought the remote weapons platform into play. After unleashing a few rounds the desired effect was quickly achieved. The rebels abandoned their vantage point and the firing stopped. It was all very matter of fact.

Meanwhile, at the height of the clashes and with over 250 Irish troops already deployed, a request for evacuation was made by some humanitarian NGOs whose compound inside Goz Beïda was being looted by rebels. Lieutenant Colonel Paddy McDaniel immediately committed his reserve, the Dutch Marines in their Viking all terrain armoured vehicles. Fifteen minutes later they had travelled the 5 km and were at the NGO compound. On arrival they found between 100 and 120 rebels in and around the compound and a tense stand-off commenced. The rebels had peeled off from the main body and stormed into Goz Beïda looking to loot rich pickings from wherever they could find them. They entered the compound, firing their AK-47 assault rifles, and began stealing vehicles, fuel and satellite phones, only for the Dutch to arrive, As the Dutch marines and the rebels confronted one another, both were on the verge of going head-to-head – a nervously twitching trigger-finger could inadvertently transform the scene from tension into carnage in a split-second. It was time to get the Dutch some support and now.

With APC Company having protected the perimeter of the refugee camp, they slowly and gingerly went to assist, since the sudden arrival of more armoured personnel carriers onto the scene could set off a tense situation. The APC Company stood off at the market square near the UNICEF building, established contact with the NGOs and began the process of evacuating the humanitarian aid workers. The refugee camp secure, the rebels had withdrawn and as APC Company was available they moved into town to join Recce Company. During the hour-long stand-off, two Irish APCs had entered the town's market square to assist the Dutch. With the Dutch refusing to blink the rebels left, for the most part empty-handed.

With face-offs, stand-offs and shoot-outs, the Irish and Dutch were pushed to the limit but remained calm and focussed. They showed enough strength, resolve and willingness to return fire when fired upon and all was sufficient to deter an attack without escalating or inflaming the situation. They had passed the test. They had demonstrated impartiality by not intervening between the rebels and Chadian army, displayed resolve by standing firm to protect the refugees and later, on request, evacuated humanitarian aid workers and exhibited capability in returning fire. EUFOR was seen to be credible and the operation was a turning point that was all the more significant for its occurring early on. That was as may be, there were still 800 rebels out there and more beyond. This was day three of their incursion and of a very dangerous situation.

Buoyed by their success at Goz Beïda, four rebel columns pushed westwards, stating they would carry the war to the interior of the country. Believing that this hit-and-run incursion demonstrated their relevance to their sponsors, they claimed they were prepared to call off their attack if France and the European Union forced President Déby to round-table talks on Chad's political future. Their attempt to forge a foothold inside eastern Chad had been a success from the beginning. On day one they had been successful in scoring rare hits on two of Déby's attack helicopters at Modeyna. Having inflicted heavy casualties on the approaching rebel column shortly after crossing the border, the pilots of the Chadian attack helicopters went for the kill within range of the rebel vehicles. The crews of the jeep mounted anti-aircraft weapons couldn't believe their luck. Ordinarily, attack helicopters would stand off, hovering out of range with all weapons delivering from afar their deadly payloads of rockets and bombs to devastating effect. This time they got cocky and were caught. Managing to nurse their sick helicopters home to Abéché airfield, the lead helicopter carried out a controlled crash-landing but the second landing, due to the damage sustained, was ill-controlled and fatal. The rebels pushed inwards and onwards via Goz Beïda, then onto Am Dam, 700 km from N'Djamena.

For the rebels this was as good as it was going to get. Finding their way forward blocked by a heavy concentration of government troops and having made their point, it was time to head back. They headed northwest, aiming to swing back east, unaware that they were now being canalised and led into a killing zone with Chadian government forces massed for the attack. The ambush was ruthlessly executed and less than half of the rebels limped back across the border. As this scenario was being played out, the Irish again came under fire – this time sharp criticism from President Déby. He was unimpressed, not unexpectedly, by the demonstration of EUFOR impartiality as displayed by the Irish and Dutch. Had he expected EUFOR to bolster up his troops? To see intervention in association with, and supportive of, his own forces during the confrontation at Goz Beïda? From Brussels Javier Solana, EU foreign policy chief, replied that EUFOR had done a fantastic job. Incredibly, however, there was criticism from an UNHCR spokeswoman in Abéché, claiming the Irish should have prevented the rebels from threatening their staff and looting their offices in Goz Beïda during the confrontation since UN Security Council Resolution 1778 gave EUFOR a clear mandate to protect refugees, internally displaced persons, humanitarian actors and civilians in danger. Given both the size of the area of operations and the military force, and the humanitarian NGO policy of non-association with military forces, it was never intended that EUFOR would physically guard every NGO compound, refugee camp and IDP site. Therefore, a delicate balance had to be struck with the NGO community to provide security where required and not compromise their impartial stance in pursuit of their laudable humanitarian mission.

Irish Defence Minister, Willie O'Dea, and Irish Defence Forces Chief of Staff, Lieutenant General Dermot Earley, having arrived in Chad on a visit to the Irish Battalion were being interviewed on RTÉ radio's *Morning Ireland* programme by Paul Cunningham in relation to these criticisms, included in a front-page article in that morning's *Irish Times*. As a telephone conversation between the Irish Battalion Commander, Lieutenant Colonel Paddy McDaniel, and the Deputy Force Commander in EUFOR HQ in Abéché Chad, Irish Colonel Derry Fitzgerald, was happening at the same time, Lieutenant Colonel McDaniel was asked if he had seen the article in the *Irish Times*. He stated that he had and had spoken with the head of UNHCR in Goz Beïda who when shown a copy of the article had apologised immediately.

So informed, Colonel Fitzgerald hurried to where the Minister's RTÉ radio interview was in progress and a note to this effect was handed to him live on air: 'I have just now been told that the UNHCR has actually apologised this morning, so I think that speaks for itself.' This was the first of a round of apologies from the UNHCR. The UN Secretary General's Special Representative to Chad, José Victor de Silva Angelo, personally apologised later that day when they met in the Chadian capital N'Djamena, shortly before the Minister's departure for Ireland after his three-day visit. Later that evening he issued a second apology to Lieutenant Colonel Paddy McDaniel, making it clear he did not support the criticism. Both Minister O'Dea and Lieutenant Colonel McDaniel accepted the apology and considered the matter closed.

In Goz Beïda the Irish were still on high alert. A tense atmosphere lingered and there was an edginess about the place. The town walls were pockmarked by RPG impacts and thin smoke trails still drifted upwards from the fires. Twenty-four locals had been wounded and one woman killed. The Irish in Camp Ciara were accommodating 235 humanitarian staff until they felt secure enough to return to their responsibilities. Importantly, the Irish were also patrolling and reassuring the locals, helping to absorb their fear. The rattle of the heavy machine guns and the crumps of rocket-propelled grenades had faded but were not gone completely from their minds. It was to put their minds at ease, to hearten and encourage them that the Irish were there and would remain.

Practically also, to check for the unexploded debris of war: rockets, shells and anything dangerous. When sighted they would be marked and noted, and when circumstances allowed they would be destroyed by the ordnance experts. The locals and refugees had witnessed for themselves the Irish resolve, not offensive but determinedly defensive. The humanitarian aid workers had been evacuated safely and the rebels had seen EUFOR's impartiality when tested. The incident underlined the complexity of the EUFOR operation and demonstrated the importance of the presence of a professional multinational force to meet the challenge. The greatest weapon the Irish brought with them to Chad was their extensive experience of peace-enforcement around the globe, dating back to Ireland's first major UN troop-contributing mission to the Congo in Africa in 1960.

Recovery and Rebel Re-engagement

That the juxtaposition between normality and war, tranquillity and tension, commonplace and conflict coexisted side by side on the same Chadian canvas was hugely unnerving. It was difficult to reconcile the banal with the brutal, the peace with precariousness and the everyday with disarray and yet that's how it was. A battle was looming in parallel with the final recovery phase of those EUFOR forces and assets that had not been 're-hatted' (where regional or multinational forces are redeployed or re-designated) to the UN. Given the significant level of re-hatting, the elements to be recovered proved to be less than foreseen, which meant that in early May 2009 EUFOR no longer had a footprint east of Abéché, and recovery was effectively looking to be completed by the end of that month. The current hostilities had an indirect impact on EUFOR, however, as there were still over 100 EUFOR personnel in Abéché alone and the outcome of the conflict was uncertain. What was certain was that the rebels were coming, the Chadians were waiting, and Déby was well prepared. He had forged a formidable defensive force for what he knew was to be a determined rebel attack. As the arrival of the rebels loomed, and the opposing forces prepared to face each other at Am Dam, an increasingly murderous momentum had gathered and was about to unleash itself.

Technology facilities forces to inflict fearsome firepower on each other, causing terrible carnage and casualties. The rebels were well supplied and they had learned bitter lessons from previous clashes, since their assembled arsenal now included anti-aircraft weapons. But so too had Déby, who had amassed an array of mechanised weaponry capable of firing at longer ranges over distance. As the rebels approached Déby's troops, their withering fire raked the rebels on arrival and immediately slowed the momentum of their attack. Surprised, the rebels became increasingly exposed and crumbled under the intensity of fire raining down upon them. The Chadian bombardments and volley fire continuously tore into them, smashing the initial rebel attack. The rebels responded, fiercely returning fire but with weapons that were falling well short of their mark. An unequal fire fight can only have one outcome. As Déby kept up the pressure, the rebel reply became more frenzied and desperate and they were compelled to seek retreat. Not satisfied with a major and quick victory over the rebels, Déby wanted them annihilated. The Chadian forces seized their opportunity and a subsequent rebel attempt to regroup turned instead into a rout as Déby unmercifully unleashed barrage after barrage.

Hundreds of rebels were killed and captured, their vehicles damaged and destroyed. Those that survived fled, first south then eastwards, some on foot most mobile with the Chadians in hot pursuit. The military and mechanised gap had been too great, technically, professionally and also in terms of close air support. Déby's massive investment in military hardware, especially air assets, was yielding a deadly dividend. His huge expenditure had been facilitated by oil revenues and granted him a decisive military superiority. His army, re-armed, reorganised and tactically more astute, had been primed for the rebel assault and continued to harry and harass them for days, all the way back to the border. The rebels were dispersed and desperately tried to regroup, out of logistical support range and worn down by the fighting, and were faced with a perilous retreat back across the border. But still Déby came on, pursuing them relentlessly with his attack helicopters and fighters. An army in retreat is never more vulnerable and hundreds more rebels were killed and captured, their pickups put out of action. The rebel attack was not so much beaten as decisively defeated, what was left attempting to limp lamely over the border with the Chadians still after them.

The engagement was a resounding success for Déby and his regime but there was a resultant increase in tensions between Chad and Sudan. Chad accused Sudan of sheltering, re-arming and resupplying the incursion of rebels into eastern Chad, of protecting rebels as they fled back across the border and providing medical treatment to them. Chadian and Sudanese relations were to remain volatile, involving much mistrust with the potential for further incidents on the border. The rebels, however, had lost their strike capability and it was considered very likely that the Chadian rebel alliance would descend into internal disputes about leadership and future direction.

The rebel tactics, thought innovative, had not worked and neither did their strategy. The rebels thought their presence and persistence, perhaps even some prior preparations, would have inspired many of the disaffected people in Chad, particularly those amongst the lower ranks of Déby's forces, to 'rally' to them and come over to their side, only they didn't. The spark failed to ignite the momentum towards rebellion and now, weakened by their defeat, the rebels were unlikely to pose a military threat for some time to come. Neither had all the rebel stragglers yet made it back across the border. Some would, eventually, others would not. The 'mop up' continued for some more days as the retreating rebels, desperate to evade their pursuers who were continuing to conduct 'search and destroy' operations, limped across the border into Sudan. The Irish, already out giving reassurance to the local population, refugees, IDPs and aid workers, were mindful that such desperation could threaten those already vulnerable people.

Departure

It was time for EUFOR to go. The UN force, MINURCAT, was now as well established as it was going to be and there was little more EUFOR could do and no time left to do so. EUFOR now had to fully complete the recovery phase and concentrate on getting the last of its forces out of Chad before month's end. There was concern expressed by some nations in relation to 'teething problems' initially experienced by MINURCAT: fuel was in short supply and for a while had to be rationed, the UN mission was undermanned – with less than half its intended strength of 5,225 – and there were inevitably equipment shortages, especially helicopters. After struggling for a while, the first 'weak' peacekeeping operation settled into its stride and began to iron out its difficulties, but was to remain seriously under strength. Before year's end, UN member states were presented with an initiative by the UN head of the Department of Peacekeeping Operations (DPKO) and the Department of Field Support (DFS) seeking to improve the way they operated not just in Chad but in the wider world domain, identifying key challenges currently underpinning operational dilemmas for UN peacekeepers. All at a time when their services were in greater demand than ever. Deployment was at an all-time record, with more than 113,000 peacekeepers serving in eighteen operations on four continents with an approved support budget of over eight billion US dollars.

By the end of May 2009, the EU Operational Headquarters (OHQ) for its military operation in Chad and Central African Republic at Mont-Valérien in Paris would officially close, though a small number of staff would remain to finalise budgets and continue liaison with the EU Military Staff in Brussels and with the United Nations. There were no great drum rolls in Mont-Valérien, the EU military effort ending without euphoria or triumphalism, but instead a quiet but strong sense of 'job done' pervaded the headquarters. A sluggish start, there was nothing lethargic or humdrum about the commitment, and while the circumstances of the operation led many ingredients to go drastically astray in the midst of the helter-skelter, there existed a quiet determination to see these challenges as something to be dealt with. By using its limited assets well, with honesty of effort and endeavour, the force applied itself and turned promise into performance over a horizon that was new to many.

During the lifetime of EUFOR's mandate Chad experienced three unsuccessful rebel incursions. The initial Chadian rebel attack against N'Djamena, the capital, in February 2008 very nearly succeeded in toppling president Déby's regime. As a consequence the government of Chad injected substantial funding into restructuring its armed forces and Chad's military strength improved significantly with extensive military equipment acquisitions, modifications in tactics and restructuring of forces, especially in eastern Chad in the EUFOR area of operations. This shifted the regional military balance of force in favour of Déby over the rebels and Sudanese Arab militias. The fighting over and the crisis of conflict ceased, Chad paradoxically was now at a crossroads more so than ever. The tactical threat of rebel incursion, despite the continuing tensions and much mutual mistrust between Chad and Sudan, was lessened for the time being. With the threat from his restive eastern border reduced for now, would Déby with the support of the UN and EU, seek to begin to foster the conditions for good governance and economic social and political development in Chad or would he continue to put clan before country?

Challenge and Change: From Chad to Worse

The sharpness of the orders of the officer in charge of the 500-strong formation from the French armed forces echoed loudly around the vast cobblestoned courtyard of Les Invalides in Paris. Outside, seventy-two horsemen of the Republican Guard stood vigil, their ceremonial swords glistening gloriously in the afternoon sun, their mounts immaculately groomed to a gleaming textured plushness and their crimson plumes resplendent. The sun kissed square was lined with sixty eighteenth-century bronze cannons, a mixture of 12-, 14- and 24-pounder calibres. The vast enclosure, hushed after the rendition of 'La Marseillaise' by the band of the Republican Guard, now fell completely silent. President

Nicolas Sarkozy took the medal from the red velvet cushion and with great solemnity pinned it to the chest of Lieutenant General Pat Nash as he declared: 'In the name of the French Republic, we make you an officer of the Legion of Honour.' On cue, the military master of ceremonies read the tribute over the loudspeaker: 'Patrick Nash was particularly committed to making this military operation of the European Union a success, in a complex and sensitive environment.'

Built as a hospital for the wounded and ageing soldiers of Louis XIV, Irish among them, four centuries later the restless spirits of the ghosts of these 'Wild Geese' who served and died on foreign fields under foreign flags could settle and find an enduring pride in seeing a fellow countryman in Ireland's national uniform at the head of a European Force receiving such loud and enthusiastic approval, fighting for peace, not waging war. Despite Europe's pride in the Chad endeavour and the acclamation of its commander, EUFOR was not going to end the 'proxy' war, the internal strife, the tribal, clan and ethnic conflicts. Instead it was a clear and honest humanitarian-driven military crisis management operation of limited duration. It was a twelve-month military mercy mission, a bridging operation to protect refugees, IDPs and UN personnel. It involved huge distances, significant degrees of danger and often high tension.

Chad was a disconcerting place, awful yet awe-inspiring, feudal yet fascinating, full of horror and hope. Chad, Sudan and the Central African Republic – the 'Darfur Complex' – still faces an unpalatable but inescapable future, further fragility, friction and fighting a terrifying truth. Fractionalisation could well result from the complex political, military and socioeconomic dynamics that continue to produce a persistently unstable and volatile environment. The 'Darfur Complex' has not developed to the advantage of the peoples who live there but to that of the ruling regimes, and has remained all too vulnerable to outside interventions. It will become increasingly important for the EU to be concerned about future developments there, across the Sahel and also in sub-Saharan Africa, not only for humanitarian reasons but also because it supplies energy to meet Europe's and the world's growing demand and because its poverty breeds terrorism. Terrorism already had a footprint in North Africa but not yet in central Africa: Osama Bin Laden was based in Sudan during the early 1990s. Poverty, a population perpetually in penury, impoverished and powerless because the power is held by the few to their own advantage, the resources turned to wealth for them alone. This region is a dangerous place, fraught with risks. Modernisation, democracy and political change can only come from the minds of the people.

The EU-coordinated defence, diplomacy and development policies must positively address the underlying causes of the regions difficulties, but do these problems run too deep? Delivering democracy to a country that is unready, unable and unwilling to receive it is an unachievable objective. It is not possible to simply superimpose a western world model, to understand the Chadian situation you must learn to think differently ... to think Chadian. However, the validity of this approach begins to break down almost from the start, but in so doing reveals a deeper truth about the nature of the problem. Culturally many in Chad think tribal, which is their tradition and the essence of their identity, and theirs is a disparate heritage. Impose this background on a state, or rather impose a state on this background, and you are trying to modernise an anarchical situation without the years of necessary developmental layers in between.

The simple truth is the Chadians do not believe they belong to a country ... yet. Chadians do not believe in a Chadian citizenship or constituency, it does not really exist in the minds of the people, and the years of misrule have resulted in a mismatch, a major disconnect. A corresponding polarisation brought a lack of a sense of empowerment of the people and an absence of any onus to provide a functioning government and good governance by the regime. There is no one Chad, there are many Chads. It is a complex society with complicated tribal peoples that can only be influenced to change for themselves when they are ready, able and willing to do so. In the interim, other influences may lead Chad elsewhere. The inherent chronic instability could give way to further barbarity and brutality, the Justice and Equality Movement (JEM) could once again strike eastwards towards Khartoum and that could all end in a calamitous war with Sudan. Sudan itself has since imploded and fractured. Trouble between the secessionist oil-rich south and the north-based government erupted, as did disputes over the allocation of current and future oil reserves and the largest country in Africa may well fall apart!

Africa's troubled heart has a bloody history and an uncertain, perhaps unhappy future. You must not view Chad and its surrounding region through European eyes, they are two different worlds with a chasm between them. The respective regimes and rebels of both Chad and Sudan don't yet want peace, they want power, and what results is poverty and primitiveness for the many millions therein. The countries of the 'Darfur Complex' are at an early stage of statehood. Their developmental progress is retarded by regional instability, by inter-ethnic disharmony and by increased militancy; the situation constantly changing but mainly deteriorating. The latter-day discovery of oil resources and the resulting outside interventions all give cause for ample anxiety. The priority is regime maintenance rather than nation building and human security. This undermining of the State's capacity to improve state infrastructure and social development copper-fastens the causes for unrest, promising a continuous cycle of underdevelopment and an immense scale of suffering.

In the beginning the political convergence between European states that gave rise to this French-sponsored EU intervention was awkward, uncomfortable, and fragile. The long-drawn-out Force Generation Process presented little basis for optimism. All this suggested the EU force wasn't going to be a success and it was almost stopped in its tracks by the sudden, almost successful, surprise rebel assault on N'Djamena. An assault that sent shock waves throughout Europe's already wavering capitals, fearful of allowing their troops to become entangled in a complex web of conflict. It had to overcome the suspicions of some EU member states about possible ulterior motives by the French and some nations thought deployment difficulties would be insurmountable; logistical and sustainment requirements too challenging, achieving its operational objectives too great and the possibility of a UN follow-on force too unlikely. Bring to this unholy, mind-boggling mix the impact of the International Criminal Court's arrest warrants for Sudanese President Omar al-Bashir in 2009 and 2010 on the level of regional tension and you'll have some idea of the overall set of circumstances that would make even the most optimistic go into decline.

But restless for results, and possessing an endless energy, General Nash demonstrated an ability to maximise the impact of the sum of its parts and made, by force of will, the concept of a multinational European military force work. Decisive, diplomatic and dedicated, General Nash knew that in order to get a handle on the situation and end the early months of uncertainty, a deployed EUFOR had to wade in and grapple with the state of insecurity and instability in whatever form it presented itself. By acting fast and energetically, EUFOR took on these challenges and defied the gravity of popular public opinion by demonstrating professional patience as the perception of its performance slowly turned positive. Its strategy was planned that way and EUFOR 'let the results do the talking'.

At all levels its leaders had the confidence, skill, leadership and courage to hold their nerve and see the strategy through, even during its trickier moments. EUFOR fulfilled its mission to protect refugees, internally displaced persons and aid workers. While it could never claim to free its area of operations of banditry and criminality, the culture of impunity was too deeply ingrained for that, EUFOR did have a tangible effect on improving overall stability by underpinning a feeling of security providing a new sense of confidence and setting out a new standard of behaviour. EUFOR was one tiny link in a multidimensional chain trying to anchor safety and security in the shifting sands of instability in the region. EUFOR, a multi-national military force, put into practice what looked good on paper, not something always achievable. It persevered through the problems and succeeded in shining a light into a very dark place and nothing in Chad can ever be the same again. During the twelve-month period of its operation, prime ministers, ministers, politicians, diplomats, and over 450 international media also went to Chad and Europeans now knew more about what was going on in the region than ever before. Chad was now centre-stage, no longer the poor new relation of Darfur.

By maintaining the mandate, staying true to the military mission, and preserving the force's impartiality from the outset, the operation was a major projection of European Security and Defence Policy (ESDP). For over a year, General Nash was the keeper of the ESDP flame and the guarantor of European impartiality in eastern Chad and north eastern CAR. Political psychological gamesmanship and pressure was a fact of life for an Operation Commander at the military strategic level and he had to counter anyone seeking to manipulate EUFOR or in any way interfere in its impartiality. EUFOR passed the logistical litmus test and achieved a high operational tempo, reaching a successful end-date in handing over seamlessly to a UN follow-on force. Its performance brought a perception of credibility to a force that at the outset many suggested was not going to succeed. Twenty-six countries, three of them non-EU, were moulded together to produce results and contributed to a safe and secure environment for those most vulnerable in its area of operations. Ireland brought experience, a 'hard-work' ethic and a little bit of luck in producing a small military force, but nonetheless one to be reckoned with, that was recognised throughout the EU and the UN as a major success. If General Nash and the Irish at all levels in the EU force brought energy to the operation, they also brought the experience to stay the course, which was to prove invaluable in preserving the European character of the operation, not as a façade but as a fact.

Afterword

by Lieutenant General Pat Nash (retired)

On becoming Operation Commander of the proposed EU Force in Chad and the Central African Republic, it became abundantly clear to me that the operation was certainly going to be difficult and extremely complex. The formal tasks as set out in EUFOR's mandate were to contribute to the protection of refugees and Internally Displaced Peoples, facilitate the delivery of humanitarian aid, assist in the deployment of the UN (Police Force) Mission MINURCAT and, finally, be prepared to hand over to a possible UN follow-on force.

In this section of the book, Dan Harvey has dealt with the difficulties which the mission encountered, but I wish here to refer to some of the complexities a multinational, multifaceted operation must tackle if success is to be contemplated. Complexities manifested themselves at the very outset of EUFOR's mission and were primarily associated with the key objectives of the operation. One strategic objective was to contribute to a safe and secure environment (SASE). It was important to establish what the various actors understood SASE to mean; regrettably this was not possible due to conflicting interests and priorities. EUFOR was also challenged to be neutral in its dealings with stakeholders and impartial in the conduct of the operation. In defining its approach to the framing of the Concept of Operations, EUFOR had to marry the most onerous task of contributing to a safe and secure environment, in an enormous area of operations, while being neutral and impartial.

Quite evidently, it was not possible to engage in open conflict with an adversary. EUFOR, therefore, had to adopt a deterrent posture and approach and so discourage any potential spoilers by the threat of overwhelming military retaliation. This was to be achieved by putting in place serious information-gathering agencies and equipment, while generating a force of highly trained, manoeuvrable troops with the necessary organic combat support and service support to operate in such a vast area, with maximum effect. The approach was to have an extensive information campaign and quality intelligence work, to include comprehensive liaison with all parties, while conducting vigorous patrolling. All the above was to be backed up by a standby reserve composed of at least company strength, with the necessary air, armour, medical and command structure.

Deterrence was a key concept underpinning the operation; deterrence was also extremely important from the Force's own protection perspective. We had to be extremely mindful that European troops were deploying to what had already been proven to be a dangerous part of the African continent for UN troops. Strategic back-up resources had potentially 4,000 kilometres to travel. Therefore, EUFOR had to be sufficiently robust so as not to be embarrassed by any prospective protagonist.

A second complexity arose immediately following deployment when it became evident that the UN police force which was scheduled to deploy in conjunction with EUFOR, and which had the task of ensuring security within refugee and IDP camps (the camps being specifically excluded from EUFOR's mandate), was experiencing serious delays in its rollout. At the same time, a new security pattern began to emerge. Large groups of would-be spoilers had obviously noted EUFOR's capabilities and rather than expose themselves to possible retribution on a serious scale, which EUFOR's Rules of Engagement allowed it to undertake, they broke into small groups of two to four people and commenced common banditry. EUFOR, being the only credible security force in the region, was morally bound to intervene, and did, even though it was neither mandated nor structured to do so.

The force commander, Brigadier General Philippe Ganascia, made major adaptions to his operation plan and publicly announced: 'There is a discrepancy between what contributed to the initial set up of the forces deployed here and the actual reality. The background situation has changed enormously … It is, therefore, essential that we adapt our methods of action in order to counteract the *coupeurs de route* (highwaymen) whilst still remaining within the framework we were given.'

EUFOR found itself operating in the most unenviable circumstances, whereby proper governance by State authorities in Eastern Chad was in an almost shambolic state, due in large part to the upheaval from the rebel incursion of late February and the aforementioned difficulties of UN police deployment. All this meant that EUFOR was criticised for not providing blanket security. The problem was, of course, that EUFOR could not provide a permanent 'police role' presence throughout the whole area, but was confident that its new approach of targeting specific areas, while also using surprise tactics, would give the local population a sense of security as well as assuring other actors on the scene. It is to the great credit of the nearly 11,000 troops that served with EUFOR that they were able to adapt to such a change, and as the mission progressed, it was almost without exception expressed that excellent progress was made.

Another complexity for EUFOR was the question of an 'end date' as distinct from an 'end state'. The EU were at pains to stress that EUFOR CHAD/CAR would be a bridging operation with a definitive end date, one year from when initial operational capability was declared. EU countries did not want to get bogged down with a long-drawn-out mission in Africa; also countries paying large shares of the common costs were not prepared to endorse the mission unless an early end date was visualised. The end-date option was further complicated by the UN Resolution only referring to a possible follow-on force. The actual decision from the UN's perspective was long-fingered until such time as a mid-mandate review had been produced. These political requirements placed the OHQ (Operational Headquarters in Mont-Valérien, Paris) in a very difficult position from the point of view of issuing strategic guidance: traditional military operations are geared towards the achievement of a defined end-state.

An unfortunate fallout from the gap created in strategic guidance was that some actors and agencies wished to benchmark EUFOR's performance by measuring the number of IDPs who had returned to their home villages. Considerable time and effort had to be given to explaining to a raft of stakeholders the constraints placed upon the mission, while emphasising the progressive pallet of objectives the force had set itself.

EUFOR CHAD/CAR had the great benefit of being a mission planned at the highest level in Brussels, using a policy known as the comprehensive approach, whereby ownership of the decision-making process, as well as the strategic direction of the operation, were decided with full input from all interested agencies, but primarily the constituent countries of the EU. Our task at the OHQ was to define the political objectives and give military expression to the mandate and mission as outlined, in other words, to achieve effects on the ground and to make happen militarily what the EU had politically committed to. It was a daunting prospect, particularly when it transpired that the OHQ would eventually have staff from twenty-three contributing countries in all.

In facing down the challenge, I resurrected the mantra of a former commanding officer of mine when I was a young officer. In frustration at our lack of get up and go, he would extol: 'Do not come to me with problems, come to me with your solutions.' At the OHQ in Mont-Valérien, the staff took pride in being 'solution finders rather than problem posers'; their can-do attitude became a badge of pride. An unwelcome side effect occurred, however, when many national military HQs changed their up-and-coming staff far too regularly in order to maximise their exposure to HQ, which blended to become possibly more effective than the total of its diverse constituent parts.

EUFOR CHAD/CAR was seen in many quarters as a test mission for the development of the EU Security and Defence Policy. Many observers were keen to see whether Europe could construct a multinational, multifaceted operation with sufficient air armour medical as well as situational awareness assets and transport those assets into a potential hostile but proven debilitating environment, 4,000 km from home capitals. The dynamics of the world from a military perspective have changed dramatically over the past twenty years or so, the consequences of which are that military assets are overstretched. Traditionally, wars or major military operations were followed by a period of recovery, replenishment and reflection; the lessons learned were studied, and preparations were made for any future potential campaigns. However, with the spread of numerous insurgencies and major terrorist activities the world scene has changed and there is now a continuous low-level war ongoing in various parts of the world. The consequence of this is that soldiers, assets and equipment are in short supply. This difficult situation has been compounded by the current financial crisis in the western world. It is to the great credit of the European Union that a mission such as EUFOR could be launched in such circumstances; it is of even further significance that three non-member states should contribute forces. The contribution by Russia, taking into account the Georgia crisis at the time, was a major accomplishment.

A considerable amount of academic study has already been conducted into EUFOR CHAD/CAR and various lessons have been learned. Seminars have been held and the consensus emanating from them is that the operation was a major success in many fields, but that its greatest contribution may well be in the development and rollout of the European Union's Security and Defence Policy.

Lieutenant General Pat Nash (retired)
Operation Commander EUFOR CHAD/CAR, 2007–9

PART V
SYRIA (2013–14)

CHAPTER 7

Hull Down

Intuitively the Irish convoy escort commander ordered 'hatches closed'. Whether it was instinct, presentiment, a sixth sense, a feeling, a hunch, or an unconscious ability to understand or know something with subconscious reasoning, whatever it was, something inclined him towards taking the precaution to go 'hull down' and minimise the profile of an armoured vehicle leaving only the turret and cannon exposed. This was another routine, nothing-out-of-the-ordinary, convoy-escort patrol. Only on 28 November 2013, unknown to the Irish, they were driving into a fire fight. An ambush had been set by armed anti-Assad regime elements near the village of Ruihinah and they waited for the Irish patrol with patient determination.

In July 2013, after a thirty-nine-year involvement, the Austrian government decided to withdraw from the United Nations Disengagement Observer Force (UNDOF) mission on the Golan Heights because of the deteriorating security situation in Syria and the Irish government responded to an urgent request from the UN for a replacement national contingent. The decision to deploy, taken by the Cabinet and supported by a vote in the Dáil Éireann, all on the foot of a UN mandate (the so-called triple lock policy that must be adhered to before any overseas military deployment), was given legal status within the Defence Forces by what is termed a Raising and Concentration Order (RCO), which is itself the result of deliberations by a joint operations planning group. The task of raising the necessary troops was given to the 2nd Brigade based at Cathal Brugha Barracks in Rathmines, Dublin. The core of the 48th Infantry Group was to come from the 28th Infantry Battalion based at Finner Camp in Donegal, with personnel attached to it from other units of the Defence Forces. The RCO for Ireland's involvement in UNDOF was issued on 19 July 2013 and the unit was ready to be deployed seven weeks later, but was not in fact dispatched for another two weeks because of events in Syria. At the time of writing (February 2017), Irish troops are still participating with the UNDOF mission. An early incident in this involvement was to underline the seriousness of the situation the Irish had deployed into and was to severely test their skills.

UNDOF maintained a Zone of Separation between Israel and Syria on the Golan Heights, a mission that has been in place since 1974. The UN force predated the civil war in Syria between the government of President Bashar al-Assad and those who wish to overthrow him, and had no role in or around that conflict. The original mandate did not envisage a vicious civil war in Syria and did not cater for the reality of the ensuing de facto armed conflict in the area of operations. The 43rd Infantry Group had found out early that they could not escape the fallout of that war. Three weeks previously, in the chaos gripping Syria, they were caught in the civil war's crossfire during an ongoing fire fight between government and anti-government forces as another of their armoured convoys drove through the Durbol area. A number of artillery rounds landed within 200m of the convoy of ten armoured vehicles. They continued on after this 'near miss', but when it became obvious there were many localised fire fights ongoing between Syrian forces a decision was made to return to base at Faouar. While returning to base via a different route they were again fired on. None of the Irish or other UN troops were injured or their vehicles damaged but there had been similar incidents involving small arms fire leading up to that.

At the same time as the 43rd Infantry Group were receiving pre-deployment briefings at the Defence Forces United Nations Training School Ireland (UNTSI) and undergoing a Mission Readiness Exercise (MRE) in the Glen of Imaal, County Wicklow, news reports were filled with stories and footage of a chemical attack in the Syrian capital Damascus. Many thousands of people were being killed in the conflict and the first of what was to become well over two million Syrians began fleeing the country. Worryingly, there were also media reports of growing concerns that al-Qaeda linked fighters in Syria could overrun and exploit chemical and biological weapons storage facilities before all of these materials were removed. So there were a number of elements complicating an already complex, difficult and dangerous situation. As well as all this, reports of grave breaches of international law and war crimes were emerging.

Ready to Roll. An Irish MOWAG APC preparing to join a patrol along the Syrian–Israeli border. Courtesy of *An Cosantoir*

On 28 November 2013, two months into the six-month deployment of 119 Irish troops of the 43rd Infantry Group under Lieutenant Colonel Brendan Delaney, a routine escort patrol consisting of thirty-six Irish peacekeepers in five MOWAG armoured personnel carriers set out as part of the UNDOF on the heavily fortified border between Israel and Syria. Adhering to standard procedures a set sequence of practices and movements were conducted during its task, from start point to destination, in the customary manner. While conscious of the general backdrop of situational volatility and the known presence of a convoluted array of anti-government armed elements, some supposedly backed by Western powers, there was nothing specific to raise concerns above those already prevailing. Only on approaching an area where activity had occurred previously something suggested itself to that day's convoy escort commander, resulting in the 'hatches closed' order being given before it became apparently necessary to do so. Progressing forward for a while, the lead armoured MOWAG vehicle driver and car commander noticed an array of anti-tank land mines loosely strewn, openly and in plain sight, across the full width of the tarred surface of the road ahead of them.

These formed an obvious and highly dangerous obstacle to progress and reporting the unusual occurrence, the car commander ordered the vehicle to stop. Because of good inter-car communications, the other vehicles in the convoy also stopped, all maintaining a correctly spaced distance between each other and so did not bunch up. Immediately on halting the lead car came under intense and sustained fire. A dramatic gun battle with Islamic militants had begun. The hail of bullets had an immediate and obvious deadly intent behind it and rounds impacted heavily on the armour protecting the crew inside. The crew of the first MOWAG and those in the second armoured vehicle both used their secondary weapons, the co-axial 7.62mm twin machine guns, to reply and returned fire in unison, laying down a heavy covering barrage.

As the two lead vehicles continued to lay down highly effective covering fire, all of the convoy vehicles, still maintaining tactical spacing between them, prepared to reverse out of the killing zone. Textbook style they deployed smoke, left and right of the road, to screen their withdrawal and skilfully and steadily began to reverse to a safe distance. As the third vehicle was turning it reversed slightly off the road's hard surface onto the soft margin and detonated an anti-tank landmine, blowing off its rear right wheel. The driver, having initially passed the land mine on the road's hard surface, had reversed onto it while turning. The shockwave from the blast went straight through the vehicle, resulting in one Irish soldier suffering a slight soft tissue injury but no further injuries. Fortunately, all inside were wearing their safety harnesses and the vehicle minus one wheel successfully continued to safety. With the two forward APCs continuing to lay down covering fire and the smoke providing adequate cover against the attackers, all of the patrol steadily maintained their progress away from the hot spot.

Getting caught in the crossfire was one thing, appearing to be a legitimate target and having to defend themselves from often unpredictable and heavily armed anti-government warring factions was quite another. The Irish peacekeeping force, while maintaining force-protecting measures and having to engage armed elements to do so, had not become embroiled in the wider civil war. This incident, the most dramatic in recent memory, did not result in serious injury or loss of life and upon examining the impacts on the lead vehicle in particular there was an appreciation that going into unexpected contact 'hatches closed' served the convoy escort personnel well.

Regional events (the brutal ethno-sectarian Syrian civil war) had overtaken UNDOF's original mission design and rationale (maintaining a demilitarised buffer Zone of Separation between Israel and Syria on the Golan Heights) and the operational environment on the Golan Heights continued to deteriorate. As the conflict rapidly evolved, Islamist rebels stepped-up attacks on the UN and intensified their military campaign within what they termed the 'southern front' of Syria's Golan Heights, and the risks to the 1,200 members of the UN Force from six countries: Fiji, India, Ireland, Nepal, Netherlands and the Philippines, the now 130 Irish of the 44th Battalion amongst them, were escalating. In the early hours of Saturday, 30 August 2014, Irish troops were again in the line of fire when they necessarily became involved in another shoot-out in one of the fiercest engagements involving Irish troops on foreign soil in decades.

Already on 'high alert', the Irish as the UN Force Mobile Company, or emergency response unit, were involved in a dramatic rescue and extraction operation when thirty-five Filipino troops became beleaguered in their platoon base at Breiqa and a further forty-five Fijian peacekeepers were taken hostage by members of the al-Qaeda affiliated Jabhat Al-Nusra forces. The Filipino UN position at Breiqa, along with another at Rwihana, were surrounded by Islamist insurgents including, it was believed, Al-Nusra after anti-Assad regime rebels seized a Syrian border crossing at Quneitra having killed twenty Syrian army troops. During exchanges of gunfire, the Filipino peacekeepers at Rwihana succeeded in escaping from their predicament on foot under cover of darkness. Those at Breiqa, however, were seriously compromised and were coming under huge pressure, and the likelihood of them being captured was increasing. It was then the UN Force Commander ordered 130 Irish troops from the 44th Infantry Group to mount a daring, difficult and dangerous armoured operation to extract the remaining Filipino platoon.

The Irish troops engaged the Islamist rebels from their armoured MOWAG vehicles in a number of sustained fire fights as they moved in to successfully provide the fleeing Filipino peacekeepers with an exit route. During this heavy exchange of fire, Irish personnel secured the route, provided security as the beleaguered Filipino UN peacekeepers withdrew from their compromised position, and escorted them to the Force Headquarters in Camp Faouar. There were no Irish casualties suffered during the action and all safely returned and were accounted for. Two weeks after the Irish action the Fijian peacekeepers, after originally being threatened with trial under Sharia law by the jihadists, were released unharmed to a heroes welcome.

As the possibility of the UN Force being drawn into a Syrian civil war, and otherwise caught up in a regional conflict, increased the worsening security situation naturally raised concerns for the safety of Irish peacekeepers. Despite the raised risks, heightened danger, and volatility of the deteriorating situation Ireland did not withdraw its commitment to the UN mission with UNDOF on the Golan Heights, and Foreign Affairs Minister, Charlie Flanagan, reinforced Ireland's commitment to UN peacekeeping when he said: 'Support for the UN is a cornerstone of Irish foreign policy and any decision will be made in partnership with them.' The UN reviewed the viability of the mission and highly prudent operational changes were made due to the escalating violence.

Former UN Secretary-General Dag Hammarskjöld once remarked that 'peacekeeping is not a job for soldiers, but only soldiers can do it'. The Irish experience of their past sixty-year involvement in Peace Support Operations all around the world has borne out the wisdom of this observation and the Irish in turn have been largely observed to be very good at it, prepared as they are to sometimes go 'into action' and fight for peace.

Epilogue

Much has been written about UN peacekeeping and there has been a lot of academic review, hypothesis, categorisation, description and analysis of its evolution over the years. While this has a place and much has changed, in essence peacekeeping operations have mostly been hastily organised responses to assorted crises, and once launched they have more or less taken on a life and character of their own. Peacekeeping practitioners know that in the main the effectiveness of Peace Support Operations is largely dependent on strong mandates, adequate resources, good quality command and leadership. Even then much depends on the reaction of the parties to the dispute and international developments.

The contribution of Irish peacekeepers operating in the field over the last half century and more can only be judged in the light of how their involvement has contributed to the accomplishment of past peacekeeping missions. It also holds true that the Irish have displayed a suitability for peacekeeping and have developed practical experiences in the handling of various situations and adapted these from one peacekeeping mission to another. This perceived value of their particular peacekeeping participation has gained a certain stature, one curiously more acknowledged abroad than at home. This can only be further developed by ongoing participation and its continued practice should never be taken for granted. The future development of the peacekeeping craft is uncertain, however, what is certain is that the practice of practical peacekeeping, per se, will always remain in demand.

Roll of Honour

CONGO - ONUC
July 1960–June 1964

Rank	Name	Date
Company Sergeant	Felix Grant (DSM)	03 Oct 1960
Colonel	Justin McCarthy (DSM)	27 Oct 1960
Lieutenant	Kevin Gleeson	08 Nov 1960
Sergeant	Hugh Gaynor	08 Nov 1960
Corporal	Liam Dougan	08 Nov 1960
Corporal	Peter Kelly	08 Nov 1960
Private	Matthew Farrell	08 Nov 1960
Trooper	Thomas Fennell	08 Nov 1960
Trooper	Anthony Browne (MMG)	08 Nov 1960
Private	Michael McGuinn	08 Nov 1960
Private	Gerard Killeen	08 Nov 1960
Private	Patrick Davis	10 Nov 1960
Corporal	Liam Kelly	24 Dec 1960
Corporal	Luke Kelly	30 Aug 1961
Trooper	Edward Gaffney	13 Sep 1961
Trooper	Patrick Mullins	15 Sep 1961
Corporal	Michael Nolan	15 Sep 1961
Corporal	Michael Fallon	08 Dec 1961
Sergeant	Patrick Mulcahy (DSM)	16 Dec 1961
Lieutenant	Patrick Riordan (DSM)	16 Dec 1961
Private	Andrew Wickham	16 Dec 1961
Corporal	John Geoghegan	28 Dec 1961
Corporal	John Power	07 Mar 1962
Captain	Ronald McCann	09 May 1962
Corporal	John McGrath	21 Mar 1963
Commandant	Thomas McMahon	28 Sep 1963

CYPRUS - UNFICYP
March 1964–May 2005

Rank	Name	Date
Company Sergeant	Wallace MacAuley	22 Feb 1965
Sergeant	John Hammill	07 Apr 1965
Corporal	William Hetherington	19 Jul 1965
Company Sergeant	James Ryan	04 Oct 1966
Captain	Christopher McNamara	16 Jan 1968
Corporal	James Fagan	10 Jun 1968
Lieutenant	Ronald Byrne	28 Oct 1968
Trooper	Michael Kennedy	01 Oct 1969
Private	Brendan Cummins	11 Oct 1971

UNTSO - UNITED NATIONS TRUCE SUPERVISION ORGANISATION
18 December 1958 to date

Rank	Name	Date
Commandant	Thomas Wickham	07 Jun 1967
Commandant	Michael Nestor	25 Sep 1982

LEBANON - UNIFIL
May 1978 to date

Rank	Name	Date
Private	Gerard Moon	25 Aug 1978
Corporal	Thomas Reynolds	24 Dec 1978
Private	Philip Grogan	10 Jul 1979
Private	Stephen Griffin	16 Apr 1980
Private	Derek Smallhorne	18 Apr 1980

Roll of Honour

Rank	Name	Date
Private	Thomas Barrett	18 Apr 1980
Sergeant	Edward Yates	31 May 1980
Corporal	Vincent Duffy	18 Oct 1980
Private	John Marshall	17 Dec 1980
Company Sergeant	James Martin	10 Feb 1981
Private	Kevin Joyce	27 Apr 1981
Private	Hugh Doherty	27 Apr 1981
Private	Niall Byrne	23 Jun 1981
Private	Gerard Hodges	20 Mar 1982
Private	Peter Burke	27 Oct 1982
Corporal	Gregory Morrow	27 Oct 1982
Private	Thomas Murphy	27 Oct 1982
Corporal	George Murray	09 Oct 1984
Trooper	Paul Fogarty	20 Jul 1986
Lieutenant	Aengus Murphy	21 Aug 1986
Private	William O'Brien	06 Dec 1986
Corporal	Dermot McLoughlin	10 Jan 1987
Sergeant Major	John Fitzgerald	24 Feb 1987
Corporal	George Bolger	29 Aug 1987
Gunner	Paul Cullen	17 Mar 1988
Private	Patrick Wright	21 Aug 1988
Private	Michael McNeela	24 Feb 1989
Corporal	Fintan Heneghan	21 Mar 1989
Private	Thomas Walsh	21 Mar 1989
Private	Mannix Armstrong	21 Mar 1989
Sergeant	Charles Forrester	21 May 1989
Commandant	Michael Hanlon	21 Nov 1989
Corporal	Michael McCarthy	15 Nov 1991
Corporal	Peter Ward	29 Sep 1992
Corporal	Martin Tynan	13 Dec 1992
Company Quartermaster Sergeant	Declan Stokes	14 Jun 1993
Artilleryman	Stephen O'Connor	03 Oct 1993

Sergeant	John Lynch	06 Aug 1997
Private	Michael Dowling	16 Sep 1998
Private	Kevin Barrett	18 Feb 1999
Private	William Kedian	31 May 1999
Trooper	Jonathan Campbell	05 Sep 1999
Private	Declan Deere	14 Feb 2000
Private	John Murphy	14 Feb 2000
Private	Matthew Lawlor	14 Feb 2000
Private	Brendan Fitzpatrick	14 Feb 2000

EAST TIMOR - UNMET/UNTAET
July 1999–May 2004

Rank	Name	Date
Private	Peadar O'Flatharta	15 Apr 2002

LIBERIA - UNMIL
November 2003–31 May 2007

Rank	Name	Date
Sergeant	Derek Mooney	27 Nov 2003

EU/NORDIC BATTLE GROUP - EU/NBG

Rank	Name	Date
Lieutenant Colonel	Paul Delaney	23 Jul 2007

Author's Note

The encounters expanded upon in this book are not the extent of the exposure of Irish peacekeepers to conflict and confrontation; rather they are the more noteworthy events over the passage of the Defence Forces' continuous unbroken peacekeeping experience since 1958. There have been very many other incidents and episodes, all with their own share of challenges, tensions and degrees of danger and difficulty. Neither is this the full story of Irish peacekeeping involvement in mission areas worldwide, because many have seen peace maintained successfully without Irish soldiers as peacekeepers necessarily becoming embroiled in violent exchanges, stand-offs and other incidents involving adversity. However, when and where the exposure to harm, danger and death was to the extent of becoming recorded in the previous pages, it has been done so that others may be made aware, understand and benefit from the peacekeepers' experiences. It is part of one generation of Irish peacekeepers' concern for another's not yet tested. If not challenged, what happens when they are? Will they stand?

Hard training, good equipment, leadership and clear Rules of Engagement, among other essentials, will clearly allow soldiers to deal well with the uncertainty of any outcome. However, it is crucial to know what has gone before if one is properly able to manage those situations of not knowing what will happen next; what reactions are appropriate and proportionate; to be able to cope with actually felt fear and to know that it can be overcome by demonstrated courage, having first found it within oneself.

Into Action: A History of the Fighting Irish Peacekeepers, 1960–2014 presents the less familiar 'harder edge' of Irish Peacekeeping involvement, necessarily bringing the reader into a world of conflict, of fear and facing it, of coming into 'contact' and containing it, of engaging in the fire fight and winning it. In so doing it grants an awareness and appreciation of how hard-earned the proud tradition of Irish Peacekeeping was to achieve and, more especially today in this conflict-ridden era, to maintain. It is not every day that Irish soldiers 'open fire' to keep the peace, but it is every day in the mission areas in which they operate that they are prepared to do so, and at home they train hard to be able to do just that.

The seven incidents mentioned in *Into Action* vary between skirmishes to independent company-level actions, either standalone or as part of a larger formation involvement. Baluba tribesmen, emboldened native Congolese warriors, mercenaries and Kataganese Gendarmaries, Israeli-backed militias, rioting Kosovar Albanian mobs, unidentified Chadian gunmen, and armed Syrian anti-government elements all form part of the role of protagonists to peace in this narrative, a situation not necessarily prevailing in the present day but certainly one in need of being addressed.

In November 1960, the Irish people were devastated by the news that nine of an eleven-man patrol under Lieutenant Kevin Gleeson, soldiers of the 33rd Irish Battalion sent to the Congo as part of a UN peacekeeping mission, had been killed in an ambush by Baluba warriors near Niemba. In the days that followed, nearly a quarter of a million people watched as the funeral cortège passed through Dublin in what was one of the biggest public displays of emotion ever witnessed in Ireland. Less than a year later, in September 1961, the men of A Company, 35th Irish Battalion led by Commandant Pat Quinlan, tasked with protecting the European population at Jadotville, were attacked by Katanga Gendarmerie troops loyal to the Katangese Prime Minister, Moise Tshombe, became cut off and surrounded and had to hold their ground and fight for four days. On 16 December 1961, their successors, the men of A Company, 36th Battalion under Commandant Joe Fitzpatrick, found themselves within days of arrival already having suffered casualties and involved in hostilities as lead advance Company, of a lead Battalion, of a lead Brigade in the famous Battle of the Tunnel in Élisabethville.

Later, in South Lebanon in April 1980, aggressive Israeli-backed militiamen pushed too far in an attempt to forcefully take over the Irish-occupied strategically-important village of At-Tiri. Following disciplined restraint by Irish peacekeepers, the militia became ever more aggressive and reckless until finally force met force and they faced Irish gunfire. The week-long action by C Company, with Irish and UNIFIL reinforcements under Commandant Dave Taylor, was where eventually enough was enough and the Irish turned defence into attack and retook the village.

On Saint Patrick's Day, 2004, in Kosovo, south-eastern Europe, Irish troops of the 27th Infantry Group under Lieutenant Colonel Mick Finn stood firm during serious ethnically-motivated rioting in Caglavica. Four years later, in March 2008, a UN-mandated European military bridging operation, EUFOR Chad/CAR, arrived deep into war-torn and impoverished Chad; the dead heart of Africa. Chad was caught up in the bitter and bloody conflicts raging across its border in the Darfur region of Sudan, and every day traumatised refugees streamed into the country, seeking a respite from their woes. But Chad had its own problems, with growing unrest and instability, internal tensions and rivalries, and fearsome Janjaweed raiders. It was EUFOR's mission to rescue Darfur's refugees and Chad's most vulnerable from the clutches of conflict. During June 2008, the 97th Irish Battalion under Lieutenant Colonel Paddy McDaniel, had to intervene in the midst of a clash between Chadian government forces and rebel attackers in Goz Beïda, in the vicinity of the D'Jabal refugee camp. Doing what they had gone there to do, they placed themselves between the refugee camp and the fighting and inevitably became caught in the conflict's crossfire. More recently, in November 2013 Irish soldiers of the 43rd Infantry Group, part of a peacekeeping mission on the heavily fortified border between Syria and Israel – a mission which predates the civil war in Syria between the government of president Bashar al-Assad and those wishing to overthrow him – and with no role in or around that conflict, were to discover that they could not escape the fallout of that war. First by becoming caught up in 'near-miss' crossfire and later becoming the target of warring factions in an ambush.

The first and the latest occurrences, both ambushes, fifty-three years apart, neatly bookend the seven incidents described. Belonging to different centuries, different continents, and different contexts, the unpredictability of the susceptibility to an ambush scenario for the Irish peacekeepers involved was largely the same, though the outcomes were significantly different. Yet the lessons were learned, and in the year 2058, when it becomes time to chart a hundred years of unbroken peacekeeping service by Irish soldiers, the commentary may well attempt to evaluate the continuing contribution of the Irish Defence Forces and Ireland's place in the world. In the intervening years, future generations of Irish peacekeepers may well 'have stood' the evolving challenges and tests, and they too, in turn, may well record some of these incidents so that the generation of peacekeepers who come after them may be alert to what may be required of them. To all Irish peacekeepers, present and future, stay safe, but most importantly also, stay true.

Acknowledgements

I am of an age to have children studying and working abroad, as it happens in countries that have high regard for their militaries; the UK, USA and France. This societal respect for military service was a phenomenon new to them and stimulated a fresh regard for what I had always considered 'my vocation', and developed an entirely new perspective, indeed a new-found appreciation, of the Irish Defence forces' role, reputation and relevance. This recognition, an acknowledgement from the people that mattered most to me, was important to me, a serving Irish soldier.

More respected abroad than at home, this new-found perspective extended particularly to what many abroad considered to be an Irish art: peacekeeping. As to exactly why the Irish seemed to enjoy a particular suitability to it, was this a myth or a reality, I am not the one to say, but I do know that at times peacekeeping requires that the peace be kept, sometimes by forceful means.

To relate this aspect of the Irish peacekeeping story, one held deep within the Irish Defence Forces unspoken subculture, many peoples' efforts need to be acknowledged and I do so gratefully. Having conducted in excess of a hundred interviews over several years, I wish to recognise the trust of those who shared their experiences. To listen to their extraordinary accounts (some officially deemed 'heroic') was humbling, and all the more so because they were related so matter-of-factly, as if their actions were ordinary when they were anything but. I was also hugely relieved that their accounts could be captured for others to learn from, but almost as soon acutely realised the burden of responsibility placed upon me to do justice to their truth.

For their enormous assistance in attempting to do this I wish to say a sincere thank you to the ever helpful members of the Military Archives, past and present, under the direction of Commandants Padraic Kennedy, Stephen MacEoin, Commandant (retd.) Victor Laing and Commandant Peter Young (RIP); Commandant John Gaffney, Commandant Dave O'Neill (retd.) and Private Tom Mc Sweeney (retd.) of the Defence.

Forces Printing Press; to the Defence Forces Press Office, in particular, Lieutenant Colonels Gavin Young and Neill Nolan, Commandant Sean O'Faherty, Denis Hanley and Commandant Pat O'Connor; Alexander Mattalaer of the Institute of European Studies and Daniel Keohane of the Centre for Security Studies, ETH Zurich; Cyril Brennan, Department of Foreign Affairs; Lieutenant General Bill Callaghan (RIP); Major Generals Michael Minihane (RIP), Vicent Savino and Pat Nash; Brigadier Generals (retd.) Jack Kissane, Johnny Vize, Jim Saunderson, Seamus O'Giollain, Ger Ahern, Derry Fitzgerald; Brigadier General Joe Mulligan; Colonels (retd.) Sean Norton, Peter Feely, Tommy Dunne, Harry Crowley, Michael Shannon, Con McNamara, George Kerton, Paddy McDaniel and Tuncay Sevim; Colonels Joe McDonagh, Tom Aherne, Tony Bracken and Peter Marrion; Lieutenant Colonels (retd.) Dermot Igoe, Noel Byrne, Johnny Molloy, Dan Murphy and Kiernan McDaid; Lieutenant Colonels Mark Brownen, Brian Cleary and John O'Loghlen; Commandants (retd.) Ned Kelly, Adrian Ainsworth, Declan Lawlor, Dick Murtagh, Paddy Gore, Pat Brennan, George Kirwin and Liam Donnelly; Commandants Earnan Naughton, Garry McKowen, John Kilmartin, Caimin Keogh, Louise Flynn, Tom McGuinness and David Hathaway; Lieutenant Commander Paddy Harkin; Captains (retd.) Noel Carey, Liam Murphy and Dr Ray Murphy; Captains John Tynan, Morgan Mangan and Ed Holland; Barrack Quartermaster (retd.) Billy Hutton; Company Sergeant (retd.) Jim Clarke; Sergeants (retd.) Michael Butler, Peter Fields and Thomas 'TC' Martin; Corporal (retd.) Gerald Francis RIP; Privates (retd.) Pat Liddy, John Wooley and John Grace; Private Paddy Cloherty.

A special word of thanks to Margaret Devlin, for her unstinting early clerical support, and finally to my children, Eva, Lynn, Mary-Claire and Hugo, that they may know when I needed inspiration both at home and especially overseas, they were it. The views represented in this book are those of the author only and do not represent those of the Defence Forces.

Dan Harvey, February 2017

Index

60mm mortars, 22, 30, 34
84mm anti-tank recoilless rifle, 86–8, 92–3, 104, 122, 142, 178–9

Ade standoff, Chad, 264–7
Adoula, Cyrille, 18
Agnew, Capt. Harry, 65
Ahern, Lt. Ger, 168, 198, 224, 225
Aherne, Lt. Tom, 128, 140, 144, 145–6, 149, 162, 186; and the DFF break-in, 120, 121–2, 123, 124, 175, 176
Ahtisaari, Martii, 230
Ainsworth, Capt. Adrian, 123, 129, 136, 164–5, **171**, 173, 179–81
airport infrastructure in Chad, 254, 260
al-Assad, President Bashar, 292, 304
al-Bashir, President Omar, 282
Al-Nusra, 295
Albanian Muslims of Kosovo, the, 213
Allen, Cpl. Bob, 44
AMIS (African Union Mission in Sudan), 239
ammunition supply, 45, 46, 56, 102–3
ANC (Armée Nationale Congolaise), 14, 65
Annan, Kofi, 238–9
AO (Area of Operations) in South Lebanon, 115, 116
APCs (armoured personnel carriers), 35, 55–6, 59, 123, 127, 131, 146, 150, 177, 221, 272; MOWAG APC, 258, 267, 268, **269**, 270, **293**, 293–4, 295
APIHC (armour piercing incendiary hard core) ammunition, 134
Arafat, Yasser, 201
Askander, Abu, 125, 141, 144, 145, 147, 163, 187

At-Tiri, battle of, 112, 118, 130–3, 134–8, 140–4, 154–6, 162–74, 186, 196–8, 303–4; and ceasefire, 184–5; and standoff, 145–51, 152–3
attack on UNIFIL HQ at Naqoura, 181–4
Austerlitz Bridge riot, the, 215
Austrian withdrawal from UNDOF, 291

Bahrain Declaration, the, 120
Baluba tribe, the, 16, 17, 107; and attack on Irish patrol, 6–8, 9–12, 13
Barak, Ehud, 201
Barrett, Pte. Tom, 187, 188, 190, 191
battalion rotation, 49–50, 54, 68–9, 102
Battle of Kosovo (1389), the, 208, 209
Baudouin, King, 5
Bayeke tribe, the, 17
Bazzi, Mahmoud, 186–7, 188
Belgian intervention in Congo, 6
Belgian officer corps of the Katangan Gendarmerie, 23
Berlin Conference, the, 3
Berry, Capt. 'Chuck', 222–3
Bin Laden, Osama, 280
black birds of Kosovo, the, 207–8
border policing in Kosovo, 231–2
Bracken, Lt. Tony, 133, 141, 143, 150, 155, 177, 197
Brannstrom, Brig-Gen. Anders, 229
break-in by DFF at At-Tiri, 120–5, 126–7, 130–1, 175, 176
Bren (light machine) gun, 29, 30, 34, 93–4, 97
briefing for UN strategy in Elisabethville, 56
British mandate for Palestine, the, 112
Browne, Dick, 15

Index

Browne, Trooper, 12
Brownen, Cmdt. Mark, 269, 270
Butler, Sgt. Michael, 78–9
Byrne, Capt. Noel, 129, 142, 173, 189

Callaghan, Cmdt. 'Bill,' 73–4
Camp Ciara, Goz-Beïda, Chad, 258, 261, 267–72, 275
Campbell, Capt. Billie, 163
CAR (Central African Republic), 236, 237, 239, 240, 262, 283; and EUFOR CHAD/CAR, 286, 287–8
Carey, Lt. Noel, 26, 30–1, 32, 33–4, 37, 41, 42, 44, 47
Carey, Lt-Col. Paul Jude, 42
Carter, President Jimmy, 151, 190, 192
Casement, Roger, 4
casevacs, 136–7, 143
casualties and losses, 49, 54, 101, 103, 143, 165, 188, 189, 190, 191–2, 200, 294; at the battle for the Tunnel, Elisabethville, 55, 61, 62–3, 66, 73, **75**, 77, 90; death of Pte. Stephen Griffin, 135, 136–7, 138, 140, 191; from the Niemba ambush, 11, 12–13, 303; at the siege of Jadotville, 32, 34–5, 38, 41
Cati, Sgt. Ben, 197
CB ('counter battery') fire, 61, 65
ceasefire at At-Tiri, 184–5
Chad crisis and the Darfur Complex, the, 236, 243–4, 245–8, 277, 280–1, 282, 304; and the Ade standoff, 264–7 (*see also* EUFOR (European Union Force) and intervention in Chad)
Chad National Army, the, 269, 276–7
Chadian society, 281–2
Christmas dinner, 1961, 106, 107, 108
Clark, Gen. Wesley, 211
clearing of railway carriages at the Tunnel, Elisabethville, 98
Cloherty, Pte. Padraigh, 169
Clune, Cmdt. Joe, 31
colonial exploitation of Congo, 3–5

combat styles in Chad, 244–5
Compagnie Internationale, the, 15–16
conditions for a ceasefire at Jadotville, 44–5
Congolese independence and political instability, 5–6, 13–14, 18
Conlon, Fr. Sean, 137
Connolly, Cpl. Charlie, 64, 89
Coughlan, Cmdt. Larry, 123, 126, 128, 129, 150, 167
courage of soldiers, the, 63–4, 105
CPs (checkpoints), 116, 121, 126, 129, 130, 132
Crean, Fr., HCF, **12**
criticism of EUFOR impartiality in Chad, 273–4
Crowley, Capt. Harry, 102, 105, 106, 107
Cruise O'Brien, Dr. Conor, 19, 31, 53

Daly, Pte. Michael, 137
Daly, Pte. Mick, 84
Darfur Complex and Sudanese suppression, 236, 238–41
Darfur rebel campaign in Chad, 245–52
de Bruin, Cmdt. Enda, 260
Déby, Idriss, 241–3, 244, 245, 247, 248–9, 250, 252, 273, 276–7, 279
defence cuts in Ireland, 258
defensive entrenchments in Elisabethville, 96
Delaney, Lt-Col. Brendan, 293
Denard, Bob, 15
Detention Centre, Kamina, 20
determinants for maintaining the peace, xv
deterrence as a peacekeeping objective, 285
DFF (De Facto Forces) of South Lebanon, 114–15, 116, 118, 138, 153, 157, 158–9, 160; attack at UNIFIL HQ, Naqoura, 181–2; break-in at At-Tiri, 120–5, 126–7, 130–1, 175, 176; and imprisonment of Irish soldiers, 136, 141, 181; and murder of Irish soldiers, 187, 188, 189, 190, 191, 193; negotiations with the Irish Defence Forces, 125–6, 145;

reaction to Irish recapture of At-Tiri, 175–81; removal of Sherman tank at At-Tiri, 145, 146–7; and tensions with Irish forces, 119, 120, 159
Dillon, Capt. Ronan, 224, 225
diplomatic initiative by the Irish government after murder of Irish soldiers, 190–1, 193–4, 196
discipline and mindset of Irish soldiers, x–xi, 75, 101–2, 116, 134–5, 162, 189, 197, 265, 303
Dogs of War, The (book), 15
Donnelly, Capt. Liam, 25, 31, 38
Douala port, Cameroon, 256, 259–60
Douglas C-124 Globemaster II transport aircraft, 49–50
downsizing of KFOR, the, 230–1
Dunne, Lt. Tommy, 81–2, 84, 89
Dutch involvement in Chad, 272

Earley, Lt-Gen. Dermot, **241**, 274
Emile, Abu, 142, 145, 147
Enclave post evacuations, 156–61
'end date' of EUFOR operations in Chad, 286
Erskine, Gen., 186, 189
ESDP (European Security and Defence Policy), 283, 287
Ethiopian battalions, 16, 55, 69, 76–7, 103, 104, 107
ethnic conflict in Kosovo, 209–10, 215–28, 229
ethnic groups in Kosovo, 212–13
ethnic violence in Pristina, 207
EUFOR (European Union Force) and intervention in Chad, 245, 262, 263, 266, 273–4, 276; aftermath and achievements, 280, 283–8; OHQ of, 246, 278, 287; planning and logistics for, 236–7, 240–1, 253–4, 256–7
EULEX (European Rule of Law Mission), 231
Europa Camp at N'Djamena, Chad, 256

European patronage of Katangan secession, 19
evacuation of Irish soldiers at OP Ras, 187–8
evasive tactics of the Darfur rebels, 246
Evening Herald (newspaper), 14–15

FAK (Katangese Air Force), 21, 24, 38, 40, 65
Fallon, Cpl. Michael, 49, 55, 63
Fallon, Pte. James, 63–4
'fan' tactic of evasion in Chad, 246, 247
Faulques, Col. Roger (René), 96, 97, 100
Feely, Col. Peter, 74, 80, 89, 98, 104
Feith, Peter, 229
Ferguson, Cpl. Paul, 66
Fields, Signalman Peter, 102–3, 107–8
fighting conditions, 66–7, 72, 76, 77–9, 80, 84, 165–6, 271
Fijian Army at the battle of At-Tiri, the, 197–8
Finn, Lt-Col. Michael, 229, 304
fire plans of heavy mortars, 76
First Battle of Katanga, the, 19–22
Fitzgerald, Col. Derry, 274
Fitzpatrick, Cmdt. Joe, 73, 80, 81, 84, 85, 94–5, 99, 103, 105, 303
Flanagan, Charlie, 296
FMR (Force Mobile Reserve), 117, 130, 132, 139, 181, 184
FN automatic rifle, 30, 90, 263
Foley, Cpl. Sean, 33, 37
'Force Keane,' 35, 36
'Force Keane 2,' 42, 45
Foster, Pte. Tom, 97
Fouga Magister jet trainer plane, 24, 38, 40, 42, 45
Francis, Cpl. Gerard, 59, 80–1, 82, 88–9, 90, 92, 94, 95, 102
Frederick the Great, 101
French intervention in Chad, 245, 246, 247, 249
friendly fire, 93–4

Gal, Lt-Col. Gary, 127–8
Ganascia, Brig-Gen. Philippe, 286
Gaynor, Sgt. Hugh, 7, 9, 11
Gill, Cpl. Johnny, 142, 143
Gilleran, Capt. Tony, 123, 129, 167
Gleeson, Lt. Kevin, 6, 7, **8,** 9, 10, 11, 12, 303
Glen of Imaal, Co. Wicklow, 81, 292
Gore, Capt. Paddy, 182–3, 188–9
Gormley, Pte. Edward, 39–40
GPMG (7.62mm General Purpose Machine Gun), 16
'Gravy Train' of At-Tiri, the, 142, 143
Gregan, Cpl. Sammy, 102, 105
Griffin, Pte. Stephen, 135, 136–7, 138, 140, 191
Guerin, Cpl. Paddy, 66, 77
guerrilla raids in Israel, 113–14
Gustav sub-machine gun, 30, 33, 59, 89, 98, **99,** 102, 104

Habré, Hissène, 242, 243, 247
Haddad, Major Saad, 114–15, 120, 125, 145, 147, 149, 150, 156, 177, 181, 186; military tactics of, 127, 128, 162–3, 194; and the murder of Irish soldiers, 190
half-track at At-Tiri, 167, 168, 169, 171–2
Hammarskjöld, Dag, 19, 52–3, 296
Harrington, Lt. Billy, 189
Hartigan, Capt. Thomas, 22
Hathaway, Capt. David, 222, 223, 224, 225–6
Heery, Capt. Kevin, 142
Hegarty, Sgt. Willie, 26, 36, 37
helicopter support, 43–4
Henry, Cpl. Cyril, 133
Hezbollah, 201, 202, 203
Hill 880 at At-Tiri, 112, 122, 125, 126–7, 142, 147, 150, 153, 162, 199–200; Dutch missile launches from, 166, 178
Hindy, Steve, 187

HMG (.5 Browning Heavy Machine Gun), 16, 133–4, 263
Hogan, Cmdt. PD, 7–8, 9
Hogan, Lt-Col. Michael, 54, 70–1, 72
Holland, Lt. Ed, 217, 218–19
Hovden, Lt. Bjorn, 43
Hurley, Cmdt. Seán, 144, 159
Hutton, Sgt. Billy, 144, 169, 177–8

ICC (International Criminal Court), 239, 282
IDF (Israel Defence Forces), the, 114, 127–8, 142, 146, 147–8, 150, 151, 178, 189–90, 201; occupation and withdrawal from Lebanon, 198–9, 200–2, 203; and support for the DFF, 190, 193, 194
IDP (Internally Displaced People) of Chad, 237–8
imprisonment of Irish soldiers by the DFF, 136, 141, 181
Indian Ghurkhas, 53, 54, 77, 103
infantry tactics, 28–30, 38–9, 57–9, 67–8, 69, 73, 74, 81, 84
Initial Entry Forces of EUFOR, 262
intelligence in warfare, 68, 71–2, 130
international intervention in Kosovo, 210–12
intimidation of At-Tiri villages to riot, 163–4, 170
Irish Army Rangers, 262–7
Irish Battalion HQ Operations Section, 139
Irish Defence Forces: in Chad, **241,** 251, 253, 258–9, **260,** 262–4, 284; 97th Bn, 257, 267–72, 273–4, 275, 304; in Congo, 6–7, **8,** 19–22, **298**; 1st Infantry Group, 20; 32nd Bn, 13; 33rd Bn, 6–12, **30,** 77, 303; 35th Bn, 25–6, 50, 54, 87; B Company, 26, 54, **90**; A Company, 25–6, 27–48, 303; 36th Bn, 49–50, 59, 65, 69, 106–7; B Company, 59, 62, 69, 76, 79, 81–2, 92, 93, 101, 104; A

Company, 49, 50, 51–2, 53, 54–7, **58,** 59, 61–4, 65, 66, 67, 68, 69–70, 73–5, **75,** 77, 79–89, 93, 96–8, 99–100, 101, 103, 105, 107, 303; 37th Bn, 102; in Kosovo, 207, **209,** 212; 27th Infantry Group, 214, 304; C Company, 220, 228; in Lebanon, 111–12, 115, 117–18, 124–5, 196, 199–200, 202, 204; 46th Bn, 116, 119, 122, 152–3, 200; B Company, 156–61; C Company, **113,** 121, 122–3, 124–5, 128–33, 135–47, 175–6, 185, 303–4; 56th Bn, 198–9; 89th Bn, 200; in Syria, 291, **293;** 43rd Infantry Group, 292, 293–4, 304; 44th Infantry Group, 295–6; 48th Infantry Group, 291
Irish Force Commander in EUFORS, 255
Irish-Israeli relations, 189–90
Israel, state of, 112–13, 194 (see also IDF (Israel Defence Forces), the)
Israeli support for the DFF, 190

Jackson, Maj-Gen. Michael, 21
Jadotville, Congo, 24–5, 26–8, **27, 37, 40, 41** (see also Siege of Jadotville, the)
Janjaweed of Darfur, Sudan, 235–6, 238
JEM (Justice and Equality Movement) of Darfur, 238, 281
Jones, Cpl. Michael, 143
Jones, Trooper Tom 'Deno', 172–3
Joyce, Pte. Kevin, 200

Kasavubu, President, 17
Katanga struggle for independence from Congo, 13–14, 17–18, 19
Katangan Gendarmerie, **21,** 22, 23, 50, 52, 54–5, 106, 303; and foreign mercenaries, the, 14–17, 20, 23, 24, 31, 32, 39, 51, 64–5, 96, 100; and the Tunnel, Elisabethville, 56, 61, 67, 68–9, 87, 89, 90–1, 92, 94, 95, 97
Keane, Cmdt. Johnny, 35
Kelly, Cpt. Eamon 'Ned', 122–3, 175–7, 185

Kelly, Pte. Gerry, 89, 90
Kelly, Sgt. Tom, 34, 37
Kerton, Capt. George, 137
KFOR (Kosovo Force), 207, 211, 212, 214, 215, 216–22, 227, 228, 230–2; SISU Company, 217, 224–6
Kissane, Lt-Col. Jack, 126–7, 144, 145, 153–4, 186, 189
KLA (Kosovo Liberation Army), 210, 216
Klein, Maj. Harry, 187
Knightly, Lt. Kevin, 26, 38, 39
Kolwazi airstrip air strike, 75–6
Kosovo, 207–8, 212–14, 231–2 (see also KFOR (Kosovo Force))
Kreuzlingen remote weapons platform, 270
Kumanovo Military Technical Agreement, 230

Lally, Pte. Pat, 93–4
landing of USAF transport aircraft amid Katangese fire, 50–1
landline communications in Chad, 254–5
landscape and climate of Chad, 261–2
Lawlor, Capt. Declan, 157–61
leadership qualities, 70, 71, 86, 91–2
Lebanese civil war, the, 113, 114
Leech, Lt. Joe, 26
Leopold Farm (Irish Camp), 54–5
Leopold II, King, 3, 4
'Les Affreux' and French mercenaries, 15
liaison effectiveness, 118
Liberian deployment of Irish Army Rangers, 263–4
Liege crossroads, Elisabethville, 61–3
LMTs (Liaison and Monitoring) elements of KFOR, 231
Logistic Section of the Irish Defence Forces and military operations in Chad, 253
logistics of military operation in Chad, 253–8, 259–61, 283, 284–5
Long, Pte. John, 142
Lualaba, Sgt., 6, 8

Lufira Bridge and Force Keane relief support, 36, 42, 44
Lumumba, Patrice, 5, 18
Lunda tribe, the, 17

Mac Seoin, Cpl., **171**
machinations in the UN, 52–3
MacMahon, Cmdt. Kevin, 22
Manning, Pte. John, 38
Mannix, Cpl. Dan, 95
marksmanship, 185
Marron, Lt. Peter, 173, 177
Martin, Trooper Thomas 'TC,' 170–2, 198
Massaguet desert battle, Chad, 247–8
McCarthy, Lt-Col. Justin, 204
McDaniel, Lt-Col. Paddy, 268, 269, 270, 274, 304
McDonagh, Trooper, 175–6
McGuinness, Cmdt. Tom, 268, 270
McKeon, Cmdt. Gary 'Tex,' 257, 261
McKeown, Cmdt. Larry, 214, 220
McKeown, Lt-Col. Sean, 18
McMullan, Trooper, 49
McNamee, Lt-Col. Hugh, 31
medals and commendations, **171**, 229, 279–80
mercenaries in the Katangan Gendarmerie, 14–17, 20, 23, 24, 31, 32, 39, 51, 64–5, 96, 100
MFC (Mobile Fire Controller), 61
military investment in Chad, 279
military procedures, 102
military roles in a changing environment, 287–8
military strategy in Lebanon, 140–1, 152, 153, 167, 168–9, 174–5, 185
Military Technical Agreement between NATO and Yugoslavia, 211
Mills 36 hand grenades, 98
Miloševic, Slobodan, 208–9, 210
Minehane, Cmdt. Michael, 20, 196
mineral resources of Katanga province, Congo, 4–5, 6

MINURCAT (UN Mission in Central African Republic and Chad), 256, 263, 278, 284
Misgav Am kibbutz attack by the PLO, 147–8, 193
Mitten, Trooper Gerry, 143
MNBGs (Multinational Battle Groups) of KFOR, 231
Mobutu, Col. Joseph, 18
Molloy, Lt. Johnny, 136, 166–7, 168, 169, 198
Monahan, Sgt. John, 35, 38, 39–40
Moore, Trooper Paddy, 133
mortar fire, 41, 49, 54–5, 100, 103–4, 176–7; nature of, 56, 60–3, 76, 78, 105, 175, 183–4
Mott, Cpl. Charlie, 172–3
MOWAG APC, 258, 267, 268, **269**, 270, **293**, 293–4, 295
Mpola, Maurice, 18
MRE (Mission Readiness Exercise), 292
Mulcahy, Sgt. Paddy, 49, 62, 63, 64
Munongo, Godefroid, 18, 19, 46
Murphy, Capt. Dan, 123
Murphy, Capt. Liam, 123
Murray, Pte. James, 64

Nash, Lt-Gen. Pat, **241**, 245–6, 249, 255, 280, 282–3, 284–8
NATO air campaign against Serbia, 211
Naughton, Cmdt. Earnan, 259
NCOs, 105
negotiations between the DFF and Irish Defence Forces, 125–6, 145
neutralising Katangese mortar positions, 65–6
Neville, Sgt. Pat, 34, 44
Niemba ambush at the River Luweyeye, Katanga, Congo, **4**, 6–7, 8–13, **12**, 17, 77, 303
NorMainCoy (Norwegian Maintenance Company), 188

Norton, Lt. Sean, 62, 80, 87, 93, 94, 95, 96, 101, 104, 105, 107; military decision-making of, 83, 84, 86, 91–2, 97
Norwegian KFOR troops, 218, 219, 220, 222, 226, 227
Norwegian medical staff and support, 137, 182, 188

O'Boyle, Capt. Conor, 147
O'Dea, Willie, **241**, 255, 274
OHQ of EUFOR, the, 246, 278, 287
Okito, Joseph, 17
O'Mahoney, Pte. John, 187, 188
Omar, Abu, 125, 145
ONUC (UN Operation in the Congo), 14, 18, 52
Operation Litani, 148
Operation Morthor, 32, 53, 54, 57
Operation Rampunch (Rum Punch), 19, 20, 23–4, 57
Operation Sarsfield, 69, 73, 85
Operation Unokat, 66, 69–70, 76
OPs (Observation Posts), 119, 142, 158
Oueddei, Goukouni, 247

pack rations, 106
Page, Capt. Kevin, 73
Pakenham, Col. Paul, 255
peace enforcement and passive peacekeeping, 18, 118–19, 134–5
peace talks, 106–7
peacekeeping and the Irish Defence Forces, xii–xiv, 202–4, 229, 296, 297, 302–5; characteristics of, 122, 134–5, 196, 275; and negotiation over confrontation, 139–40, 196–7; and returning fire, 144, 162 (*see also* rules of engagement)
peacekeeping as a secondary duty of the Army, x–xi
PLO (Palestinian Liberation Organisation), the, 114, 117, 120, 147, 148, 157, 198
policing in EUFOR area in Chad, 285–6

post-blocking from Veternik Ridge after Pristina riots, 226–7
Powell, Colin, 239
Power, Cpl. John, 102
Power, Sgt. John, 161
Prendergast, Sgt. Jack, 35, 38, 45
primary duties of the Army of the Republic, x, xi
prisoner exchange after ceasefire at At-Tiri, 184–5
Pronk, Johannes 'Jan,' 239
proposed UNIFIL inquiry into At-Tiri standoff, 186
'proxy war' between Chad and Sudan, 237 (*see also* Chad crisis and the Darfur Complex, the)
Puren, Jerry, 64–5

Quinlan, Cmdt. Pat, 25, 28, 30–1, 32, 64, 303; military qualities at Siege of Jadotville, 35, 36, 38, 39, 42, 44–6, 47
Quinlan, Lt. Tom, 26, 33, 47, 53, 64

radio communications, 16, 29–30, 33, 85, 96, 135, 220, 268
RCO (Raising and Concentration Order), 291
rebel incursions in Chad, 246–53, 267–72, 273, 279; defeat by Chad National Army, 275–7
reconnaissance, 130, 262, 270, 271
recreations, 111–12
Red Cross, the, 106–7
Reidy, Pte. Bill, 34
release of Irish soldiers at Bayt Yahun, 145
removal of Sherman tank at At-Tiri by the DFF, 145, 146–7
rescue and extraction operation of Filipino troops at Breiqa, Syria, 295–6
rescue of APC at west end of At-Tiri, 131–2
returning fire, 144, 149, 152, 154, 162, 194–5, 272

right of self-defence, 192
Riordan, Lt. Paddy, 74, 80, 82, 83, 101
riot at Bayt Yahun, 155-6
riot control drills, **209**
riots south of Pristina, March 2004, 217-22
roadblock placed by Gendarmerie in Elisabethville, 52, 53
roll of honour, **298-301**
rules of engagement, 18, 105-6, 116, 117, 118-19, 136, 142, 149, 157, 192, 240 (*see also* returning fire)
Russian interest in Kosovo, 211-12

Saab fighter planes, 57
Sarkozy, Nicolas, 245, 249, 279-80
SASE (safe and secure environment) as a peacekeeping objective, 284
Searson, Pte. Michael, 89
securing of the Tunnel at Elisabethville, 96-103, **99,** 104, 107-8
Serbian nationalism, 208-9, 210
Serbs of Kosovo, the, 213
SFOR (Stablization Force) in Bosnia, 211
Sharon, Ariel, 198
Sherrif, Capt. Dermot, 183-4
shock and mental distress, 146
Siege of Jadotville, the, 24-48, **27, 37, 40, 41**
Silva Angelo, José Victor de, 274
Six Day War, the, 113
SLA (South Lebanon Army), 201
SLA/M (Sudan Liberation Army/ Movement), 238, 239
Slatina Air Base, Kosovo, 211-12
Smallhorne, Pte. Derek, 187, 188, 190, 191
Socopetrol petrol and oil depot attack, 64
Solana, Javier, 273
Sornaivalav, Pte. Seveti 'Sorro,' 165, 191
Sreenan, Brig-Gen. Jim, 202
Stanley Avenue ambush, Elisabethville, 53-6
Steyr AUG A3 rifle, 263
street fighting techniques, 251

Sudan, 280, 281, 304; relations with Chad, 277, 279, 281
Sudanese government suppression of Darfur rebels, 238-9 (*see also* Chad crisis and the Darfur Complex, the)
sulha, tradition of, 186-7
supply of meals and other essentials, 142, 176, 188
Swedish battalions in Congo, 17, 22-3, 56, 64, 68-9, 76, 101, 103; transport and APC support, 26, 35, 53, 55, 59
Swedish KFOR troops, 217, 218, 219, 220-1, 222, 223, 226, 227
Syrian civil war, the, 291, 292, 294, 295, 304

T-55 tank, 249, 250
Tahany, Pte. James, 39
Taylor, Cmdt. Dave, 123, 128, 149, 164, 167, 168, 170, 174-5, 176; military strengths of, 124, 169; and negotiations with the DFF, 125, 126, 141, 144-5, 147
Tebnine, Lebanon, 115
technology and firepower, 276
territorial dispute between Kosovo and Serbia, 207-8
terrorism and poverty, 280-1
Thors, Warrant Officer Eric, 43, 45
Tito, Gen. Josip, 210
TOW missile, the, 178, 179
training, xiii, 29, 59, 68, 84, 112, 116, 134, 161-2, 258, 262, 271, 292
trenches as defensive infantry tactic, 28-30, 38-9, 105
tribal fights and displacement of people, 237-8
tribal thought and Chadian society, 281
triple lock policy, the, 291
Tshombe, Moise, 6, 13, 14, 17, 19, 20, 53, 75-6, 303
Tunnel at Elisabethville, the, 56, **58,** 59, 62-4, 66, 71, 76-8, **90,** 96-9, **99,** 106,

303; and Operation Unokat, 66, 69–70, 79–96
Tynan, Capt. John, 270

ultimatum from Munongo to Quinlan to cease fighting, 46–8
UN, the, 13, 18, 52, 53, 68, 76
UN Charter and peacekeeping, the, xvi, 105–6, 118
UN Security Council Resolutions, 6, 114, 190, 191, 192, 197, 201, 230, 274
UNAMID (UN African Mission in Darfur), 239
UNDOF (UN Disengagement Observer Force), 186, 291–2, 293, 295, 296
UNHCR, the, 273–4
UNIFIL mission in Lebanon, the, 112, 115, 119, 128, 148, 189, 190–1, 200, 202–4, **299–301**; Irish request for Force Mobile Reserve, 124, 129, 130, 139; purpose of, 114, 117; terms of reference of, 119, 195–6
UNMIK (UN Mission in Kosovo), 214, 217
UNMIK-Police, 226
UNOGIL (UN Observer Group in Lebanon), 118, 187, 204
UNTSI (Defence Forces UN Training School Ireland), 292
UNTSO (UN Truce Supervision Organisation), 118, 145, 185, **299**

urban fighting, 67
US interests and UN Security Council resolutions, 192–3
US pressure for IDF withdrawal from At-Tiri, 151–2

Vartam, Zavan, 187
Vickers machine gun, 30, 38, 39, 46, 59
Vincent, Capt. Patrick, 187
Vize, Cmdt. Johnny, 137–40, 147

Waldheim, Dr. Kurt, 189
weaponry, 16, 21, 22, 30, 63, 86–7, 90, 133–4, 178–9, 263, 265, 270
Whyte, Lt-Col. Frank, 137
Wickham, Pte. Andy, 89, 101
Wild Geese, The (film), 15
Woodcock, Pte., 63
Woolley, Pte. John, 77–8
wreaths at Albertville airport, **11**

YU Flats evacuation of Kosovar Serbs in Pristina, 222–6
Yugoslavia, 209, 210

Zaghawa tribe, the, 242, 243, 248
Zone of Separation, Golan Heights, 291, 292, 295